ADVANCES IN DIGITAL GOVERNMENT

Technology, Human Factors, and Policy

edited by

William J. McIver, Jr.
University at Albany (SUNY)

Ahmed K. Elmagarmid
Hewlett-Packard and Purdue University

KLUWER ACADEMIC PUBLISHERS
Boston / Dordrecht / London

Distributors for North, Central and South America:
Kluwer Academic Publishers
101 Philip Drive
Assinippi Park
Norwell, Massachusetts 02061 USA
Telephone (781) 871-6600
Fax (781) 681-9045
E-Mail < kluwer@wkap.com >

Distributors for all other countries:
Kluwer Academic Publishers Group
Post Office Box 322
3300 AH Dordrecht, THE NETHERLANDS
Telephone 31 786 576 000
Fax 31 786 576 254
E-Mail < services@wkap.nl >

 Electronic Services < http://www.wkap.nl >

Library of Congress Cataloging-in-Publication Data

Advances in digital government : technology, human factors, and policy / edited by
William J. McIver, Jr., Ahmed K. Elmagarmid.
    p. cm. -- (Kluwer international series on advances in database systems; ADBS 26)
    Includes bibliographical references and index.
    ISBN 1-4020-7067-5 (alk. paper)
    1. Public administration--Information resources management. 2. Electronic government
       information. 3. Internet in public administration. I. McIver, William J.,
    1963- II. Elmagarmid, Ahmed K. III. Series.

    JF1525.A8 A38 2002
    352.3'8'0285—dc21   2002021856

Contents

Contributors   ix

Acknowledgements   xiii

Preface   xv

Introduction   1
  WILLIAM J. MCIVER, JR. AND AHMED K. ELMAGARMID

Supporting Data and Services Access in Digital Government
Environments   37
  ATHMAN BOUGUETTAYA, MOURAD OUZZANI,
  BRAHIM MEDJAHED, AND AHMED K. ELMAGARMID

Cooperative Architectures   53
  CARLO BATINI, ELETTRA CAPPADOZZI, MASSIMO MECELLA,
  MAURIZIO TALAMO

Automating the Delivery of Governmental Business Services Through
  Workflow Technology   69
  VIJAYALAKSHMI ATLURI, SOON AE CHUN,
  RICHARD HOLOWCZAK, AND NABIL R. ADAM

Data Integration and Access   85
  JOSÉ LUIS AMBITE, YIGAL ARENS, WALTER BOURNE,
  STEVE FEINER, LUIS GRAVANO,

VASILEIOS HATZIVASSILOGLOU, EDUARD HOVY,
JUDITH KLAVANS, ANDREW PHILPOT,
USHA RAMACHANDRAN, KENNETH A. ROSS, JAY SANDHAUS,
DENIZ SARIOZ, ROLFE R. SCHMIDT, CYRUS SHAHABI,
ANURAG SINGLA, SURABHAN TEMIYABUTR, BRIAN WHITMAN
AND KAZI ZAMAN

Scalable Data Collection for Internet-based Digital Government
Applications   107
    LEANA GOLUBCHIK

Security and Privacy Challenges of a Digital Government   121
    JAMES B. D. JOSHI, ARIF GHAFOOR, WALID G. AREF,
    EUGENE H. SPAFFORD

Digital Democracy through Electronic Petitioning   137
    ANN MACINTOSH, ANNA MALINA, AND STEVE FARRELL

Compliance Analysis for Disabled Access   149
    CHARLES S. HAN, JOHN C. KUNZ AND KINCHO H. LAW

COPLINK   163
    ROSLIN V. HAUCK, MICHAEL CHAU AND HSINCHUN CHEN

Web-Based Systems that Disseminate Information from Databases but
    Protect Confidentiality   181
    ALAN F. KARR, JAEYONG LEE, ASHISH P. SANIL,
    JOEL HERNANDEZ, SOUSAN KARIMI AND KAREN LITWIN

WebView   197
    AIDONG ZHANG, LEI ZHU AND DAVID MARK

The Federal Government   215
    YOLANDA L. COMEDY

Policy and Portals   231
    PATRICIA DIAMOND FLETCHER

Citizens' Perspectives on E-government   243
    SHARON STROVER

Building Collaborative Digital Government Systems   259
    SHARON S. DAWES AND THERESA A. PARDO

Contents

E-Government in Canada 275
JEFFREY ROY

Laying out the Foundation for a Digital Government Model Case Study 289
NOUREDDINE BOUDRIGA AND SALAH BENABDALLAH

Aveiro - Digital Town 305
NELSON PACHECO DA ROCHA

Index 315

Contributors

Nabil R. Adam, *Rutgers University, Newark, New Jersey USA*
José Luis Ambite, *University of Southern California,*
                    Los Angeles, California USA
Walid G. Aref, *Purdue University, West Lafayette, Indiana USA*
Yigal Arens, *University of Southern California,*
              Los Angeles, California USA
Vijayalakshmi Atluri, *Rutgers University, Newark, New Jersey USA*
Carlo Batini, *Autorità per l'Informatica nella Pubblica Amministrazione*
               (AIPA), Roma, Italy and
               Università di Roma "La Sapienza", Italy
Salah Benabdallah, *National Digital Certification Agency (ANCE) and*
                    University of Carthage, Tunisia
Noureddine Boudriga, *National Digital Certification Agency (ANCE) and*
                      University of Carthage, Tunisia
Athman Bouguettaya, *Virginia Tech, Falls Church, Virginia USA*
Walter Bourne, *Columbia University, New York, New York USA*
Elettra Cappadozzi, *Autorità per l'Informatica nella Pubblica*
                     Amministrazione (AIPA), Roma, Italy
Michael Chau, *University of Arizona, Tucson, Arizona USA*
Hsinchun Chen, *University of Arizona, Tucson, Arizona USA*
Soon Ae Chun, *Rutgers University, Newark, New Jersey USA*
Yolanda L. Comedy, *IBM, Washington, DC USA*
Sharon S. Dawes, *University at Albany, Albany, New York USA*
Ahmed K. Elmagarmid, *Hewlett-Packard, Palo Alto, California USA*
Steve Farrell, *The Scottish Parliament, Edinburgh, UK*

Steve Feiner, *Columbia University, New York, New York USA*
Patricia Diamond Fletcher, *University of Maryland, Baltimore County, USA*
Arif Ghafoor, *Purdue University, West Lafayette, Indiana USA*
Leana Golubchik, *University of Maryland, College Park, Maryland USA*
Luis Gravano, *Columbia University, New York, New York USA*
Charles S. Han, *Autodesk, Inc., San Rafael, California USA*
Vasileios Hatzivassiloglou, *Columbia University,*
                        New York, New York USA
Roslin V. Hauck, *University of Arizona, Tucson, Arizona USA*
Joel Hernandez, *MCNC Research Triangle Park, North Carolina, USA*
Richard Holowczak, *Rutgers University, Newark, New Jersey USA*
Eduard Hovy, *University of Southern California,*
                        Los Angeles, California USA
James B. D. Joshi, *Purdue University, West Lafayette, Indiana USA*
Sousan Karimi, *MCNC Research Triangle Park, North Carolina, USA*
Alan F. Karr, *National Institute of Statistical Sciences*
                        Research Triangle Park, North Carolina, USA
Judith Klavans, *Columbia University, New York, New York USA*
John C. Kunz, *Stanford University, Stanford, California USA*
Kincho H. Law, *Stanford University, Stanford, California USA*
Jaeyong Lee, *National Institute of Statistical Sciences*
                        Research Triangle Park, North Carolina, USA
Karen Litwin, *MCNC Research Triangle Park, North Carolina, USA*
Ann Macintosh, *Napier University, Edinburgh, UK*
Anna Malina, *Napier University, Edinburgh, UK*
David Mark, *State University of New York at Buffalo*
                        Buffalo, New York USA
William J. McIver, Jr., *University at Albany, Albany, New York USA*
Massimo Mecella, *Università di Roma "La Sapienza", Italy*
Brahim Medjahed, *Virginia Tech, Falls Church, Virginia USA*
Mourad Ouzzani, *Virginia Tech, Falls Church, Virginia USA*
Nelson Pacheco da Rocha, *Universidade de Aveiro, Portugal*
Theresa A. Pardo, *University at Albany, Albany, New York USA*
Andrew Philpot, *University of Southern California,*
                        Los Angeles, California USA
Usha Ramachandran, *University of Southern California,*
                        Los Angeles, California USA
Kenneth A. Ross, *Columbia University, New York, New York USA*
Jeffrey Roy, *The University of Ottawa, Ottawa, Ontario Canada*
Jay Sandhaus, *Columbia University, New York, New York USA*
Ashish P. Sanil, *National Institute of Statistical Sciences*
                        Research Triangle Park, North Carolina, USA

Deniz Sarioz, *Columbia University, New York, New York USA*
Rolfe R. Schmidt, *University of Southern California,*
                 Los Angeles, California USA
Cyrus Shahabi, *University of Southern California,*
                 Los Angeles, California USA
Anurag Singla, *Columbia University, New York, New York USA*
Eugene H. Spafford, *Purdue University, West Lafayette, Indiana USA*
Sharon Strover, *University of Texas, Austin, Texas USA*
Maurizio Talamo, *Autorità per l'Informatica nella Pubblica*
                 Amministrazione (AIPA), Roma, Italy and
                 Università di Roma "Tor Vergata", Italy
Surabhan Temiyabutr, *Columbia University, New York, New York USA*
Brian Whitman, *Columbia University, New York, New York USA*
Kazi Zaman, *Columbia University, New York, New York USA*
Aidong Zhang, *State University of New York at Buffalo*
                 Buffalo, New York USA
Lei Zhu, *State University of New York at Buffalo*
                 Buffalo, New York USA

Acknowledgements

A number of people have been instrumental in this project. Melissa Fearon of Kluwer Academic Publishers has been a most helpful and patient editor. Scott Delman, also of Kluwer Academic Publishers, gave the green light for this project. Scott Hamilton at IEEE Computer magazine was the editor of our special issue on digital government, which provided the impetus for this book. We must also acknowledge Larry E. Brandt, Program Director for Digital Government at the National Science Foundation, for the encouragement and direction he has given to our research community.

William McIver would like to acknowledge the generous support of the Indiana Center or Database Systems at Purdue University, the Scholarly Technology Group at Brown University, and the School of Information Science and Policy at the University at Albany, State University of New York for help in completing this project; and most importantly the patience of my partner Joy James, and the life-long support of my parents William and Edna McIver.

Ahmed Elmagarmid's research is supported by the grant 9983249-EIA from the National Science Foundation's Digital Government program.

Several figures used in this book have been reused by permission of IEEE.

Preface

Motivation

In February 2001, *IEEE Computer* magazine published a collection of articles on digital government that we had edited. The issue was a success for the digital government community; however, in the process of preparing the issue, we received more important contributions than could be accommodated. That motivated us to edit an extended collection of articles, including full articles on the research that was presented in *Computer*. This volume is the result.

Objectives

The primary objective of this edited volume is to present a collection of in-depth articles that addresses a representative cross-section of the matrix of issues involved in implementing digital government systems. Specifically, the articles presented in this book constitute a survey of both the technical and policy dimensions related to the design, planning and deployment of digital government systems. The research and development projects within the technical dimension represent a wide array of governmental functions, including the provisioning of health and human services, management of energy information, multi-agency integration, and criminal justice applications. The technical issues dealt with in these projects include database and ontology integration, distributed architectures, scalability, and security and privacy. Human factors research presented here emphasizes compliance with access standards for the disabled. The policy articles contained in this volume cover both conceptual models for developing digital government systems as well as real management experiences and results in deploying them.

A corresponding objective of this volume is to present digital government issues from the perspectives of different communities and societies. The hope is that through geographic and social diversity, this collection of articles will illuminate a wider array of policy and social perspectives than might otherwise be made available to the reader. This should expose practitioners to new and useful ways of thinking about digital government and the values and assumptions that those outside of their societal sphere bring to this area of research. Collectively, the articles presented here represent projects and issues from North America, Europe and North Africa; and they present results that impact on urban and rural communities; people who have disabilities; and, in general, a broad spectrum of citizens and government officials.

The Contributions in this Volume

The articles in this volume represent a broad cross-section of topic domains in digital government research. They also address many dimensions of digital government research, including: national versus local contexts, developed versus developing nations, broad software substrates versus specific application domains, policymaking, collaborative design and development processes, citizens' attitudes toward digital government, and the requirements for providing services to disabled and elderly populations.

We begin in, chapter 1, with an introduction, which includes a history of digital government; a survey of major technical, human factors and policy concepts and issues involved in the development and operation of digital government systems; and linkages to the research of the contributors to this volume. This collection is organized into four groups: foundation systems, specific application domains, policy issues, and case studies.

Foundation Systems

The first group of articles in this volume focuses on systems designed to implement broad aspects of government.

In chapter 2, Bouguettaya, Ouzzani, Medjahed, and Elmagarmid present a Web-based system that is designed to support the performance of cooperative tasks between different government agencies whose data have different structure and semantics, and to which different rules and processes are applied. Examples of these types of cooperative tasks abound within social services, where citizens are often required to interact with multiple agencies to attain a goal. Their system, called *WebDG*, takes an ontology-based approach to managing interactions between diverse databases that may exist across multiple agencies involved in a cooperative task.

In chapter 3, Batini, Cappadozzi, Mecella, and Talamo present an overview of the Italian government-wide Nationwide Public Administration Network and the corresponding Nationwide Cooperative Information System. These systems were mandated by the Italian Parliament in 1993 in the creation of the Authority for Information Technology in the Public Administration (AIPA) and are intended to increase the overall effectiveness and efficiency of the ministries that comprise the Italian government, particularly in the context of inter-ministry actions.

In chapter 4, Atluri, Chun, Holowczak, and Adam discuss their research on inter-agency workflow and decentralized workflow management. The goal of their work is to eliminate the submission of redundant requests to multiple government entities in the process of attaining a complex goal, such as the establishment of a business. Their approach is designed to allow customization and automatic execution of workflows.

In chapter 5, Ambite, Arens, Bourne, Feiner, Gravano, Hatzivassiloglou, Hovy, Klavans, Philpot, Ramachandran, Ross, Sandhaus, Sarioz, Schmidt, Shahabi, Singla, Temiyabutr, Whitman and Zaman describe their research on the integration and access of statistical data across government agencies. Their *Digital Government Research Center (DGRC)* system performs the mapping of ontologies across organizations, multi-database access planning and automated terminology analysis. The DGRC provides a Web-based query input interface that is designed to bridge the gap between general query mechanisms appropriate for experts and mechanisms that allow non-experts to be productive.

In chapter 6, Golubchik presents her research on scalable data collection over the Internet. This work is motivated by the fact that government organizations are now allowing citizens to file forms electronically. Scalability of such services is of particular concern when there are deadlines for citizens to upload their data (e.g. a tax filing deadline). Golubchik's framework, called *Bistro*, is designed to provide scalable data collection over the Internet both with and without deadlines.

In chapter 7, Joshi, Ghafoor, Aref, and Spafford present an overview of the challenges in providing security and privacy in digital government. They focus in particular on the difficulties that multiple heterogeneous security regimes pose in this context. They present various solutions to providing security in a multi-domain digital government environment and focus in particular on the role-based access control (RBAC) model.

Special Domains

The second group of articles in this volume focuses on research and development of systems that implement governmental functions within focused domains.

In chapter 8, Macintosh, Malina and Farrell discuss the design and evaluation of a Web-based system they have implemented to support the most representative of the functions of a democratic government: participatory decision-making by voting. Their system, called *e-petitioner*, enables citizens of Scotland to create, view, discuss, sign, and submit petitions to the Scottish parliament.

In chapter 9, Han, Kunz and Law discuss their on-line system for testing the compliance of building and facilities designs with the Americans with Disabilities Act. They use a hybrid approach to evaluate designs from both compliance and usability perspectives. Their Web-based prototype system replaces the traditional compliance and permit approval process with one that is semi-automated.

In chapter 10, Hauck, Chau, and Chen discuss their research in knowledge management within the domain of law enforcement. Their *COPLINK* Project is a collaboration between the Tucson, Arizona USA police department and the Artificial Intelligence Lab at the University of Arizona. The project has developed the *COPLINK Connect Database* application, which facilitates information sharing within and between law enforcement agencies; Detect Criminal Intelligence Analysis application, which is designed to analyze collections of intelligence data and identify important relationships (e.g. between a crime suspect and some other object or concept); and, a collaboration framework for law enforcement agencies.

In chapter 11, Karr, Lee, Sanil, Hernandez, Karimi, and Litwin describe a prototype system they have developed for disseminating statistical data while protecting confidentiality of organizations or individuals referenced in the data. Protecting the confidentiality of data collected by governments has long been a major concern. Their system employs geographical aggregation and Bayesian statistical analysis methods of the aggregated methods to preserve confidentiality.

In chapter 12, Zhang, Zhu, and Mark discuss their research in the efficient content-based retrieval of images from very large distributed databases. The goal of their system, called *WebView*, is to improve access to the massive amounts of image data collected by various government agencies by augmenting existing systems. WebView uses a new approach called *keyblock*, which they show to be superior to several well-known approaches.

Policy Issues

The third group of articles in this volume focuses on policy issues in the development of digital government.

In chapter 13, Comedy examines the role of the federal government in the development of information technology, from encouraging research and development to policymaking. She looks in particular at the work of the President's Information Technology Advisory Committee in supporting the transformation of society and government through innovations in information technology.

In chapter 14, Fletcher discusses the role of policymaking in the evolution of digital government. She focuses in particular on the policies that have addressed requirements for high availability and "understandability" of government information. This has resulted in the adoption of the portal model of information access – most prominently in the FirstGov Web portal -- as a means of providing highly available, single points of entry into broad collections of government information.

In chapter 15, Strover discusses the results of a survey of citizens' attitudes toward digital government. This survey consisted of interviews of over 1,000 randomly sampled respondents across Texas, including a special random sample of rural counties. The results showed that while citizens value the potential benefits of digital government, they are concerned about a number of issues, including Internet access, privacy and the quality of services offered.

In chapter 16, Dawes and Pardo examine critical success and failure factors for collaborative design, development, and deployment of digital government systems. These factors were identified through in-depth examinations of 18 collaborative digital government projects across the state of New York.

Case Studies

The articles in the fourth and final group present case studies of digital government policy and systems development. Collectively, the articles address the development of digital government in the context of both developed and developing nations and at the town level (i.e. the creation of a digital city).

In chapter 17, Roy examines the evolution of digital government in the Canadian context. He discusses key policy documents that have established the foundation for Canada's digital government plans. He also presents the views of a cross section of senior Canadian government officials on the development of digital government. The views discussed address issues of system and organizational capacities, cultures of innovation and technological adoption, competencies, drivers and inhibitors of the evolution of digital government, and design principles.

In chapter 18, Boudriga and Benabdallah discuss the Tunisian government's planning model for developing digital government. The major facets of the model address: the definition of the objectives for their digital government, the upgrading of their telecommunications infrastructure to accommodate, the modification of the Tunisian legal system to accommodate new concepts brought about by on-line services, and the digital divide that exists within their country. Their article presents a workflow for these tasks, which might serve as a template for other developing nations.

In chapter 19, Pacheco da Rocha discusses the development of a digital city in the mid-sized Portuguese town of Aveiro. The primary goals of the Aveiro Digital Town project are economic and social development. Particular emphasis is given by Pacheco da Rocha to requirements that must be addressed within digital governments to meet the needs of disabled and elderly populations.

WILLIAM J. MCIVER, JR. and AHMED K. ELMAGARMID

Chapter 1

Introduction

Advances in Digital Government: Technology, Human Factors, and Policy

William J. McIver, Jr.[1] and Ahmed K. Elmagarmid[2]
[1]*School of Information Science and Policy University at Albany, State University of New York, Albany, New York 12222 USA. E-mail: mciver@albany.edu*

[2] *Office of the Chief Technology Officer, Hewlett-Packard, 1501 Page Mill Road, Palo Alto, CA 94304-1185USA and Department of Computer Sciences, Purdue University, West Lafayette, Indiana USA. E-mail: ahmed_elmagarmid@hp.com*

Abstract: This chapter provides an introduction to the book *Advances in Digital Government: Technology, Human Factors, and Policy*. It presents a brief history of digital government; and it outlines major technical, human factors and policy concepts and issues involved in the development and operation of digital government.

Key words: history of digital government, digital government technology, human factors issues, policymaking

1. INTRODUCTION

Digital government can be defined as the civil and political conduct of government using information and communication technologies (ICT). This includes the provisioning of services and the management of legislative processes. Such technologies can empower citizens with greater access to services and more flexible and effective means of participating in government, leading to improved citizen-government interaction.

Developed nations first began making use of computers in government for non-military applications in the 1950s. These were mostly batch processing applications, however (Ashley 1999). The goal of these efforts, of course, was to improve the efficiency of government and the processes that they managed. It would take pioneering efforts in interactive computing beginning in the early 1960s and computer-based communications later in that decade before a vision of citizen-centered digital government applications could begin to evolve. This included work by J.C.R. Licklider (1960), Douglas Englebart (Press 1993), and Robert W. Taylor (with Licklider) (1968).

The period from 1965 to the early 1970s saw the development of a number of technologies that would help lead to the development of this vision. Researchers at MIT, the RAND Corporation, and the National Physical Laboratories in Britain helped to develop packet switching, which would be crucial in the development of data networks. These efforts lead the inception of the ARPANET in the U.S. in 1969, which would by 1975 connect over 50 computers in the U.S. and in several NATO countries in Europe (Press 1997).

The ARPANET was crucial to the evolution of modern conceptions of digital government. While it was not developed for use by average citizens, it along with its direct descendant -- the present day Internet -- bracket the development of a number of technologies that have subsequently been used to provide public services, including e-mail, FTP, TCP/IP, and HTTP; and the Internet that has become the dominant communication technology for digital government systems.

Other technological developments also played a role in the evolution of digital government. Between 1973 and 1977, a number of major experiments with interactive cable television were conducted in the U.S. and Japan, culminating in the release of the first commercial interactive television service in 1977 called *QUBE* (Dutton 1994). These experiments attempted, in part, to demonstrate the use of public services by people in their homes.

In 1970, the BBC and the Independent Broadcasting Authority in Britain began to develop a technology known as *teletext*, which allows people to simultaneously view textual and video data on their television screens. Text is transmitted by broadcasters along with a standard video signal and is displayed in an unused part of the screen using a decoder installed on the television. This technology evolved into the commercial CEEFAX and ORACLE services and has, since 1976, been used to transmit information – some of it government-related – to viewers across Britain (Dodson 2001). Related to the development of teletext was the development of *videotext*, which allows textual data to be superimposed on video frames and still images. Unlike teletext, videotext data are typically accessed via a telephone and modem. In Britain, videotext was first offered as a commercial service in 1978 by the Post Office under the name Viewdata, which was later changed to Prestel. Germany started its own videotext service, called

Bildschirmtext, in the 1980s. Ultimately, both Britain's and Germany's videotext efforts failed to catch hold (Spurgeon 2001). It would take an effort by the French to make this communication modality work.

In 1978, Simon Nora and Alain Minc, two French civil servants, published a critically important report in the history of computing -- *L'Informatisation de la société* (The Computerization of Society) – which had been commissioned by Valéry Giscard d'Estaing, the president of France at the time (1980). Their report defined a new industrial policy necessary to restructure civil and political society in France via the synthesis of telecommunications and computing technologies, a concept they called télématique. In L'Informatisation de la société, Nora and Minc argued, in part, that the social and economic forces unleashed by the rapid evolution and deployment of these technologies must be channeled through a coherent public policy concerned with balancing the interests of citizens, the government, and the private sector. Nora and Minc's report was so influential that it spurred the development and widespread deployment of the Télétel/Minitel videotext system by the French government in 1979, despite the previous failure of the British government to do the same. Their report was also, arguably, the genesis of a comprehensive vision of what has come to be known as digital government. Minitel by 1995 provided over 26,000 on-line services, many of which are government services (Kessler 1995).

Between 1969 and 1990, use of the ARPANET and its technological and organizational offshoots such as CSNET and NSFNET remained largely outside of the realm of average citizens. Mostly academic, government, and industrial scientists had access to these networks (Zakon 2001). In addition, personal computing technologies did not start to become widely available until the late 1970s. Without exposure to the capabilities of these technologies, the consciousness of the broader public (at least outside of France) would, arguably, remain at a nascent stage with respect to conceptions of digital government. Other avenues existed, however.

During the 1980s, the emergence of the personal computer and the establishment of community networks and proprietary dial-up on-line information services allowed the broader public to become familiar with technologies such as e-mail, electronic bulletin boards, chat rooms, and other on-line services. In 1986, the first FREENET was started in Cleveland, Ohio in the U.S, which provided free access to a virtual community in which people could share information and discuss issues. The original conception of the Cleveland FREENET was as a forum for citizens to communicate with public health officials. The Cleveland FREENET was soon followed by the creation of many community networks in North America and around the world. Also during the 1980s, existing and new on-line information services such as CompuServe and AOL began offering dial-up services geared toward personal computer users. All of these developments helped to expose citizens to the notion of on-line services – including government services – and it paved the way for wider use of the Internet.

Bracketing the efforts to deploy the Télétel/Minitel in France was the move by average citizens to use the Internet and the development of software technologies that made its use more convenient. In 1990, commercial dial-up access to the Internet finally became available to the public through the Internet service provider called The World (Zakon 2001); others would soon follow. In 1992, the World Wide Web was released for public use by CERN (European Organization for Nuclear Research) and by 1993 the first general purpose Web browser – Mosaic – was made available to the public (W3C 2000).

These developments would make the world ripe for the development of digital government technologies. Several factors eased the adoption of Internet-based approaches to digital government -- especially Web-based solutions – over earlier technologies such as Minitel. Unlike Minitel, the base technologies that implemented Internet standards such as TCP/IP, telnet, FTP and HTTP, are non-proprietary and they have been ported to a wide spectrum of computing platforms, including personal computers. In addition, Internet-based services offered a better means of connecting people and systems than did isolated dial-up bulletin board systems. The World Wide Web standards HTTP and HTML in conjunction with "backend" Web standards such as CGI enabled a truly platform-independent and extensible means of providing on-line services and information (see http://www.w3.org).

These developments culminated in 1993 in the National Information Infrastructure (NII) initiative of the United States Government. The NII initiative had a much broader focus than creating digital government. The agenda was to create a "seamless web of communications networks, computers, databases, and consumer electronics that will put vast amounts of information at users' fingertips" (NRC 1994). The agenda called for the creation of an open data network – the NII – so as to improve many facets of life, including job creation, education, and communication. The goals of the NII initiative with regard to digital government included establishing the ability to: "coordinate with other levels of government and with other nations," and "provide access to government information and improve government procurement" (NTIA 1993).

Development of a distinct area of research in digital government began in the 1990s (Elmagarmid & McIver 2001). Several major research centers were established during this time, including the Center for Technology in Government (CTG) at the State University of New York, Albany; the Digital Government Research Center, jointly operated by Columbia University and the University of Southern California Information Sciences Institute; and the International Teledemocracy Centre at Napier University in Scotland. Several critical conferences and funding sources also emerged during this time. In 1997, the Ford Foundation funded an invitational workshop on digital government hosted by the CTG and attended by researchers from Europe and North America (see http://www.ctg.albany.edu). The U.S. National Science Foundation (NSF) started its Digital Government research grant program in 1997 (see http://www.nsf.gov). NSF held interdisciplinary workshops on digital government in May 1997 and October 1998. The participants of the latter workshop issued a major report on digital government in March 1999 (see Dawes et al. 1999).

Major initiatives to deploy digital government systems were also undertaken in the 1990s. In 1991, Singapore's government commissioned its IT2000 Master Plan for research and development of a comprehensive e-government ("No Pain without Gain," 2000). In 1993, the Italian government established the Italian Authority for Information Technology in the Public Administration (AIPA), an independent body charged with planning, promoting, and monitoring IT in the public sector (see Chapter 3).

In 1994, a quasi-digital government movement began to emerge out of Amsterdam's *De Digitale Stad* (Digital City) project. A digital city system is variously characterized as a "local social information infrastructure," a "communication medium," a tool for enabling "local democracy," or as a tool for accessing local resources (van den Besselaar et al. 2000). They might be best classified as quasi-digital government systems (or projects) since their functionality usually extends beyond government to civil and commercial society, and they are sometimes managed by non-governmental organizations. The idea for digital cities has its roots in the FREENET (or community network) movement discussed above (Rustema 2001). Since 1994, over 100 digital city projects have been started in Europe, Japan and the U.S. (Ishida 2000). One example -- the Aveiro Digital Town project in Portugal – is discussed in this volume in chapter 18.

1.1 Digital Government as a Unique IT Environment

All sectors in society have long been undergoing social, economic and technological transformations by ICTs, yet the domain of government is unique in this respect. Government transcends all of the sectors in a society. It provides not only the legal, political and economic infrastructure to support other sectors, but it also has a significant influence on the social factors that contribute to the development of those sectors. Digital government, as a result, has the potential to profoundly transform citizens' conceptions of civil and political interactions with their governments in societies around the world. Unlike commercial service offerings, digital government services must be made accessible to all in many societies. Furthermore, the implementation of a public service often requires the integration of intra-government ICTs. Because of all of this, a matrix of human factors, geographic, organizational, ontological, security, data quality, policy, social and other issues must all be dealt with in ways that may be more complex than in other application domains. All of these factors make digital government a highly unique environment for technological and policy research.

1.2   Progress

Appraisals of digital government solutions must be made, at minimum, in the dimensions of technology, functionality and policy. Progress made thus far in each other these dimensions has been mixed. In the United States, unprecedented levels of citizen interaction with government agencies are now possible over the Web. Congressional records, information about agency activities, forms, statutes and regulations can now be retrieved over the Web with relative ease. Digital government is also facilitating two-way communication and more complicated processes. A number of U.S. government agencies now make it possible for citizens for file comments to proposed regulations. The U.S. Department of Agriculture, for example, received over 100,000 electronically filed comments in 1998 for its proposed organic foods regulations. Citizens in Scotland are now able to create and file on-line petitions with their Parliament.

The broad picture for digital government is still wanting for better solutions, however. Many of the problems are ultimately of a technical nature such as data integration or the interoperability of security mechanisms, but they are most apparent at developmental and functional levels. The head of IBM's worldwide government services, Todd Ramsey, was quoted in the July 24, 2000 edition of the Economist as saying that "[a]bout 85% of all public-sector IT projects are deemed to be failures."

The Taubman Center for Public Policy and American Institutions at Brown University released a widely-cited study -- *Assessing E-Government: The Internet, Democracy, and Service Delivery by State and Federal Governments* (West 2000) -- that examined of over 1800 state and federal Web sites in the United States. Their study focused on identifying the major functional shortcomings of Web-based digital government through a site-by-site examination of features and a survey of Web managers of those sites. According to their report, the areas that require major improvements include disability access, the development of security and privacy policies, foreign language translation, and consistency and standardization of Web site designs across government organizations.

Progress has been made in the policy arena with regard to current digital government efforts, as is reported by several articles in this volume. This progress includes policy formation in many governments to spur structural and process changes necessary to make government more receptive to and capable of deploying digital government solutions. Policy formation has also been key in defining visions of digital government. These efforts are discussed below in section 4.

2. DIGITAL GOVERNMENT TECHNOLOGY

A wide spectrum of technologies – both hardware and software -- can be considered to exist within the category of digital government systems. This volume focuses on digital government technology from a software perspective. These include technologies that: "externalize" government by enabling citizens or government officials to interact with governmental processes, and those technologies that perform internal governmental processes. We will refer to the former type of digital government technologies as *externalizing* systems and the latter as *internal* systems. The prime examples of externalizing digital government systems technologies are the Web-based services that have become prominent in the past few years. Internal digital government systems technologies include novel applications of computing techniques in geographic information systems (GIS), database management and image processing to solve critical tasks within government agencies. Of course, many externalizing systems employ the services of internal systems. The contributors to this volume discuss examples of both externalizing and internal systems technologies.

The architectures of systems in both the categories of externalizing and internal digital government systems are in most cases database-centric. It is, therefore, useful to discuss digital government technologies along the dimensions of system architectures and data management. A critical third dimension of digital government technologies that is orthogonal to these other two is security. All of these are discussed below.

2.1 System Architectures

In this section, we discuss digital government system architectures within each part of our taxonomy of externalizing and internal systems.

2.1.1   Externalizing Systems

The dominant vision of externalizing digital government systems has become -- like many other areas of the information technology (IT) sector -- Web-centric. Commercial Web service offerings have clearly raised citizens' expectations of the level of service provided by government agencies over the Web (Cook 2000). Digital government systems can generally be characterized along two dimensions: the architectural relationship they have with their clients and the type of service they are capable of providing for their clients. Architectures include intranets to support intra-governmental processes, public network access to facilitate government-citizen interactions, and extranets for supporting interactions between government and non-governmental organizations (e.g. government-to-business).

Four basic types of Web architectures are seen among current externalizing digital government systems, each corresponding to one of four levels of service ("No Pain without Gain," 2000):

- **Level 1 Externalizing Services**. Level one services provide one-way communication for displaying information about a given agency or aspect of government.
- **Level 2 Externalizing Services**. Level two services provide simple two-way communication capabilities, usually for simple types of data collection, such as the registration of comments with government agencies.
- **Level 3 Externalizing Services**. Level three services extend on level two services to provide the ability to carryout complex transactions that may involve intra-governmental workflows and legally binding procedures. Examples include voter and motor vehicle registration.
- **Level 4 Externalizing Services**. The fourth level of service is characterized by the emergence of government portals that seek to integrate a wide range of services across a whole government administration. The *eCitizen* portal developed by the government of Singapore is a prime example of this type of system (see http://www.ecitizen.gov.sg).

Several systems that support level 3 externalizing services are presented in this volume. Macintosh, Malina and Farrell present, in chapter 8, the *e-petitioner* system, which supports citizens in the function that most represents democratic governments: the process of decision making through voting. E-petitioner allows citizens of Scotland to create, view, discuss, sign, and submit petitions to the Scottish parliament. Han, Kunz and Law present, in chapter 9, an on-line system for testing the compliance of building and facilities designs with the Americans with Disabilities Act. Karr et al.

present, in chapter 11, a Web-based system designed to provide citizen access to statistical data, such as agricultural data, in a manner that protects the confidentiality of those data. Zhang, Zhu and Mark present, in chapter 12, the *WebView* system, which provides officials and citizens efficient access to very large geographic image databases.

Two systems presented in this volume can be classified as level 4 externalizing services. Bouguettaya et al. describe, in chapter 2, *WebDG*, which consists, in part, of Web-based facilities that allow citizens to more easily access information and processes across related and often geographically disparate social service agencies. WebDG is capable of supporting level 4 services in that it performs ontological and process integration between different government agencies. Italy's *National Public Administration Network* and domain-specific *Cooperative Information Systems* (CIS) presented by Batini et al., in chapter 3, supports Web-based externalization of services for government officials within an overall framework that seeks to integrate ministries across the whole government.

2.1.2   Internal Systems

A wide spectrum of technologies can be considered to fall within the category of internal digital government systems, including those that perform tasks common to large organizations, such as financial management, document processing, and communications (e.g. e-mail). Our focus in this volume is on systems that provide novel solutions to functions that are unique to government. Such systems fall generally into two categories:

– **Integrative and communicative systems**: These are systems that provide support for inter-agency (or ministry) integration and cooperation.
– **Domain-specific processing and knowledge management systems**: These are systems that provide support for processing and interpretation of data within ontologies that are unique to government, such as agricultural statistics, data used by law enforcement agencies, social services policies (i.e. rules) and data, and geographic images from government geological surveys.

Several integrative and communicative systems are presented in this volume. The WebDG system (chapter 2) of Bouguettaya et al. (discussed above in the context of externalizing services) also features internal digital government functions designed to integrate information and processes across disparate social service agencies. This capability is critical when citizens require a set of related services, each provided by separate agencies (e.g. financial assistance together with childcare). Atluri et al. describe, in chapter

4, a decentralized workflow management system called *DWFMS*, which is designed to support inter-agency workflows involved in the registration of businesses. Ambite et al. describe, in chapter 5, the DGRC System, which is designed to capture and integrate statistical information across different government agencies, each represented by different ontologies. In chapter 6, Golubchik describes a system called *Bistro*, which supports scalable uploading of documents (e.g. tax returns) – with or without deadlines -- across the Internet.

Several domain-specific processing and knowledge management systems are presented in this volume. The systems of Han, Kunz and Law (chapter 9); Karr et al., (chapter 11); and Zhang, Zhu and Mark (chapter 12) -- discussed above in the context of externalizing services – can be classified in this category. In addition, Hauck, Chau and Chen, in Chapter 10, describe a collection of software technologies they have developed, called *COPLINK*, which enables "information sharing and criminal analyses within and between law enforcement agencies."

Of course, it is possible for systems to span these two categories. Also discussed above in the context of externalizing services, the *National Public Administration Network* and domain-specific *Cooperative Information Systems* (CIS) of Batini et al. (chapter 3) are components of an overall framework that span the categories of integrative and communicative systems and domain-specific processing and knowledge management. This framework, developed by Italy's Authority for Information Technology in the Public Administration (*Autorità per l'Informatica nella Pubblica Amministrazione*) or AIPA is designed to "increase organization efficiency and overall effectiveness of administrative actions" by facilitating greater inter-ministry cooperation through software-centric solutions.

2.2   Data Management

The development of improved semantic data modeling, more powerful management of relations between documents, and more sophisticated data access and retrieval mechanisms are at the core of developing and expanding digital government. The high level goal is to provide digital government services that don't simply fit within a read-only paradigm of interactions between citizens, government officials and government sources of information, but to allow a paradigm that achieves more interactive, process-oriented dissemination and viewing of government information.

Governments maintain extraordinary amounts of information, much of which could potentially be made available to citizens and officials via digital government services. Providing effective access to large collections of information for a large community of users has always presented significant technical challenges. Yet, providing access to government information for citizens and officials constitutes a unique set of requirements (or desired functionality), which we outline in the following subsections.

2.2.1 Document Transfer

Many digital government systems are fundamentally document transfer applications, involving downloading or uploading of government forms, reports or other types of documentation. As more citizens begin to retrieve documents from and submit forms to government agencies, contention for common resources will increase and the need for efficient and scalable document management will become evermore critical. A number of general approaches have been developed to address these issues. Popular documents can be cached at sites across the Internet to place them closer to potential clients (see Wang 1999). Various approaches are taken to handle high volumes of requests: the processing of requests can be distributed across a cluster of Web servers to provide load balancing, a single centralized high capacity platform might be used, or some combination of these two approaches might be taken (see Ferreira 1998). These approaches are applicable to digital government; however, digital government poses special problems with regard to document downloading and uploading.

Government agencies are increasingly making documents available for downloading over the Web (West 2000). Many government documents, such as pending legislation, tax codes, and related collections of rules or statutes (e.g. as in the U.S. Federal Register), are very large relative to documents managed by many other types of Web sites. To facilitate more efficient downloading and use of such documents, data management services within digital government systems are needed to support both the automatic generation of digests of multiple documents and the user's ability to select sections of monolithic documents, which would then be automatically extracted and downloaded.

Conversely, more government agencies are also allowing citizens to file documents (i.e. to upload them) on-line. Unlike downloading, the uploading of documents may often be associated with time constraints, such as tax filing deadlines, which makes efficiency and scalability in this context all the more critical. A framework for supporting efficient and scalable uploading is presented by Golubchik in chapter 6.

2.2.2 Classification and indexing

Locating desired information within collections of government documents – as in any other domain – requires that they be organized in such a manner that relevant ones can be precisely identified and they can be located efficiently on secondary or tertiary storage. Documents in a collection may be characterized according to some classification scheme to increase the probability that information relevant to a query can be identified. The techniques that are chosen must support good *precision* and good *recall*. Precision is the ratio of the number of relevant documents to the total number of documents returned by a query. Recall is the ratio of the number of relevant documents returned by a query to the total number of relevant documents that exist in a collection. Precision or recall cannot each be improved without sacrificing the other.

Many Web-based government sites allow full-text searching of documents, which allows querying to be performed independent of a classification scheme; that is, terms and phrases are not restricted. However, classification schemes are still highly useful for identifying relevant information. Various government information classification schemes exist. Some are used to classify documents. The U.S. Library of Congress scheme for cataloguing documents is a prime example (see http://www.loc.gov). MAchine-Readable Cataloging (MARC) was developed by the Library of Congress as an extension of this scheme to allow the automated interchange of bibliographic information (see http://www.loc.gov). MARC, it should be noted, is widely used outside of the domain of government, as it is supported by most library catalog systems today.

Other types of classification schemes may be used to characterize information to which documents refer, such as types of businesses or legal codes. The North American Industry Classification System (NAICS) is one such government classification scheme. It was adopted in 1997 jointly by the U.S., Canada, and Mexico as a result of the North American Free Trade Agreement (NAFTA) for classifying businesses. It is used to locate government information associated with businesses and to allow governments themselves to analyze statistics on industrial activity throughout North America (see http://www.census.gov). The U.S. Law Code is yet another classification scheme, where laws) are classified under sections (or domains) of law, such as general provisions, bankruptcy, or the presidency (see http://www.nara.gov/fedreg). This scheme is used widely by people who perform legal research.

Of course, the proliferation of government classification standards may itself become a source of the problems generally associated with heterogeneous systems. Attempts have been made to address this issue. A comprehensive classification scheme was developed in 1994 in support of the Global Information Locator Service (GILS). GILS defines a way of describing any information produced by the government so that it is easier for users to locate. It is based on the ISO 23950 search standard (see http://www.gils.net). XML DTDs have been developed to allow the semantic information represented by various government information classification schemes such as MARC to be embedded in on-line government documents. The MARC 21 version of the MARC standard, adopted in the late 1990s, has been mapped to various other meta-data standards, including the XML-based Dublin Core and ONIX standards, GILS and the Digital Geospatial Metadata standard.

The information used to classify documents – whether it be the full text of the documents or metadata -- must then be represented in data structures that will allow them to be located efficiently. Indexing and access method techniques have been widely studied in the field of database systems (see Salzberg 1996).

The classification issues discussed here tie in strongly with ontologies and query mechanisms, which are discussed below.

2.2.3   Ontologies

An ontology in the context of database systems is a collection of metadata that describes the semantics and structure of the data that are managed within a particular application domain (e.g. health insurance, social services, and agriculture). Bouguettaya et al. (2001) refer to ontologies, in this volume, as "conceptual schemas against which queries are formulated." Appropriate ontologies must be designed so as to allow querying and presentation of government information for a broad spectrum of needs by citizens and officials. This issue is addressed in chapter 2 of this volume by Bouguettaya et al.

2.2.4   Integrated ontologies

The management of multiple application domains within an organization (e.g. a government) often eventually leads to calls for their integration and, hence, there becomes a concomitant need to integrate their ontologies. Within a government, of course, there are potentially a very large number of such application domains and associated ontologies, making their integration more complicated than other ontology integration tasks. These information spaces are also likely to be distributed, both administratively and geographically, complicating the problem of their management even further. Ambite et al., in chapter 5, and Bouguettaya et al., in chapter 2, address these issues.

2.2.5   Query mechanisms

Government data exists in many formats. Citizens and officials must, therefore, have the ability to perform queries over a variety of data types, including the full text of documents, geographic information, images and audio. In addition, query mechanisms over these data types must support users having different levels of expertise. Mechanisms to support a diversity of user abilities might include keyword-based searching with Boolean operators, natural language querying, and content-based image searching.

2.2.6   View construction and view management

Searching for and monitoring a given content domain within a digital government remains fairly complex, involving manual accesses to multiple data sources and parsing large documents. A view mechanism analogous to those available in traditional database management systems would be useful within the data management services layer of a digital government system. It would enable a user to construct customized interfaces for locating and examining data using a single interface that has coherence for them. For example, a citizen or government official should be able to construct a view over multiple sources of data for a particular item of pending legislation. Such a view might contain instructions from the user about how, when, and from what sources data are to be retrieved; and instructions on how the resulting data are to be reformatted and presented. This type of view mechanism could be designed to work in concert with other mechanisms discussed above. For example, a view might be attached to a trigger that monitors the modification of a source of government information in which a user is interested, such as a legislative item or a policy document.

2.2.7   Dynamic relations

Dynamic relationships exist between many government documents, the management of which is critical to users' understandings of certain kinds of issues or events. There are, for example, dynamic associations between a piece of legislation that has passed into law and the regulations that are subsequently developed to implement and enforce that law. There are also associations between pending legislation and discussions about them in government forums. In the United States, for example, the *Congressional Record* serves the function of reporting daily actions taken with respect to all legislation. Citizens and government officials would benefit from automated and semi-automated data management services that could be used to dynamically discover information from such a source and notify them of associations between items discovered and other units of government information in which they are interested.

2.2.8 Temporal relations

There exist temporal relations over many government documents that are important to users. For example, many government agencies make *requests for comments* on regulations they are proposing via their Web sites and through other media; these requests usually have deadlines by which people must respond. Another type of temporal relation exists with respect to the versioning of pending legislation, from its initial introduction through various markups, amendments and final passage. Document delivery services are needed within digital government systems to enable users to access and manage government information more effectively with respect to these types of temporal constraints. For example, citizens concerned about an issue being managed by a particular government ministry would benefit from the availability of *temporal triggering mechanisms,* which they could invoke at appropriate Web sites to notify them of the existence of new requests, and to remind them of approaching deadlines. Legislative (or parliamentary) staff members and citizens tracking particular legislative items would benefit from *temporal tracking mechanisms* which they could invoke to achieve better process management involved in working on the legislation and understanding its historical and administrative trajectories.

2.2.9 Geographic views and geo-correlated accesses

Geographic relationships exist implicitly within many government documents. While these relationships are important to understanding them, they are often not explicitly represented in such documents, nor are many documents indexed in geo-correlated ways. The introduction of geo-correlated indexing of government documents might prove helpful to users' understandings of legislation, regulations, or other types of information. For example, using such a data management service, a citizen unfamiliar with a particular governmental districting structure could begin their search for information about a particular issue by submitting a query relative to geographic entities with which they are familiar.

2.3 Security

Security services are necessary in digital government systems to enable data privacy, privacy of communications, and authentication. Many collections of government data contain information that is sensitive with respect to citizens or the government itself. This type of information must obviously be managed using cryptographic methods to increase the probability that only authorized parties can view it. The communication of such data via digital government systems must also be protected from unauthorized eavesdropping.

Authentication – beyond simple identity verification (e.g. password-based logins) – is becoming increasingly necessary as more complex transactions are being handled by digital government systems. These types of transactions include the level 3 and level 4 externalizing services discussed in section 2.1.1. Necessary authentication services include the following:

- **Authentication and Digital Signatures**: It must be possible to verify the identity of someone or the ownership of information created by, transmitted through, or stored in a digital government system during the processing of a transaction.
- **Repudiation/Non-repudiation:** A digital government system must have a method for authenticating the originator of a transaction in a way that is verifiable by third parties, and in a way that does not allow the originator to later refute that they originated the transaction.
- **Certification Authorities**: It is necessary to bind the identity of the originator of a transaction in a way that is verifiable by a third party together with any information associated with authentication, non-repudiation or any other security processes during a transaction. Such information includes public keys and digital certificates. If, for example, a user or process presents a digital certificate, its validity and ownership by that user or process must be verifiable.

These issues are addressed in greater depth by Joshi et al. in chapter 7 of this volume (see also Rivest, Shamir and Adelman 1978).

Statistical database security is another critical security issue in digital government systems. Statistical queries apply aggregate statistical measures (e.g. averaging, locating a mean value for an attribute, or finding a maximum value for an attribute) to collections of data. A database system might be configured using standard database management system security mechanisms to restrict access to individual records containing confidential data; however, it might still be possible to deduce confidential information through the creative application of statistical queries over that same data if no special precautions are taken. Suppose, for example, a government agency were to store statistical data about a population – say home owners in Albany, New York – but allowed only aggregate queries over sensitive attribute values such as income and disallowed access to attributes such as name. A user might still be able to deduce an individual's income by submitting a query for average income while restricting other attribute values such that the targeted individual's record is isolated (e.g. by address, occupation, or some combination of attributes). This issue and effective countermeasures are discussed in greater depth by Karr et al. in chapter 11 of this volume (see also Denning and Denning, 1979; and Adam and Worthmann, 1989).

3. HUMAN FACTORS

Digital government systems must be flexible enough to facilitate access by citizens over a wide range of abilities and skills, including those having disabilities or disabling conditions, and those lacking sophisticated computer technology and skills. Human factors research has produced useful technical approaches to solving these types of problem. This section focuses on the technical aspects of these issues. A discussion of policy issues surrounding accessibility, particularly for the disabled, is given below in section 4.2. The key human factors issues surrounding digital government systems concern accessibility, universal design, and information use.

3.1 Usefulness, Usability, and User-Centered Systems

The noted cognitive psychologist and human factors researcher Thomas K. Landauer (1995) points to the "failure to design well" as the central cause of problems with usefulness and usability of computer-based systems and processes. These failures, he points out, are often due to a lack of focus on users in the design, development and operational phases of systems.

Other major factors Landauer cites as impacting usefulness and usability include the following:

– **Hardware and software limitations:** Usefulness and usability are often limited by the functional limitations of software systems and in some cases the technical limitations of the hardware systems that they control. The case literature is replete with examples of software systems that overly constrain the ways tasks can be performed or that do not allow them to be performed at all. Media rich Web sites often tax the limited processing power and bandwidth limitations of many users' hardware. Bandwidth limitations remain of particular concern for those who use rural, analog telephone lines.

– **Unreliable systems:** Systems fail due to software errors, user errors, and hardware failure, with the first two factors being the most common. Landauer assigns responsibility for user error to computer systems; they should be designed so as to prevent users from causing erroneous conditions.

- **Incompatible systems and data types**: While standardization of
  software systems and data types (e.g. file formats) has become
  widespread, particularly in the context of Web technologies and desktop
  environments, incompatibility problems continue to limit the usefulness
  and usability of many systems. Though Web clients (e.g. browsers) have
  brought about a significant improvement in the interoperability of data
  sources from different applications and operating systems, the use of data
  sources such as PDF files and RealAudio streams now requires clients to
  support special adjunct software systems (e.g. plugins). Compatibility
  problems due to this issue are likely to be more acute for economically
  disadvantaged citizens and community organizations (e.g. schools and
  libraries) that cannot upgrade from older or relatively low-end
  equipment. Only until recently, for example, has the relatively
  economical WebTV Internet appliance begun to support audio streaming
  applications such as RealAudio.
- **Negative ergonomic and social impacts of computer systems:**
  Computer systems are now recognized as potential sources of ergonomic
  problems such as repetitive stress injuries and fatigue. Many negative
  social impacts have been attributed to the deployment and use of
  computer systems. These include impacts on work and work life, privacy,
  culture, and the natural environment (see Greenbaum 1995; Kling 1996;
  and Postman 1992).

Landauer and many others have long recommended user-centered
approaches to design, development, and deployment as necessary to the
creation of useful and usable computer systems. Using these approaches,
designers, developers, procurers, and maintainers of digital government
systems would engage in iterative processes of systems analysis,
implementation, and operation, with each process having users as their
central focus. Unfortunately, these approaches are not used often enough.
Financial and time constraints are common reasons for foregoing user-
centered processes.

Designers of digital government systems would first interact directly with
users in the design phase to gain an in-depth understanding of their needs
and to explore possible approaches to meeting them. In the second phase, or
development phase, developers would engage in iterative cycles of
implementation, evaluating usability, and design modification based on test
results. Once a system is ready for operation, the deployment phase, user-
centered processes should be used to determine how best to integrate it into
human work flow processes, to determine what skills are necessary to use it,
and to periodically monitor its usefulness and usability. Deployment also
includes procurement of software systems and hardware developed by other

organizations. This process should also be user-centered, having inputs from the people who would use and manage such systems.

3.2   Accessibility and Universal Design

The concept of accessibility in the context of digital government encompasses not only the direct human-ICT interactions used to conduct transactions with government, but also factors that limit citizens' physical interactions with government. Barriers to physical interaction include both disabilities and disabling conditions, and problems of geography and time, independent of disabilities, that prevent people from travelling to sites where government services and information are offered. The integration of telecommunications and computing technologies has, of course, served greatly to reduce barriers of geography and time, though many infrastructure issues remain (see section 4.4). We will focus on accessibility issues for people with disabilities in this section.

The Trace Center for Research & Design at the University of Wisconsin identifies four major categories of disabilities or impairments:

– **Visual impairments**
– **Hearing impairments**
– **Physical impairments**
– **Cognitive/Language impairments**

It is also often the case that people have multiple impairments. Visual impairments range from low vision to blindness. Some visually impaired people are able to see light, but can discern no shapes; the vision of some people is dim or fuzzy; some people cannot differentiate between certain colors; and others can see no light at all. Hearing impairments range from partial hearing impairment to deafness. Two major types of physical impairments exist: skeletal and neuromuscular. Those with skeletal impairments may have a limited range of movement for certain joints or they may have small or missing limbs. Those with neuromuscular impairments may have paralysis in all or part of their body or they may have poor neuromuscular control. Cognitive/language impairments include problems with memory, perception, problem solving, conceptualizing, and comprehension and expression of language.

Digital government offers many potential advantages over existing modes of citizen-government interaction for equalizing opportunities for people who have disabilities to make use of government services. ICTs are the basis for a wide array of solutions for accommodating people with disabilities. Solutions include text-to-speech and speech-to-text conversion devices and software, text magnification features offered in desktop operating systems and applications, voice-activated controls for computer applications, telecommunication devices for the deaf (TDDs), closed captioning for video data, and computer-based Braille devices for the blind.

Approaches to accommodating specific types of impairments (or combinations thereof) are not always obvious and, therefore, deserve the attention of specialists. For example, many people who are hearing impaired use American Sign Language (ASL) to communicate. It cannot be assumed, however, that ASL speakers understand English, as it is a completely different language from ASL. A detailed discussion of such issues is beyond the scope of this article. For an introduction to specific ICT-based approaches to accommodating people with disabilities, see the following publications: "A Brief Introduction to Disabilities" by the Trace Research & Development Center at the University of Wisconsin (http://trace.wisc.edu); "Towards Accessible Human-Computer Interaction" by Bergman & Johnson, 1995; and "Computers and People with Disabilities" by Glinert and York, 1992.

The concept of *universal design* has evolved out of the objective of designing systems that can accommodate people with disabilities. The goal of universal design is to develop systems that can be used by the widest possible range of people without design modifications. General principles for universal design have been developed by a number of organizations (Bergman & Johnson 1995; Connell 1997; NYNEX n.d.; Pacific Bell AGPD 1996). Universal design principles have also been developed for the specific software engineering domain of Web applications (W3C 2001a). Web site accessibility is discussed later in this section. Two points must be stressed in motivating the use of universal design:

- **Universal design should be applied from project inception.** It is critical that universal design principles be applied from the inception of a project. Better usefulness and usability of accessibility features can be realized when they are made integral parts of a design. It is also usually far more cost-effective to include accessibility features into a design than to retrofit them into a completed system.
- **Universal design benefits all people, not just those who have disabilities.** Techniques developed to provide those having a specific type of impairment with access to some system are often found to be useful to others. For example, text-to-speech conversion has been found to be useful for "hands free" applications, such as having e-mail messages read to people as they drive. Closed captioning is useful not only to those with hearing impairments, but also to hearing people working in noisy environments.

The National Institute on Disability and Rehabilitation Research (Connell 1997) has developed the following universal design principles, some of which may not be applicable to all digital government systems:
- systems should accommodate a wide range of user abilities and preferences;
- it should be easy to adapt systems to a broad spectrum of user preferences and abilities;
- system interfaces should be intuitive and simple to use;
- systems should be able to employ different input and output modes according to user abilities and ambient conditions;
- systems should be designed to minimize hazards and to be tolerant of user errors;
- systems should be usable with minimum physical effort; and
- the size and spatial placement of system elements should accommodate a wide range of body size, posture and mobility.

Pacific Bell's Advisory Group for People With Disabilities (1996) has recommended that universal design processes be used throughout the entire development process and that they be user-centered by including people with disabilities in usability evaluations.

Special attention has been paid to accessibility in the context of Web content. Web content such as HTML or XML documents must be carefully designed so that people who use special devices or software to compensate for impairments can use them. Certain encoding techniques can render Web content "unreadable" by such compensating systems. For example, if an image element (i.e. <IMG>) contained in a document is not associated with descriptive text (e.g. using the ALT attribute), it will be of little use to citizens who employ systems to compensate for vision impairments.

Different aspects of markup languages pose problems for various adaptive systems. Some text readers, for example, have difficulty processing HTML tables. Guidelines for designing accessible Web content have been developed by the World Wide Web Consortium (W3C) and are continuously revised as markup languages evolve (see W3C 2001a). A number of tools are available for validating Web content against these and other accessibility guidelines (see http://trace.wisc.edu).

Many specialized browsers and devices have been developed that provide alternate ways for people to use the Web. These include special browsers for the visually impaired that allow Web content to be read aloud or displayed on devices such as Braille bars; more general screen-reader devices and software that allow users to have any on-screen content read to them; and other adaptive technologies, such as voice input systems, telephone-based Web browsers, and systems that transform or filter existing Web content to make it more accessible (see www.w3.org/WAI).

3.3   Information Needs, Uses and Seeking Strategies

The designs of digital government systems must also take into account sociological phenomena that can impact their use. In particular, it is important for designs to factor in the ways in which people view and use information. These considerations are particularly important for citizens who lack experience in using ICTs and those who are socially, economically or linguistically marginalized.

A significant body of research in the field of communication exists on the relationships between social environments and the information needs of people in them and their approaches to meeting those needs. One useful collection of literature in this area centers on models of *information use environments* (see Agada 1999 and Metoyer-Duran 1991).

Information use environment models examine information needs and uses by examining the contexts of the subjects (i.e. people or communities) whom are seeking and using that information. A key concept identified here is the concept of a *gatekeeper*, a knowledgeable and trusted person in a community through which people can acquire information and interpretations of that information. Information is often sought through gatekeepers to meet critical government services and information needs of citizens.

The concept of gatekeepers has been recognized as being more common in economically, linguistically or socially marginalized communities, but it has applicability for all citizens and government officials in their use of sources of government information. For example, it is common for the average citizen to have difficulty finding and interpreting certain domains of government information. Legislation and regulations often contain what is considered arcane and hard to read language, or references to highly specialized concepts. Government officials, on the other hand, may be unfamiliar with a particular domain of governmental information from another agency or they may want only to quickly view an interpretation of a particular document or section contained therein. Citizens and government officials in these circumstances might benefit from automated and semi-automated mechanisms that serve as on-line gatekeepers, acting as arbiters and interpreters associated with a given source of information.

One type of mechanism that could be used to implement digital government gatekeepers is an *annotation service* that would run as a Web browser companion. Such facilities allow third parties to create annotations and to associate them with existing, independently maintained Web content. Examples of this kind of technology include *the Annotation Engine* (http://cyber.law.harvard.edu), *CritSuite* from the Foresight Institute (see http://crit.org), *JotBot* (http://windspirit.com/jotbot), the now defunct Third

Voice (http://www.thirdvoice.com) and *Xanadu* (http://xanadu.com). Using this type of service, citizens or government officials would be able to attach comments or interpretations to government documents, without having administrative access to Web sites from which the documents are published. These interpretations could then be sought and viewed by anyone at their discretion while visiting a government Web site.

4. POLICY

Policies are sets of principles and plans of action that are designed to achieve an associated set of goals. Policy making with its relationship to a set of goals can be, as the well-known sociologist and public planner Herbert Gans declared, a "rational" process in that "policies can be proved to implement the goals being sought" (1993:x). The overriding goal toward which digital government policymaking is aimed is, perhaps, best stated in the August 31, 2000 report of the Panel on Transforming Government, of the U.S. President's Information Technology Advisory Committee (PITAC PTG). The goal as stated in the report is to "harness the power of advanced information systems to make government's stores of information and vital services easily accessible to and usable by all U.S. citizens 'regardless of their physical location, level of computer literacy, or physical capacity'" (2).

There are three major areas in which digital government policymaking has been focused:

– **Government transformation**: These are policies that help transform governmental organizations to make them more receptive to the deployment of digital government systems.
– **Public infrastructure**: These are policies that guide the transformation of public infrastructure to facilitate the deployment and use of digital government systems.
– **Social and economic Issues**: These are policies that address the social impacts or economic issues that arise in the development, deployment and use of digital government technologies.

L'Informatisation de la société in France and the National Information Infrastructure (NII) initiative of the United States Government (see NRC 1994) are examples of policy documents that addressed some aspects of these three areas.

In this section, we provide an overview of some key policy issues involved in the development and operation of digital government. These are freedom of information, accessibility for the disabled, privacy and security, and digital divides. These and a number of other policy issues are addressed in this volume in articles by: Comedy, in chapter 13; Fletcher, in chapter 14; Strover, in chapter 15, Dawes and Pardo, in chapter 16; Roy, in chapter 18; Boudriga and Benabdallah, in chapter 18; and Pacheco da Rocha, in chapter 19.

4.1   Freedom of Information

The concept of digital government is for many people premised upon the notion that citizens have the right to access the information that their government produces. The earliest expression of this right is in the Universal Declaration of Human Rights (U.N. 1993a), which was adopted in 1948 by the United Nations (U.N.) . Article 19 of the declaration states:

> Everyone has the right to freedom of opinion and expression: this right includes freedom to hold opinions without interference and to seek, receive and impart information and ideas through any media and regardless of frontiers.

In 1976, the U.N. adopted the International Covenant on Civil and Political Rights, of which Article 19 of the Universal Declaration of Human Rights is a part. This covenant is binding for those states party to it, of which there were 147 as of January 2002 (U.N.H.C.R. 2002).

A number of countries and regional bodies have enacted corresponding freedom of information (FoI) laws since the 1950s, including Australia, Austria, Canada, Finland, France, Ireland, Japan, South Africa, and the U.S. Finland passed a law in 1951 giving its citizens the right to access public documents. The U.S. Congress passed its Freedom of Information Act in 1966, which has since been amended several times. The treaty of the European Union was amended with a code of conduct that gives citizens access to its documents, with some exceptions. Efforts exist in a number of other countries to enact FoI laws, including Israel and the United Kingdom (Freedom of Information Center 2001).

Policymaking around FoI has mainly been concerned with balancing citizen's information needs with the national security needs of their country and the privacy concerns of individuals and organizations referenced in such information. Two modes of publication of information covered by FoI laws exist: *routine publication* of designated information and *publication on request*. Digital government systems have facilitated the publication of increasing amounts of information in the first category (West 2000). Publication on request processes, on the other hand, have historically been contentious, with government agencies often resisting publication due to claims of risk to national security. The terrorist events in the U.S. of September 11, 2001 have raised concerns about freedom of information, particularly the routine publication of information via the Web. Some policymakers feel that even unclassified information could aid people in perpetrating terrorist acts.

The costs for searching and reproduction of information are also an issue for enactment of FoI laws (see Section 4.4). Some laws require citizens to bear some of the costs in meeting a request for publication. These requirements usually come into play when the information being sought exists only on paper or some other physical medium. The immediate costs for searching for and transferring (i.e. duplicating) documents may be greatly reduced in a digitized government relative to paper-based administrations. Long-term costs will likely be incurred, however, by the special challenges of preserving digital information (see Task Force on Archiving of Digital Information 1996).

Fletcher, in chapter 14, discusses freedom of information requests within the broader framework of government policy on making information available via the Web.

4.2   Accessibility for the Disabled

As discussed above in section 3.2, digital government systems must be made accessible to the widest possible spectrum of user capabilities, including the functional or physical limitations of those who are disabled or who have disabling conditions. A disabled person is defined, in part, under the Americans with Disabilities Act (ADA) as someone who has "a physical or mental impairment that substantially limits one or more major life activities" (U.S. Congress 1990).

In 1997, the U.S. Census Bureau estimated that 19.7% (52.6 million) of Americans had some kind of disability, with over 3% requiring personal assistance; over 2.2 million Americans used a wheelchair; and among Americans age 15 years and older, 1.8 million were blind and 5.9 million had difficulty seeing newsprint (McNeil 2001). The World Health Organization (W.H.O.) estimated in 1997 that 180 million people worldwide are visually impaired and 121 million are hearing impaired. Over 80% of people in both categories were living in developing nations (W.H.O. 1997).

An overwhelming body of evidence suggests that disabled citizens everywhere have suffered serious disadvantages in employment, education, and most other aspects of life (U.S. Congress 1990). Digital government must play a role in removing these disadvantages.

Laws and policies have been established in a number of societies to address the broad issue of access for the disabled. The Canadian Human Rights Act, passed in 1977, prohibits discrimination on the basis of disability and it requires that persons with disabilities be accommodated in: the workplace, the provisioning of public services, and in the design of public facilities (1976-1977). The Americans with Disabilities Act (ADA) (U.S. Congress 1990) was enacted in 1990 to provide an environment of non-discrimination for people with disabilities in public and commercial accommodations and employment. The European Union has also enacted a comprehensive set of policies to equalize opportunities for people with disabilities (see http://europa.eu.int). In 1993, the United Nations General Assembly adopted a non-binding resolution in the spirit of the ADA (U.N. 1993b). The U.S. Telecommunications Act, passed in 1996, requires that telecommunications products and services be made accessible to the disabled. More recently, legislation in the U.S. has brought disability access requirements into the realm of digital government. Section 508 of the Rehabilitation Act (29 U.S.C. 794d) was amended in 1998 to require that federal systems and services be made accessible to citizens and federal employees who have disabilities. A comprehensive list of laws and policies of different nations that address accessibility is maintained by the Web Accessibility Initiative of the W3C (see http://www.w3.org/WAI/Policy).

Despite these laws and growing public concern about accessibility, many governments remain out of compliance with Web accessibility standards (West 2000; West 2001). Further education of information technology professionals and more vigilant enforcement of accessibility laws will be necessary to correct this situation.

Pacheco da Rocha, in chapter 19, discusses accessibility issues in the context of the design of a digital city. Comedy, in chapter 13, discusses accessibility as an issue within a comprehensive policy framework for digital government developed in the Clinton administration.

4.3   Privacy and Security

The need for security technologies in digital government was motivated in section 2.3 above. It is necessary to enable data privacy and authentication in digital transactions between citizens and government and within government. Security is traditionally viewed as a technical issue, whereas privacy is viewed as an often desirable and expected social condition that can be enabled by security. Privacy is, thus, addressed as a goal to be met through social policies and laws that guide the deployment and use of technologies. These social policies may in turn mandate certain technical policies.

Strover, in chapter 15, and Comedy, in chapter 13, discuss privacy issues and attitudes toward privacy.

4.3.1 Data privacy and privacy of communications

Data privacy and privacy of communications are the aspects of privacy that are key in digital government. Laws and policies have evolved in many countries that address data privacy and privacy of communications. Though in many countries, it should be noted, citizens do not have a general right to privacy. That is, a right that explicitly encompasses all aspects of privacy: bodily privacy, territorial privacy, data privacy and privacy of communications. Banisar (2000) provides a comprehensive examination of privacy laws across the world.

Data privacy policies are concerned with both the collection and processing of data. A *preference-based* model is often employed to describe the privacy status of data that are collected from users. There are two variations of this model: data are either assumed to be private or they are not assumed to be private. Users should be entitled to either *opt in* to or *opt out* of the respective privacy regime. This, of course, does not address the issue of enforcing data privacy.

Countries employ two models of data privacy enforcement relevant to digital government. Some countries have passed laws that focus narrowly on the conduct of government agencies with regard to data privacy. Such laws generally require the government to protect personal data that it collects from citizens and to require agencies to justify (internally) the transfer of and use of such data by other agencies. The U.S. Privacy Act of 1974 is an example of such a law. Other countries, such as the members of the European Union (E.U.), take a more comprehensive approach by providing data privacy protection laws that encompass both private and public sectors, and that provide for a centralized agency to enforce these laws. Countries have also handled communications privacy using these models.

The differences between these two models of data privacy enforcement can pose potential conflicts in an international context. How, for example, are the data regarding a citizen involved in immigration to be handled between two countries that have different data privacy standards? Commerce, which is regulated by governments, is also subject to this type of conflict. The E.U. and the U.S., as a result of each having incongruent data privacy laws, were forced to negotiate a "safe harbor" agreement that addressed the handling of personal data that are transmitted between the U.S. and E.U. member states (Banisar 2000).

A working group within the World Wide Web Consortium (W3C) is developing a standard called P3P (Platform for Privacy Preferences Project) designed to ease the publication by Web sites of their data privacy policies and the interpretation by users or software agents of those privacy policies (W3C 2001b). Under this standard, Web sites encode their privacy policies according to the P3P protocol, which provides for encoding policies using XML-based elements. The P3P protocol also defines, among other things, the process by which a privacy policy is located and the semantics of P3P elements. As of this writing, the P3P specification had reached the Last Call Working Draft for version 1.0.

4.3.2   Authentication and non-repudiation

Authentication as a digital government policy issue is concerned with the use of sound methods of verifying identification and achieving non-repudiation – just as it is from a technical perspective (see section 2.3 above). Digital signatures and encryption provide sound technical approaches for addressing both concerns. Governments, such as the E.U.. and various states within the U.S., have in recent years passed laws that make digital signatures legal forms of authentication and that, in some cases, allow government to serve as a certification authority for such signatures (EU 1999; State of California 1995).

Non-repudiation policies address a person's rights and abilities to refute a claim that a signature belongs to them. In other words, under sound conditions for non-repudiation, a person would be legally and technically unable to repudiate a signature they made. From a technical perspective, digital signatures created using public key encryption can implement non-repudiation because a message and its reputed sender's public key can be used in combination to verify that a digital signature used to "sign" the message was created using both the sender's private key and the message. The traditional legal concept of non-repudiation presents conflicts with this technical concept of non-repudiation, however.

Under the traditional concept, a person can repudiate a signature on a document by claiming that it is either a forgery or that the signature is not a forgery, but was obtained illegally (e.g. through coercion). Non-repudiation can be achieved by having a third party, such as a notary, witness the creation of a signature. Another conflict has arisen over the burden of proof for non-repudiation. The burden of proof under traditional non-repudiation has been the receiver of the signature, not the alleged signatory. Within the digital realm, however, the legal meaning of non-repudiation has been evolving such that an alleged signatory either has the burden of proof or they have no right of repudiation at all (McCullah and Caelli 2000). Clearly, this is an issue that must be resolved in the context of digital government, as digital signatures are certain to become more commonplace in citizen-government interactions.

4.4   Digital Divides

Arguably, one of the most critical policy issues facing implementers of digital government is the phenomenon known as the *digital divide*: the so-called gap between those citizens having access to Internet technologies and those who lack such access. Many citizens still do not have basic access to Internet technologies. Democratic access to and use of digital government services cannot be truly realized in a society as long as there remain citizens who lack access to both appropriate technologies and technical skills to make use of these services.

A number of critically important studies have been performed in the United States to characterize this gap. The most influential studies in this category are, perhaps, the *Falling through the Net* surveys conducted by the National Telecommunication and Information Administration (NTIA 1995, 1998, 1999, 2000). These studies have consistently revealed that significant gaps in access to Internet technologies exist along dimensions of race, income, gender and educational attainment.

Access to information (e.g. digital government services) is not only characterized by access to technologies, however. Access to information has been studied on several levels, including the properties and characteristics of access, as well as the means and availability of access. Means and availability of access are linked not only to demographics (e.g. as in the results of the NTIA studies), but also to information usage skills and geography. Access to the equipment, software and telecommunications necessary for Internet access must obviously be accompanied by skills to make use of them.

Telecommunication-based information technologies have come to be seen as spatial systems that change space (and time) relations to create new "virtual" geographies (Gillespie and Robins 1989; Kitchin 1998). These include geographies defined by communication, economics and social formations. Access to digital government services clearly requires access to a geography in which access points (e.g. telephones, computers or kiosks) or other appropriate telecommunications infrastructures exist. Such geographies include work environments, libraries, and schools where access points likely exist.

Less obvious are the relationships between the deployment of these technologies and urban planning by both public and private sectors. Urban geographies must have an evolving infrastructure to provide the more advanced telecommunications services necessary for citizens to conveniently make use of advanced government services. It is becoming less practical, for example, to download government documents using 56K modems as the sizes and quantities of these documents increase, but newer technologies may not be practical either. Certain advanced data communications standards such as ISDN, DSL, and cable television-based Internet access, which provide solutions to bandwidth problems, may be unavailable in certain areas due to a lack of necessary telecommunications infrastructure.

A digital divide that prevents access to government information can also be characterized by the information itself: its costs, representations, communication processes used to convey it, and ways it is collected from one's surrounding environment. These issues have been examined extensively at both conceptual (McReadie and Rice 1999a & b) and implementation levels (December 1996). Of particular concern here are potential cost barriers for information and representations of government information. Thus far, most, if not all, digital government Web sites in the U.S. offer information free of charge. It is the case, however, that certain sources of public information are not free. Large collections of legal briefs and other documentation about legal cases are available through subscription services such as Westlaw (http://www.westlaw.com). Such arrangements raise serious questions about the ability of citizens to access government information they need.

Communication researchers have demonstrated that the valuation of information in general presents a unique problem for those who are economically disadvantaged (McCreadie & Rice 1999a: 68). Beyond the basic consideration of whether one can afford to pay for information, the value of information is more uncertain than most other types of goods; its usefulness cannot be conclusively determined until it can be used (e.g. read). Those who are less able to afford information are also less likely to take chances buying it because its usefulness may be highly uncertain to them.

Finally, the cost of technology may present a barrier to government information. Policymaking to address the digital divide within digital government must mandate the leveraging of World Wide Web and other document delivery technologies and newer metadata technologies to provide access points via more widely available technologies. These include telephony-based applications and low cost Internet appliances such as the handheld computing devices or Internet appliances. Policies must also encourage innovations that allow electronic government documents to be used in the context of human agent environments, wherein citizens can still communicate directly with government officials.

Digital divide issues are discussed in this volume by: Comedy, in chapter 13; Strover, in chapter 15; Roy, in chapter 17; and Boudriga and Benabdallah, in chapter 18.

5.   CONCLUSIONS

Digital government can be defined as the civil and political conduct of government using information and communication technologies (ICT). The development and operation of advanced systems of digital government requires a holistic approach, taking into account information and communication technologies, human factors, and policy. Many of the individual technical and policy issues seen in the domain of digital government are not new, but the domain of government does present unique problems in terms of scope, scale, and the complexity of technological and organizational interactions necessary to implement ICT-based solutions. Solutions must often transcend many sectors, requiring the integration of multiple intra-governmental systems. Digital government services must also be made accessible to all citizens in most societies, requiring the collection, organization and presentation of information to a wide variety of types of users. This includes presenting potentially complex government information to non-experts and providing appropriate interfaces for people with physical impairments. The intersection of technology with the civil and political aspects of a society causes a number of critical policy issues to be raised. These include policies on freedom of information, accessibility for the disabled, privacy and security, digital divides, and collaboration and development processes.

This introduction presented a survey of these issues and provided references between them and the articles in this volume that address them.

REFERENCES

"No gain without pain." The Economist, June 24, 2000.

Adam, Nabil and Worthmann, John C. (1989). "Security-control methods for statistical databases: a comparative study." ACM Computing Surveys. Volume 21, No. 4. December.

Agada, John. (1999). "Inner-City Gatekeepers: An Exploratory Survey of Their Information Use Environment." Journal of Information Science. 50(1):74-85.

Ashley, Kevin. (1999). Preserving the History of Government Computing: Social and Technological Change. Digital Resources for the Humanities 1999 (DRH'99). University of Edinburgh, Scotland. September 12-15, 1999.

Banisar, David. (2000). Privacy & Human Rights 2000: An International Survey of Privacy Laws and Developments. Washington, D.C., USA: Electronic Privacy Information Center and London, UK: Privacy International. http://www.privacyinternational.org/survey/.

Bergman, Eric and Earl Johnson. (1997). Towards Accessible Human-Computer Interaction. Sun Microsystems Accessibility Program. http://www.sun.com.

Bouguettaya, Athman, Ahmed Elmagarmid, Brahim Medjahed, Mourad Ouzzani. 2001. "A Web-based Architecture for Government Databases and Services." National Conference on Digital Government Research. Los Angeles, California. May 21-23.

Canadian Human Rights Act. (1976-1977). C. 33, s. 1. http://laws.justice.gc.ca.

Cheng, W.C. , C.-F. Chou, L. Golubchik, S. Khuller, and H. Samet. 2001. "Scalable Data Collection for Internet-based Digital Government Applications." National Conference on Digital Government Research. Los Angeles, California. May 21-23.

Connell, Bettye Rose, Mike Jones, Ron Mace, Jim Mueller, Abir Mullick, Elaine Ostroff, Jon Sanford, Ed steinfield, Molly Story, and Greg Vanderheiden. (1997). *The Principles of Universal Design, Version 2.0.* North Carolina State University, The Center for Universal Design. April 1, 1997.

Cook, Meghan E. (2000). What Citizens Want From E-Government: Current Practice Research. Center for Technology in Government. October.

Dawes, S., Bloniarz, P., Kelly, K., & Fletcher, P. (1999). *Some Assembly Required: Building a Digital Government for the 21ˢᵗ Century*, Albany, NY: Center for Technology in Government, University at Albany/SUNY.

Dodson, Sean. (2001). "A short history of interactive TV Fron Winky Dink to Sky Sports." *Guardian Unlimited, Guardian Newspapers Limited.* April 5, 2001. (URL: http://www.guardian.co.uk).

Dutton, William H. (1994). "Driving into the Future of Communications? - Check the Rear View Mirror." Paper delivered at 'POTS to PANS: Social issues in the multimedia evolution from Plain Old Telephony Services to Pictures and Network Services', *the BT Hintlesham Hall Symposium*, Hintlesham, Suffolk, 28- 30, March 1994. (URL: http://infosoc.informatik.uni-bremen.de).

eCitizen. Singapore's Citizen Service Portal. http://www.ecitizen.gov.sg.

Elmagarmid, Ahmed K. and William J. McIver, Jr. (2001). The Ongoing March Toward Digital Government. *IEEE Computer.* Vol. 34, No. 2, February.

European Union (EU). (1999). DIRECTIVE 1999/93/EC OF THE EUROPEAN PARLIAMENT AND OF THE COUNCIL OF THE EUROPEAN UNION of 13 December 1999 on a Community framework for electronic signatures. http://europa.eu.int.

Ferreira, Luis. (1998). Load-Balancing Internet Servers. IBM International Technical Support Organization. ISBN 073840313X.

Freedom of Information Center (2001). *International Freedom of Information Resources.* http://foi.missouri.edu.

Gans, Herbert J. (1993). *People, Plans, and Policies: Essays on Poverty, Racism, and Other National Urban Problems.* New York: Columbia University Press.

Gillespie, Andrew and Kevin Robins. (1989). "Geographical Inequalities: The Spatial Bias of the New Communications Technologies." Journal of Communication. 39(3), Summer.

Glinert, Ephraim P. and Bryant W. York. (1992). Computers and People with Disabilities. *Communications of the ACM.* Vol . 35, No. 5, May.

Greenbaum, Joan. (1995). *Windows on the Workplace: Computers, Jobs, and the Organization of Office Work in the Late Twentieth Century.* New York: Monthly Review Press.

Hovy, Eduard, Andrew Philpot, Jose Luis Ambite, Yigal Arens, Judith Klavans, Walter Bourne, and Deniz Saros. 2001. "Data Acquisition and Integration in the DGRC's Energy Data Collection Project." National Conference on Digital Government Research. Los Angeles, California. May 21-23.

Ishida, Toru. (2000). Understanding Digital Cities. In T. Ishida and K. Isbister (Eds.). Digital Cities: Technologies, Experiences, and Future Perspectives. Heidelberg: Springer-Verlag, LNCS 1765.

Kessler, Jack. (1995). The French Minitel: Is There Digital Life Outside of the "US ASCII" Internet? A Challenge or Convergence? D-Lib Magazine. December.

Kitchin, Robert M. (1998). "Towards geographies of cyberspace." Progress in Human Geography. 22, 3. pp. 385-406.

Kling, Rob. (1996). *Computerization and Controversy: Value Conflicts and Social Choices (Second Edition)*. New York: Morgan Kaufmann.

Landauer, Thomas K. (1995). Cambridge, Massachusetts: The MIT Press.

Library of Congress. Thomas -- U.S. Congress on the Internet. (http://thomas.loc.gov). 1999.

Licklider, J.C.R. (1960). "Man-Computer Symbiosis." *IRE Transactions on Human Factors in Electronics*. March 1960, 4-11. (re-published as URL: http://memex.org/licklider.pdf).

Licklider, J.C.R. and Taylor, Robert W. (1968). "The Computer as a Communication Device." *Science and Technology*. April 1968, 21-31. (re-published as URL: http://memex.org/licklider.pdf).

Marchionini, Gary, Carol Hert, Ben Schneiderman, Liz Liddy. 2001. "E-Tables: Non-Specialist Use and Understanding of Statistical Data." . National Conference on Digital Government Research. Los Angeles, California. May 21-23.

McNeil, Jack. (2001). Americans With Disabilities 1997: Household Economic Studies. *United States Census Bureau Current Population Reports*. P70-73, February 2001.

Metoyer-Duran, C. (1991). "Gatekeepers in ethnolinguistic communities: Methodological considerations." Public Libraries. 32: 18-25.

McCullagh, Adrian and William Caelli. (August 2000). Non-Repudiation in the Digital Environment. First Monday, volume 5, number 8. URL: http://firstmonday.org/issues/issue5_8/mccullagh/index.html

National Research Council (NRC). (1994). *Realizing the Information Future: The Internet and Beyond*. Computer Science and Telecommunications Board, National Research Council.

National Telecommunications and Information Administration (NTIA). (1993). The National Information Infrastructure: Agenda for Action. URL: http://www.ntia.doc.gov/opadhome/infohigh.html.

National Telecommunications and Information Administration (NTIA). (1995). Falling Through the Net: A Survey of the 'Have Nots' in Rural and Urban America, Washington, DC: U. S. Commerce Department, (July).

National Telecommunications and Information Administration (NTIA). (1998). Falling Through the Net II: New Data on the Digital Divide, Washington, DC: U. S. Commerce Department, (July).

National Telecommunications and Information Administration (NTIA). (1999). Falling Through the Net: Defining the Digital Divide, A Report on the Telecommunications and Information Technology Gap in America, Washington, DC: U. S. Commerce Department, (July).

National Telecommunications and Information Administration (NTIA) . (2000). Falling Through the Net, Toward Digital Inclusion, A Report on Americans' Access to Technology Tools, Washington, DC: U. S. Commerce Department, (October).

Nora, Simon and Alain Minc. (1980). The Computerization of Society: A Report to the President of France. Cambridge, Massachusetts: The MIT Press. Originally published as L'Informatisation de la société. © 1978, La Documentation Française, Paris.

NYNEX . (n.d.) NYNEX Accessibility and Universal Design Principles. Available from the Trace Research & Development Center Web Site. http://trace.wisc.edu.

Pacific Bell Advisory Group for People with Disabilities (AGPD). (1996). Universal Design
    Policy: The Advisory Group's Recommendations and Pacific Bell's Response. Available
    from the Trace Research & Development Center Web Site. http://trace.wisc.edu.
Postman, Neil. (1992). *Technopoly: The Surrender of Culture to Technology*. New York:
    Knopf.
President's Information Technology Advisory Committee / Panel on Transforming
    Government (PITAC PTG). (2000). "Transforming Access to Government Through
    Information Technology." *Executive Office of the President*, August 21. (Prepublication
    Copy).
Press, Larry. (1993). "Before the Altaire: The History of Personal Computing."
    Communications of ACM. Vol. 36, No. 9. September 1993, 27-33.
Press, Larry. (1997). "Seeding Networks: The Federal Role." *On the Internet.*
    January/February 1997. (URL: http://www.isoc.org/oti/articles/0197/press.html).
Qubit Technology. (www.qubit.net). 1999.
Rivest, R., Shamir, A. and Adelman, L. (1978). "On Digital Signatures and Public Key
    Cryptosystems." Communications of the ACM, Vol. 21, No. 2, February.
Rustema, ReindeR (2001). The Rise and Fall of DDS: evaluating the ambitions of
    Amsterdam's Digital City. Doctoral Thesis in the Communication Science. University of
    Amsterdam. November 2001.
Salzberg, Betty. (1996). Access Methods. *ACM Computing Surveys*. Vol. 28, No. 1., 117-120.
Spurgeon, Brad. (2001). "Minitel Hangs On in Internet Age." International Herald Tribune
    Monday, March 12, 2001. (URL: http://www.iht.com/articles/13149.htm).
State of California. (1995). *Digital signatures*, AB 1577, chapter 594., Chaptered October 4,
    1995.
Stefanidis, Anthony, Panayotis Partsinevelos, Peggy Agouris. 2001. Using Lifelines for
    Spatiotemporal Summaries. . National Conference on Digital Government Research. Los
    Angeles, California. May 21-23.
Task Force on Archiving of Digital Information. (1996). *Preserving Digital Information.*
    Report Commissioned by the Commission on Preservation and Access and the Research
    Libraries Group, Inc. May 1. http://www.rlg.org/ArchTF.
Third Voice. (1999). Third Voice Beta 1 Client. (http://www.thirdvoice.com/about).
Trace Research & Development Center. (n.d.). A Brief Introduction to Disabilities. *University
    of Wisconsin-Madison.* http://trace.wisc.edu.
United Nations (U.N.). (1993a). *Human Rights: The International Bill of Human Rights:
    Universal Declaration of Human Rights; International Covenant on Economic, Social and
    Cultural Rights; and International Covenant on Civil and Political Rights and Optional
    Protocols.* New York, NY: United Nations.
United Nations (U.N.). (1993b). The Standard Rules on the Equalization of Opportunities for
    Persons with Disabilities. Resolution 48/96, annex, of December 20, 1993.
United Nations High Commissioner for Human Rights (U.N.H.C.R.). (2002). *Status of
    Ratifications of the Principal International Human Rights Treaties.* January 8.
    http://www.unhcr.ch.
United States Congress. (1990). Americans with Disabilities Act, Public Law 101-336.
    http://www.usdoj.gov/crt/ada/pubs/ada.txt.
United States Department of Justice (U.S. DoJ) (1994). ADA Standards for Accessible
    Design: Nondiscrimination on the Basis of Disability by Public Accommodations and in
    Commercial Facilities. 28 CFR Part 36. Revised as of July 1, 1994.
van den Besselaar, Peter, Melis, Isabel and Beckers, Dennis. (2000). Digital Cities:
    Organization, Content, and Use 1. In T. Ishida and K. Isbister (Eds.). Digital Cities:

Technologies, Experiences, and Future Perspectives. Heidelberg: Springer-Verlag, LNCS 1765.

Wang, Jia (1999). A survey of web caching schemes for the Internet. *ACM Computer Communication Review*, 29(5):36--46, October 1999.

WebTV. http://www.webtv.com.

Weinberg, Bella Hass. (1996). Complexity in Indexing Systems – Abandonment and Failure: Implications for Organizing the Internet. ASIS 1996 Annual Conference Proceedings. October 19-24.

West, Darrell M. (2000). Assessing E-Government: The Internet, Democracy, and Service Delivery by State and Federal Governments. A Alfred Taubman Center for Public Policy and American Institutions, Brown University.

West, Darrell M. (2001, September). An Assessment of City Government Websites. A Alfred Taubman Center for Public Policy and American Institutions, Brown University.

West, Darrell M. (2001, September). State and Federal E-Government in the United States, 2001. A Alfred Taubman Center for Public Policy and American Institutions, Brown University.

World Health Organization (1997). *World Health Report 1997: Conquering Suffering Enriching Humanity.* World Health Organization: Geneva. http://www.who.int.

World Wide Web Consortium (W3C). (1998). "Extensible Markup Language (XML) 1.0." W3C Recommendation. 10 February 1998. (http://www.w3.org).

World Wide Web Consortium (W3C). (1999). " Extensible Stylesheet Language (XSL) Specification." W3C Working Draft. 21 April 1999. (http://www.w3.org).

World Wide Web Consortium (W3C). (2000). "A Little History of the World Wide Web: from 1945 to 1995." http://www.w3.org/History.html.

World Wide Web Consortium (W3C). (2001a). Web Content Accessibility Guidelines 2.0. W3C Working Draft 24 August 2001. http://www.w3.org/TR/WCAG20/

World Wide Web Consortium (W3C). (2001b). The Platform for Privacy Preferences 1.0 (P3P1.0) Specification. W3C Working Draft 28 September 2001. http://www.w3.org/TR/2001/WD-P3P-20010928.

Zakon, Robert H. (2001). Hobbes' Internet Timeline v5.4. http://www.zakon.org

Zhang, Aidong and Lei Zhu. 2001. "Metadata Generation and Retrieval of Geographic Imagery." National Conference on Digital Government Research. Los Angeles, California. May 21-23.

William J. McIver, Jr. is Assistant Professor of Information Science and Policy at the University at Albany, State University of New York (SUNY). His main research foci are in the areas of database systems and social informatics. Professor McIver's current research covers the areas of universal service, information needs and uses, human rights, digital government and XML database applications. His previous research has been in the areas of database integration, telecommunications (for which he is co-holder of a patent), agent-based systems and software reusability. He was co-editor with Ahmed K. Elmagarmid of the *IEEE Computer Special Issue on eGovernment* in February 2001.

Professor McIver has held research positions at U S WEST Advanced Technologies (now Qwest Communications), the University of Colorado at

Boulder, Purdue University and Brown University. He has also held teaching positions at Morehouse College, Spelman College, the Atlanta University Center, the University of Colorado at Boulder, and the University of Colorado at Denver.

Professor McIver's memberships include the ACM Special Interest Group on Computers and Society (SIGCAS), The IEEE Society on Social Implications of Technology (SSIT), IEEE Computer Society, The Society for Philosophy and Technology, National Society of Black Engineers, and Computer Professionals for Social Responsibility.

Professor McIver has a B.A. degree from Morehouse College in Computer Science, an M.S. degree in Information and Computer Science from the Georgia Institute of Technology, and a Ph.D degree in Computer Science from the University of Colorado at Boulder. Contact him at mciver@albany.edu.

Ahmed K. Elmagarmid is Director of Information Technologies in the office of the Chief Technology Officer at Hewlett-Packard. He is also Professor of Computer Sciences and the Director of the Indiana Center for Database Systems and the Indiana Telemedicine Incubator at Purdue University. He received a Presidential Young Investigator award from the National Science Foundation, and distinguished alumni awards from Ohio State University and the University of Dayton in 1993 and 1995, respectively. Dr. Elmagarmid received the B.S. degree in Computer Science from the University of Dayton in 1977, and the M.S. and Ph.D. degrees in Computer and Information Science from Ohio State University in 1981 and 1985, respectively.

Dr. Elmagarmid is the editor-in-chief of *Distributed and Parallel Databases*: An International Journal, editor of *IEEE Transactions on Knowledge and Data Engineering, Information Sciences Journal, Journal of Communication Systems*, and editor of the book series on *Advances in Database Systems*. He has chaired and served on several program committees and served on several editorial boards.

Dr. Elmagarmid's research interests focus on applications of database technology to telemedicine, digital government, and electric power management. He has done work in video databases, data quality and confidentiality, and multidatabase systems.

Chapter 2

Supporting Data and Services Access in Digital Government Environments

Athman Bouguettaya[1], Mourad Ouzzani[1], Brahim Medjahed[1]
Ahmed K. Elmagarmid[2]
[1]*Department of Computer Science, Virginia Tech, Falls Church, Virginia USA*
[2] *Office of the Chief Technology Officer, Hewlett-Packard, 1501 Page Mill Road, Palo Alto,,*
CA 94304-1185USA and Department of Computer Sciences, Purdue University, West Lafayette,
Indiana USA

Abstract: We describe a Web-based architecture, named *WebDG*, to support emerging
Digital Government applications. We use an *ontological* approach to organize
government data and services (applications). The data space is segmented into
logically inter-related clusters of databases to accelerate *metadata* and data
discovery. Equally, services are segmented into *vocabulary*-based taxonomies
to provide a fast mechanism for their retrieval and enactment. As a proof of
concept, we use government social services, namely, the Indiana Family and
Social Services Administration (FSSA), as a case study for the deployment of
our novel techniques. The implementation uses several state-of-the-art, Web-
based middleware and e-services technologies as building blocks for *WebDG*.
These include, CORBA, EJB, and HP's e-speak products.

Key words: Database, E-Service, Ontology, Digital Government

1.   INTRODUCTION

The use of databases has taken a new level of importance with the
widespread use of the Web. The efficient and effective use of databases has
as a result become a central target to government services. The considerable
growth in the US economy has largely been possible because of the
increasing use of information technology. The use and management of data
plays a central role in the created dynamics. Because of the strategic
importance of data management in the context of the Web, two recent

reports underlined the strategic importance of Internet-based technologies that ought to be supported by government agencies. The first report, a government sponsored report to tackle the issues facing the nation at the dawn of the 3rd millennium, called IT^2 [Gro99], stresses that the efficient access of data on the Web is of utmost importance to both citizens and government agencies. The second report submitted to the President of the United States, called the PITAC report [JK99], and prepared by eminent US scientists makes a very strong argument in investing in strategic IT areas. Specifically, they make a strong statement with regard to investing in data management.

The information revolution has led organizations all over the world to heavily rely on large numbers of databases to conduct their everyday business. These databases are usually deployed in wide-area network based environments. In such highly dynamic environments it has been very difficult to exert any formal control over the changes taking place in the information space (e.g., registration of new information sources), let alone elicit cooperative tasks. The most prominent application requiring this type of environment is Digital Government. To really take advantage of the abundant connectivity generated by the widespread use of the Internet, there is a need to empower both novice and expert users. This requires a sophisticated infrastructure that can support flexible tools to manage the description, location and access to Internet/Web databases.

We propose the use of *distributed ontologies* of information repositories. In a large network of autonomous databases that would potentially span the globe, a meaningful organization and segmentation of databases would have to be based on simple ontologies that describe coherent slices of the information space. This meta-information would represent the domain of interest of the underlying information repositories. In this approach, collections of databases that store information about the same topic are grouped together. These ontologies are used to capture the structure and semantics of the information space. In general, they act as a global conceptual schema against which queries are formulated. We propose to investigate the design and implementation of these distributed ontologies for government databases in the context of the Web. The result is a Web-based infrastructure, called *WebDG* that elicits the transparent access to government databases where each database would be presented to the user as one homogeneous element of a much larger database.

Government welfare and social services within the Indiana *Family and Social Services Administration* (FSSA) are used in this research as a case study. This government agency consists of dozens of autonomous departments providing services to needy and indigent citizens. The current process of serving citizens is inefficient. In addition, it is costly to both the agency and citizen. One of the major challenges facing this agency has been the seamless interoperation of multiple, isolated, heterogeneous, and autonomous information systems. We have teamed up with the Indiana Family and Social Services Administration (FSSA) to help move their database management technology to a level where the FSSA and the citizens would be served effectively and efficiently.

The remaining of this chapter is organized as follows. In Section 2, we discuss issues and challenges in moving government to the Web era. Section 3 describes the FSSA's information systems, services, applications, and goals. In Section 4, we present an ontology-based approach for databases and applications (services). In Section 5, we present the deployment of WebDG, a Web-based Digital Government System. We describe the implemented architecture and an accompanying scenario.

2. DIGITAL GOVERNMENT

Governments are by far the most complex organizations in a society. They provide the legal, political, and economic infrastructure to support the common daily needs of citizens and businesses. Governments consist generally of a large and complex network of institutions at different levels, i.e., local, tribal, state, and federal. This opens tremendous opportunities for information technology to profoundly improve and transform the way governments function. In this context, Digital Government has emerged as a distinct research area. Digital government or e-government is defined as the civil and political conduct of government using information and communication technologies [EM01]. Some of the most important issues in enabling Digital Government are reported in different reports and workshops [DBK99, EM01, JK99]:

1. **Data Integration**: Governments usually store large amounts of information over distributed, autonomous and heterogeneous databases. The objective would be to provide an efficient integrated access to this information. It should be accessible to both lay citizens and experts. Different aspects need to be investigated including ontological integration, middleware support, and query processing.

2. **Scalable Information Infrastructure**: A Digital Government infrastructure should be able to scale with respect to the growing numbers of underlying systems and users (potentially all citizens and businesses). Adding a new information system should not require major modification in the infrastructure. In addition, the infrastructure needs to support a large spectrum of heterogeneity and high volumes of information.

3. **Access to Government Services**: Governments provide a large number of services to help citizens. Discovering and accessing services that best fit citizens' needs often require expert knowledge. The aim would be to enable a seamless and transparent access to government services through a Web-based infrastructure.

4. **Privacy and Security**: These two issues are very critical because of the very sensitive information (e.g., citizens' personal information) and the nature and requirements of some government services (e.g., Internet voting). Failure to provide adequate solutions to privacy and security challenges may hinder the wide deployment of Digital Government.

5. **Accessibility**: One of the major goals of Digital Government is to be accessible to all citizens regardless of their physical and social conditions. This means that particular attention should be given to disadvantaged citizens.

Our proposed architecture, *WebDG*, addresses all the above issues save security, privacy, and accessibility.

3.   CASE STUDY: GOVERNMENT SOCIAL AND WELFARE SERVICES

While the outcomes of this research are generic enough to be applicable to a wide range of applications, we specifically target the general area of government social services as a case study. The Indiana *Family and Social Services Administration* (FSSA) is our partner in this research. We have worked very closely with the FSSA to address the problem of organizing and accessing the glut of information generated by the variety of departments and other autonomous entities the agency deals with.

The FSSA is moving ahead to help strengthen the ability of families to succeed in their communities. It provides services to families who have issues associated with low income, mental illness, addiction, mental retardation, disability, aging, and children who are at risk for healthy development. The FSSA has several programs to assist citizens for their special needs. These programs interact with their federal counterpart to address issues requiring access to data from other agencies (state and local governments). Federal agencies also need this information for better planning and budgeting. This interaction is also required for reporting and auditing purposes. It is important to note that each program usually maps to a separate information system that in turn maps to several databases. The most important systems used by FSSA are summarized in *Table 1*.

All systems mentioned in *Table 1* interact with the *US Department of Health and Human Services* (HHS) information systems as mandated by law. The purpose has so far been largely for reporting and auditing purpose. However, this is expected to include other goals (e.g., planning and budget allocation). Additionally, some systems interact with other federal agencies such as the *Internal Revenue Service* (IRS) to intercept money owed for child support. Some systems also interact with the Justice Department systems for fraud detection and enforcement. Interfaces between the FSSA systems and other state and federal systems are all dissimilar and no standard interfacing for data transfer and exchange exists. Problems of scalability and extensibility are a direct consequence of *ad hoc* solutions. To expeditiously respond to the citizens' needs, the FSSA must be able to seamlessly integrate geographically distant, heterogeneous, and autonomously run information systems. In addition, FSSA applications and data need to be accessed through one single interface: *the Web*. In such a framework, case officers and citizens would transparently access data and applications as homogeneous resources.

4.   ONTOLOGY-BASED SUPPORT FOR GOVERNMENT DATABASES AND SERVICES

Part of FSSA case officers' task is to interact with local and state agencies to extract government information and provide government services. However, the large number of FSSA databases and applications (services) makes it extremely difficult to query the available information space.

The Indiana FSSA consists of dozens of autonomous departments located in different cities and counties. Each department's information system consists of a myriad of databases and applications. To access government information, case officers first need to locate the databases of interest. This process is often complex and tedious due to the heterogeneity, distribution, and number of FSSA databases.

The FSSA provides several rehabilitation programs to help disadvantaged citizens. Currently, FSSA case officers must deal with different situations that depend on the particular needs of each citizen (disability, children health, housing, employment, etc). For each situation, they must typically delve into a potentially large number of applications and determine those that best meet the citizens' needs.

Table 1. Overview of FSSA Systems. (Reprinted by permission of IEEE. Athman Bouguettaya et al. "Managing Government Databases." *IEEE Computer*, February 2001. © 2001 IEEE.)

Agency	Application	Architecture	DBMS	# of Sites	# of Stations
Family and Children	Indiana Client Eligibility System	Mainframe	IMS	140	3,800
	Indiana Child Welfare Information System	Client-server	Oracle	95	1,200
Child Support	Indiana Support Enforcement Tracking System	Mainframe and distributed AS/400s	DB2 and DB2/400	184	900
	Providers	N/A	N/A	N/A	N/A
	County operations	N/A	N/A	N/A	N/A
Disability, Aging, and Rehabilitative Services	Client Rehabilitative Information system	Client-server	N/A	30	400
	Vocational Rehabilitation Claims	Client-server	MS Access	1	10
	Bureau of Disabilities and Determination Services	Client-server	N/A	9	100
	Bureau of Aging and In-Home Services	Islands of LANs	MS FoxPro	17	100
Mental Health	State operating facilities	Client-server	N/A	9	880
Family Resources	Temporary Assistance for Needy Families	Mainframe batch	IBM DB2	N/A	N/A
Family and Social Services Admin.	Data Warehouse	N/A	N/A	400+	7,500

To elicit the filtering and reduction of the overhead of discovering FSSA databases and applications, we propose the use of distributed ontologies. The uniform use of distributed ontologies is the core of the proposed approach. Each ontology focuses on a single common information type (e.g., disability). It dynamically groups databases into a single collection, generating a conceptual space with a specific content and scope. Furthermore, each FSSA application is wrapped by an *e-service*. Simply put, an *e-service* is an application functionality that can be programmatically invoked from the Web [CDS00]. Similarly to FSSA databases, we organize the e-service space into *distributed ontologies*, also called *vocabularies*. Each vocabulary is composed of a set of attributes that describe the basic properties of FSSA e-services.

4.1   Modeling Government Databases into Distributed Ontologies

WebDG adopts an *ontology*-based organization of the diverse databases to filter interactions, accelerate information searches, and allow for the sharing of data in a tractable manner. Key criteria that have guided our approach are: scalability, and design simplicity.

An *ontology* defines a taxonomy based on the semantic proximity of information interest [Bou99]. Ontologies describe coherent slices of the information space. Databases that store information about the same topic are grouped together. For example, all databases that may be of interest to disabled people (e.g., *Medicaid and Independent Living*) are members of the ontology *Disability* (*Figure 1*). This topic-based ontology provides the terminology for formulating queries involving a specific area of interest. It aims to reduce the overhead of locating and querying information in large networks of databases. As an information source may contain information related to more than one domain of interest, it may belong to more than one ontology. Note that our definition of an ontology is a little different from those found in other areas of research (e.g., linguistics or AI). In our approach, a concept is defined locally and its definition may change over time. The participating information systems are responsible for the meaning of a concept.

Each ontology focuses on a single common area of interest. It provides domain specific information and terms for interacting within the ontology and its underlying databases. This generates a *conceptual space* that has a specific content and scope. The formation/modification of an ontology is a semi-automatic process. Privileged users (e.g., the database administrators) are provided with tools to maintain the different ontologies. For the purpose of this project, we have identified eight ontologies within FSSA, namely, *Family, Visually Impaired, Disability, Low Income, At Risk Children, Mental Illness and Addiction, Health and Human Services*, and *Insurance*. A representative sample of these ontologies is presented in *Figure 1*.

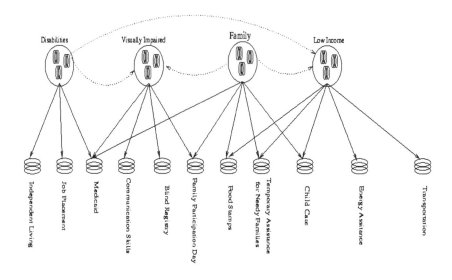

Figure 1. Example of Ontologies within FSSA

The FSSA ontologies are not isolated entities. They are related by *inter-ontology relationships*. These relationships are dynamically established based on user requests' patterns. They allow a query to be resolved by member databases of remote ontologies. The inter-ontology relationships are initially established statically by the ontology administrator. They essentially depict *functional* relationships that dynamically change over time.

Locating databases that fit users' queries requires detailed information about the content of each database. For that purpose, the concept of *co-databases*} are introduced. These are metadata repositories (data about groups of databases) that surround each FSSA database. To avoid the problem of centralized administration of information, metadata repositories are distributed over information networks.

A *co-database* is an object-oriented database that stores information about its associated database, ontologies and inter-ontology relationships. A set of databases exporting a certain type of information (e.g., *disability*) is represented by a class in the co-database schema. This class inherits from a pre-defined class, *OntologyRoot*, which contains generic attributes. Examples of such attributes include *Information*-type} (e.g., ``Disability'' for all instances of the class *Disability*) and *Synonyms* (e.g., ``Handicap'' is a synonym of ``Disability''). In addition to these attributes, every subclass of the *OntologyRoot* class has some specific attributes that describe the domain model of the underlying databases. For example, a subset of the class *Disability* is defined as follows:

Class Disability *ISA* OntologyRoot {
     attribute String County;
     attribute Person Citizens;
      ....

}

4.2   Ontological Organization of Government Services

The current process of collecting social benefits within the FSSA is *ad-hoc* and time-consuming. Typically, the case officers must manually execute different FSSA applications related to the welfare programs. Since the number of applications is large, locating the ones that best fit citizens' needs is usually a cumbersome task. Furthermore, the applications are distributed over different FSSA departments. This makes this task even more complex. To address this issue, we wrapped each FSSA application participating in *WebDG* by an *e-service*. The main benefits of adopting the e-service approach are the following: (1) E-services allow the use of pre-existing (legacy) FSSA applications without requiring their modification. (2) They allow the bridging of the heterogeneity of FSSA applications. Heterogeneity occurs at different levels that include the interface, programming language, business logic, and back-end systems. (3) They cater for the dynamic discovery of FSSA applications that best meet citizens' needs.

To facilitate e-service discovery, we define a vocabulary for FSSA e-services. The vocabulary is composed of a set of attributes that describe the basic properties of FSSA e-services. Each e-service is advertised using XML according to the defined vocabulary (*Figure 2*). The use of XML is a natural fit because of its growing popularity as a standard for encoding and exchanging information over the Web. The following example shows a subset of the XML document used to advertise an FSSA e-service:

```
<?xml version="1.0"?>
    .......
    <attr name="Bureau" required="true">
        <value >Vocational Rehabilitation </value>
    </attr>
    <attr name="Disability" required="true">
        <value> true </value>
    </attr>
    .......
```

Figure 2. FSSA Vocabulary

The aforementioned attributes are of three types: *location-based*, *topic-based*, and *assistance-based* (*Figure 2*). *Location-based* attributes specify the division (e.g., family and children, mental health) and bureau (e.g., child support, disability determination) the e-service belongs to. Citizens and case officers can also query e-services based on the city the e-services are offered in. For example, a disabled citizen may be interested in registering for an *independent living* course only if this course is offered in her/his city. *Topic-based* attributes allow the specification of the type of e-services users are interested in. For example, a single mother can get the benefits she is entitled to by selecting the *family* and *children* attributes. *Assistance-based* attributes allow the specification of the kind of assistance users prefer. The assistance would be either in cash (e.g., TANF- *Temporary Assistance for Needy Families*) or in kind (e.g., WIC- *Women Infant and Children*).

5.   DEPLOYMENT OF WEBDG

In this section, we describe the details of *WebDG*, an architecture to support Digital Government applications. We also describe real FSSA application using *WebDG*.

5.1   WebDG Architecture

In Figure 3, we present the global architecture of *WebDG* using the FSSA scenario. A representative set of eight FSSA databases (Family Participation Day, Communication Skills, TANF, Food Stamps, Medicaid, Blind Registry, Job Placement, and Independent Living) has been identified. These databases are either under Oracle or Informix DBMSs. We have also deployed four FSSA applications. These are wrapped by e-services.

Users (i.e., citizens and case officers) access *WebDG* through a Web browser. They download a Java applet that opens a socket connection to the rest of the system. Two types of requests can be submitted: querying FSSA databases or invoking FSSA applications. The data/service manager receives all requests. The data/service manager is composed of five components: *request handler*, *data locator*, query *processor*, *service locator*, and *service engine*.

The *request handler* is responsible for routing requests to either the *data locator* or the *service locator*. The data locator's role is to educate users about the information space and discover relevant databases. Three ontologies are currently implemented in the prototype: *family*, *visually impaired*, and *disability*.

Information necessary to locate and access FSSA databases is stored in *distributed metadata repositories* (one repository per database). These repositories contain information such as ontology membership, database name and location, etc. The metadata repositories are stored in object-oriented databases (ObjectStore DBMS). They are registered as CORBA objects to three different Orbix ORBs (one ORB per ontology). CORBA provides a robust distributed object infrastructure for implementing distributed applications.

While browsing the available information space, users can learn about the content of each database by displaying its documentation in the format provided by the database (e.g., HTML/text, audio, or video formats). Once users have located a database of interest, they can submit SQL queries directly to individual databases. The *query processor* handles these queries by accessing the appropriate database via JDBC gateways. Like the metadata repositories, FSSA databases containing the actual data are registered as CORBA objects. *WebDG* uses two ORBs, namely OrbixWeb and VisiBroker.

The service locator and engine components deal with application requests. Because the number of applications offered within FSSA is large, helping users to find applications of interest is of prime importance. To facilitate this discovery, each application is wrapped by an *e-service*. We have used *Hewlett-Packard's e-speak*, an e-service platform to define and invoke e-services.

Users can locate e-services by specifying either the e-service name or properties. Frequent system users usually use the first alternative. Service properties are part of a vocabulary defined for government welfare services. Examples of properties include the *service category* (e.g., *health*, *housing*) and the *bureau* the service is member of (e.g., *VRS*). All e-services are registered in an *e-speak core* by specifying their interfaces and properties using the defined vocabulary. Once users have located the e-service of interest, they can directly interact with it by invoking its operations through the *service engine*. Examples of operations for the *Job Finder* e-service include searching for jobs and setting up interviews. The current prototype includes four e-speak compliant e-services: *FPD* (*Family Participation Day*), *CS* (*Communication Skills*), *JF* (*Job Finder*), and *IL* (*Independent Living*). The e-services wrap proprietary FSSA applications. These applications use two communication middlewares, namely EJB (WebLogic server) and RMI, to implement social and rehabilitation programs.

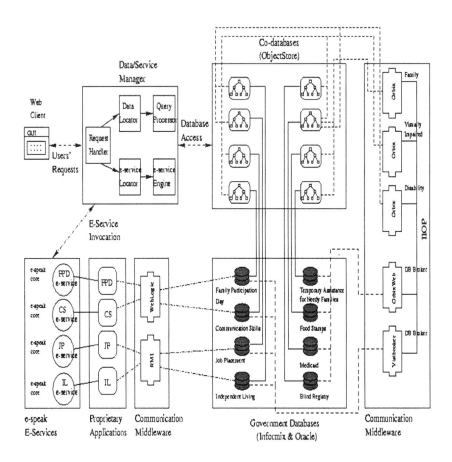

Figure 3. The Global Architecture

5.2   Application Scenario

Citizens come to the FSSA for specific needs. They may be unemployed, unable to support their families, have children with disability, etc. Based on the ontological approach in organizing data and services, the *WebDG* system helps case managers ensure that applicants receive all benefits they are entitled to. We describe a scenario in which a disabled citizen visits an FSSA officer looking for a job and other rehabilitation programs within FSSA.

In a first step, the case officer checks if the citizen is registered within the Vocational and Rehabilitation Services bureau. The officer browses the existing ontologies and finds that the disabilities ontology is relevant. Three databases, Job Placement (JP), Independent Living (IL), and Medicaid (MDAID) are displayed. The case officer selects the Job Placement (JP) database and submits a query to this database (see *Figure 4*). The query's result shows that the citizen is registered within the JP database.

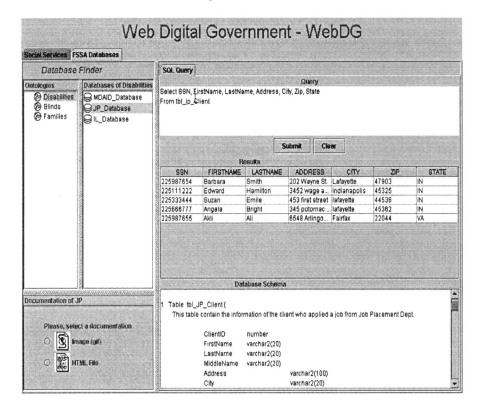

Figure 4. Database Finder

Next, the case officer looks for e-services that provide job openings for disabled people. The disability and job properties of the FSSA vocabulary are used. The system returns the Job Finder e-service. The case officer invokes a Job Finder's operation (Job Search) that looks for job openings. Appropriate search criteria such as skills, minimum hourly wage, and number of hours are specified. The case officer invokes the Job View operation (see *Figure 5*) of the Job Finder e-service to view the different openings relevant to the citizen's expertise. Openings can be discarded, hidden from the citizen, or made available for browsing.

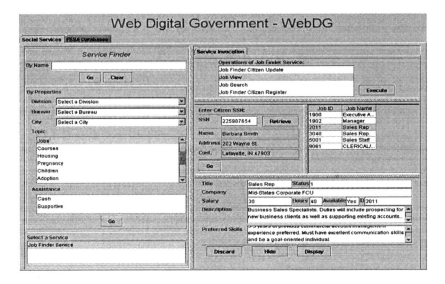

Figure 5. Service Finder

6.   CONCLUSION

Digital Government environments are characterized by a large number of interacting databases and applications (e-services). In this chapter, we described *WebDG*, a system that seamlessly integrates databases and e-services based on an ontological approach. We implemented the system to support government welfare and social services within the Indiana FSSA. Case managers use a Web-based one-stop shop to serve needy citizens to have access to the different FSSA programs and services. Citizens have access to the system to check the application status and invoke operations on selected e-services (e.g., set up a job interview). The *WebDG* system has been fully implemented using different technologies including CORBA, Java, RMI, EJB, and HP e-speak. A demo is available online at http://www.nvc.cs.vt.edu/~dgov.

ACKNOWLEDGMENTS

This research is supported by the grant 9983249-EIA from the National Science Foundation's Digital Government program. The second author is partly supported by a USENIX scholarship.

REFERENCES

[Bou99] A. Bouguettaya, editor. Introduction to the Special Issue on Ontologies and Databases, Distributed and Parallel Databases Journal, 7(1). Kluwer Publishers, July 1999.

[CDS00] F. Casati, U. Dayal, and M. C. Shan. Report on the VLDB Workshop on Technologies for E-Services. ACM SIGMOD Record, 29(4), December 2000.

[CS01] F. Casati and M.-C. Shan. Models and Languages for Describing and Discovering E-Services. In SIGMOD 2001, May 2001.

[DBK99] S. S. Dawes, P. A. Bloniarz, and K. L. Kelly. Some Assembly Required: Building a Digital Government for the 21st Century. Technical report, Centre for Technology in Government, http://www.ctg.albany.edu/research/workshop/, March 1999.

[EM01] A. Elmagarmid and W. J. McIver. The Ongoing March Toward Digital Government. IEEE Computer, 34(2), February 2001.

[Gro99] IT2 Working Group. Information Technology for the Twenty-First Century: A Bold Investment in America's Future. National Coordination Office for Information Technology Research and Development, http://www.ccic.gov, January 1999.

[HP] HP. E-speak Developer Site. http://www.e-speak.net/.

[JK99] Bill Joy and Ken Kennedy. IT Research: Investing in our Future. President's Information Technology Advisory Committee Report to the President, February 1999.

Athman Bouguettaya received a Master's degree in Computer Science, and a Ph.D. in Computer Science in 1987 and 1992, respectively, from the University of Colorado at Boulder (USA). He is the Program Director of Computer Science at Virginia Tech in Falls Church, Virginia. He has published widely in the field of databases, including in *IEEE Transactions on Knowledge and Data Engineering*, *IEEE Transactions on Computers*, *IEEE Internet Computing*, *Very Large Databases (VLDB) Conference*, *Special Interest Group on Management of Data (SIGMOD) Conference*, and the *Conference on Extending Database Technology (EDBT)*. He is on the editorial board of the *Parallel and Distributed Databases Journal* and the *Technical Committee of the IASTED*. He was the guest editor of the special issue of the *IEEE Internet Computing* on Web Databases. He has served in various official positions for numerous international conferences, including VLDB and ICDE.

Mourad Ouzzani is a Ph.D. candidate in the Department of Computer Science at Virginia Tech. His research interests include query optimization for Web databases, digital government, and Web services. He received MSc and BSc degrees in Computer Science from USTHB, Algiers, Algeria. He is the recipient of a USENIX scholarship.

Brahim Medjahed is a Ph.D. candidate in the Department of Computer Science at Virginia Tech. His research interests include Web services, Web databases, and digital government. He received his Bachelors' and Master's degrees in Computer Science from the University of Algiers. He is a student member of the IEEE and ACM.

Ahmed K. Elmagarmid is Director of Information Technologies in the office of the Chief Technology Officer at Hewlett-Packard. He is also Professor of Computer Sciences and the Director of the Indiana Center for Database Systems and the Indiana Telemedicine Incubator at Purdue University. He received a Presidential Young Investigator award from the National Science Foundation, and distinguished alumni awards from Ohio State University and the University of Dayton in 1993 and 1995, respectively. Dr. Elmagarmid received the B.S. degree in Computer Science from the University of Dayton in 1977, and the M.S. and Ph.D. degrees in Computer and Information Science from Ohio State University in 1981 and 1985, respectively.

Dr. Elmagarmid is the editor-in-chief of *Distributed and Parallel Databases*: An International Journal, editor of *IEEE Transactions on Knowledge and Data Engineering, Information Sciences Journal, Journal of Communication Systems*, and editor of the book series on *Advances in Database Systems*. He has chaired and served on several program committees and served on several editorial boards.

Dr. Elmagarmid's research interests focus on applications of database technology to telemedicine, digital government, and electric power management. He has done work in video databases, data quality and confidentiality, and multidatabase systems.

Chapter 3

Cooperative Architectures
The Italian Way Along e-Government

Carlo Batini[1,2], Elettra Cappadozzi[1], Massimo Mecella[2], Maurizio Talamo[1,3]
[1]*Autorità per l'Informatica nella Pubblica Amministrazione (AIPA), Roma, Italy*
[2]*Dipartimento di Informatica e Sistemistica, Università di Roma "La Sapienza", Italy*
[3]*Centro Interdipartimentale per il Calcolo Avanzato nella Scienza e nella Tecnica,
Università di Roma "Tor Vergata", Italy*

Abstract: In Italy, the need for a better coordination of efforts and investments in the
              area of government information systems motivated the Italian Parliament in
              1993 to create the Authority for Information Technology in the Public
              Administration. The initiatives undertaken by AIPA include: the definition,
              design and deployment of a Nationwide Public Administration Network to
              connect public administrations; and the definition and deployment of a
              Nationwide Cooperative Information System atop the network to facilitate
              increased organizational efficiency and effectiveness of administrative actions.
              In the last few years, some cooperative projects aiming at the development of
              specific cooperative systems in different areas have been experimenting with
              different technologies, architectures, and approaches to cooperation. This
              chapter describes and compares these projects, focusing on the organizational
              characters of their approaches to cooperation; and it proposes some guidelines
              for the future Nationwide Cooperative Information System of the Italian Public
              Administration.

Key words: cooperative process, cooperative information system, cooperative project

1.   INTRODUCTION

In Italy, the need for a better coordination of efforts and investments in
the area of government information systems motivated the Italian Parliament
in 1993 to create the Authority for Information Technology in the Public
Administration (Autorità per l'Informatica nella Pubblica Amministrazione,
AIPA) with the aim of promoting technological progress by defining criteria

for planning, implementation, management and maintenance of the information systems of the Italian Public Administration (PA). More recently, the Italian Government has set up the *e*-Government Action Plan (Italian Government 2000) with the aim of achieving inter-administration cooperation by the end of 2002.

The establishment of an *e*-Government strategy requires that a number of government-specific constraints and problems be addressed. First, autonomous administrations must be able to cooperate with other administrations since they do not have complete control over data and services needed to reach their own goals. Such goals are typically set up by external entities or events (e.g. the passage of a law). Second, administrations must be able to share a common semantic view of the "real world" concepts on which they cooperate. Finally, many administrations own legacy information systems, but there is no real opportunity for forcing and/or coordinating migrations away from legacy systems.

In order to increase organization efficiency and overall effectiveness of administrative actions, given the constraints discussed above, it would be useful to develop a Cooperative Information System (CIS) (Brodie 1998, Mylopoulos and Papazoglou 1997). In such a way, it will be possible to consider the set of distributed, yet independent systems of public administrations as a Nationwide Cooperative Information System (*Nationwide CIS*) of Italian PA in which each subject can participate by exchanging services with other subjects.

Among the various initiatives undertaken by AIPA and carried out through the *e*-Government Action Plan, the definition, design and deployment of a *Nationwide Public Administration Network* able to connect public administrations among them, is central in order to reach such an objective. Currently the Nationwide PA Network is providing essential interconnection services (e.g., www access, e-mail, file transfer) to public administrations as basic services.

In the last few years some projects have been undertaken aiming at the development of specific CISs for different areas (e.g., territorial and cadastral systems, services to enterprises, etc.). Such *domain-specific CISs*, and others that will be developed in the near future will be integrated later in order to constitute the baseline of the Nationwide CIS.

Previous works (Mecella and Batini 2001a, Mecella and Batini 2001b) have compared some of these projects focusing mainly on technological and architectural issues; conversely the aim of this chapter is to present the overall integration strategy underlying the Italian *e*-Government initiative by widening the set of projects considered and by focusing on the characterization of their organizational models of cooperation. Some guidelines stemming from such experiences will be also described.

Section 2 describes the Nationwide PA Network, some architectural guidelines and possible approaches to cooperation. Section 3 outlines the different Domain-specific CISs and compares them according to dimensions related to the cooperative approaches adopted by them. Finally, section 4 discusses some lessons learned from these experiences and proposes some guidelines useful for the future Nationwide CIS.

2. THE NATIONWIDE PUBLIC ADMINISTRATION NETWORK

2.1 Layers

The architecture of the Nationwide PA Network consists of three layers, as shown in *Figure 1*, offering Transport Services, Basic Services and Cooperative Services. The Transport and Basic Service layers, which are currently deployed, offer the technological infrastructure that allows the interconnection of different administrations. The Cooperative Service layer will offer the set of technologies, application protocols and services (e.g. repositories, gateways, etc.) enabling the effective cooperation among administrations. The design for this layer has not yet been completed, as different projects are validating and experimenting with different solutions. As current technological trends are moving towards the merging of different technologies in an overall web infrastructure, it is possible that the Cooperative Service layer will overlap with the Basic Service layer. The Nationwide CIS, which will partially integrate the domain-specific CISs, will be developed on top of the Cooperative Service layer. In the remainder of this chapter, the term "Cooperative Architecture" refers to the distributed computing model on which the development and deployment of all new cooperative applications among administrations will be based. Some basic principles of the Cooperative Architecture (to be described in the following sections) have already been applied in the various domain-specific CISs described in this chapter, whereas other issues still need to be investigated.

2.2 Domains and Cooperative Gateways

The basic principle underlying the Cooperative Architecture is the one of domain. A domain includes all of the computing resources, networks, applications and data that belong to a specific administration, regardless of the technical nature of the information system. Each such domain is modeled as a single entity, regardless of its internal complexity, and is connected to the Nationwide PA Network through the Domain Cooperative Gateway, that exports the set of data and application services offered by the domain through Cooperative Interfaces. The interfaces may be designed according to different paradigms and modeling approaches (Mecella and Batini 2001b, Arcieri, Cappadozzi, Naggar et al. 2001, Mecella and Batini 2000, Mecella and Pernici 2001), and deployed through various technologies. The application components that export the cooperative interfaces through the different cooperative gateways of the various administrations are the basic building blocks for the development of the different CISs (both of Area and Nationwide). New applications among administrations are built by suitably assembling such components. Even if implementation details are very different in the various projects, domain-specific CISs consist of the different components hosted on the cooperative gateways and of the "glue" applications necessary to integrate and coordinate such components.

2.3   Systems and Cooperative Processes

Cooperative systems among different administrations can be classified into *Administration-to-Administration (A2A)* and *Administration-to-User (A2U)* (Mecella and Batini 2001a); A2U systems are targeted towards customers (e.g. citizens, private companies, non-profit organizations, etc.), whereas A2A systems are targeted towards operators of the same or of different administrations. These can be both front office and back-office operators.

A further classification can be made between *human-centered-automation* systems and *application-centered-automation* systems. The former type of systems require significant human intervention for realizing the activities supported by the systems; whereas the latter type of systems operate completely at the application level, requiring only a trigger from a human user. In order to further clarify the differences between the two categories, the reader should consider the following examples:

– **Example 1**: Some administrations make their information accessible through web sites. Suppose an operator of another administration then accesses these web sites during the execution of an administrative activity, possibly cutting and pasting data from different web pages into others. The exposition of information through web sites is a human-centered-automation system: operator intervention, acting as the "glue" for the different pages, is crucial in this type of system.

– **Example 2:** Some administrations make their information accessible as application components on their cooperative gateways. Suppose another administration develops a workflow application that supports the operator. In such a case, the different components are application-centered-automation systems. The new workflow application is a cooperative application that needs only to be triggered by the operator.

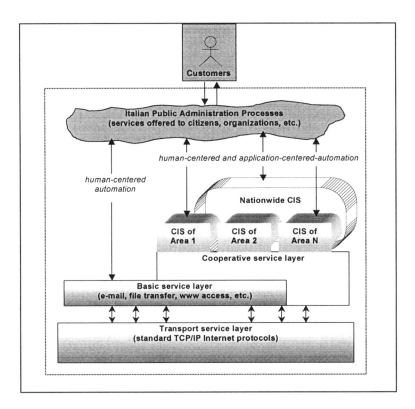

Figure 1. The Architecture of the Nationwide PA Network; grey elements (Transport service and Basic service layers, some domain-specific CISs) have been completed, white elements (Cooperative service layer and the Nationwide CIS) are under construction.

Both types of systems enable the automation of cooperative processes (Schuster et al. 2000, Mecella and Batini 2001a). These are sequences or aggregations of processes that have to be executed jointly by different organizations (i.e., administrations) in order to satisfy a service request from a customer.

The fragmentation leading to cooperative processes is caused by frequent interruptions implied either by laws that assign to some other administrations the responsibility of actions or by request of information owned by other administrations. It has been shown that in about 40% of the cases, the operator of the process does not know all the information she needs in order to complete it and, therefore, must request such information from other subjects. Currently, most of the exchange of information occurs using paper documents and often through ordinary mail. Conversely, in about 15% of the cases other administrations are required to be involved in specific tasks. Finally, in 35% of the cases, administrations are required to be notified of particular events when they occur in some other administration.

Due to the strong constraints described in the Introduction, a Business Process Reengineering (BPR) strategy is not applicable on a large scale in the short and medium term to the Italian PA. Therefore, the automation of the cooperative processes through cooperative applications is the more effective solution for improving services offered to customers.

2.4   Approaches to Cooperation

The design of domain-specific CISs can be carried out through different approaches:

- **Workflow-based**: The different cooperative components of the cooperative gateways export data and application services necessary to carry out specific cooperative processes among administrations involved in the workflow. Such components and the overall CIS mainly support A2A applications. It is preferable to use application-centered-automation support, which requires a strict agreement on technologies, schemas, etc. to be adopted for the cooperative components by all the administrations involved.

- **Lagging consistency-based**: Cooperative components asynchronously expose updated data to other administrations when the internal databases of an administration are updated. The cooperation agreement concerns only update notifications, not the coordination and the synchronization of internal workflows with the external ones (as in the workflow-based approach). The focus is on the knowledge of the event in opposition to its direct control. Such systems can be both A2U and A2A, possibly with application-centered-automation.

- **Publish-based**: Cooperative components are autonomously developed by an administration mainly to export data and application services which might be interesting to some other subjects (administrations or customers). Such components can support both A2U and A2A systems, possibly with human-centered-automation.

In both workflow-based and lagging consistency-based cooperation, each administration remains autonomous, and the cooperative system manages the propagation of both query results and updates (Relly et al. 1998, Arcieri et al. 2001a, Arcieri, Cappadozzi, Naggar et al. 2001). When an update is performed in an administration (e.g., the change of address of a citizen that produces a change of data in the information system of the City Council the

citizen resides in), an update notification needs to be sent to some other administrations (e.g., the Department of Finance and the Department of Justice), as required by laws and regulations. Such an update notification can be propagated using different approaches, including:
- **Publish & Subscribe architecture** (Mecella and Batini 2000): In this approach, the administrations agree on the schema of the events, the technologies to be adopted both for the event description (e.g., XML) and the communication infrastructure (message oriented middleware, distributed object middleware, etc.).
- **Access Key Warehouse architecture (AKW)** (Arcieri, Cappadozzi, Naggar et al. 2001): In this approach, a database of identifiers acts as an index of the data locations and access paths, which then enables the cooperative system to control the dissemination of updates from sources to other databases distributed among different administrations, by correlating data identifiers. Administrations have to agree on the identifiers to be used.

Publishing-based cooperation typically leverages the huge amount of data and application services owned by a leader administration (e.g., the Department of Justice), which autonomously decides to develop and export components. Generally, application services offered by components allow only query access to the data exported by the administration. The vision supporting this approach is that each administration, in a bottom-up fashion, will be able to export, in successive iterations, more and more of its data and application services by following some guidelines and common cooperative patterns (Mecella and Batini 2000). In turn, other administrations will develop new applications or processes (not yet considered) by using such application services. The availability of data and application services is the trigger for new cooperative applications.

We now discuss organizational issues that push towards an approach in turn of the other. Workflow-based cooperation is suitable when there is a clearly defined cooperative process to be automated, and a strong commitment (e.g., a new law mandates the development of the cooperative system). In a few cases, this approach is also adopted by autonomous administrations, which agree and develop the cooperative system for their own common benefit (e.g., expense reduction). The components developed by each administration are targeted towards the specific workflow application.

Lagging consistency-based cooperation can be adopted in order to assure data coherence among overlapping data managed by different administrations involved in cooperative processes. As an example, the Department of Finance, holding a large amount of cadastral and property data in its legacy systems, can adopt the lagging consistency-based cooperation approach in order to assure coherence across all databases belonging to the over 8200 Italian city councils. In such a way, each city council can directly work on updated cadastral and property data without the need to directly cooperate with the legacy systems of the Department of Finance.

Experience shows that the publish-based cooperation approach is possible through an autonomous initiative of an administration, which then becomes a leader administration. The leadership of the exporting administration is required in order to have a critical mass of data and application services enabling the exposition and the bottom-up adhesion of other minor administrations to the initiative. In such a case, the development process of the components inside the administration is not based only on user requirements (there are no clearly identified users whose needs must be modeled as use cases), but on a bottom-up analysis of its own data and application services. Moreover, reuse-oriented and "pluggability"-oriented engineering methodologies for such components are crucial, as possibly new inter-administration applications, yet to be designed, will be based on them. These issues may imply high costs and risks of this approach.

3.   COOPERATIVE PROJECTS

In the years 1998 through 2000, several projects were undertaken, aiming at the development of domain-specific CISs. All projects are based on the concepts of domain and cooperative gateway, but they have adopted different approaches to cooperation, different technologies and types of target applications, as shown in *Table*.

Specifically, the technologies that have been evaluated in the cooperative projects are OMG Common Object Request Broker Architecture (CORBA, OMG 1998), SUN Enterprise JavaBeans (EJB, Monson-Haefel 2000) and Java Message Service (JMS, SUN 2000), Microsoft Component Object Model (COM+, Trepper 2000), traditional technologies (e.g., file transfer, message switching, etc.) and Web technologies (e.g., servlets, script server pages, HTML/HTTP, XML).

In *Tables 1 and 1b*, each project is described along with its target CIS, typical project data (length, start date and current phase), the approach to cooperation (see Section 2.4), the interaction type of the target applications (see Section 2.3) and some technological details. The reader interested in specific details can refer to Mecella and Batini 2001b, Arcieri et al. 2001a, Arcieri et al. 2001b.

Table 1. Brief description of cooperative projects

	Arconet	SICAP	WebArch	RAE
Project Target	Prototype of the Cooperative Gateway of the Italian Social Security Service	CIS of the Department of Justice	Document Register and workflow management of the Prefectures	CIS for the notification of events related to the enterprise
Start Date	Summer 1998 (1st prototype) Summer 1999 (2nd prototype)	Spring 1999	Late 1998	Autumn 2000
Length	10 months (1st prototype) 8 months (2nd prototype)	2 years	Less than 1 year	Expected 1 year
Current Phase	Both prototypes were ended; both never entered into production	1st release ended; 2nd release in the implementation phase	Operative	Implementation
Cooperation type	Publish-based	Publish-based	Publish-based	Workflow-based and Publish-based
Interaction Type	A2A, application-centered-automation	A2A, application-centered-automation	A2A, application-centered-automation	A2A and A2U, application-centered and human-centered-automation
Architectures and Technologies	CORBA and DCOM (1st prototype) EJB and COM+ (2nd prototype)	CORBA	CORBA	XML, EJB, Message Oriented Middleware and JMS, Publish & Subscribe architecture

Table 1b. Brief description of cooperative projects (continued)

	e-Payment Order	SICC	SIM	SAIA
Project Target	CIS for the management of employees and suppliers payment orders	CIS for cadastral data exchange among Italian City Councils, Department of Finance, Notaries and Certified Land Surveyors	CIS for data exchange among Central Administration, Mountain Communities, Mountain City Councils and other local administrations located in mountain territory	CIS for access and interchange of citizen data among Italian City Councils and Central Administrations
Start Date	Spring 2000	1998	1998	1999
Length	2 years	Over 1 year	2 years	Over 2 years
Current Phase	Prototyping	Operative	Operative	Operative
Cooperation type	Workflow-based	Lagging consistency-based	Lagging consistency-based	Workflow-based, Publish-based and Lagging consistency-based
Interaction Type	A2A, application-centered-automation	A2A and A2U, application-centered-automation	A2A and A2U, application-centered-automation	A2A and A2U, application-centered-automation
Architectures and Technologies	Traditional technologies (message switching, file transfer) and proprietary cooperative gateway	AKW, Web technologies, TCP/IP socket	AKW, Web technologies, message queuing with dynamic queues and JMS	AKW, Web technologies and XML, message queuing with dynamic queues and JMS

A subtle issue addressed by all the projects is the management of the semantic and technological heterogeneity. As domain-specific CISs and the Nationwide CIS assemble cooperative components, possibly autonomously deployed by different administrations, semantic and technological homogeneity is not assured. As stated in the Introduction, all administrations have the same semantic background on the "real world" they are working on, but this does not assure that the semantics of the data exported by the cooperative components is homogeneous; moreover the technologies adopted by the various administrations are very different. Publishing-based and lagging consistency-based approaches can lead to multiple semantics, which must later be integrated and resolved by "glue" applications (this is especially critical in publishing-based cooperation). Conversely, workflow-based cooperation requires the definition of a single semantics since the project start-up. Historically some projects have addressed technological heterogeneity, leaving partially unresolved the problem of semantic heterogeneity. In such projects, reconciliation processes and migrations were started. Other projects have been broadening the scope of domain-specific CISs, then moving towards higher complexity. In *Figure 2* the heterogeneity of the different CISs is shown, together with the evolution processes of a few of them.

4. LESSONS LEARNED AND GUIDELINES FOR THE NATIONWIDE COOPERATIVE SYSTEM

The domain-specific CISs developed in Italy during the years 1998 through 2000 have been designed with poor inter-project coordination, leading to different cooperation approaches and adopted technologies, as pointed out in *Tables 1 and 1b*. This lack of coordination has been partially helpful by allowing the experimentation of different solutions and, therefore, a critical mass of experiences.

Recently the *e*-Government Action Plan (Italian Government 2000) has defined a strategic vision towards the overall Nationwide Cooperative Information System, by establishing priorities, milestones and additional funding. In this section, we briefly describe some guidelines that should be useful in developing the Nationwide CIS of the Italian Public Administration. They stem from the experiences of the different domain-specific CISs.

Currently some issues hamper the definition of a universal platform for the Nationwide CIS. They are:

- technological platforms for applications change very fast, involving muddle in the marketplace;
- organizational and management issues are not focused enough, due to the use of complex technologies in administrations with different dimensions and abilities;
- the unavailability of interoperable products sometimes binds choices to only a single supplier.

The maturity lacking in technologies and the complex sharing of responsibilities among administrations tend to increase costs (in terms of time, technical and organizational resources) in order to reach and manage *universal agreement*.

Conversely, there are agreements among subjects involved in specific domain-specific CISs. Such agreements should be progressively extended towards a greater number of administrations and towards different areas. Extensions of agreements need to be justified by strong interactions among different areas or by reductions of managerial costs. Such agreements regard both the semantics and the technologies to be used in the cooperation.

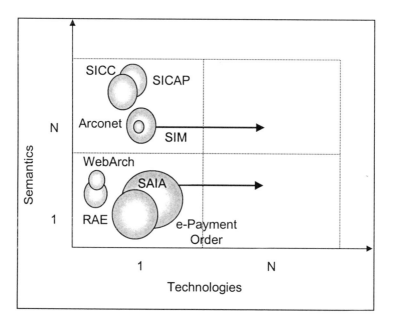

Figure 2. Semantic and technology heterogeneity of the cooperative projects. The radius measures the complexity of the project through a composite, qualitative measure, which includes the length of the project, the cost of the project, and the number of administrations involved. The arrows depict the evolutionary direction of the domain-specific CISs. The relative position inside each square is unimportant.

The Nationwide CIS will reuse data and application services already supplied by domain-specific CISs. Therefore, different semantics and technologies need to be managed. Moreover, the process of development of the Nationwide CIS cannot be totally centralized and homogenous, as it is very difficult to quickly obtain a generalized agreement from all of the administrations and on all the areas. The solution should be to consider a cyclic and iterative development process in which the cycles of evolution of the Nationwide CIS are in relationship to the cycles of evolution of the single domain-specific CISs (Mecella and Batini 2001a). Such coordination is possible though a rational bottom-up control, which establishes the minimum set of basic technologies, derived by all the domain-specific CISs, and develops effective area agreements defining data exchange and interfaces to application services. Of course, the set of technologies will be subject to evolution and widening during the years.

Area agreements, even if limited to single CISs, allow autonomy in the selection of different technologies for interconnection. In order to connect the different CISs, both the mapping of semantics -- to be supported by repositories -- and application backbones offering gateways have to be offered by the Cooperative Service layer.

REFERENCES

Arcieri F., Cappadozzi E., Naggar P., Nardelli E., Talamo M. (2001): Coherence Maintenance in Cooperative Information Systems: the Access Key Warehouse Approach. International Journal of Cooperative Information Systems, vol. 10, no. 3&4, September 2001 (a preliminary version with the title "Access Keys Warehouse: a New Approach to the Development of Cooperative Information Systems" in Proceedings of the 4th IFCIS International Conference on Cooperative Information Systems (CoopIS'99), Edinburgh, Scotland, 1999).

Arcieri F., Cappadozzi E., Nardelli E., Talamo M. (2001a): Distributed Territorial Data Management and Exchange for Public Organizations. Proceedings of the 3rd International Workshop on Advanced Issues of E-Commerce and Web-based Information Systems (WECWIS'01), San Jose, CA, USA, 2001.

Arcieri F., Cappadozzi E., Nardelli E., Talamo M. (2001b): SIM: A Working Example of an E-Government Service Infrastructure for Mountain Communities. Proceedings of DEXÀ01 Workshop "On the Way to Electronic Government" (DEXA-eGov'01), Munich, Germany, 2001.

Autorità per l'Informatica nella Pubblica Amministrazione (AIPA): http://www.aipa.it/english[4/.

Brodie M.L. (1998): The Cooperative Computing Initiative. A Contribution to the Middleware and Software Technologies. GTE Laboratories Technical Publication, 1998, available on-line (link checked July, 1st 2001): http://info.gte.com/pubs/PITAC3.pdf.

Italian Government (2000): e-Government Action Plan. Rome, Italy, June 23, 2000, available on line (link checked July 1, 2001): http://www.funzionepubblica.it/download/actionplan.pdf.

Kossmann D. (ed.) (1998): Special Issue on Interoperability. IEEE Bulletin of the Technical Committee on Data Engineering, vol. 21, no. 3, 1998.

Mecella M., Batini C. (2000): "Cooperation of Heterogeneous Legacy Information Systems: a Methodological Framework". Proceedings of the 4th International Enterprise Distributed Object Computing Conference (EDOC 2000), Makuhari, Japan, 2000.

Mecella M., Batini C. (2001a): Enabling Italian e-Government Through a Cooperative Architecture. In Elmagarmid, A.K., McIver Jr, W.J. (eds.): Digital Government. IEEE Computer, vol. 34, no. 2, February 2001.

Mecella M., Batini C. (2001b): A Review of the First Cooperative Projects in the Italian e-Government Initiative. Proceedings of the 1st IFIP Conference on e-Business, e-Commerce, e-Government, Zurich, Switzerland, 2001.

Mecella M., Pernici B. (2001): Designing Wrapper Components for e-Services in Integrating Heterogeneous Systems. To appear in VLDB Journal, Special Issue on e-Services, 2001.

Monson-Haefel R. (2000): Enterprise JavaBeans (2nd Edition). O'Reilly, 2000.

Mylopoulos J., Papazoglou M. (eds.) (1997): Cooperative Information Systems. IEEE Expert Intelligent Systems & Their Applications, vol. 12, no. 5, September/October 1997.

Object Management Group (1998): The Common Object Request Broker Architecture and Specifications. Revision 2.3. Object Management Group, Document formal/98-12-01, Framingham, MA, 1998.

Relly L., Schuldt H., Schek H.J. (1998): Exporting Database Functionality. The CONCERT Way. In Kossmann 1998.

Schuster H., Georgakopoulos D., Cichocki A., Baker D. (2000): Modeling and Composing Service-based and Reference Process-based Multi-enterprise Processes. Proceedings of the 12th International Conference on Advanced Information Systems Engineering (CAISE 2000), Stockholm, Sweden, 2000.

SUN Microsystem (2000): Java Message Service. http://java.sun.com/products/jms/.

Trepper C. (2000): E-Commerce Strategies. Microsoft Press, 2000.

Carlo Batini is a Full Professor at the Università di Roma "La Sapienza", and since 1993 he is on leave from university, currently serving as a member of the executive board of the Autorità per l'Informatica nella Pubblica Amministrazione (AIPA). His research interests include methodologies for conceptual data base design, visual interfaces, information systems engineering and evaluation, methodologies for cooperative information systems. He received a Graduation (Laurea) in Engineering from the Università di Roma "La Sapienza" and a Post Graduation in Systems Engineering and Computer Science from the School of Engineering, Università di Roma "La Sapienza". Contact him at batini@aipa.it.

Elettra Cappadozzi is a manager of the Autorità per l'Informatica nella Pubblica Amministrazione (AIPA). Her research interests include technical and organizational methodologies for cooperative information systems among different public administrations. She currently works in many projects coordinated by AIPA. She received a Graduation (Laurea) in Mathematics from the Università di Roma "La Sapienza" and a Post Graduation in Processing Systems Engineering from the School of Engineering, Università di Roma "La Sapienza". Contact her at cappadozzi@aipa.it.

Massimo Mecella is a Ph.D. student in Computer Engineering at the Dipartimento di Informatica e Sistemistica, Università di Roma "La Sapienza". The thesis dissertation is scheduled to be completed by Spring 2002. His research interests include *e*-Government, software engineering for cooperative information systems, middleware technologies, component-based and Web architectures. He received a degree (Laurea) in Computer Engineering from the Università di Roma "La Sapienza". Contact him at mecella@dis.uniroma1.it.

Maurizio Talamo is a Full Professor of Databases and Information Systems at the Università di Roma "Tor Vergata". His research interests concern organizational issues and design techniques and methodologies of inter-administrative distributed systems, databases and operations research. He currently is consultant of the Autorità per l'Informatica nella Pubblica Amministrazione (AIPA) for some national projects; during the years 1998 to 2000 he has been the CEO of the Initiative for the Development of an IT Infrastructure for Inter-Organization Cooperation promoted by AIPA. Contact him at mautala@gmx.it.

Chapter 4

Automating the Delivery of Governmental Business Services Through Workflow Technology

Vijayalakshmi Atluri, Soon Ae Chun, Richard Holowczak, Nabil R. Adam
Center for Info Management, Rutgers University, Newark, New Jersey USA

Abstract: Governments provide a wide range of services to individual citizens, businesses and to other agencies within the same government. Information required to obtain government services is available, but is scattered across many web pages, documents, forms, news, rules and regulations, maps, and other sources, maintained by different government agencies. As a result, it is often quite challenging to extract the relevant information from these abundant and/or hidden sources, to determine which agencies need to be contacted, what exact steps are needed, and in which order they must be taken. Although many government agencies have their own web sites that can process citizens' requests, entrepreneurs must independently contact each agency and submit business information to each one redundantly as user information is rarely shared across agencies. In this chapter, we describe an approach based on workflow technology that guides entrepreneurs through the process of obtaining a government service, in particular, establishing a new business. This approach has many desirable characteristics: *customized* workflow generation, *decentralized* workflow management and *automatic* execution of the workflow, which are essential for an effective eGovernment environment.

Key words: workflow, workflow customization, decentralized workflow management

1. INTRODUCTION

Governments provide a wide range of services to individual citizens, businesses and to other agencies within the same government. Services in well-established governments such as in the US support virtually every aspect of a citizen's life from programs to support basic life necessities

(Health and Human services), education, employment, retirement, national defense and so on. Traditional dealings with these services have not been through online interaction but rather through telephone, mail and in-person interactions.

Driven by US government mandates to streamline service delivery and by citizens' expectations (e.g., [GSA00]) for more "citizen-centric" (as opposed to bureaucracy-centric) services, the federal and state level agencies have been pressured to provide more efficient ways for citizens to interact. These service delivery efforts focus on building so-called eGovernment systems that provide a single electronic interface to a wide range of services that are tailored for the individual.

Many of the challenges facing agencies aiming to deliver eGovernment services are similar to those of any large corporation. Over time, different agencies (corporate divisions) have adopted a wide range of internal information systems (both commercial off-the-shelf software (COTS) and systems developed in-house) to support business functions. Such systems generally manage large amounts of data in a variety of data types including spatial, temporal and multimedia. In most cases, these systems were designed and implemented to support specific agency needs (a "stove-pipe" fashion) with agency employees as the target users. Transitioning these systems to support eGovernment is not a trivial task. Streamlining business processes requires data interoperability among information systems. Opening up such information systems for direct use by constituents outside of the agencies requires careful attention to user interface design and security issues. In addition, from the citizen's perspective, there are many processes (such as registering a new business) that involve interaction with a number of agencies at federal, state and local jurisdictions. Thus, constituents require guidance as to the specific agencies equipped to carry out each step of a process, the specific sequence of those steps and facilities to keep them apprised of the status of each task.

Contribution to eGovernment Research: Our work in eGovernment has focused on workflow technology and interoperability. Specific workflow research topics include customized workflow generation, workflow visualization and decentralized workflow management. Workflow customization combines inputs from user requests and preferences (e.g., from an on-line interview) with a database of business rules to generate a workflow tailored to the user's specific requirements and goals. Workflow visualization provides facilities where the user can interact with the workflow and track task progress. Decentralized workflow management introduces the notion of a self-describing workflow that is automatically forwarded from one processing agent to the next without relying on a central workflow server to manage the task sequence.

Many agencies at all levels of government are actively engaged in developing eGovernment systems. Our approach to decentralized workflow management allows us to build upon existing systems and infrastructure without the need for individual projects to adapt to a single specific standard. As we describe below, we have provided a range of interface options with several degrees of automation (from completely automated to no automation at all) designed to accommodate any agency regardless of their technology resources or development trajectories.

Motivating Example: Our focus is on eGovernment initiatives at the State level. Specifically, we model an example of a very common and economically important process: establishing a new business. The process of establishing a new business requires interaction between the entrepreneur and several State agencies. There are a large number of general references (books, magazines, State published literature and web sites, and independent web sites) that may assist an entrepreneur in first determining what steps are required and that also provide some general instructions on how to carry out each step. However, many factors such as the type of business (corporation, sole proprietorship, etc.), and the intended line of business exert tremendous influence on the specifics of these steps and instructions.

Consider a specific example. An entrepreneur, John Smith, would like to start a new business in New Jersey, namely an auto body repair facility. Another entrepreneur, Jane Carlson, wants to open a convenience store. John Smith wants to locate his business in downtown Newark, Essex County, while Jane Carlson wants to have her shop nearby her home in Mercer County. John wants to have the business incorporated with several employees, while Jane wants to have it in sole proprietorship without any employees.

While both must perform some similar tasks such as registering with their state's Department of Revenue (for tax purposes), Jane faces a short list of tasks while John faces a lengthy process of obtaining construction permits from the local government, an air quality permit from the Department of Environmental Protection, a license from the Division of Motor Vehicles, and employer related insurance from the Department of Labor. Aside from these regulatory and fiduciary requirements, the entrepreneurs may consider many other factors such as the demographics of the potential client base, incentives for opening the business in specific areas (e.g., New Jersey's tax-free enterprise zones), transportation corridors, traffic analysis and so on.

Our research work on inter-agency workflow and decentralized workflow management supports the business community with transparent interactions with various State agencies and their underlying heterogeneous systems without infringing on their autonomy and business practices.

2.   RESEARCH OBJECTIVES

Often relevant information required to register a business is available on web pages, forms, newsletters, rules and regulations, maps, and others publications, maintained by government agencies. Although all the information related to a business is available, it is very difficult to extract, either because it is abundant, or hidden. Establishing a new business may, for example, require permits from different agencies, which is in itself a complex process, as demonstrated in *Figure 1*. It is often quite challenging to determine which agencies need to be contacted, what are the exact steps needed, and in which order they must be performed. Although many government agencies have their own web sites that can process citizens' requests, entrepreneurs must independently contact each agency and submit similar business information multiple times as user information is rarely shared across agencies.

A Government service can be viewed as a process that consists of various tasks to be executed in a meaningful order. Some processes involve various work units within an agency (e.g., Motor Vehicle registration service consists of subtasks within the Department of Motor Vehicles), while others involve tasks spanning across many agencies (e.g., Business registration service involves the Department of Commercial Recordings, Department of Taxation, Department of Labor, Department of Environmental Protection, etc.). The various steps required for a specific business type, the sequence in which they need to be executed, and by which agency they are executed can be visualized as an inter-agency workflow.

In general, a workflow can be defined as a set of tasks and dependencies that control the coordination requirements among these tasks. The task dependencies can be categorized as control-flow dependencies, value dependencies, and external dependencies [GHS95,RS94].

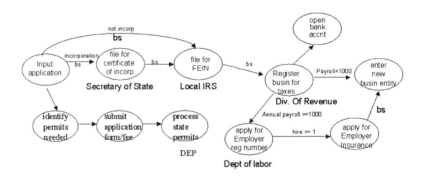

Figure 1. Business Registration Process

In the example in *Figure 1*, the "bs" dependency between "file for FEIN" and "Register business" is a control flow dependency, denoting "begin-on-success." The dependency "payroll >= 1000" between "register business" and "apply for employee reg number" is a value dependency.

Effectively, employing a workflow system will guide entrepreneurs through the process of establishing their business. Our approach comprises of three steps: (1) Generate a *dynamic* and *customized* workflow, based on user parameters, requirements and agency constraints; (2) Automatically execute the different steps involved at appropriate agencies in the appropriate sequence by authorized individuals, adhering to the business policies of those agencies; and (3) Visually report the progression of the workflow so that entrepreneurs and agencies can monitor the status.

A workflow management system (WFMS) is a system that supports process specification, enactment, monitoring, coordination and administration of workflow processes through the execution of software, whose order of execution is based on the workflow logic [WFMC]. As can be seen from Figure 2(a), the tasks that constitute the workflow are executed by different, autonomous, distributed systems. We call the system that executes a specific task a *task execution agent*, or simply *agent*. We denote the task execution agent of a task t_i as $A(t_i)$.

Traditionally, workflow management is carried out by one single centralized WFMS engine, which is responsible primarily for: (1) distributing the tasks to the appropriate agents, and (2) ensuring the specified task dependencies by sending the tasks to their respective agents only when all preconditions are satisfied. Consider for example the workflow shown in Figure 2(a). The WFMS first sends t1 to A(t1), after it receives the response from A(t1), it sends t2 and t3 to A(t2) and A(t3), respectively, and after receiving the response from A(t3), it sends t4 to A(t4), and so on. In other words, the WFMS is responsible for the control of process flow at every stage of execution.

A centralized WFMS enjoys several advantages, including thin clients, central monitoring and auditing, and simpler synchronization mechanisms. However, in an environment with inter-organizational workflows, a centralized WFMS has certain limitations, including: (i) scalability is one of the pressing needs since many concurrent workflows or instances of the same workflows are executed simultaneously, and a centralized WFMS may cause a performance bottleneck, (ii) it can be a single point of failure, and (iii) the systems at different agencies are inherently distributed, heterogeneous and autonomous in nature, and therefore do not lend themselves to centralized control. The inter-agency workflow system for eGovernment services should take into consideration diversities in culture, system heterogeneity and autonomy of agencies.

To address these problems, we propose a decentralized workflow management system (DWFMS), in which workflow control migrates from one agent to another. With decentralized control, shown in Figure 2(b), the entire workflow is first sent to A(t1) by a central system, which is responsible for merely receiving the request and forwarding the results to the user. After the execution of t1, A(t1) forwards the remaining workflow to the subsequent agents, in this case, to A(t2) and A(t3). At the end, the last task execution agent(s) need to report the results back to the central system. The percolation of workflow from one agent to the next can be seen in Figure 2(b). Note that, this way of execution results in fewer message exchanges between the central system and the task execution agents, and also minimizes the control by one single central controlling authority, which is desirable in autonomous environments.

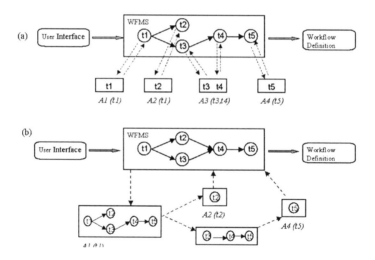

Figure 2. Centralized and Decentralized Workflow Management

3.   DECENTRALIZED WORKFLOW SYSTEMS

In this section we discuss in detail our approach to customized workflow design and decentralized workflow management.

3.1   Generation of Customized Workflows

The conventional workflow model and design steps in the business world assume that a workflow needs to be completely specified including exception cases and various conditional branches. In an eGovernment environment, the steps required to obtain government services differ widely depending on such factors as age, sex, address, business type, business structure, business location, number of intended employees, total amount of the annual payroll, and many more. Incorporating all possible cases and capturing them in one workflow at the design time is not practical. Our proposed system considers the individual customer's profile to dynamically tailor a customized workflow. It possesses the following characteristics:

(1) Component-based composition: The workflow specification is generated through composition of tasks that are autonomous services provided by relevant work units or agencies. Each task and its parameter information are published by its execution agent (e.g. input to the task, output from the task, which agency it belongs to, which agent executes the task, etc.). These tasks make up a service catalog.

(2) Rule-based generation: Workflow specification is rule-driven. Almost all government services need to comply with federal, state or local regulations. These regulations determine the necessary tasks and the order in which they must be performed. For instance, a State business registration service requires that *business entity filing* has to be done before the registration.

(3) User preference driven customization: Another factor that influences the generation of workflow specifications is the user profile and preference information. User input is used for identifying the relevant regulations mandated by the government agencies. Once a rule is identified, relevant tasks and their order determine the workflow, which is a customized workflow for that user.

The tasks are structured in a hierarchical manner in the sense that one task may include several sub-tasks. Rules are clustered and organized in a manner to facilitate identification of rules for a service. The example from a State business registration process stated in Section 1 illustrates our approach to customized workflow generation, which takes into account a variety of customer needs. According to the requirements of John and Jane, two different workflow specifications are generated as shown in figure (3a) and (3b) for John and Jane, respectively.

The process of opening a new business in NJ depends on many parameters, such as the business structure, whether it should be a sole proprietorship, a corporation or a partnership; the business type, such as restaurant, gas station, or nail shop; the business location; the number of intended employees; the total amount of the annual payroll, and many more. Specifying all these cases in workflow definitions would be tedious and error prone. Instead of predicting complete specifications for all possible combinations of tasks and dependencies, the workflow specification is generated tailored to the customer's needs.

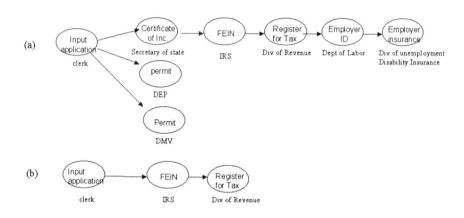

Figure 3. Customized Workflows

3.2   Decentralized Workflow Management

Workflow execution requires a workflow engine that is responsible for interpreting the workflow specification, and for scheduling and coordination of task execution. In the centralized architecture, the workflow manager is located at the central server, and it sends the tasks to appropriate agents for execution. On the other hand, in decentralized workflow management, the task execution agents have to additionally perform the role of interpreting the workflow specification, enforcing the control flow at its own site and then forwarding the remaining workflow to subsequent task execution agents, as appropriate. In other words, the task execution agents have to assume some of the functionalities of the central server, and therefore, the decentralized management requires a collection of workflow management components.

Our approach to decentralized workflow management employs (1) *self-describing workflow* and (2) *WFMS stubs*.

Self-describing workflows: Self-describing workflows are partitions of a workflow that carry sufficient information so that they can be managed by a local task execution agent rather than the central WFMS. Each self-describing workflow comprises of (1) a task t, (2) all the tasks that follow t and the dependencies among them, (3) the agent that executes t, (4) the input objects required to execute t. This information is piggybacked along with t when sending it to its execution agent.

WFMS stub: A WFMS stub is a light-weight component that can be attached to a task execution agent, which is responsible for receiving the self-describing workflow, modifying it and re-sending it to the next task execution agent. This module is responsible for interpreting the given self-describing workflow, *i.e.*: (1) evaluates preconditions and executes its task, (2) partitions the remaining workflow, constructs self-describing workflows, (3) evaluates control information and (4) forwards each self-describing workflow to its subsequent agent.

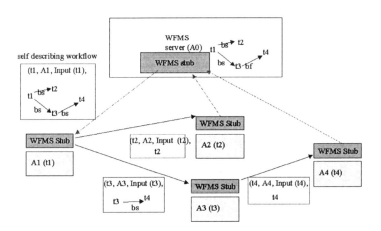

Figure 4. WFMS stub with self-describing workflow partitions

An important property of the partitioning is that it should preserve the original semantics of the workflow. In other words, it should neither remove any tasks or dependencies, nor it should add any new ones. A partitioning algorithm that preserves this property has been proposed in [ACM01]. Figure 4 illustrates the execution of a business registration workflow for an auto body repair shop using self-describing workflows and WFMS stubs. Once the application information is processed (t1), the workflow is partitioned into two: one involves the Department of Environmental Protection agency to obtain an air quality permit (t2). The second involves the local IRS agency to obtain a federal employer identification number (t3) which leads to another partition where business registration for tax (t4) begins at Department of Taxation, and so on.

4.   SYSTEM ARCHITECTURE

Our approach to transparently deliver eGovernment services that involve multiple agencies is based on a hybrid architecture consisting of a client-server architecture and an agent architecture. The architectural and functional relationships among various components are shown in figure 5. Client applications for entrepreneurs include (1) a GIS-based business location service which provides mapping and location-based information to facilitate decision making on a business location; (2) an interview interface, which dynamically elicits user information specific for a business type, and (3) a workflow interface through which a business owner can visualize the workflow and interact with its execution.

The server side feeds in GIS related data, e.g. maps and location-dependent information. It also has a component to guide interview sessions based on an interview rule base. These interview rules are embodiments of case analysts' expert knowledge such that only questions relevant to a specific business or location and user answers are asked. The server also has a workflow generation component where the user profile information gathered at the interview session and the rules and regulations database are matched to generate a customized workflow. The other server component is a central workflow management system. This component is a specialized software agent, which manages workflow execution by communicating and collaborating with various agency-specific workflow execution agents. It also handles exceptions raised in task execution agents.

Government agencies that execute a task will have a workflow execution agent software component called workflow stub. The workflow stub interprets a workflow specification and interacts with task agents, either a human clerk or a program, for task execution. Once the scheduled task at an agency is finished, the workflow stub agent generates self-describing workflows for the subsequent agencies and forwards them to their workflow stubs. We consider this agent architecture with specialized workflow stubs to be more suitable for decentralized management of workflow execution, because it allows autonomy and heterogeneity of each government agency. These workflow stubs communicate among themselves to collectively achieve the workflow execution. The server management is minimized unless communication with the central management component is necessary, as in exception handling, cancellation of execution, or notification of successful workflow execution.

The architecture in Figure 5 only shows details that are relevant to workflow generation and workflow execution. We left out modules that are concerned with security, data and information interoperability and the rules and regulations databases. The global architectural overview that contains all the modules can be found in [AD01].

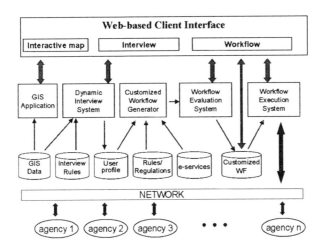

Figure 5. Architecture of Workflow based eGovernment Services

5. RELATED WORK

Distributed scheduling of workflows has been addressed in Exotica/Flowmark [MO95], INCA[BA96], Migrating Workflows[AR98], ORBWork and WebWork of Meteor system [DA97, ML98], Mentor/Mentor-Lite [MU98] and WIDE [CE97]. We discuss some that are considered most relevant to our approach. An INCA (Intelligent Information Carrier) is an object that contains the context of a workflow instance, including information relevant to the execution of the process as well as propagation of the object among the relevant processing stations. The INCA is routed from one processing station to the next according to the control flow specification that is stored in the INCA and in the processing station. This system, however, does not allow for parallel processing of the activities since each INCA implicitly serves as an exclusive token that can solely be processed at a single location at a time. A similar approach is described in Migrating Workflows [AR98].

EXOTICA/FMQM (Flowmark on Message Queue Manager) consists of a process definition node and runtime nodes. A process definition is compiled and divided into several parts and each part is distributed to a runtime node. Each runtime node has a node manager in charge of communicating with the process definition node. The definition node sends to each involved node manager only the information pertaining to the activities that will be executed at that node. Upon receiving its part of the process, a runtime node manager maintains a process table, which stores the partitioned process definition needed for the execution of instances of each process. The communication between runtime nodes takes place through message queues.

ORBWork and WebWork in the Meteor system make use of a workflow scheduler and task managers that manage individual tasks based on CORBA and the web as its respective infrastructure. The scheduling information is distributed among the individual task managers. Each task scheduler has the necessary information about its immediate predecessor and successor tasks.

While the EXOTICA and Meteor systems illustrate decentralized and distributed architectures, the partitions are done statically and the partitions are distributed to each execution agent before execution begins. Our approach focuses on the methodology for dynamic partitioning in runtime environment.

6.   FUTURE RESEARCH DIRECTIONS

Our work has focused on inter-agency workflows generated in response to a user's request. There is a need, however, for the agencies to be able to initiate the generation of a workflow on behalf of the user, such as ongoing reporting, quarterly tax payments, employee tax withholding, insurance payment, re-certification procedures and so on. This necessitates automatic generation of workflows in response to some event (based on external constraints), such as an approaching deadline for re-certification.

Another area of future work is concerned with collaborative work on tasks. For example, a corporate or partnership start up may wish to work on parallel tasks. This requires underlying groupware supporting concurrency control, redundancy and consistency checking, etc.

Changes in the underlying rules and regulations can have a significant impact on customized workflow generation. This calls for the ability to trace the origins of a rule to the source agency, propagating the change to the rule base, adapting changes dynamically to currently executing workflows, and validating them to ensure completeness and feasibility.

Dynamic adaptability and exception management in decentralized workflow control models are still in its infancy. A suitable recovery mechanism (as in transactional databases) needs to be devised for exceptions due to errors and failures in decentralized control model. The dynamic nature of workflow execution could arise due to the user's modification of requirements, or due to changes in the execution environment (such as resource availability or requirements.) A decentralized workflow model needs a theory and mechanisms for adapting to this dynamism.

A workflow authorization mechanism must not only ensure that tasks be executed only by authorized individuals, but also has to make sure that users gain access only during the execution of the specific task. Without the latter, an applicant, for example, may change the location of the plant after a permit has been granted by the DEP for a specific plant at a specific location. The *Workflow Authorization Model* (WAM) [AH96] addresses such problems by *dynamically* changing the time interval during which the authorization is valid, to achieve the desired synchronization. However, WAM assumes central security administration to enforce security policies. Therefore, there is a need to develop methodologies to support decentralized security administration, in effect, enabling enforcement of policies that span more than one agency without requiring centralized control.

ACKNOWLEDGEMENTS

This work is supported in part by the US National Science Foundation under grant EIA-9983468. We extend our gratitude to Dr. Francisco Artigas for his expert knowledge on GIS applications and to our collaborators in the State of New Jersey, specifically W. Rayner, A. Abeid, O. Marcopolous, S. Colbert. We would like to thank Pietro Mazzoleni and Timuchin Bakirtas for their assistance in the prototype development.

REFERENCES

[ACM01] V. Atluri, S. Chun, and P. Mazzoleni, "A Chinese Wall Security Model for Decentralized Workflow Systems," submitted for publication, 2001.

[AD01] Adam et al. "E-Government: Human Centered Systems for Business Services", in Proceedings of the first National Conference on Digital Government Research, Los Angeles, CA, May 2001.

[AH96] V. Atluri and W-K. Huang, "An Authorization Model for Workflows," Lecture Notes in Computer Science, No.1146, Springer-Verlag, September, 1996, pp. 44-64.

[AR98] Andrzej Cichocki and Marek Rusinkiewicz, "Migrating Workflows", in Workflow Management Systems and Interoperability, Ed. A. Dogac and L. Kalinichenko and M.Tamer Ozsu and A.Sheth, Springer, 1998, pp. 339-355.

[BA96] D. Barbara, S. Mehrotra and M. Rusinkiewicz, "INCAs: Managing Dynamic Workflows in Distributed Environments", Journal of Database Management, special issue on Multidatabases 7 number 1, 1996.

[DA97] S. Das, K. Kochut, J. Miller, A. Sheth and D. Worah, "ORBWork: A Reliable Distributed CORBA-based Workflow Enactment System for METEOR2", Technical Report, Computer Science, University of Georgia, UGA-CS-TR-97-001, 1997.

[GHS95] Dimitrios Georgakopoulos, Mark Hornick, and Amit Sheth, "An Overview of Workflow Management: From Process Modeling to Workflow Automation Infrastructure." Distributed and Parallel Databases, 1995, pp. 119-153.

[GSA00] US General Services Administration, "Citizens Expectations for Electronic Government Services." September 2000.

[ML98] J. Miller et al, "WebWork: METEOR2's Web-based Workflow Management System", Journal of Intelligent Information Systems 10, number 2 , 1998.

[MO95] G. Alonso, D. Agrawal, A. El Abbadi, C. Mohan, R. Gunthor and M. Kamath, "EXotica/FMQM: A Persistent Message-Based Architecture for Distributed Workflow Management", Proceedings of the IFIP WG8.1 Working Conference on Information Systems for Decentralized Organizations, Trondheim, 1995,

[MU98] P. Muth, D. Wodtke, J. Weissenfels, G. Weikum and A. Kotz Dittrich, "Enterprise-wide Workflow Management based on State and Activity Charts", Workflow Management Systems and Interoperability (eds) A. Dogac and L. Kalinichenko and T. Ozsu and A. Sheth, Springer Verlag, 1998.

[RS94] Marek Rusinkiewicz and Amit Sheth. "Specification and Execution of Transactional Workflows." In W.Kim, editor, Modern Database Systems: The Object Model, Interoperability, and Beyond. Addison-Wesley, 1994.

Vijayalakshmi Atluri received her B.Tech. in Electronics and Communications Engineering from Jawaharlal Nehru Technological University, Kakinada, India, M.Tech. in Electronics and Communications Engineering from Indian Institute of Technology, Kharagpur, India, and Ph. D. in Information Technology from George Mason University, USA. She is currently an Associate Professor of Computer Information Systems in the MSIS Department at Rutgers University. Dr. Atluri's research interests include Information Systems Security, Databases, Workflow Management, and Digital Libraries. She has published over 40 technical papers in refereed journals and conference proceedings in these areas, and is the co-author of the book, Multilevel Secure Transaction Processing, Kluwer Academic Publishers (1999). She served on the program committees of a number of conferences in these areas. She served as program chair for the 2000 ACM Workshop on Role Based Access Control, as a program co-chair for the 1999 IFIP WG11.3 Working Conference on Database Security, and as a guest editor for the ACM Transactions on Information Systems Security, Journal of Computer Security and Distributed and Parallel Databases. Currently, she is serving on the steering committee of the ACM SIGSAC and ACM Symposium on Access Control Models and Technologies. In 1996, she was a recipient of the National Science Foundation CAREER Award to investigate issues related to incorporating multilevel security into database management systems for advanced application domains such as office information systems, CAD/CAM, workflow systems. Dr. Atluri is a member of the IEEE Computer Society and the Association for Computing Machinery.

Soon Ae Chun is a Ph.D. candidate of Information Technology in the MS/IS Department at Rutgers University. She received a B.A. from Pusan National University, S. Korea, and an M.A. in Linguistics and an M.S. in Computer Science from the State University of New York at Buffalo. Her research interests include Workflow Management and Electronic Commerce, Information Systems Security, Geo-spatial information and satellite image Database systems. Her dissertation focuses on the decentralized workflow management for delivering eGovernment Business Services, which is funded by a dissertation fellowship at School of Management at Rutgers University. She is a student member of the IEEE Computer Society and the Association for Computing Machinery (ACM).

Richard D. Holowczak holds a B.S. in Computer Science from the College of New Jersey, an M.S. in Computer Science from the New Jersey Institute of Technology, and M.B.A. and Ph.D. degrees from Rutgers University. He is presently an Assistant Professor of Computer Information Systems at Baruch College, CUNY. Dr. Holowczak's research focuses on digital libraries, electronic commerce and networked information systems. He has published articles in IEEE Transactions on Knowledge and Data Engineering, IEEE Computer Journal, Online Information Review and ACM Computing Surveys and his research has been supported by the Professional Staff Congress-CUNY, NASA and the National Science Foundation. He is a member of the IEEE Computer Society and the Association for Computing Machinery (ACM).

Nabil R. Adam is a Professor of Computers & Information Systems and the Director of the Rutgers CIMIC center in Newark. Dr. Adam published numerous technical papers in such journals as IEEE Transactions on Software Engineering, IEEE Transactions on Knowledge and Data Engineering, ACM Computing Surveys, Communications of the ACM, Information Systems, Journal of Management Information Systems, International Journal of Intelligent and Cooperative Information Systems. He co-authored/co-edited nine books including ``Electronic Commerce: Technical, Business, and Legal Issues", Prentice Hall, 1998, a book on

Databases Issues in GIS, Kluwer Academic Publisher, 1997 and one on Electronic Commerce (1996), published as part of the Springer Verlag Lecture Notes Series in Computer Science. Dr. Adam is Editor-in-Chief of the International Journal on Digital Libraries and serves on the Editorial board of the Journal of Management Information Systems and the Journal of Electronic Commerce. He served as a guest editor for the Communications of the ACM, Operations Research, and Journal of Management Information Systems. He is the co-founder and current chair of the IEEE Technical Committee on Digital Libraries. He served as General Chair and Program Chair of various international conferences related to Digital Libraries and Electronic Commerce. Dr. Adam was elected as a distinguished speaker in the IEEE Computer Society's Distinguished Visitors Program (DVP) for the period 1997-2000. He was invited to lecture on Digital Libraries, Electronic Commerce and other related topics at several national and international institutions.

Chapter 5

Data Integration and Access
The Digital Government Research Center's Energy Data Collection (EDC) Project

José Luis Ambite[1], Yigal Arens[1], Walter Bourne[2], Steve Feiner[2], Luis Gravano[2], Vasileios Hatzivassiloglou[2], Eduard Hovy[1], Judith Klavans[2], Andrew Philpot[1], Usha Ramachandran[1], Kenneth A. Ross[2], Jay Sandhaus[2], Deniz Sarioz[2], Rolfe R. Schmidt[1], Cyrus Shahabi[1], Anurag Singla[2], Surabhan Temiyabutr[2], Brian Whitman[2] and Kazi Zaman[2]
[1]University of Southern California [2]Columbia University

Abstract: This chapter describes the progress of the Digital Government Research Center in tackling the challenges of integrating and accessing the massive amount of statistical and text data available from government agencies. In particular, we address the issues of database heterogeneity, size, distribution, and control of terminology. In this chapter we provide an overview of our results in addressing problems such as (1) ontological mappings for terminology standardization, (2) data integration across data bases with high speed query processing, and (3) interfaces for query input and presentation of results. The DGRC is a collaboration between researchers from Columbia University and the Information Sciences Institute of the University of Southern California employing technology developed at both locations, in particular the SENSUS ontology, the SIMS multi-database access planner, the LEXING automated dictionary and terminology analysis system, the main-memory query processing component and others. The pilot application targets gasoline data from the Bureau of Labor Statistics, the Energy Information Administration of the Department of Energy, the Census Bureau, and other government agencies.

Key words: ontologies, multi-database systems, data integration

1.   INTRODUCTION: THE DIGITAL GOVERNMENT RESEARCH CENTER

As access to the Web becomes a household commodity, the government (and in particular Federal Agencies such as the Census Bureau, the Bureau of Labor Statistics, the Energy Information Administration, and others) has a mandate to make its information available to the public. But the massive amount of statistical and text data available from such agencies has created a set of daunting challenges to the research and analysis communities. These challenges stem from the heterogeneity, size, distribution, and disparity of terminology of the data. Equally, they stem from the need to provide broad and easy access to (and support proper understanding of) complex data.

The Digital Government Research Center (DGRC; www.dgrc.org) was established to address these problems. The DGRC consists of faculty, staff, and students at the Information Science Institute (ISI) of the University of Southern California and Columbia University's Computer Science Department and its Center for Research on Information Access, and builds on the mandate of the Digital Government program as set out in (Schorr and Stolfo, 1998). The goals of the DGRC are to conduct and support research in key areas of information systems, to develop standards/interfaces and infrastructure, build pilot systems, and collaborate closely with government service/information providers and users.

Figure 1 shows these three system components:

Information Integration. We have addressed effective methods to identify and describe the contents of databases so that useful information can be accurately and efficiently located even when precise answers are unavailable. We have wrapped over a hundred sources for testing the first stage of information integration, performed research on computational properties of aggregation, and investigated the extraction of information from footnotes embedded in text.

Ontology Construction. We have extended USC/ISI's 70,000-node terminology taxonomy SENSUS to incorporate new energy-related domain models, and have developed automated concept-to-ontology alignment algorithms. Term extraction from glossaries involves the automatic analysis of 7000 terms across agencies (EIA, Census SICS and NAICS codes, EPA) and the automatic handling of acronyms towards the creation of a cross-agency ontology.

User Interface Development. We have designed and implemented a completely new user interface with the capability of handling integrated querying and presentation of results.

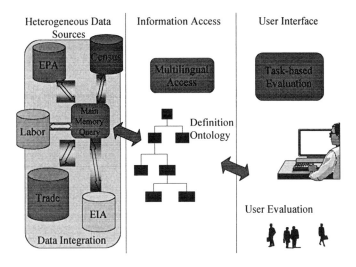

Figure1. DGRC System Components

2. INFORMATION CAPTURE AND INTEGRATION

In this section we discuss the issues of source wrapping, domain modeling, the SIMS query access planner, aggregation queries, and the extraction of information from footnotes. We do not address the very important question of data uncertainty and error in this chapter.

2.1 The SIMS Planner and Domain Models

The retrieval of information dispersed among multiple sources requires familiarity with their contents and structure, query languages and location. A person (or system) with need for distributed information must ultimately break down a retrieval task into a collection of specific queries to databases and other sources of information (e.g., analysis programs). With a large number of sources, individuals typically do not possess the knowledge or time required to find and process the information they need.

Our approach to integrating statistical databases builds on research performed by the SIMS group at ISI (Arens et al., 1996). SIMS assumes that the system designer specifies a global model of the application domain and describes the contents of each source (database, web server, etc.) in terms of this global model. A SIMS mediator provides a single point of access for all the information: the user expresses queries without needing to know anything about the individual sources. SIMS translates the user's high-level request, expressed in a subset of SQL, into a *query plan* (Ambite and Knoblock, 2000), a series of operations including queries to sources of relevant data and manipulations of the data. Queries are expressed internally in the Loom knowledge representation language (MacGregor, 1990). The SQL subset is limited in its treatment of aggregation operators (such as sum, average, etc.). The problem is that distributing such operators over multiple databases is difficult and potentially inefficient.

2.2   Incorporating and Modeling New Data Sources - Creating a Data Warehouse

In the first phase of the EDC project we developed a mediator architecture that integrates time-series data from several web sites and databases from agencies such as the Bureau of Labor Statistics (BLS), the Census Bureau, and the Energy Information Administration. Since 1999, we[1] have incorporated over 100 tables, from sources in various formats, (including Oracle and Microsoft Access databases, HTML web forms and pages, and PDF files). Details of our data wrapping techniques are given in (Hovy et al. 2001).

To date, we have wrapped 53 series from the Bureau of Labor Statistics (BLS); 3 series from the California Energy Commission (CEC); and 25,000 modeled EIA OGIRS (Oil and Gas Information Resource System) series. In addition to the time series concepts (the MEASUREMENTs), the EDC system also provides footnote information, by joining through parallel ANNOTATION and FOOTNOTE concepts, which share the definitional metadata above but have a few different retrievable attributes. All this data is organized into a single Data Model, which in turn is embedded into SENSUS. Each measurement concept thus possesses all of the following attributes, which can be retrieved as if they exist in an end source.

Table 1. Attributes

Name	Type	
AGENCY-NAME	String	agency providing data
AREA-NAME	String	locale of data
FAMILY-NAME	String	subgroup of series within agency
FREQUENCY-NAME	String	how often/when measured, e.g. monthly
POINT-OF-SALE-NAME	String	where in the supply chain measured
PRODUCT-NAME	String	what product e.g. unleaded regular
PROVENANCE-NAME	String	how data obtained: web, RDBMS, etc.
QUALITY-NAME	String	what kind of measurement: vol, price
SEASONAL-ADJUSTMENT-NAME	String	is data seasonally adjusted
UNIT-NAME	String	units of measurement: Mbbl/mo, etc.

We wrapped some 15,000 location-specific series from a collection of data tables defined as text for EIA[2]. In order to publish all monthly values for each state individually, the original webpages had to be wrapped, merged into a single large collection, and reaggregated as required by appropriate extraction. Details on this process can be found in (Hovy et al., 2001).

A large amount of the information is in the form of semi-structured web pages. These web sources were 'wrapped' automatically using technology from the Ariadne system (Muslea et al., 1998). Ariadne allows a developer to mark up example web pages using a demonstration-based GUI. Then the system inductively learns a landmark grammar that is used to extract the marked-up fields from similar pages and generates all the necessary wrapper code. The resulting wrapper acts as a simple relational database that accepts parametrically-defined SQL and dynamically retrieves data from the associated web pages and forms.

In SIMS, each of these data sources, whether natively relational or wrapped by Ariadne, is modeled by associating it to an appropriate domain-level concept description. A set of approximately 500 domain terms, organized in 10 subhierarchies, constitutes the domain model so far required for the EDC domain. A fragment of the EDC domain model is shown in Figure 2. The dimensions can be seen as metadata that describes the series. The actual data is modeled as a set of measurements (i.e., date and value pairs). The domain model also describes whether a source has footnotes for some of the data. The answer to a query will also return the footnote data associated with the corresponding tuples if so requested.

2.3   Aggregation Queries

We[3] have been investigating how to integrate data sets/sources with information aggregated at different 'granularities' and with different 'coverage'. For example, a data source might have gasoline-price information for the whole United States reported by month for the last ten years; another source might have the same type of information for the whole United States reported by year up to 1990; finally, yet another source might have yearly gasoline-price information discriminated by state. The goal of our work is to conceptually present users with a reasonably uniform view of the available data without necessarily exposing all this heterogeneity in aggregation granularity and coverage.

The main challenge of our integration is dealing with data sets exhibiting *varying* granularity and coverage. Data sets might have information at different granularities of time (e.g., month vs. year), of geography (e.g., cities vs. states vs. countries), of product (e.g., unleaded regular gasoline vs.

'general' gasoline), and so on. Numerous statistical techniques, ranging from imputation to sophisticated forms of averaging, have been developed to deal with data on mismatched scales. We develop a new approach as follows. We present users with a simple, unified view of the data. This view is sufficiently fine-grained to allow users to exploit most of the information that is available, but also sufficiently coarse-grained to hide most of the granularity and coverage differences of the data sets. Users pose queries against this view. Most of the time we will be able to correctly answer queries with the available data sets. But sometimes have to reformulate a query if the data needed to answer it is not available. For example, this situation is possible if the unified view is not at the coarsest level of granularity of all data sets. Defining such a coarse view is undesirable because it might result in valuable data not being available for users to exploit.

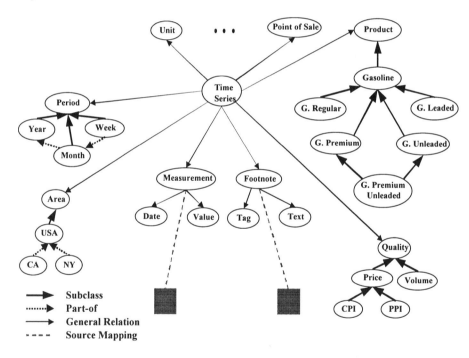

Figure 2. Fragment of the Domain Model. (Reprinted by permission of IEEE. José Luis Ambite et al. "Simplifying Data Access: The Energy Data Collection Project." *IEEE Computer*, February 2001. © 2001 IEEE.)

In such a case, we relax and reformulate the query to find the *closest* query for which we have all required data, and provide exact answers for that. Our key observation for such reformulation is that data attributes (e.g., time, geography, product) often follow natural granularity hierarchies (e.g., day->month->year for time, city->state->country for geography). Combining each of these granularity hierarchies results in a granularity *lattice* (Harinarayan et al., 1996) where a node might correspond to leaded gasoline data by month and state, and another node might correspond to leaded gasoline data by year and country, etc. We have developed algorithms to identify, for each of these nodes, the queries that we can answer exactly at the node's level of granularity. For example, given a set of data sources, we might conclude that we can answer any query on leaded gasoline by month and state as long as the query is about the 1990–1999 time period, and about the states of California and New York. At run time, we can then decide whether we can answer a user query exactly as is, or whether we need to reformulate it and find the 'closest' query in the lattice for which we can provide exact answers, using some distance function over the granularity lattice. Initial results and algorithms are illustrated on four BLS data sets, all on average price of unleaded regular gasoline, at http://db-pc01.cs.columbia.edu/digigov/Main.html.

2.4 Data Warehousing for Efficient Evaluation of Decision Support Queries

Types of queries of particular interest are decision-support queries, also known as datacube queries, or on-line analytical processing (OLAP) queries. A datacube is a set of data measurements that are defined by the values of a set of dimensions in a way similar to our domain models. It can be thought as a multidimensional matrix. Datacube queries involve aggregations (sums, averages, etc, on groupings) of the data across one or several of the dimensions.

Datacubes compute aggregates of a set of database records at a variety of different granularities. For example, a datacube on census data might be broken down by age, rating of English proficiency, and number of children, also finding the maximum income including subtotals across each dimension. This implies that in addition to computing the maximum income over all the data, we would also have to compute the maximum income over all ages, all English proficiency ratings, all (age, proficiency) pairs, etc. Since we have 3 dimensions there are 2^3 granularities at which we would have to compute subtotals.

Datacubes are useful for many kinds of data analysis in which one can "slice and dice" multidimensional data to observe patterns. Such an approach is useful in many digital government contexts, including any large multidimensional data set over which aggregates are needed at various granularities. Datacubes can also be used to analyze data for privacy issues. An analysis of the datacube can help identify cells in which the population is too small for safe disclosure of the detailed data; only aggregated data would be released in such a case.

In order to efficiently evaluate decision-support queries on our integrated statistical data, our architecture has a dual mode of operation. This extended architecture is shown in Figure 3. First, our system can retrieve live data from databases and web sources. This allows the users to obtain completely up-to-date data. However, for complex analytical queries that typically require large amounts of data and processing, live access does not offer the level of interactivity that some users require. Second, our system can warehouse the information from the data sources to allow for complex analytical queries to be executed much more efficiently. However, the data would be only as recent as the last update to the data warehouse. Figure 3(a) shows the process of loading the data warehouse. Once we have the sources modeled in our ontology we can retrieve all the available time-series and store them in a local data warehouse normalized under our common schema. On this local warehouse we can evaluate queries much more efficiently as we describe in the next section. Figure 3(b) shows how we propose to use the data warehouse. The user interacts with a friendly interface that passes formal queries (e.g. SQL) to the query planner (SIMS). Then the query planner analyzes the query and decides whether to retrieve the data live or to use the local data warehouse.

We are exploring two approaches to efficiently evaluate decision-support queries once we the data is in our local data warehouse. The first approach provides very fast responses when the warehouse data can be loaded into main memory (Ross and Zaman, 2000). The second approach can be used with large warehouses that must be stored on disk and provides very fast approximate answers that converge quickly to the exact answer (Ambite et al., 2001). In this chapter we do not address the reasoning task that allows the mediator to decide whether to use the warehouse or the live sources.

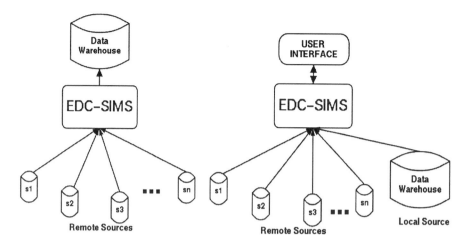

Figure 3. Extending our integration system with a Data Warehouse (a) Loading the Data Warehouse (b) Using the Data Warehouse

2.4.1 Main Memory Datacube Aggregation

For large datasets with many dimensions, the complete datacube may be very large. In order to support on-line access to datacube results, one would like to perform some precomputation to enhance query performance. Past datacube precomputation schemes (Harinarayan et al., 1996, Gupta et al., 1997, Shukla et al., 1998) materialize selected datacube tuples on disk, choosing the most beneficial cuboids (i.e., combinations of dimensions) to materialize given a space limit. However, in the context of a data-warehouse receiving frequent "append" updates to the database, the cost of keeping these disk-resident cuboids up-to-date can be high.

In (Ross and Zaman, 2000) we propose a main memory-based framework that provides rapid response to queries and requires considerably less maintenance cost than a disk-based scheme in an append-only environment. For a given datacube query, we first look among a set of previously materialized tuples for a direct answer. If not found, we use a hash-based scheme reminiscent of partial match retrieval to rapidly compute the answer to the query from the finest-level data stored in a special in-memory data structure. We[4] use a two-level materialization scheme, which is discussed in detail in (Ross and Zaman, 2000). Our approach yields rapid query responses for the important class of applications in which the finest granularity tuples of the datacube fit in main memory.

2.4.2   Progressive Evaluation of OLAP queries

We[5] build on our previous work in the EDC project and we propose an architecture for fast evaluation of OLAP (On-Line Analytical Processing) queries on our integrated data. We have developed a very efficient method of processing range-sum queries based on wavelet techniques (Schmidt and Shahabi, 2001a, 2001b). Range sum queries are one of the most basic types of decision support query, but even the best proposed techniques for their evaluation scale poorly with the dimension of the data domain. (Schmidt and Shahabi, 2001a, 2001b) introduced POLAP, a new algorithm that produces exact range sum query results as efficiently as the best known methods, but also produces accurate estimates of the query result long before the exact computation is complete. This combination allows us to deliver progressive query evaluation: we provide a quick approximate query response that becomes increasingly accurate as the computation progresses. In this project we apply POLAP to statistical data integrated from multiple agencies.

The fundamental idea behind POLAP is that we can express these range functions as a sum of basic component functions. Our algorithm can be used as an exact, approximate, or progressive range-sum query evaluator. Details on POLAP can be found in (Ambite et al., 2001).

When our system works as a mediator the integration is virtual in the sense that the actual data reside in the remote sources. The data become integrated only through the models and query processing in the mediator. Our system can also materialize all the available data in a local warehouse. Once the data is in the warehouse, the system can process complex analytical queries very efficiently even for very massive data sets by using POLAP.

3.   ONTOLOGY CONSTRUCTION

Practical experience has shown that integrating different term sets and data definitions is fraught with difficulty. The U.S. Government has funded several metadata initiatives with rather disappointing results. The focus has been on collecting structural information (formats, encodings, links), instead of content, resulting in large data collections (up to 500,000 terms) that are admirably neutral, but unsuitable as 'terminology brokers'.

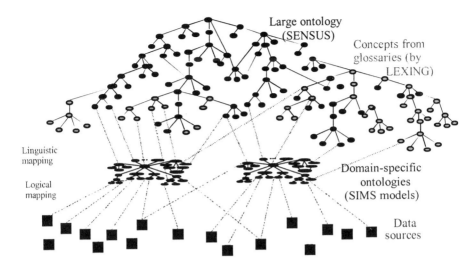

Figure 4. Ontology and Domain Models. (Reprinted by permission of IEEE. José Luis Ambite et al. "Simplifying Data Access: The Energy Data Collection Project." *IEEE Computer*, February 2001. © 2001 IEEE.)

We are following a different approach, one that has been tested, on a relatively small scale, in various applications in the past two years. Rather than mapping between domains or collecting metadata, we create mappings between the domain and an existing *reference ontology*. This choice allows us in the future to make available to statistics agencies (and eventually to the general public) any other domains that have also been mapped into the reference ontology. Furthermore, by making publicly available the reference ontology with our merging tools, we hope to encourage others to align (or even to merge) their term banks, data dictionaries, etc., as well.

We are collecting, aligning, and merging the contents of several large term banks, placing them under the high-level structure of an existing large (70,000-node) and fairly general ontology called SENSUS, built at USC/ISI (Knight and Luk, 1994)[6]. The ontology for the EDC project has the structure shown in Figure 4. To deploy the version of SENSUS used for the EDC project, we[7] (1) defined a domain model of approximately 500 nodes to represent the concepts present in the EDC gasoline domain, (2) linked these domain concepts into SENSUS using semi-automated alignment tools, and (3) defined a new type of ontology link called *generally-associated-with* to hold between concepts in the ontology and domain model concepts, allowing the user while browsing to rapidly proceed from high-level concepts to the concepts associated with real data in the databases.

3.1 Definition Analysis: Extracting Glossary Entries with LEXING

Several problems with terminology require that special attention be devoted to terms in a cross-agency endeavor. In particular, and especially confusing to non-specialist users, is the proliferation of terms, and the fact that agencies define ostensibly identical terms differently. What is called *wages* in one database may be what another calls *salary* (even though it may have a *wages* too, as well as an *income*). Reading the glossaries' definitions may or may not be of help; lengthy term definitions often contain important information buried away.

To achieve our goals for the EDC project, we have identified three steps:

- Identification of the definitional material from a web page or other online source (*identification*)
- Parsing of the definition for its most salient properties and features (*LEXING generation, genus finding*)
- Incorporation of the structured information into a larger ontology, including linking and merging definitions from different agencies and sources.

We[8] have built a system that extracts the genus word and phrase from free-form definition text, entitled LEXING, for **Lex**ical **In**formation from **G**lossaries (Klavans and Whitman, 2001). We combine statistical and semantic processes to extract these terms, and demonstrate that this combination allows us to predict the genus even in difficult situations such as empty head definitions or verb definitions. For example, the following definition appears in our data set:

> **Motor Gasoline Blending Components:** Naphthas (e.g., straight-run gasoline, alkylate, reformate, benzene, toluene, xylene) used for blending or compounding into finished motor gasoline. These components include reformulated gasoline blendstock f or *{sic}* oxygenate blending (RBOB) but exclude oxygenates (alcohols, ethers), butane, and pentanes plus. *Note:* Oxygenates are reported as individual components and are included in the total for other hydrocarbons, hydrogens, and oxygenates.

Our model of building a lexical knowledge base (LEXING) from machine-readable dictionaries (MRDs) is influenced by the work done in (Byrd et al., 1989) and (Neff and Boguraev, 1989), in which the authors propose a hierarchical structure to represent the complex information found in MRDs. To determine the genus, LEXING uses knowledge gained from the part-of-speech tagging and noun-phrase (NP) chunking (Evans et al., 2000) components. Below we show an abbreviated parse of our sample definition, showing the semantic separators *used-for* and *excludes* as well as the genus term (Napthas) and acronym:

> (term: Motor Gasoline Blending Components (full-def: ...) (core-def: ...)
> (is-a Napthas) (properties (used-for blending) (excludes oxygenates))
> (acronym RBOB))

We have performed two evaluations on LEXING output:

1. Definition Content Analysis: we ran our system on various definitional sources to determine if our ideas of content were correct, and which fields are frequent.
2. LEXING Accuracy: we evaluated the genus term identification algorithm against a "gold standard".

Our main definition sets came from two government agencies: the Energy Information Administration (data on energy sources such as gasoline or coal), and the Environmental Protection Agency (glossaries on environmental concerns); we also tested over heart-disease related definitions from definition extraction work done in (Klavans and Muresan, 2000). Inputs ranged from web pages to flat ASCII documents.

The results in Table 2 show that definitional content hinges largely on the genus. Semantic properties are found in well-edited glossaries (such as EIA edited). This evaluation indicates the profile of source definitions in terms of complexity.

Table 2. Definitional Content Analysis

	Term	Genus Phrase	Properties	Quantifiers	Include Exclude
EIA	19	18	15	7	2
Edited		**95%**	**79%**	**37%**	**11%**
EIA	127	121	38	50	9
Web		**95%**	**30%**	**39%**	**7%**
EPA	1054	1029	56	24	75
Web		**98%**	**5%**	**2%**	**7%**
Medical	90	83	0	0	0
Auto		**92%**	**0%**	**0%**	**0%**

For the second evaluation to determine the accuracy of LEXING, we manually tagged 500 definitions, 100 each from 5 domains (Civil Engineering, Computer Terms, Biomedical Information, General Medical Information, and Energy Information) in order to establish a measurement standard or "gold standard". A match was defined as both the human tagger and the computer choosing the same genus term. This is shown in Table 3. What is novel is our processing of heterogeneous glossary input from different sources to be merged into a large on-line ontology.

Table 3. Genus Term Finding Results

Domain	Civil Eng.	Comp.	Biomedical	Medical	Energy
Genus	93/99	81/101	93/102	100/103	85/102
Term	**94%**	**80%**	**92%**	**97%**	**83%**

3.2   Semi-Automated Term-to-Ontology Alignment

In linking agency-specific domain models (as required by SIMS) to SENSUS (and hence to one another), the central problem is term alignment. Determining where a given term belongs in a 90,000-node ontology is a challenging problem. At first glance, it might seem impossible to align two ontologies (or taxonomized term sets) automatically. Almost all ontologies depend to a large degree on non-machine-interpretable information such as concept/term names and English term definitions. However, recent research has uncovered a variety of heuristics that help with the identification and alignment process. We[9] are using a 5-step procedure that is partially automated, including heuristics that make initial cross-ontology alignment suggestions, a function for integrating their suggestions, a set of alignment validation criteria and heuristics, a repeated integration cycle, and an evaluation metric

In the EDC project we have re-implemented two existing matching heuristics (NAME and DEFINITION MATCH) and developed a new one (DISPERSAL MATCH). NAME MATCH performs an exhaustive (sub)string match of the concept name to be linked against every concept name in SENSUS, with special rewards for beginning and ending overlaps of substrings. Since this match is very slow, we have implemented an algorithm used to match gene sequences to obtain a two order of magnitude speedup.

In recent work, we[10] have greatly refined NAME-MATCH. We tried to match 3882 terms extracted by LEXING (see Section 4.3) from EIA's 'Glossary of Energy and Energy Related Terms' (EIAGOE) to the SIMS domain model, consisting of 426 concepts. We implemented seven variants of NAME-MATCH, which are outlined in (Hovy et al., 2001). Briefly, these include variants on substring, trigram, character bag, and edit distance matching.

Figure 5 illustrates the accuracy for each of ten subgroups of domain concepts, measured against human alignment of the same concepts. The almost-perfect accuracy of 8 of the 10 subgroups provides cause for optimism.

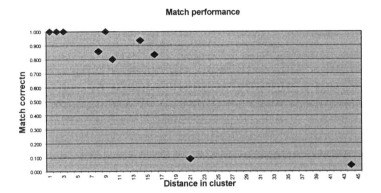

Figure 5. Accuracy of alignment of 98 domain model concepts (organized in 10 groups) against SENSUS (90,000 concepts), using automated alignment heuristics.

4. USER INTERFACE DEVELOPMENT

It is currently extremely difficult for users to make productive use of the statistical data available on the web. Because of the sheer wealth of information, current systems typically offer two fundamentally different user interfaces to access it. One method attempts to trade off generality for ease of use by relying on a collection of ready-made presentations, consisting of tables and charts that have been designed in advance to answer typical questions. However, there may be hundreds of these presentations, making it difficult for users to find the one that provides the closest answer. At best, these systems provide a keyword searching mechanism to help users discover relevant presentations; in many cases, none of them may address the user's specific query.

The other method for finding information achieves generality by allowing users to construct their own queries. However, these user interfaces are for experts only, requiring intimate knowledge of the domain and structure of the database, the meaning of the attributes, the query language, and the ways in which resulting information is presented.

To address the user interface issues, we[11] are developing a unified web-based user interface for querying and presenting statistical information. Our focus has been on the development of a robust, portable, and efficient user interface that facilitates user access to data from multiple sources/agencies. The interface addresses the following main tasks: support for adaptive, context-sensitive queries via a system of guided menus; display of tables created by the integration back-end from one or multiple individual databases, along with footnotes and links to original data sources; and browsing of the ontology that supports the entire integration model, with the capability of displaying concept attributes, relationships, and definitions in graphics and text. This method allows users to construct complete queries by choosing from a dynamically changing set of menu options, composed dynamically with reference to the domain models in SENSUS. The design is obviously extensible: as new databases are added to the system, their domain models are linked into SENSUS, and their parameters are immediately available to the user for querying. The taxonomization in SENSUS ensures appropriate grouping for menu display by the interface.

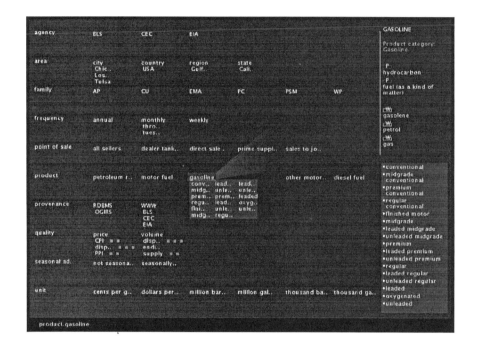

Figure 6. Snapshot from the User Interface in Development

Our recent work has focused on the query interface, and how it can be linked with the ontology to improve users' understanding of the information that is available. Conventional cascaded "walking" menus, which are often used to navigate hierarchical menu structures, result in a limited "peep-hole" view of the choices that are available. As shown in Figure 6, we have attempted to eliminate this problem by laying out all choices in a tabular representation. Each entry in the leftmost column of the figure represents a top-level menu. Each row to the right of that entry includes the items in that menu's second level. A column below a second-level item corresponds to that item's next level, and so on. When the number of items at a particular level exceed a threshold, the items are organized in multiple rows or columns. When the user selects an item, such as "gasoline" in the figure, it is highlighted (along with items at its next level, if it is not a leaf), and information about it from the ontology is presented in an area on the right of the display. This additional information is visually linked to the selected item by a beam, and includes the item's definition, its ancestors in the ontology, its wordnet links, and its children.

Because of the potentially large size of the menu hierarchy being displayed, and the limited amount of screen space available, many of the entries shown are shortened by eliding final characters (e.g., most of the items below "gasoline") or by displaying them as iconic boxes (e.g., several of the items in the "quality" row). To address the need to examine these items in detail, we are implementing a "fish-eye" view capability (Furnas 1986), which allows a user to selectively increase or decrease the level of detail presented in any portion of the menu hierarchy. Modifying the level of detail smoothly increases or decreases the screen space dedicated to that portion of the hierarchy. In the next phase of the project, we will be designing and performing formal user experiments with both professional analysts and lay users to obtain feedback on our design. Future areas for research include determining how to reuse and modify previous queries, developing ways to pose more complex queries than the single conjunction of individual terms that we currently support, and attempting to exploit the ontology to highlight potentially interesting relationships among items that the user has selected

5. FUTURE WORK

In our future work, shown also in Figure 1, we will address additional foundational issues in the task of making available complex statistical data to a wide (and not always expert) public:

Improvement of database query management. We will develop a main-memory query processing engine that will allow users to rapidly filter and aggregate data in order to answer their data analysis queries. We will also develop our research in returning an approximate result to the query very efficiently and for fast convergence to the exact result. Database expertise lies both at Columbia University and at USC.

Multilingual access of information. Given appropriate funding, we plan to develop multilingual question answering capabilities, extending question-answering work being done by the Natural Language Group at USC's

Information Sciences Institute. Possible languages include Spanish and Chinese.

Formal testing of usability and of system performance. We propose to perform testing at three levels: glass box evaluation of components, black box system evaluation, and usability testing. We will measure user satisfaction given new interfaces to complex databases. We will draw on the long-standing expertise of the Electronic Data Service along with evaluation expertise on presentation technologies of the Center for Research on Information Access at Columbia University (Jacobsen et al., 1994).

NOTES

1. This work was performed by Andrew Philpot and José Luis Ambite, with the help of domain experts at EIA and BLS.
2. For example, see http://www.eia.doe.gov/emeu/states/ main_ca.html
3. This work is led by Luis Gravano, in collaboration with Vasilis Vassalos of New York University, and Anurag Singla.
4. This work was performed by Kenneth Ross, from Columbia University, with the assistance of a graduate student, Kazi Zaman.
5. This research has been performed by Jose-Luis Ambite, Cyrus Shahabi, Rolfe R. Schmidt, and Andrew Philpot.
6. SENSUS can be accessed using Ontosaurus, the ontology browser at http://mozart.isi.edu:8003/sensus/sensus_frame.html (Swartout et al., 1996).
7. This work was performed by José Luis Ambite, Eduard Hovy, and Andrew Philpot.
8. This work is led by Judith Klavans, Brian Whitman, Walter Bourne, and Deniz Sarioz.
9. This work was performed by Eduard Hovy and Usha Ramachandran. Refinements and recoding of the algorithms are being performed by Andrew Philpot.
10. This work was performed by Andrew Philpot, with discussions with Jose Luis Ambite and Eduard Hovy.
11. This work was initially performed by Vasileios Hatzivassiloglou and Jay Sandhaus. A new interface has been built by Steve Feiner and Surabhan Temiyabutr.

REFERENCES

Arens, Y., C.A. Knoblock and C.-N. Hsu. 1996. Query Processing in the SIMS Information Mediator. In A. Tate (ed), *Advanced Planning Technology*. Menlo Park: AAAI Press.

Ambite J.L. and C.A. Knoblock. 2000. Flexible and Scalable Cost-Based Query Planning in Mediators: A Transformational Approach. *Artificial Intelligence Journal*, 118 (1-2).

Ambite, J. L., Y. Arens, E. Hovy, A. Philpot, L. Gravano, V. Hatzivassiloglou, and J.L. Klavans. Simplifying Data Access: The Energy Data Collection Project. IEEE Computer 34 (2), Special Issue on Digital Government, February 2001.

Ambite, J. L., C. Shahabi, R. R. Schmidt, and A. Philpot. Fast Approximate Evaluation of OLAP Queries for Integrated Statistical Data. Proceedings of the First National Conference on Digital Government (dg.o 2001), Redondo Beach, May 2001.

Byrd, R.J., B.K. Boguraev, J.L. Klavans and M.S. Neff. 1989. From Structural Analysis of Lexical Resources to Semantics in a Lexical Knowledge Base. U. Zernik (eds.) *Proceedings of the First International Workshop on Lexical Acquisition*. Detroit, Michigian.

Evans, D., Klavans, J. and Wacholder, N. 2000. *Document Processing with LinkIT*. RIAO Paris, France, 1336-1345.

Furnas, G. 1986. Generalized Fisheye Views. Proceedings of CHI 86. April 1986, pp. 16-23.

Gupta, H. et al. 1997. Index Selection for OLAP. *Proceedings of the 13th ICDE*.

Harinarayan, V., A. Rajaraman, and J. D. Ullman, 1996. Implementing Data Cubes Efficiently, *Proceedings of the 1996 ACM SIGMOD Conference*.

Hovy, E.H., A. Philpot, J.-L. Ambite, and U. Ramachandran. 2000. Automating the Placement of Database Concepts into a Large Ontology. In preparation.

Hovy, E.H., A. Philpot, J.-L. Ambite, Y. Arens, J.L. Klavans, W. Bourne, and D. Sarioz. 2001. Data Acquisition and Integration in the DGRC's Energy Data Collection Project. Proceedings of the dg.o 2001 Conference. Redondo Beach, California.

Jacobsen, Lynn, D. Millman, and W. Bourne. 1994. Providing Access to a Data Library: SQL and Full-Text IR Methods of Automatically Generating Web Structure. *Proceedings of the Second World Wide Web Conference '94: Mosaic and the Web*.

Klavans, J. L. and Muresan S. 2000. "DEFINDER: Rule-Based Methods for the Extraction of Medical Terminology and their Associated Definitions from On-line Text". *Proceedings of 2000 American Medical Informatics Association (AMIA) Annual Symposium*, Los Angeles, California.

Klavans, J. L and B. Whitman 2001 "Extracting Taxonomic Relationships from On-Line Definitional Sources Using LEXING"

Knight, K. and S.K. Luk. 1994. Building a Large-Scale Knowledge Base for Machine Translation. *Proceedings of the AAAI Conference*.

MacGregor, R. 1990. The Evolving Technology of Classification-Based Knowledge Representation Systems. In John Sowa (ed.), *Principles of Semantic Networks: Explorations in the Representation of Knowledge*. Morgan Kaufmann.

Muslea, I. and S. Minton and C. A. Knoblock. 1998. Wrapper Induction for Semistructured Web-based Information Sources. Proceedings of the Conference on Automated Learning and Discovery. Pittsburgh, PA.

Neff, Mary and Bran Boguraev. 1989. Dictionaries, dictionary grammars and dictionary entry parsing. *Proceedings of the 27th Meeting of the ACL*. Vancouver, Canada.

Ross, K. A. and K. A. Zaman. 2000. Serving Datacube Tuples from Main Memory. *12th International Conference on Scientific and StatisticalDatabase Management*, pp. 182-195.

Schmidt, R. R. and Shahabi, C. (2001a). Polap: A Fast Wavelet-based Technique for
    Progressive Evaluation of OLAP Queries. Submitted.
Schmidt, R. R. and Shahabi, C. (2001b). Wavelet Based Density Estimators for Modeling
    OLAP Data Sets. In *Third Workshop on Mining Scientific Datasets* in conjunction with
    FirstSIAM Int'l Conference on Data Mining.
Schorr H. and S. J. Stolfo, Towards the Digital Government of the 21st Century,
    Communications of the ACM, CACM, Nov. 1998.
Shukla, A. and P. Deshpande and J. Naughton. 1998. Materialized View Selection for
    Multidimensional Datasets. *Proceedings of the 24th International VLDB Conference.*
Swartout, W.R., R. Patil, K. Knight, and T. Russ. 1996. Toward Distributed Use of Large-
    Scale Ontologies. *Proceedings of the 10th Knowledge Acquisition for Knowledge-Based
    Systems Workshop.* Banff, Canada.

Jose Luis Ambite is a Senior Research Scientist at the Information Sciences
Institute of the University of Southern California and at the Digital
Government Research Center a joint effort of the University of Southern
California and Columbia University. He received his Ph.D. in Computer
Science from the University of Southern California in 1998. His Ph.D.
dissertation research focussed in general plan optimization techniques which
were applied to query optimization in the SIMS and Ariadne mediator
systems as a special case. His research interests include information
integration, automated planning, databases, and knowledge representation.

Yigal Arens is Co-director of DGRC, the USC/Columbia University Digital
Government Research Center and Director of the Intelligent Systems
Division of the University of Southern California's Information Science
Institute in Marina del Rey, California, USA. Dr. Arens received his Ph.D.
from the University of California at Berkeley. His primary research interests
are information integration, planning in the domain of information servers,
knowledge representation, and human-machine communication. In 1983, he
joined the faculty of the Computer Science Department at the University of
Southern California. He joined USC's Information Sciences Institute
(USC/ISI) in 1987, where he first worked on the Integrated Interfaces
project, a multimedia presentation design system combining text, tables,
maps, and other graphics. For almost ten years he headed the SIMS (Single
Interface to Multiple Sources) research group specializing in integration of
heterogeneous databases and other information sources.

Walter Bourne is Assistant Director of Academic Information Systems,
head of its Research Computing Support group, and advisor to the Electronic
Data Service. He received a Ph.D. in Political Science from Columbia
University in 1976. His interests include analysis of computer and network
performance, computer-assisted data finding and retrieval, and the
automated application of existing meta-information and intermediary

expertise to these tasks. Dr. Bourne co-developed Columbia's online numerical data search and retrieval "DataGate" engine.

Steven Feiner is a Professor of Computer Science at Columbia University, where he directs the Computer Graphics and User Interfaces Laboratory. He received a Ph.D. in Computer Science from Brown University in 1987. His research interests include virtual environments and augmented reality, knowledge-based design of graphics and multimedia, information visualization, wearable computing, and hypermedia. Prof. Feiner is coauthor of Computer Graphics: Principles and Practice (Addison-Wesley, 1990) and of Introduction to Computer Graphics (Addison-Wesley, 1993). He is also an associate editor of ACM Transactions on Graphics.

Judith Klavans is Co-director of DGRC, the USC/Columbia University Digital Government Research Center and Director of the Center for Research on Information Access (CRIA) at Columbia University. Dr. Klavans received her Ph.D. from University College at the University of London in 1980. Her primary research interests are computational linguistics and natural language processing. Prior to joining Columbia University, she was on the research staff at IBM T.J. Watson Research Center. In 1995, she became the director of the newly formed interdisciplinary research center, CRIA, the goal of which is to build research that cuts across computer and information science. Her current interests include natural language analysis for building ontologies, multilingual information access, and summarization.

Andrew Philpot is a Research Scientist at the Information Sciences Institute of the University of Southern California. Prior to ISI, he was at NASA Ames Research Center. He received an M.S.C.S. (Artificial Intelligence) from Stanford University in 1990. His research interests include automated planning, information integration, and ontology construction and integration.

Kenneth A. Ross is an Associate Professor of Computer Science at Columbia University, where he directs the Database Research Group. He received a Ph.D. in Computer Science from Stanford University in 1991. His research interests include database query processing, query language design, and main-memory databases. He is the recipient of an NSF Young Investigator Award, a Packard Foundation Fellowship, and a Sloan Foundation Fellowship.

Cyrus Shahabi is currently an Assistant Professor and the Director of the Distributed Information Management Laboratory at the Computer Science

Department and the Integrated Media Systems Center (IMSC) at the University of Southern California. He received his Ph.D. degree in Computer Science at the University of Southern California in August 1996. He participated in the design and the implementation of the Omega object oriented parallel database machine. His Ph.D. dissertation is on scheduling the retrievals of continuous media objects, which is applicable in a number of multimedia applications (e.g., video-on-demand and digital editing). Dr. Shahabi's current research interests include multimedia databases and storage servers, spatial and temporal databases, and data mining.

Chapter 6

Scalable Data Collection for Internet-based Digital Government Applications

Leana Golubchik
Department of Computer Science, University of Maryland at College Park

Abstract: Data collection (or *uploading*) is an inherent part of numerous digital
             government applications. Solutions that have been developed over the years
             for *download* problems do not apply to uploads. Hence, scalable uploading of
             data over the Internet is an important, and until now an open, research
             problem.

Key words: Data collection, scalable uploads, digital government applications

1.   DATA COLLECTION APPLICATIONS IN DIGITAL GOVERNMENT

Government at all levels is a major *collector* and provider of data. There are clear benefits to disseminating and collecting data over the Internet, given its existing large-scale infrastructure and widespread reach in commercial, private, and government domains. In this chapter, we focus on the *collection of data over the Internet*, and specifically, on the *scalability* issues which arise in the context of Internet-based massive data collection applications. By data collection, we mean applications such as Internal Revenue Service (IRS) applications with respect to electronic submission of income tax forms.

The U.S. Congress wants 80% of tax returns to be filed *electronically* by 2007. Electronic returns are easier to process and contain far fewer errors. Clearly, with (on the order of) 100 million individual tax returns being filed by April 15th, where each return is on the order of 100 KBytes [IRS, 2001], *scalability* issues are a major concern.

The Integrated Justice Information Technology Initiative facilitates information sharing among state, local, and tribal justice components. This program coordinates with a number of other Department of Justice's technology initiatives, including the Global Criminal Justice Information Network Initiative. An integrated (global) information sharing system involves collection, analysis, and dissemination of criminal data. The sizes of the data being collected in this application have a wide variance, for instance they can include text and images. Clearly, in order to facilitate such a system one must provide a *scalable* infrastructure for collection of data.

A number of government agencies support research activities, where the funds are awarded through a grant proposal process, with deadlines imposed on submission dates. For instance, agencies like the National Science Foundation (NSF), which currently uses FastLane, and the National Institute of Health (NIH) have a fairly large number of proposals submitted on regular basis. The entire process involves not only submission of proposals, which can involve fairly large data sizes, but also a review process, a reporting process (after the grant is awarded), and possibly a results dissemination process. All these processes involve a data collection step.

Digital democracy applications, such as online voting during federal, state, or local elections, constitute another set of massive upload applications. These are also deadline-driven applications, with relatively small file sizes, whose results (i.e., outcome of an election) are expected to be computed soon after the uploading deadline. These applications provide opportunities for application-specific data aggregation.

There are numerous examples of digital government applications with large-scale data collection needs. Throughout this chapter we will use the IRS example to illustrate our points, mainly due to its familiarity.

1.1   Working within the Current Internet Technology

Given the current state of upload applications, i.e., everyone uploads directly to the data's final destination server (refer to Figure 1), a specific upload flow, from some client to the destination server, can experience the following potential bottlenecks: (a) poor connectivity of the client, (b) congestion somewhere between the client and the server, or (c) overload on the server, or a combination of these bottlenecks. Given these bottlenecks, traditional solutions (or a combination of these solutions), such as buying a bigger server, buying a bigger pipe, and co-locating the server(s) at the ISP(s), exhibit shortcomings including lack of flexibility and lack of scalability.

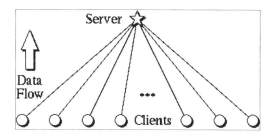

Figure 1. A large number of users uploading their data to the same Server (as in the IRS example).

The poor performance that can be potentially experienced by users of digital government applications, given the existing state of technology, is largely due to how (independent) data transfers work over the Internet, i.e., TCP/IP. That is, TCP/IP is very good at equally sharing the bandwidth between all flows using the same link. To illustrate this point, consider the following example.

Suppose 1 million (out of the possible 100 million) users submit their income tax forms to IRS servers at about the same time. Suppose that IRS places 2,500 servers around the country, with an average of 400 users uploading to each server simultaneously. And, suppose further that these 400 users share the same *bottleneck* link during the simultaneous uploads to one of these servers (as depicted in Figure 1) while trying to beat the deadline to submit their income tax forms, each receiving $(1/400)^{th}$ of the bottleneck link's bandwidth. If in isolation the user would have been able to complete the upload in 30 seconds, then on the *average* a user would have to wait on the order of 2 hours to complete his or her transfer, and in the *worst* case he or she will have to wait on the order of 3 hours. Furthermore, placing 2,500 servers around the country dedicated to what is essentially a *one day* event is not the most cost-effective approach. (Not to mention that predicting how many are needed this year, and how many more will be needed next year is no small matter.) Thus, the users suffer due to poor performance, and the IRS suffers due to high costs.

Although TCP/IP is here to stay (at least for the foreseeable future), much can be done at the application layer to circumvent this problem. An application layer solution, in the context of data collection applications, is the focus of this chapter.

1.2   Hotspots in the Internet

Hotspots are a major obstacle to achieving scalability in the Internet. At the application layer, hotspots are usually caused by either (a) high demand for some data or (b) high demand for a certain service. This high demand for data or services is typically the result of a *real-life event* involving availability of new data or approaching deadlines; therefore, relief of these hotspots may improve quality of life. For instance, imagine again those 1 million people trying to make the deadline for submitting their tax returns on April 15th, all at 5 minutes to midnight (as depicted in Figure 1). This would not only flood the IRS servers and result in many people not making the deadline, but it would also create sufficient traffic on the Internet to interfere with many other Internet-based applications that have no relationship with income tax form submissions.

At the application layer, hotspot problems have traditionally been dealt with using some combination of (1) increasing capacity; (2) spreading the load over time, space, or both; and (3) changing the workload. Some examples of these are data replication (e.g., web caching [Karger et al., 1997], ftp mirroring), data replacement (e.g., multi-resolution images, audio, video), service replication (e.g., DNS lookup, Network Time Protocol), and server push (e.g., news download, software distribution).

We note that the classes of solutions stated above have been studied mostly in the context of applications using the following types of communication (a) one-to-many (data travels primarily from a server to multiple clients, e.g., web download, software distribution, and video-on-demand); (b) many-to-many (data travels between multiple clients, through either a centralized or a distributed server, e.g., chat rooms and video conferencing); and (c) one-to-one (data travels between two clients, e.g., e-mail and e-talk). However, to the best of our knowledge there is no existing work, except ours, on making applications with *many-to-one* communication scalable and efficient. Existing solutions, such as web-based submissions, simply use many independent one-to-one transfers. Moreover, although many-to-many data transfers can be achieved using a set of one-to-many, a set of many-to-one, or both types of data transfers, to the best of our knowledge, existing work on many-to-many data transfer applications is focused on making the one-to-many communication efficient and scalable.

Many-to-one communication corresponds to an important class of applications, whose examples include the various *upload* applications such as submission of income tax forms, conference paper submission, proposal submission through the NSF FastLane system, NIH proposal submission system, homework and project submissions in distance education [Thomas et al., 1996], voting in digital democracy applications [Watson et al., 1999], voting in interactive television [Press, 1993], and many more.

1.3   Why Does *Upload* Require New Solutions?

We can view hotspots in most *download* applications as being due to a demand for popular *data objects*. We can view hotspots in most *upload* applications as being due to a demand for a popular *service*, e.g., the income tax submission service, as the actual data being transferred by the various users is distinct. The two main characteristics which make upload applications different from download applications are as follows: (1) in the case of uploads, the real-life event which causes the hotspots often imposes a *hard deadline* on the data transfer service, whereas in the case of downloads, it translates into a desire for low latency data access; and (2) uploads are inherently data *writing* applications while downloads are data reading applications. Traditional solutions aimed at latency reduction for data *reading* applications are (a) data replication (using a variety of techniques such as caching, prefetching, mirroring, etc.) and (b) data replacement (such as sending a low resolution version of the data for image, video, audio downloads). Clearly, these techniques are not applicable in uploads.

Additionally, *confidentiality* of data as well as other security issues are especially important in write-type applications (e.g., in uploading tax forms, papers, and proposals). Another important characteristic of uploads is that, unlike most downloads where data is intended to be consumed immediately upon receipt, uploaded data is often stored at the server for some time before its consumption. We will explain how we exploit this characteristic in the next section.

1.4   Scalable Framework

In this section we briefly outline the basics of our framework intended as a solution to the scalable data collection problem. A number of important and difficult research problems remain open within this framework, as outlined in [Bhattacharjee et al., 2000], as well as within the context of the general problem of data collection over the Internet. Our goal in this chapter is to illustrate the importance of this, until now neglected, research problem as well as present one possible solution.

Two types of upload applications exist, those with deadlines and those without deadlines. Our framework, termed the *Bistro* system, under development at the University of Maryland [Bistro, 2001], can accommodate both types of applications. Below, we discuss our framework in the context of deadline-driven applications with reasonably large data transfer sizes, such as the IRS application described earlier.

We observe that the existence of hotspots in uploads is largely due to approaching deadlines. The hotspot is exacerbated by the long transfer times. We also observe that what is actually required is an assurance that specific data was submitted before a specific time, and that the transfer of the data needs to be done in a timely fashion, but does *not* have to occur by that deadline because the data is not consumed by the server right away, i.e., IRS agents are not waiting to process all tax forms at one minute past midnight on April 16th.

Thus our approach is to break the deadline-driven upload problem into pieces. Specifically, we break up our original deadline-driven upload problem into:

a) a real-time *timestamp* subproblem, where we ensure that the data is timestamped and that the data cannot be subsequently tampered with;

b) a low latency *commit* subproblem, where the data goes *somewhere* and the user is assured that the data is safely and securely *on its way* to the server; and

c) a timely *data transfer* subproblem, which can be carefully planned (and coordinated with other uploads) and must go to the original destination.

This means that we have taken a traditionally *synchronized client-push* solution and replaced it with a *non-synchronized* solution that uses some combination of *client-push* (step (b) above) and *server-pull* (step (c) above) approaches. Consequently, we eliminate the hotspots by spreading most of the demand on the server over time; this is accomplished by making the actual data transfers almost *independent* of the deadline. (Also, note that the only step that must occur before the deadline is the timestamp, i.e., the actual data does not have to be transferred before the deadline.)

For the non-deadline-driven upload problems we can modify subproblem (a) above to provide simple mechanisms (e.g., message digests) that can later be used to verify data integrity.

Lastly, note that the above solution is somewhat analogous to sending a certified letter through a postal service with the main difference being that there is an inherent trust in the postal system whereas our solution, as outlined below, involves the use of untrusted intermediaries that essentially act as untrusted post offices. Hence *security* and *integrity* of the data become an inherent part of our framework. We refer the interested reader to [Cheng et al., 2001b] for one possible security protocol for an IRS-type application.

1.5   A Case for Use of Intermediaries

In the Internet, connectivity is usually non-uniform and can be time-dependent. Such connectivity problems contribute to important obstacles to achieving efficient large-scale data collection. Poor connectivity problems are due to either high traffic or low bandwidth connections. Consequently, different hosts experience different connectivity characteristics to the same data source. And hence, an effective solution to connectivity problems over the Internet must by necessity be distributed.

As is clear from past experience with download applications (e.g., Napster-type solutions [Napster]) great benefits can be obtained through the use of host intermediaries. Furthermore, the above stated solution in the context of the *Bistro* framework also implies the use of intermediaries. The benefits of such intermediaries are as follows.

– Connectivity in the Internet is time-dependent and non-uniform. Since users can have better connectivity to some hosts (intermediaries) than others having a choice of hosts results in performance benefits.
– Hotspots occur around the destination server due to demand for data or service. Thus, simple parallelism (in the form of multiple choices of destinations/intermediaries) improves performance.
– Intermediaries can provide choices of algorithms used to collect data for a variety of possible data sources, e.g., they can provide flexibility in terms of when to use push and when to use pull for data collection, facilitate prioritization of data sources during the collection process, and so on.
– Intermediaries clearly result in the ability to share resources between multiple data collection applications and agencies, which in turn results in cost-effectiveness, facilitation of application-specific data aggregation (which can improve performance further), and so on.

1.6 Importance of Resource Sharing

We note that an important characteristic of the *Bistro* framework is the notion of *resource sharing*. It is fairly clear that a more traditional solution of, e.g., buying a bigger cluster for a *one time event* (which may not be *big enough* for the next similar event) is not the most desirable or flexible solution to the upload problem. The ability to share an infrastructure, such as an infrastructure of intermediaries or, in our case, *bistros* (as described below), between a variety of wide-area digital government data collection applications for a variety of government agencies has clear advantages over the traditional solutions described earlier.

Thus, some advantages of our approach are that: (a) it is more *dynamic* and therefore more *adaptive* to system and network conditions; (b) it provides for more resource sharing opportunities and thus can result in a more cost effective solution to wide-area upload problems; and (c) it *does not rely* on the existence of a private infrastructure but it *does not preclude* it either.

In summary, we believe that the *Bistro* framework is a more *flexible* solution that takes advantage of whatever resources are available in the system and the Internet to the *best* extent possible. Below we give a more detailed description of the *Bistro* framework.

2.   BISTRO FRAMEWORK

Our approach is to break the upload problem into the following subproblems: (a) timestamp, (b) commit, and (c) transfer, and then design and develop the *Bistro* architecture that implements solutions to these subproblems using a set of primitive services. The primitive services that are used to build an upload application are a function of that application's requirements.

Given the break-up into subproblems, the original data transfer is now done using two data transfers (1) from a client to one or possibly more hosts (intermediaries) on the Internet, which we will refer to as *bistros*, and then (2) from one or more *bistros* to the server. This flow of data is illustrated in Figure 2. Although Figure 2 only depicts a single upload, it is understood that the *bistros* may be *shared* by many simultaneous upload activities/applications, each with different deadlines, characteristics, and requirements.

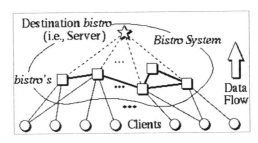

Figure 2. A *single* upload with the *Bistro* System after *Bistro* software is installed on the Server.

Note that, the client-to-*bistro* data transfer also produces the timestamp and the commit, i.e., the data is timestamped so the server has a guarantee that it cannot be tampered with after the deadline, and the client receives a commit, i.e., a *receipt* that guarantees that the data will arrive at the server and that its integrity and privacy will be preserved.

The timestamp has to be produced before the deadline; the commit has to be performed with low latency, and the data transfer from a *bistro* to the server has to be done in a timely manner. The exact constraints on all these operations are again a function of the requirements of the particular upload application. These are implemented by composing the appropriate primitive services, where we argue that a small set of such services is sufficient. We now present the set of services we are designing and implementing, and the details of each and how they fit into our *Bistro* architecture.

2.1 Primitive Services

The basic structure of our software architecture is illustrated in Figure 3, with two basic sublayers: (1) *primitive services*, which currently include timestamping (*TS*), security (*SEC*), fault tolerance (*FT*), commit (*CMT*), and data transfer (*XFR*); and (2) mechanisms and policies for implementing these services. We refer to the two layers together as the *Bistro-libraries*.

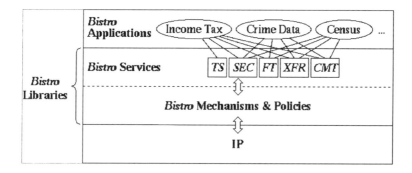

Figure 3. Bistro software architecture.

The *TS primitive service* provides mechanisms and policies for (1) timestamping the instant of an upload request and (2) ensuring that the user is not able to tamper with the data without affecting the timestamp. Depending on the upload application, either one or both of these mechanisms will be needed.

The *SEC primitive service* provides mechanisms and policies for (1) privacy/confidentiality, (2) authentication, (3) non-repudiation, and (4) integrity. Note that the need for this primitive service is partly due to the fact that data will travel through and be temporarily stored at (potentially) untrusted hosts, namely *bistros*. Depending on the upload application, only a subset of these mechanisms may be needed.

The *FT primitive service* provides mechanisms and policies for ensuring that data will not be lost or temporarily unavailable due to failures of various system components, such as network links and hosts corresponding to *bistros*, limitations on connectivity, or simply due to the possibly malicious nature of some *bistros*. This will require some degree of redundancy in the temporary storage at the *bistros*. The amount of redundancy, and therefore, degree of fault tolerance will again depend on the application.

The *XFR primitive service* provides mechanisms and policies for the actual transfer of the data from the client to the *bistro* and from the *bistro* to the server. This corresponds to the careful planning of the data movement, including choice of which *bistros* participate in the transfer, which client transfers to which *bistro*, coordination between the *bistros*, as well as the potential aggregation of the data as it is moved around. For instance, the choice of which client goes to which *bistro* may depend on the distances between clients and *bistros*. Or, in some applications, aggregation of data can reduce the overall amount of data transferred, e.g., in a voting for interactive television application all votes from clients transferring to the same *bistro* can be aggregated and only the summary needs to be transferred to the server.

The *CMT primitive service* provides mechanisms and policies for committing the upload transaction, i.e., it is analogous to issuing a *receipt* to the user, which acknowledges the transfer of responsibility for completing the upload from the user to a *bistro*. Therefore, from the user's point of view, the data transfer is completed at the time of commit.

Note that a specific upload application will require the use of some subset of primitive services. For example, uploading tax forms and grant proposals requires all the primitive services described above, while crime data collection and Census Bureau surveys applications may not require TS services that are motivated by deadlines (e.g., as in the IRS application).

Given the above description, it is also clear that each primitive service can have a number of characteristics (and/or gradations). An upload application can be constructed by combining some subset of these primitive services and appropriate choice of characteristics within each primitive service. Consequently, the resulting performance and scalability characteristics of the application are a function of the chosen primitive services and their respective characteristics.

2.2   Deployment Issues

Bistro is an application layer platform, and hence (unlike say a network layer protocol) it is easily deployable. Installing a *bistro* is as simple as installing a web server.

Our intent for deploying the *Bistro* platform is *not* to rely on adding resources (such as hosts) to the Internet. Rather, we envision that people will want to install *Bistro* on their hosts on the public Internet and contribute their resources to the overall *Bistro* infrastructure because it will improve their performance as well. In turn, the existing *bistros* will discover the new installations and integrate them into a *Bistro* infrastructure. Thus, our architecture will take advantage of *existing* resources and utilize them to their full potential for each upload application.

Note that deployment over private networks can also be done but is relatively straightforward from the deployment point of view. We also note that some applications, e.g., some of the digital government applications, might wish to employ some private servers, for a variety of purposes (i.e., *Bistro* can be deployed over a combination of public and private hosts). In this case, deployment becomes simpler as compared to deployment over a completely public infrastructure. Hence, in our work we address the most general form of the deployment problem.

We note that an attractive characteristic of the *Bistro* framework, with respect to digital government needs, is that it can be gradually deployed and experimented with over the public Internet, simply by installing the *Bistro* system on intermediaries (which can be public or private). Each application (within each agency) can have its own scalability, security, fault tolerance, and other upload characteristics, and these applications and agencies can still share available resources, if so desired, across all *Bistro* servers, with minimal interference. For example, our security protocol (refer to [Cheng et al., 2001b]) does not rely on a particular cryptographic system in order to provide the needed privacy and integrity characteristics; hence, each application and each agency can choose one that satisfies its requirements. Efficient, cost-effective, and secure sharing of resources between multiple upload applications is an important part of our work.

3. CONCLUSIONS

Scalable Internet-based data collection problem has been, until this point, a neglected research topic. The *Bistro* framework has been designed to address scalability problems in Internet-based upload applications over a wide range of applications and problem sizes. In designing, implementing, and deploying *Bistro*, we are gaining knowledge and experience that are fundamental to making large-scale data collection and dissemination, for a variety of applications, a reality.

We believe that digital government applications should be built on top of the *Bistro* infrastructure since data collection (i.e., uploads) is an inherent part of these applications. Furthermore, *Bistro* provides one infrastructure for *all* government agencies and *all* digital government data collection applications, which we believe to be a highly desirable feature.

We also believe that the *Bistro* framework is extensible to other Internet-based applications which have a many-to-one data transfer component, such as e-commerce, online auctions, Internet-based storage, and many more. Since the scalability of many-to-one data transfer has not been addressed yet, solving the many-to-one problem will improve the scalability of all these applications.

To date, we have designed the *Bistro* framework [Bhattacharjee et al., 2000] and conducted a performance study, which demonstrated the potential performance gains of this framework as well as provided insight into the general upload problem [Cheng et al., 2001a]. Since confidentiality of data as well as other security issues are especially important in upload applications and in our solution where we introduced untrusted (public) intermediaries (i.e., *bistros*), we also developed a secure data transfer protocol within the *Bistro* framework which not only ensures the privacy and integrity of the data but also takes scalability considerations into account [Cheng et al., 2001b]. However, a great number of open research problems still remain within the *Bistro* framework as outlined in [Bhattacharjee et al., 2000]; they are the topic of our ongoing efforts.

REFERENCES

Bhattacharjee, S., Cheng, W. C., Chou, C.-F., Golubchik, L., and Khuller, S. (September 2000). Bistro: a platform for building scalable wide-area upload applications. *Performance Evaluation Review (also presented at the Workshop on Performance and Architecture of Web Servers (PAWS) in June 2000)*, 28(2):29--35.

Bistro (2001). *Project Home Page*. http://www.cs.umd.edu/projects/icl/bistro/.

Cheng, W. C., Chou, C.-F., Golubchik, L., and Khuller, S. (June 2001a). A performance study of bistro, a scalable wide-area upload architecture. Technical Report CS-TR-4260, University of Maryland.

Cheng, W. C., Chou, C.-F., Golubchik, L., and Khuller, S. (June 2001b). A secure and scalable wide-area upload service. *Proceedings of the 2nd International Conference on Internet Computing*.

IRS (2001). *Fill-in Forms*. http://www.irs.ustreas.gov/prod/forms_pubs/fillin.html.

Karger, D., Lehman, E., Leighton, T., Levine, M., Lewin, D., and Panigrahy, R. (1997). Consistent hashing and random trees: Distributed caching protocols for relieving hot spots on the World Wide Web. *STOC*, pages 654--663.

Napster (2001). *Home Page, Napster, Inc.* http://www.napster.com/.

Press, L. (1993). The Internet and interactive television. *Communications of the ACM*, 36(12):19--23.

Thomas, P., Carswell, L., Petre, M., Poniatowska, B., Price, B., and Emms, J. (1996). Distance education over the Internet. *Proceedings of the conference on integrating technology into computer science education*, pages 147--149.

Watson, R. T., Akselsen, S., Evjemo, B., and Aarsaether, N. (1999). Teledemocracy in local government. *Communications of the ACM*, 42(12):58--63.

Leana Golubchik is an Associate Professor in the Department of Computer Science at the University of Maryland at College park. From fall of 1995 until summer of 1997, she was an Assistant Professor in the Department of Computer Science at Columbia University. Her research interests include computer systems modeling & performance evaluation, Internet-based computing, and multimedia storage systems. Leana received her Ph.D. degree from the Computer Science Department at the University of California at Los Angeles in 1995. She is currently the Vice Chair of SIGMETRICS (elected 2001) and a past member of its Board of Directors (1999-2001). She was a guest co-editor for special issues of the *IEEE Transactions on Knowledge and Data Engineering*, the *Parallel Computing* journal, and the *International Journal of Intelligent Systems*, a program co-chair of the 2001 Joint ACM SIGMETRICS/Performance Conference and MIS'99, as well as a program committee member of several conferences, including SIGMETRICS, SIGMOD, ICDCS, ICDE, and PDIS. Leana has received several awards, including the NSF CAREER award, the IBM Doctoral Fellowship, and the NSF Doctoral Fellowship. She is a member of the IFIP WG 7.3 (elected 2000), ACM, IEEE, and Tau Beta Pi.

Chapter 7

Security and Privacy Challenges of a Digital Government

James B. D. Joshi, Arif Ghafoor, Walid G. Aref, Eugene H. Spafford
Purdue University, West Lafayette, Indiana USA

Abstract: A digital government can be viewed as an amalgam of heterogeneous information systems that exchange high-volume information among government agencies and public and private sectors engaged in government business. This gives rise to several daunting multidomain security challenges as well as concern for citizen privacy. The success of a digital government infrastructure depends on how well it meets these challenges and its preparedness against numerous potential threats ranging from simple act of hacking to cyber-terrorism. In this chapter, we outline these crucial security and privacy issues and present various solutions that are available and need to be further investigated.

Key words: security, access control, privacy, multidomain environment

1.   INTRODUCTION

A digital government (DG) can be viewed as an amalgam of interconnected heterogeneous information systems in which government agencies and public and private sectors exchange a high volume of information. Several US government agencies have aggressively adopted information technologies in order to modernize the government's highly fragmented service-centric information infrastructure by improving information flow and the decision-making process. Efficient, flexible, interoperable, and securely integrated information systems are needed to achieve such seamless information flow and service integration. Creating such systems requires a holistic development approach to building a secure information infrastructure. Such infrastructure supports both the intricate interdependence of government programs at different levels and between government and the private and public sectors that have become essential partners in supporting government's public services.

Although Information Age technologies provide intriguing opportunities for developing DG concepts, they also create significant infrastructure security and privacy challenges. The overall grade of *"D-"* for computer security at the Federal Departments and agencies, as per the report published on September 11, 2000, by the Subcommittee on Government Management, Information and Technology, indicates the uphill path the government agencies need to take in order to transform their processes and integrate them within a secure DG infrastructure.

Various goals of information system security include confidentiality or secrecy, integrity, availability, accountability, and information assurance [13]. Three key mechanisms that provide the foundation for an information security include *authentication, access control,* and *audit.* Authentication establishes the identity of an entity and is a prerequisite for access control. Access control limits the actions or operations that a legitimate entity performs. The audit process collects data about the system's activity. Once a user is authenticated, the system should enforce access control using an established technique such as a reference monitor that mediates each access by a user to an object.

Several access-control models have been proposed to address the security needs of information systems. Traditional access control approaches fall into two broad categories: discretionary (DAC) and mandatory (MAC). DAC approach lets users grant their privileges to other users, whereas MAC approach uses a classification scheme for subjects and objects. User classification leads to several clearance levels for access control, whereas classification of objects can be established according to their sensitivity. To avoid the unauthorized flow of sensitive information, the MAC model - also referred to as the multilevel model - can enforce no read-up and no write-down rules at a given level [13].

Several security technologies that are becoming indispensable for large distributed and networked heterogeneous systems, like a DG, include *firewalls, intrusion detection systems, encryption techniques, PKI (Public Key Infrastructure) technologies,* etc. Growing privacy concerns over the Internet foreshadows the critical citizen privacy issue in a DG environment because of the huge amount of citizen information it will have in its databases. For a DG infrastructure, designing and implementing these mechanisms and technologies in an integrated manner poses a daunting challenge. We perceive the following three key concerns for a DG infrastructure:

- Secure integration of information systems belonging to government and non-government organizations,
- Citizen privacy that is key to the success of democratic process,
- Threats to the DG infrastructure that can endanger the national security, and their assessment in order to build efficient counter measures.

2. SECURE INTEGRATION OF SYSTEMS

Inherently multidisciplinary and dynamic, a DG's organizational and operational base is characterized by the coexistence of diverse information security policies employed by individual government agencies. These varied policies create a highly heterogeneous multidomain environment. Such environments should support interoperability of several security domains and allow strong inter-domain interaction. Diversity in a multidomain environment may exist in different forms [10]. For example, the environment may be composed of diverse interacting and collaborating constituent agencies with different policies. Similarly, the environment may have more than one security goals or the variations of the same goal. Furthermore, the environment may have heterogeneous system components such as operating systems, databases, etc., each with different security mechanisms [10].

The overall infrastructure must allow seamless and secure interoperation among diverse and heterogeneous security mechanisms. The infrastructure should be scalable, open and extensible. Meeting all these requirements presents several daunting challenges, the key among which include: *semantic heterogeneity, secure interoperation, risk propagation and assurance,* and *security management.*

2.1 Semantic heterogeneity

The diversity of organizational and user-specific security policies in a DG environment requires powerful formalisms for efficiently mapping security attributes across interacting domains. In a DG environment, coexistence of different security policies or the variations of a single policy can give rise to naming conflicts among similar security attributes, and structural conflicts among user/role hierarchies and access rules. These conflicts need to be resolved by employing an appropriate metapolicy [10]. Such metapolicy models should be generic and flexible enough to express a wide range of security policies and must provide a semantic basis for policy composition and modifications. Metapolicies must also allow autonomy and transparency for the policies adopted by an individual domain, which provides for the policies' continuous evolution.

2.2   Secure interoperability

Any policy change, addition, or deletion requires reevaluating the system's secure interoperability. Secure interoperability poses a major challenge when dealing with an environment where subjects from a different domain access objects in a given domain. The goal is to ensure that no security violations occur during inter-domain accesses. In particular, secure interoperation should enforce the following two principles [7]:
– The autonomy principle, which states that if access is permitted within an individual system, it must also be permitted under secure interoperation.
– The security principle, which states that if an access is not permitted within an individual system, it must not be permitted under secure interoperation.

For example, consider two systems S1 and S2, and assume that user A can access whatever user B can access in S1, and user C can access whatever user D can access in S2. Now, suppose we allow S1 and S2 to interoperate by allowing D to access A's files and B to access C's files. This results in the violation of the security principle, as B can now access A's files through transitivity (B can access C's and hence D's, and consequently A's files), which was not permitted within S1 alone. Hence, the added interoperation links between S1 and S2 result in an insecure multidomain environment.

As indicated by the undecidability result of the safety problem related to secure interoperation [7], in general, it is impossible to guarantee secure interoperation among multiple domains. Furthermore, even the problem of finding a secure solution with some optimality is NP-complete [7]. Optimization can include maximizing the amount of shared data among all domains, maximizing the number of legal accesses, or minimizing the number of conflicting domains.

2.3   Assurance and risk propagation

In a multidomain environment, users must maintain a certain degree of assurance about the entire system's security. While some risks may be acceptable in a local system, such risks can, in a larger network, propagate and increase the level of vulnerability of all interconnected systems. For example, an information system, say S, may be securely interoperating with many other systems, all of which interoperate with each other through system S. In such a case, a security breach in S renders all the interconnected systems vulnerable to attack.

A related issue, the cascading problem, also arises in multidomain environments. Consider two multi-level systems, X and Y. Suppose system X is designed for managing information classified as either *secret* or *top secret* and that all users of X are cleared for *secret* information at least. System Y can handle information classified as *confidential* or *secret*, and its users are cleared for *confidential* information at least. Now, suppose their owners integrate the two systems, and the resulting three levels of clearance include *confidential*, *secret*, and *top secret*. In the merged system, the *secret* information can pass between the two systems. If a penetrator overcomes the protection mechanisms in both the individual systems, then he can downgrade the *top secret* information of system X to the level of *secret* and pass it to system Y. In system Y, the same penetrator can then downgrade that information to *confidential*. Thus, users having the lowest clearance in either system can access the *top secret* information. This shows that in a DG environment each system should maintain high assurance and be aware of the security assurances of the other systems.

2.4 Management challenges

Security management in a DG infrastructure presents a challenging task because of the large number of administrative domains, subjects, and objects. One characteristic of a DG is that it essentially forms an open system where the entities that represent users, objects, policies, security domains, and other components are transient. This inherent dynamism makes the task of overall management and, in particular, security configuration management, and the management of metapolicies and policy evolution very difficult. Practical and efficient methodologies for security management will be crucial for the success of a DG.

3. APPROACHES TO SECURE INTEGRATION

Several approaches to information security exist that aim to meet the challenges we have described. Here, we profile the strengths and limitations of the most prominent methods, which Table 2 summarizes.

3.1 Policy-metapolicy specification

In a multidomain environment, establishing semantically correct relationships among security policies is essential to ensuring secure cooperation. Metapolicies can specify such relationships as cooperation rules and guidelines for conflict resolution and interaction.

Hosmer [10] proposes several conflict-resolution methods, including manual, standard form, and rule-based strategy approaches. The manual approach, used most commonly, assigns a security officer the responsibility for manually integrating multiple policies and resolving conflicts. In the standard-form approach, the organization adopts some generic or policy-neutral guidelines to ensure secure interoperability. Each domain uses a conversion logic to translate its local rules to a global metapolicy schema. In a rule-based strategy, the conflict resolution mechanism uses a predefined set of rules such as voting or informal guidelines. For policy mediation, Kuhnhauser's framework uses conflict and cooperation matrices [14]. A conflict matrix provides a ranking mechanism to resolve conflicts between two policies. The cooperation matrix stores the information about a predetermined policy to be used when two domains interact.

Traditional DAC and MAC models lack capabilities for expressing a domain's arbitrary security requirements. Increasingly, flexible approaches are being sought that allow user-defined security policies. One such model is the newly emerging *role-based access control* (RBAC) model that has generated great interest in the security community. Recently, Sandhu and colleagues have proposed the National Institute for Science and Technology RBAC as a standard reference model [17]. RBAC's policy neutrality, constraints, and role hierarchies make it a powerful model for specifying policies from other models such as DAC and MAC and for specifying arbitrary user-specific access rules [17, 19].

RBAC's flexibility and similarity with organizational concepts make it a good candidate for addressing access control issues in a multidomain environment [15]. Further, models for administrative roles provide efficient mechanisms for distributing security management functions to a number of administrators [19]. Other new access control models that have shown potential for supporting a multipolicy environment include *type enforcement*, *multiple-policy schematic protection* (MSP), *typed access matrices* (TAM), and *dynamically typed access control* (DTAC) models, which use subject and object types [13]. However, these models have reached only the initial phases of their development.

Applications and services in a DG environment require automated transactional functions and workflow-based processing. To support access control in such transaction-intensive environments, Thomas and colleagues [21] propose an initial *task-based access control (TBAC) family of models in which the authorization unit is a task. However*, much needs to be done for making TBAC useful for real world applications. A viable access control solution proposed by Bertino and colleagues for workflow-based systems is to assign roles to workflow tasks [3].

Public-key infrastructure technology is maturing, and the use of PKI certificates is expected to be ubiquitous in the near future. Certificates issued by a PKI facility can be used for facilitating access control in the networked DG environment. For example, an extended X.509 certificate, issued by a certification authority, can carry user information [17]. These techniques can be used to either support a host's access control method by carrying access control information or provide a separate access control mechanism based on trust centres. Table 1 summarizes various access control approaches discussed and their important features.

Table 1. Access control approaches and features compared

Approach	Features
DAC	Ownership based, flexible, most widely used, does not provide high degree of security, and hence low assurance
	Typed versions such as SPM, TAM and DTAC are expressive but have little or no experience base
	DTAC can handle dynamic changes and task based control
	Most cannot be used where classification levels are needed
	Typed versions have tried to include classification levels
MAC	Administration based,
	Information flow control rules; uses classification labels
	High level of security, and hence high assurance, but less flexible.
RBAC	Policy-neutral/flexible; Principle of least privilege
	Separation of duty; Easy administrative features
	Able to express DAC, MAC and user-specific
	Can be easily incorporated into current technologies
	Good potential for use in multidomain environments when policies are expressed using role hierarchies and constraints
Access control tasks/workflow systems	Task-oriented authorization paradigm, RBAC for WFMS
	TBAC is at an initial stage of development
	Key for success of transaction intensive DG environment
Certificate-based	Utilization of existing PKI facilities
	Complements the host's access control model
	Can use trust centers in the WWW

3.2 Architectural methods

Approaches that address the challenges of large multidomain environments also address architectural issues. Notable among these are the Object Management Group's Common Object Request Broker Architecture (CORBA) and the Open Software Foundation's Distributed Computing Environment. CORBA offers a security policy specification but lacks formal semantics, thus making security-handling mechanisms more or less ad hoc.

DCE addresses the general issue of object interoperability by providing a middleware architecture that implements an ad hoc security mechanism.

Some other proposed architecture includes the Distributed Trusted Operating System (DTOS) and the Meta Object Operating System Environment (MOOSE) [8]. DTOS supports separation between the policy specification and policy enforcement components by using a mix of tabular representation and a language-based specification model to provide a high degree of flexibility in security policy selection. MOOSE's three-layer architecture uses a formal approach to integrate modelling, specification, verification, and implementation [8].

Software agent based architectures are emerging as possible solutions for addressing the DG's multidomain security issues. Agents are characterized by *adaptation, cooperation, autonomy,* and *mobility.* Agent communication languages, with extensions, can be used to negotiate policies during conflicts to ensure secure interoperation [HE8]. The servers and clients in a distributed environment can assign policy negotiation and security enforcement tasks to agents. Although the mobility and adaptability characteristics of agents provide essential features for the efficient use of system resources, they themselves can pose several security threats. For example, an agent can engage in malicious behaviour, thus disrupting the host's normal operation. Similarly, a host can hinder an agent's activity by denying required access to local information resources.

3.3   Database federation approach

The database federation approach, which integrates several database management systems, provides some solutions to the multidomain problem and is relatively a mature field. Several researchers have proposed approaches for developing systems that achieve the autonomy of component databases yet remain transparent at the federation level. These approaches also address a multidomain environment's security management issues. For example, Jonscher and Dittrich's federated database system allows DAC and MAC policies within component databases [12]. This system uses a global access layer to map global authorizations into the local-access rights of individual databases. The Distributed Object Kernel [20] is another example of a secure federated database system that uses a mapping technique to build a global-access policy from local DAC and MAC policies. In the DOK system, the enforcement mechanism for global security involves layered processing by agents designed to check attribute constraints and sanitize query results. Approaches for federated-database schema integration can be extended for developing metapolicy frameworks for access control in a multidomain environment and to provide a viable security management solution for a DG infrastructure.

Table 2. Digital government security challenges and potential approaches to solving them. (Reprinted by permission of IEEE. James Joshi et al. "Digital Government Security Infrastructure Design Challenges." *IEEE Computer*, February 2001. © 2001 IEEE.)

Challenges	Solution approaches
Semantic Heterogeneity	Generic language (such as Z), algebraic, security automata
	Policy neutral models such as RBAC
	Typed extensions of access control matrix models such as TAM and DTAC
	Programmable security; Export security interfaces
Secure interoperation	*Conflict types*
	Domain conflict, Rule conflict
	Conflict resolution approaches
	Manual, need-based, priority based, voting etc.
	Composition operators such as Union, Intersection, Product
	Hierarchy of security properties; Virtual roles/Role mapping in RBAC
Flexibility/ Extensibility	Separation of policy specification and enforcement components
	Policy library/Policy habitat, Layered architecture
Risk control/ Assurance	Safety analysis such as static and dynamic checking in DTAC
	Use of least privilege feature in RBAC system; Inline coding
	Retain reference monitor properties of tamperproof, complete mediation and verifiability
Management	Administrative models such as administrative role based models
	Auditing; Risk, vulnerability analysis
	Security assessment and certification, Layered architecture

4. CITIZEN PRIVACY

A fairly common definition of privacy is "the right of individuals, groups, or institutions to determine for themselves when, how, and to what extent information about them is communicated" [11]. As shown by various surveys [1], personal privacy in the Internet is a big concern for users, and it has been so for many years. The recent move towards the development and deployment of a new digital Interactive TV technology that have the capability to track each TV show a viewer watches and profile the viewing as well as spending habits of people, adds a new dimension to the already growing privacy concerns over the Internet [22]. The DG infrastructure that essentially builds on these Internet technologies thus carries over a new level of concerns for citizen privacy.

In a DG environment, user transactions for the government services will essentially use various sensitive personal information such as social security numbers, tax information, criminal records, medical information, etc. Besides, a DG environment allows increased connectivity of businesses to government information systems. This calls for extra measure on the part of the DG infrastructure to provide protection of personal information in huge government databases and sensitive information in transit. Compromising a single DG component can leak out huge amounts of personal information in its databases to the non-government systems connected to it. Access to social security numbers by identity thieves provides them with a much more power to abuse in a DG environment as this allows them to potentially access any information about a person stored in government databases. Billions of records are estimated to be available in both private and government databases that describe each citizen's finances, interests, and demographics. Privacy vulnerabilities arise even if data is available in statistical or aggregate forms that allow personal information to be inferred [11]. Furthermore, the fact that the government carefully monitors every transaction and resource access made by a citizen can discourage citizen participation.

End users are exposed to several security and privacy risks when using Web browsers, which will play an essential part as DG interfaces. Browser vulnerabilities can be used to compromise client security and user privacy [6, 16, 13]. Cookies, the data stored on the client's machine and exchanged between the clients and the server to maintain connection information, can be used for the purpose of gathering user information. Use of executable contents, such as Java applets, ActiveX controls, etc. is another source of security vulnerability [13]. Firewall technology has become the most popular defense for network servers against the open untrusted Internet. Though firewalls can prevent illegitimate traffic from travelling from the global Internet to DG networks, legitimate requests that pass through a firewall may be used for a data-driven attack on the networks or back-end systems [6, 16]. Configuration of firewalls and network servers is a formidable and error prone task.

5.   APPROACHES TO CITIZEN PRIVACY

In a DG environment, a conflicting situation is that while enhanced capability of carefully monitoring user activity is desirable to detect malicious activities against the DG infrastructure and to achieve accountability, it conflicts with the privacy concerns of citizens. The success of a DG environment will depend on how well it balances its ability to monitor malicious activities and its ability to establish itself as a fully trustworthy and secure medium. An effective solution for privacy in such an open DG environment will require a combined effort from technological, legislature and public policy sectors [11]. Encryption and PKI technologies provide reasonable solutions to the *communication privacy* that concerns with the privacy of the information in transit [11]. However, adequate technical measures do not exist that address the authorized use of sensitive personal information in databases (*database privacy*).

A forthcoming proposal is to develop new access control models or extend existing ones that are capable of addressing privacy constraints as access rules. As pointed out by Samarati [11], such an access authorization model should include: explicit permissions provided by owner, permission based on the use and purpose of information, permissions to control dissemination, permissions based on time and external conditions, etc. Such privacy-oriented mechanisms are lacking and this can become a deterrent to the success of the DG. Several tools such as web anonymizers, remailers, encrypted authentication, currently provide support for achieving some level of privacy. However, there also are tools that offset these, such as snoopware that locate personal data on the web, stealthware that essentially monitors client behaviour, etc.

6.   THREATS TO THE DG INFRASTURCURE

As Internet acts as the global platform that provides universal access to a DG infrastructure, all kinds of cyber attacks can be targeted towards the DG environment. Furthermore, as a DG environment is a monolithic multidomain system of securely interconnected heterogeneous systems, such attacks can have highly exacerbated effects. For example, a simple denial of service attack at some key government systems may have a very damaging effect on the services provided by other interconnected systems, rendering essential government services inoperative. Even bigger concern is the protection of critical infrastructure components within the DG. Thus, higher level of security assurance will be desirable for each individual domain. Further, independent as well as collaborative techniques must be developed to counter such threats. It is expected that in a few years the cyber-threats to the country will be worse than the physical threat [2]. At the worst, a DG infrastructure can be considered as a system with a single point of failure.

Potential "*info weapons*" that can be used to launch attack on a DG government, as are done over the Internet, include computer viruses, logic bombs, worms, Trojan horses, etc [2, 5, 6]. Various attacks on systems include denial of service attack, virtual sit-ins and blockades, rootkits, etc [5]. The attacks using these malicious tools range from simple hacktivism to the more damaging cyber-terrorism and info-war [5]. Cyber-terrorists can target civilian infrastrucure, military infrastructures or economic sector, or all at once to launch a complete infowar against the country.

Within the Internet, "hacktivism" refers to active hacking activities with the intent to disrupt normal operations but not causing serious damage [5], whereas cyber-terrorism refers to the use of act of terror over the cyberspace. Aimed against the DG infrastructure, a simple hacking can have grave consequences. For example, an hour-long properly coordinated hacking activity that affects the country's air traffic system, a critical infrastructure, can have very drastic consequences. Several instances of hacktivism in last few years have been discussed in [2, 5].

A recent survey conducted by Computer Security Institute (CSI) and FBI, reports that 71% of enterprises surveyed had detected unauthorized use by insiders in 2000 [16]. Similar results have been reported by the security survey conducted by Information Security Magazine (ISM) [4]. This indicates that the insider threat is real and can have more damaging effect than the external threat.   In a DG environment, such security breaches through disgruntled insiders can put the whole nation at risk. As Shaw and colleagues point out, *"staff employees pose perhaps the greatest risk in terms of access and potential damage"* to the DG environment, particularly, *"the part that constitutes the critical infrastructure of the country"* [18].

Table 3. Threats and their intent [2]

Threat level	Actor	Intent
National security threats	Information Warrior (Cyber-soldier) National intelligence (Cyber-spy)	Reduce decision making capability at the national level, National chaos and psychological terror Information leakage for political, military and economic advantages
Shared threats (government & private sector)	Cyber-terrorist Industrial espionage Organized crime (Cyber-crime)	Visibility/publicity, chaos, political changes Competitive advantage Revenge, retribution, monetary gain, institutional/political change
Local Threats (Hacktivism)	Institutional hackers Recreational hacker	Monetary gain, thrill/challenge, publicity/prestige Thrill, challenge

Table 3 shows various threat levels and the criminal intent behind them [2]. At the highest level, we see national security threats, which are essentially aimed at the nation's critical infrastructure. Threats common to both government and non-government agencies include cyber-terrorism and e-espionage. Finally, there are frequently occurring hacking incidents that can create huge losses within a DG environment. So far, there is no nationally coordinated defense capability to detect and counter strategic and well-coordinated act of cyber-terrorism against the nation [2, 5].

7. APPROACHES AGAINST THREATS TO DIGITAL GOVERNMENT

As indicated by the ISM survey [4], a key technical problem related to the insider attack is the inadequate policy specification and enforcement. Proper management of authorization policies, and policies as to the use of various software programs such as e-mails, browsers, etc. and use of up-to-date virus protections can greatly reduce insider attacks that can often be considered accidental or unintentional. Such unintentional insider security breaches can largely be avoided through education and awareness. Approaches using separation of duty and granting of least privilege to users can greatly reduce the misuse of resources by an insider. In such cases, use of formal models such as RBAC and DTAC can drastically improve the management complexity. The gravity of insider threat in a DG environment accentuates the need for proper monitoring of not just the technical activities of employees with crucial knowledge of the working of the DG infrastructure, but also their personal traits to detect any deviant behaviour. Doing that requires a careful balancing act between monitoring employee activities and maintaining citizen privacy.

A balanced and integrated use of various security technologies will be essential to secure the overall DG infrastructure from external threats. Intelligent distributed capabilities will be required to detect and counter both structured and unstructured attacks against the DG infrastructure. A difficulty, as pointed out by Denning, is the proper assessment of cyber-threats that can have national risk [5], particularly because such incidents have not been encountered.

8. CONCLUSION

Several daunting challenges exist towards the development of a secure DG infrastructure. As it facilitates the functioning of the entire country, ensuring its security is of utmost importance.

Foremost is the problem of secure integration of information systems of various government and non-government agencies in order to streamline government services. Of the many access control approaches, RBAC models appear to be the most attractive solution for securing the multidomain DG environment. In essence, RBAC models can provide a generic framework for expressing diverse security requirements. Integration of such access control models with encryption and PKI technologies can provide pragmatic solutions to the complex DG infrastructure.

Federated database management system approaches show promise and will likely be expanded to effectively address general multidomain issues. Agent systems, on the other hand, require further exploration to evaluate their security enforcement features. Developing efficient techniques to evaluate security assurance and carry out risk analysis remains a major challenge.

Threat assessment and the development of coordinated, distributed capability to detect and counter them will be very crucial for the success of the DG. There is a critical need for developing privacy models and mechanisms. Furthermore, it is essential to pursue multidimensional approach to citizen privacy that combines well-coordinated technical, legal as well as organizational and public efforts.

Acknowledgement: The research presented in this chapter has been funded by a grant from the Center for Education and Research in Information Assurance and Security (CERIAS) at Purdue University.

REFERENCES

[1] M. S. Ackerman, L. F. Cranor, J. Reagle, "Privacy in e-commerce: examining user scenarios and privacy preferences" Proceedings of the first ACM conference on Electronic commerce, 1999, Pages 1 – 8.

[2] Y. Alexander, M. S. Swetnam, Cyber Terrorism and Information Warfare I, Assessment of Challenges, Oceana Publisher Inc./Dobbs Ferry, New York,1999.

[3] E. Bertino, E. Ferrari, V. Atluri, "The Specification and Enforcement of Authorization Constraints in Workflow Management Systems," ACM Transactions on Information and System Security, Vol. 2, No. 1, Feb. 1999, pp. 65-104.

[4] A. Briney, "Security Focussed", Information Security Magazine, September, 2000, Pages 40-68.

[5] D. Denning, "Activism, Hacktivism, and Cyberterrorism:
The Internet as a Tool for Influencing Foreign Policy", Internet and International Systems: Information Technology and American Foreign Policy Decisionmaking Workshop, December, 2001.

[6] S. Garfinkel, E. H. Spafford, "Web Security & Commerce," O'Reilly & Associates, Inc., Sebastapol, CA, 1997.

[7] L. Gong and X. Qian, "Computational Issues in Secure Interoperation", IEEE Transaction on Software and Engineering, Vol. 22, No. 1, January 1996.

[8] J. Hale, m. Papa, S. Shenoi, "Programmable Security for Object-Oriented Systems"", Proceedings", Database Security XII: Status and Prospects, S. Jajodia (eds), Kluwer Academic Publishers, 1998, pp. 109-123.

[9] Q. He, K. Sycara, Z. Su, "A Solution to Open Standard of PKI", Proceedings of the Third Australian Conference, Eds. - Colin Boyd, Ed Dawson, ACISP'98, Brisbase, Australia, July 13-15, 1998.

[10]   H. H. Hosmer, "Metapolicies I", ACM SIGSAC Data Management Workshop, San Antonio, TX, December, 1991.

[11]   "Database Security XII Status and Prospects", Editor: Sushil Jajodia, IFIP TC11 WG11.3 Twelfth International Working Conference on Database Security, July 15-17, 1998, Chalkidiki, Greece.

[12]   D. Jonscher, K.R. Dittrich, "Argos – A Configurable Access Control System for Interoperable Environments" Proc. of the IFIP WG 11.3 Ninth Annual Working Conference on Database Security, Rensselaerville, NY, August 1995.

[13]   J. B. D. Joshi, W. G. Aref, A. Ghafoor, E. H. Spafford, "Security models for web-based applications", Communications of the ACM , 44, 2 (Feb. 2001), pages 38-72.

[14]   W. E. Kuhnhauser, M. K. Ostrowski, "A Formal Framework to Support Multiple Security Policies", Proceedings of the 7th Canadian Computer Security Symposium, Ottawa, Canada, May 1995.

[15]   S. Osborn, "Database Security Integration using Role-Based Access Control", IFIP WG11.3 Working Conference on Database Security, Aug. 2000.

[16]   R. Power, ""Tangled Web": Tales of Digital Crime from the Shadows of Cyberspace," Que/Macmillan Publishing, Aug. 31, 2000.

[17]   Proceedings of The Fifth ACM Workshop on Role-based Access Control, Berlin, Germany, July 26-27, 2000

[18]   E. D. Shaw, K. G. Ruby, J. M. Post, "The Insider Threat to Information Systems", Security Awareness Bulletin No. 2-98, published by Department of Defense Security Institute, September 1998.

[19]   R. S. Sandhu, E. J. Coyne, H. L. Feinstein, C. E. Youman, "Role-Based Access Control: A Multi-Dimensional View", Proceedings of the 10th Annual Computer Security Applications Conference, Orlando, FL, December, 5-9, 1994, pages 54-62.

[20]   Z. Tari, G. Fernandez, "Security Enforcement in the DOK Federated Database System", Database Security X: Status and Prospects, P. Samarati, R. Sandhu (eds), Chapman & Hall, 1997, pp. 23-42.

[21]   R. K. Thomas, R.S. Sandhu, "Task-based Authorization Controls (TBAC): A family of Models for Active and Enterprise-oriented Authorization management", Proceedings of the IFIP WG11.3 Workshop on Database Security, Lake Tahoe, California, August 11-13, 1997.

[22]   "TV That Watches You: The Prying Eyes of Interactive Television", A report by Center For Digital Democracy, http://www.democraticmedia.org/privacyreport.pdf, June, 2001.

James Joshi is a graduate student in the School of Electrical and Computer Engineering at Purdue University. His research interests are computer security and multimedia systems. He received his MS in computer science from Purdue University. He is a Student Member of the ACM and the IEEE. Contact him at joshij@ecn.purdue.edu.

Arif Ghafoor is a professor in the School of Electrical and Computer Engineering at Purdue University. His research interests are multimedia information systems, database security, and distributed computing. He received a Ph.D. in electrical engineering from Columbia University. He is a Fellow of the IEEE. Contact him at ghafoor@ecn.purdue.edu.

Walid G. Aref is an associate professor in the Department of Computer Sciences at Purdue University. His research interests are database systems, spatial and multimedia data indexing, video servers, network-attached storage devices, data mining, algorithms and data structures, and geographic information systems. He received a Ph.D. in computer science from the University of Maryland at College Park. He is a member of the ACM and the IEEE. Contact him at aref@cs.purdue.edu.

Eugene H. Spafford is a professor in the Department of Computer Sciences and the Director of Center for Education and Research in Information Assurance and Security (CERIAS) at Purdue University. His research interests are computer and network security, ethical and societal implications of computing, software validation, verification and debugging. He received a Ph.D. in information and computer science from Georgia Institute of Technology. He is a Fellow of the AAAS, the ACM and IEEE. Contact him at spaf@cerias.purdue.edu

Chapter 8

Digital Democracy through Electronic Petitioning
e-petitioner

Ann Macintosh[1], Anna Malina[1], and Steve Farrell[2]
[1]*International Teledemocracy Centre, Napier University, Edinburgh, UK.*
[2]*The Scottish Parliament, Edinburgh, UK.*

Abstract: The International Teledemocracy Centre at Napier University has designed an
              innovative e-democracy toolkit to support participation in the democratic
              decision-making process. Electronic petitioning is one of the web-based
              applications in the toolkit. It can be found at www.e-petitioner.org.uk and has
              the functionality to create petitions; to view/sign petitions; to add background
              information, to join discussion forum; and to submit petitions. On 14th March
              2000, the Scottish Parliament agreed to allow groups and individuals to submit
              petitions using the e-petitioner system for a trial period. The special
              arrangement between the Teledemocracy Centre and the Scottish Parliament
              has allowed both parties to start to evaluate the use and civic impact of
              electronic petitioning in Scotland. The development, deployment and
              evaluation of e-petitioner have demonstrated how straightforward computing
              techniques can enhance public participation in the newly established Scottish
              Parliament. As well as the system being used to submit e-petitions to the
              Scottish Parliament, it is also hosting the first ever e-petition to the British
              Prime Minister at No.10 Downing St.

Key words: electronic petitions, e-petitions, e-democracy, digital democracy, e-
              government

1.   INTRODUCTION

Widespread claims have been made that democratic politics is in crisis
as a result of public apathy, low turnout at elections, and poor levels of
public participation. These claims have coincided with the arrival of 'digital
government,' which has brought with it the now widespread concern that a
digital divide is widening in society. Our work is derived from a perceived
need to investigate how and to what extent information and communication

technology can enable a more participative system of governing, supporting both governments and citizens. "Digital Democracy through Electronic Petitioning" focuses on the design, development, and evaluation of information and communication technology to support civic representation and participation in the democratic process. This chapter describes how the International Teledemocracy Centre at Napier University has been working collaboratively with the Scottish Parliament to deploy and evaluate the e-petitioner system for the benefit of citizens in Scotland. By investigating the development and use of electronic petitioning, the Teledemocracy Centre seeks to reveal the conditions that would encourage and assist different sections of society to participate in government through the use of digital democracy systems.

Following this introductory section, section 2 in this chapter overviews the meaning of petitioning in a Scottish context. It does this by examining the petitioning processes for the Scottish Parliament and explains how electronic petitioning was introduced to the Parliament.

Section three considers the e-petitioner system in more detail. The system is one component of a web-based e-democracy toolkit, being developed in partnership with British Telecom, to motivate and facilitate public participation in governance. The toolkit is an exemplar of e-democracy applications, and comprises three web-based tools. As well as e-petitioner, the other tools are: e-consultant which is being used by the Scottish government for consultation over the internet and e-voter which is being used by Highland local authority to elect young people to a Youth Council. A prototype version of the e-petitioner system was developed in late 1999. The final system has the functionality to create petitions; to view/sign petitions; to add background information, to join discussion forum; and to submit petitions. On 14th March 2000, the Scottish Parliament agreed to allow groups and individuals to submit petitions using the Centre's e-petitioner system for a trial period. The special arrangement between the Centre and the Scottish Parliament has allowed both parties to monitor the use of electronic petitioning in Scotland. Section 4 considers the e-petitioner system from the perspective of the Scottish Parliament and describes the benefits and initial reactions of the Public Petitions Committee of the Parliament to the system.

The evaluation of the system has demonstrated how straightforward computing techniques can enhance public participation in the newly established Scottish Parliament. In our concluding section we summarise our research findings and look ahead to new developments.

2.   PETITIONING IN SCOTLAND

In many countries around the world, citizens have used petitions to make their feelings known about issues that concern them. Simply, a petition is a formal request to a higher authority, e.g. parliament or other authority, signed by one or a number of citizens. The format of petitions and the way petitions are submitted and subsequently considered by parliaments varies greatly.

In July 1999 powers in relation to specific areas of government were devolved to the new Scottish Parliament in Edinburgh from the UK Parliament in London under the Scotland Act 1998. One of the main documents setting out how the new Parliament should work was The Consultative Steering Group document (The Scottish Office, 1998). This stated that the Scottish Parliament should aspire to use all forms of information and communication technology "innovatively and appropriately" to support the Group's guiding principles of *openness*, *accessibility* and *participation*.

On the issue of petitions, the Consultative Steering Group stated:

It is important to enable groups and individuals to influence the Parliament's agenda. We looked at a number of models in other Parliaments for handling petitions and concluded that the best of these encouraged petitions; had clear and simple rules as to form and content; and specified clear expectations of how petitions would be handled.

To achieve this the Scottish Parliament established a dedicated Public Petitions Committee (PPC) to actively promote petitions as a means by which the public could effectively raise issues of concern with the Parliament. The remit of the PPC is to consider and report on whether a public petition is admissible and what action is to be taken on the petition. There are no restrictions on who can submit a petition. A petition submitted by an individual will be considered on equal terms with one submitted with a large number of supporting signatures. The PPC considers the merits of the issues raised in each admissible petition and makes a decision on the appropriate action to be taken in each case. This can involve requesting other committees in the Parliament (generally those with the remit to examine specific subject areas) to carry out further consideration of the issues raised, or requesting the views of, or action by, the Scottish Executive, local authorities and other public bodies in Scotland. Certain petitions have gone on to be debated by the whole Parliament. The Committee ensures that petitioners are kept informed of progress at each stage of the Parliament's consideration of their petition. The actions of the Committee have resulted in a range of positive outcomes, from local solutions to petitioners' concerns to amendments to legislation.

The partnership between the Teledemocracy Centre and the Scottish Parliament began in December 1999 when the PPC agreed to allow an internet-based petition from the Centre's web site sponsored by the World Wide Fund for Nature (WWF) to be the first electronic petition to collect names and addresses over the Internet. The PPC subsequently agreed to allow groups and individuals to submit petitions using e-petitioner (Scottish Parliament, 2000). Since then the partnership has worked together to ensure the requirements of the citizen wishing to petition the Parliament electronically are met whilst also ensuring the PPC has confidence in the integrity of the electronic petitioning system. The PPC's web pages have direct links to the e-petitioning system, and their published guidelines on how to petition the Parliament explain the use of electronic petitioning. Figure 1 shows the home page for the Public petitions Committee.

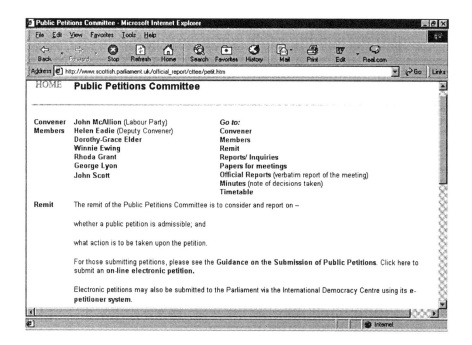

Figure 1. Public Petitions Committee web page

3.   THE E-PETITIONER SYSTEM

This section provides a description of the functionality needed in a digital democracy system to support best practice electronic petitioning. Of the key "democratic" requirements of the new Parliament, those that called for *openness*, *accessibility* and *participation* were of most importance to us in developing the system. It was important to ensure that the petitioning process was as *open* as possible. Therefore the names of all people supporting the petition needed to be easily viewed, whilst remaining within the data protection standards. Feedback on what was happening to the petition once it had collected signatures needed to be available. It was important to provide *access* for as many people as possible, in particular individuals and local community centres running slower machines, therefore flash and large graphic files needed to be excluded. The unequal technical capabilities of citizens demanded that e-petitioner was simple to use and the web pages easy to navigate through. It was also important that features that might make the system difficult for the partially sighted to use were excluded. *Participation* was important such that users could not only show their support for the petition by adding their names but also to comment on it. Also there needed to be an opportunity for those who did not agree with the aims of a petition, or who had alternative opinions, to express their views. In order to assist those who wished to participate make an informed decision on whether to support the petition and to make comments on the petition it was important to provide additional information about the petition.

These overarching democratic requirements were further expanded. In designing the e-petitioning system it was necessary to consider how technology could be used most effectively to support the Teledemocracy Centre's key enabling criteria for the digital democracy systems of accessibility, usability, security, openness and trust. Macintosh et al (2001) describe how the very nature of governance and the fact that government cannot choose its customers means that, in the design of e-democracy systems, these issues become complex.

3.1   E-petitioner Structure

The end-user e-petitioner system is at www.e-petitioner.org.uk. The main sections are the following:

e-petitioner: this is effectively the home page for the e-petitioning system. It lists the e-petitions along with the name of the individual or organisations that originally raised the petition and the current status of the petition. In other words whether is it collecting signatures, closed or whether it has been submitted to the Parliament. It gives the conditions of use for the system and links back to the main e-democracy toolkit page.

View/Sign Petition: this is the main e-petition page. It contains "name of Petition Sponsor", "the petition text", and the "sign petition" facility. Here a user who agrees with the petition issue can add their name and address to the petition. The user is requested to provide a full postal address including postcode and country. The postcodes and countries are summarised and used in the brief to the Parliament. There is also a data protection statement detailing how the gathered information will be used.

Petitioner Sponsors: here the name and address and other relevant contact details for the individual or organisation raising the petition are provided, where appropriate it provides links to the organisation's own web site.

Information: this shows important additional information, provided by the petition sponsors, which supports the petition and allows the users to be better informed about the petition issue. It was important that the users had this further information rather than just the petition text. Being able to make an informed decision is a vital part of the Centre's e-democracy work.

Comment: this gives the users the opportunity to comment further on the petition. Here they can make comments either for or against the petition and everyone can read their comments and reply to them. Having an integrated discussion forum in the petitioning system was important as it makes the system much more interactive and allows a constructive debate to occur on the petition issue. Previously petitions only provided for people to support a petition to add their name, whilst those against the petition merely withheld their signature. With the e-petitioner system, those in favour have the opportunity to add further information to support the issue and those against have an important opportunity say why the petition should not go ahead or how it should be modified.

View Signatures: this provides a list of the names, along with their countries, of all those who have signed the e-petition; giving any further details of signatories would have breached the data protection act. This allows a small level of transparency in the system with everyone knowing how many people have signed the petition.

Feedback: this important section is to ensure that everyone knows what has happened to the petition once it has closed. Far too often people support issues and then never hear of them again. This section links to the Parliaments main petitions page, gives the number of the submitted petition and allows tracking of the petition through it's life in the Parliament.

The first page of an e-petition on digital inclusion is shown in figure 2.

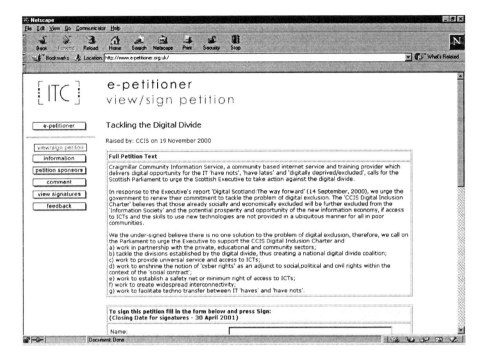

Figure 2. e-petition: Tackling the Digital Divide

As well as the end-user functionality, the management of the e-petitioner system is facilitated by additional password-protected administrative services. These include services to "create new petition", "change petition details" "view full names and addresses of those signing" and "submit petition".

3.2   E-petitioner Implementation

To be able to quickly demonstrate and try out the e-petitioner functionality the first version of the system was developed using forms and CGI scripts. It was available from both Explorer and Netscape browsers. Once e-petitioner was accepted for trial use by the Scottish Parliament, the system was updated to make it more robust and to reflect feedback from users and the Parliament. The current version of e-petitioner is hosted on the Teledemocracy Centre's Windows NT Server and uses Active Server Pages and an SQL Server database. The database comprises a number of tables for the e-petitioner system, the main ones being: Petitions, Signatures, Discussion Comments, and Evaluation.

Special mention is needed concerning security. What level of security is needed? It would be easy to say that it should match the level currently available for paper-based petitions but that then raises the issue of what level of security checks can realistically be applied to traditional paper-based petitions, particularly in terms of checking the authenticity of names and addresses. On the other hand there is always the temptation to say that everything must be checked thoroughly, which is the case for electronic voting, but not necessarily for names and addresses on petitions. Petitions to the Scottish Parliament are not legally binding therefore rigorous security checking to the level that would be needed for Internet voting is not required. Instead e-petitioner performs an internal confidence rating check to assess how secure each name and address is. The actual rating depends on a number of factors, for example, Internet Provider (IP) address and how many times the same IP address has been used to sign the petition. These confidence ratings are closely examined prior to submission of the petition to check for any irregularities. The system also automatically removes any duplicate names and addresses.

4.   PARLIAMENT'S VIEW OF E-PETITIONER

There are links to the electronic petitioning system from the Scottish Parliament's web site and links from the Teledemocracy Centre's web site to the Parliament's guidelines for petitions. The Scottish Parliament supplies a pro-forma for the submission of petitions in electronic form on its web site; however, submission of lists of signatories is not permitted in electronic format except via the special arrangement with the Teledemocracy Centre.

The Public Petitions Committee and the Centre have designed a template for a brief that is used routinely to summarise the main elements of an e-petition. An important goal was to support the Committee in making a judicious decision about the petition issue. The brief notes the petition title, the names of petitioners and dates the e-petition opened and closed. User statistics are summarised to provide an idea of numbers of signatures and their geographic locations based on postcodes. This is helpful to the Members of the PPC in that is gives them an indication of the geographical spread of those who are in support of the petition issue, both in Scotland and elsewhere in the world.   Signature validity is reported on using the confidence ratings built into the system as previously described. The full e-petition text is recorded and background information about the petition sponsors is outlined. Finally, comments made on the integrated discussion forum about the issue central to the e-petition are summarised. The brief is compiled soon after the petition closes. Details are checked by the petition sponsors before it is submitted to the Committee. Subsequently, the brief is distributed along with other authorised papers to the members of the Committee in preparation for the meeting. The brief is then dated and held on file alongside other supporting papers.

There are a number of advantages of e-petitioning. For example, people can obtain background information, make a comment about the issue, sign on-line, and receive feedback about the progress of a petition. With a traditional pen and paper petition, people do not always have very much time to consider the issues at hand. E-petitioner offers better opportunity to sit down and think about the petition's key points in depth before making an informed choice about whether or not to support and sign the petition.

In considering the discussion forum designed into the e-petitioner comments page, the Convener of the Committee, John McAllion MSP, indicated, "it gives ordinary people a chance to air their views and add to the petition issue". While the Petitions Committee always tries to obtain a balanced view from the main parties who have a relevant interest in the issues raised in a petition, e-petitioner provides the opportunity for all those signing a petition to provide their views. A traditional paper based petition only has a number of signatures and so there is no way of obtaining the detailed views of those individuals who support it.

The development of collaborations and links to e-petitioner from civic and professional bodies is considered a positive step forward. Opportunities need to be created to engage with civic society, and involve the voluntary and civic sectors more in the process of petitioning the Parliament. Increased public access to technology through learning centres combined with the collaborations the Teledemocracy Centre has initiated with the community sector to increase the scope of public awareness about e-petitioner can only benefit this process.

The partnership with the Teledemocracy Centre on this project allows the Public Petitions Committee to support the development of electronic petitioning through its active involvement in the process. It allows the Committee to keep abreast of advances in technology in this area and to evaluate the success or otherwise of the system. This may allow the Parliament to determine, in the longer term, whether it wants to develop a similar system of its own.

It is hoped that feedback from the Committee to the Centre on the way electronic petitions are managed and presented will allow the system to be developed over time and become more tailored to the Parliament's needs. In addition, statistical information that the system can provide, giving details on location of petitioners and other information, will prove useful to the Committee for research and evaluation purposes.

The Public Petitions Committee considers itself to be the gateway for public involvement in the parliamentary process in Scotland. The Committee is continuing to work with the Teledemocracy Centre to promote the development and use of electronic petitioning systems that inform people better and improve and enhance public access to the democratic process.

5.   EVALUATION

While digital democracy systems may yet radically transform the functionality, reach and usability of software tools to support democratic decision-making, it is recognised that research so far (e.g. Tsagarousianou et al, 1998) has not supported the claim that technology enhances inclusion and participation in the democratic process. Hence there is a need to undertake a detailed evaluation of the e-petitioner system. Our evaluation project was funded by the Joseph Rowntree Charitable Trust and began in October 2000 and lasted 6 months until the end of March 2001 (Malina et al, 2001). The effectiveness of e-petitioner was measured through evaluation research, and participant observations were conducted in a variety of public access settings with e-petition sponsors and users. Using this method, it was possible to watch what people did with e-petitioner, and conduct conversations with participants to take account of people's experience of use and their perceptions of e-petitioner and its function as a tool to support democratic participation. Semi-focused interviews were also arranged with Parliamentary committee members to take account of their views. While guide questions were compiled for use, interviews remained flexible enough to listen and take account of each respondent's unforeseen views. Data was subsequently extracted from observations, interview transcripts and from the on-line evaluation questionnaires that are part of the e-petitioner system.

Findings from this indicate considerable support for the e-petitioning system, with signatories applauding various advantages, in particular the opportunity to be included in what was viewed as more democratic interaction. There was, however, some marked concern that security and confidentiality may yet be problematic. Interesting data was gathered indicating how signatories found out about e-petitioner. This is likely to prove very useful in developing best practice on how to promote and publicise new e-petitions.

E-petition sponsors indicated that they viewed e-petitioner as a useful tool in influencing politicians about issues they considered important. They generally felt e-petitioner was a useful tool complimenting more traditional methods of petitioning. Indeed the ability to access at a convenient time and reach wider sections of society alongside the slower more deliberative processes made possible by e-petitioner were considered inherently more democratic.

In conclusion our collaborative work on electronic petitioning has highlighted a large number of comments and recommendations to take electronic democracy forward.

REFERENCES

Macintosh, A., Davenport, E., Malina, A. & Whyte, A.(2001); Technology Driven Inclusive Democracy. In Grönlund, Åke (2001). (ed). Electronic Government: Design, applications and management (in print).

Malina, A., Macintosh, A., and Davenport, E.; (2001) E-petitioner: a monitoring and evaluation report; Report for the Joseph Rowntree Charitable Trust; available from the International Teledemocracy Centre.

Scottish Parliament (2000). The report of the meeting of the Public Petitions Committee on 14th March 2000 to trial Internet petitions. At URL http://www.scottish.parliament.uk/official_report/cttee/petit-00/pumop0314.htm.

The Scottish Office (1998). *Shaping Scotland's Parliament.* Report of the Consultative Steering Group.

Tsagarousianou, R. Tambini, D. & Bryan C. (1998). (Eds). *Cyberdemocracy: Technology, cities and civic networks.* London & NY: Routledge.

Ann Macintosh is Director of the International Teledemocracy Centre at Napier University. She is actively involved with governmental, business and voluntary organisations concerned with the research and development of digital government systems in the UK, Europe and the Commonwealth. She was a member of the Scottish Executive's Ministerial Task Force on "Digital Scotland", and also a member of the UK-Online working group to specify e-democracy services for this government portal. She is on the Advisory Council for the Commonwealth Centre for Electronic Governance.

Anna Malina worked on a project funded by the Joseph Rowntree Charitable Trust. Her remit was to monitor and evaluate e-petitioner. She is currently finalising a doctoral thesis researching community development in cyberspace. Her study analyses the background, development and societal significance of a community based electronic network. Anna is generally interested in new relationships developing in society as a result of new ICTs and new forms of electronic communication.

Steve Farrell is Clerk to the Scottish Parliament's Public Petitions Committee. Steve joined the Parliament from the former Scottish Office (now the Scottish Executive) which he joined in 1978 and where he worked in a wide range of policy areas, including education, Historic Scotland, prisons, planning, and local government reorganisation. He worked as a Private Secretary to Scottish Office Ministers from 1996-1998, and from there moved on to the Constitution Group which was tasked with planning and setting up the new Scottish Parliament.

Chapter 9

Compliance Analysis for Disabled Access

Charles S. Han[1], John C. Kunz[2] and Kincho H. Law[2]

[1]*Autodesk, Inc., San Rafael, CA 94903*
[2]*Department of Civil and Environmental Engineering and the Center for Integrated Facility Engineering, Stanford University, Stanford, CA 94305-4020*

Abstract: Accessibility regulations are federally enacted by the Americans with Disabilities Act (ADA). Design of buildings and facilities must comply with the guidelines developed by the authors of ADA. This chapter discusses a hybrid approach using encoding prescriptive-based provisions and supplementing them with performance-based methods to support compliance and usability analysis for accessibility. The hybrid compliance analysis approach is applied to analyse a facility floor plan as a case example.

Key words: disabled access, compliance analysis, on-line code checking, performance-based code, motion planning, wheelchair simulation

1. INTRODUCTION

The handicapped accessibility regulations are federally enacted by the Americans with Disabilities Act (ADA). The intent of the handicapped accessibility regulations is to provide the same or equivalent access to a building and its facilities for disabled persons (for example, persons restricted to a wheelchair, persons with hearing and sight disabilities) and persons without qualifying disabilities. To fulfill this intent, the authors of the Americans with Disabilities Act (ADA) have developed prescriptive measures such as various clearances and reach thresholds for building components. For example, the ADA has developed guidelines for minimum clearances to allow transfer of a person from a wheelchair to a toilet and minimum lengths of grab bars associated with a toilet. Prescriptive statements are formulated to establish concrete tests for many of such measures. However, using prescriptive provisions often lead to problems such as conflicting and ambiguous statements, thus making the code difficult to parse not only by computers, but for humans as well. A design that fulfills the prescriptive code does not always imply usability. Conversely, a design that does not meet the prescriptive code could actually be accessible by a person in a wheelchair. This chapter discusses code-related compliance analysis focusing on wheelchair access.

This research examines a hybrid approach combining prescriptive-based methods in which prescriptive statements are modeled as rules where there is no indeterminacy and conflict, whereas when such problems surface, a performance-based approach using simulation is adapted. There are several motivations for this approach. First, prescriptive-based provisions capture the design intent of the building code most of the time so encoding these provisions partially addresses the goal of automated building code checking. Second, encoding these provisions and analyzing the building model is computationally inexpensive compared to using performance-based simulations. Therefore, where the prescriptive-based provisions are adequate, they should be used. However, performance-based simulations could be deployed to resolve those issues where the prescriptive-based provisions are inadequate. In addition, certain prescriptive provisions are difficult to model using a prescriptive rule-liked system. In these cases, performance-based simulation could be an alternative that can be used to test these provisions. Finally, if a building design is found to be in violation of the building code based on the encoded prescriptive provisions, the design can be analyzed against available performance-based methods so that better insight can be gained about the design.

This chapter is organized as follows: In the next section, a framework to support on-line code checking for building design is described. We then discuss the modelling of building facilities and regulations. A simulation approach for performance-based analysis of disabled accessibility is proposed. A case example is employed to illustrate the hybrid approach developed for compliance analysis for disabled access.

2. A FRAMEWORK FOR ON-LINE CODE CHECKING

Managing the code documents and allowing the documents to be accessible by users and applications are key issues to extend the usability of digital information such as regulations and codes. An important objective of this work is to provide the means to interface the regulations with usage such that the regulations are not passive but active documents that can be dynamically linked to application programs for users to search and access regulations, to perform compliance check and for supporting human functions such as design activities.

We have prototyped a proof-of-concept system that transforms the manual or on-line review process (Fig. 1(a)) and replaces it with a partially automated on-line compliance and permit approval process (Fig. 1(b)) using Internet and web-based technologies [Han97, Han98a, Han99]. The provisions in the Americans with Disabilities Act Accessibility Guide (ADAAG) [ADAAG97] are represented in HTML format with hyperlinks from the on-line code checking system. At any point in the design process, the client can send a design to the code-checking program that resides on a remote server. On the client side, the user develops a plan using a CAD package that produces design data in compliance with the Industry Foundation Classes (IFC) developed by the International Alliance of Interoperability (IAI) [IAI97]. The code-checking program examines the design data and summarizes the results in a generated web page. The web page contains a graphical representation of the building model along with "redline" information with hyperlinks to specific comments. As shown in Fig. 2, the analysis report has three frames. A VRML model of the submitted building design is displayed in the top left frame and is added with redline information if the design does not comply with the building code. These redlines have hyperlinks to associated comments. The user can click on the inaccessible building component, and the associated comment appears in the bottom frame. Finally, these comments, when applicable, have hyperlinks to the actual building code document provisions (in this case, the ADAAG [ADAAG97]) in the top right frame.

3.   BUILDING PRODUCT MODEL AND PRESCRIPTIVE CODE REPRESENTATION

For a building design to be computer-interpretable, it must be adequately described by a symbolic building model. Further, the modeling and representation of regulations and codes need to be addressed from the perspectives of both the code as well as the users and the design application. Given a building model, analysis is performed to check the design against the building code. Clearly, for automated design analysis there is a need for a standard building model that provides more information than a collection of drawing primitives.

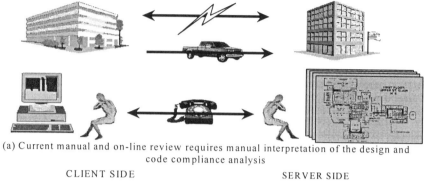

(a) Current manual and on-line review requires manual interpretation of the design and code compliance analysis

CLIENT SIDE   SERVER SIDE

CAD package

web browser

(b) On-line code checking requires automated generation of an IFC project model and automated code compliance checking

Figure 1. Manual versus On-Line Code Checking Process

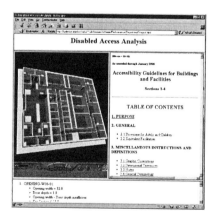

Figure 2. A Web Page Report for Disabled Access Analysis

There have been many research efforts to develop object-oriented CAD systems and object-oriented building models that contain the necessary geometric, functional, and behavioral relationships of building components. There is an on-going effort by the International Alliance of Interoperability (IAI), a consortium of CAD vendors and other AEC industry partners, to develop product model standards for facilities that enable interoperability between applications by different software vendors [IAI97]. The IAI's effort includes defining a set of objects called Industry Foundation Classes (IFC's) that adhere to the object-oriented paradigm. Fig. 3 illustrates a sample of the IFC hierarchy.

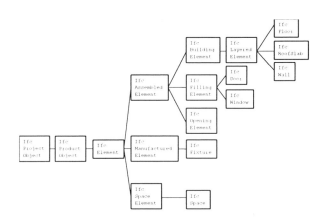

Figure 3. An Example of IFC Class Hierarchy

In our current prototype (see Fig. 1), the IFC (Release 1.5) project model is used and extended as the common product model, represented in the EXPRESS file format (in the form of a data stream as opposed to a static file). The IFC-compliant design data stream transfers from one application via the communication protocol interface to the product model interface of another service. The communication protocol interface and the common product model interface do not specify how the design data is stored. The product model interface constructs an IFC-compliant internal representation of the design data from the data stream. A Java class structure that mirrors the IFC EXPRESS schema's class hierarchy, attributes, and relationships has been constructed for the internal representation. In the prototype, the code-checking program takes an IFC project model in EXPRESS file format and sends it to the code-checking program.

The representational model implemented for the prescriptive-based encoded provisions uses the same structure as the IFC project model hierarchy. For example, all encoded provisions concerning door accessibility would be instances of a door accessibility class. Therefore, an individual component can be checked against all the applicable instances of provisions for that class of building component. By structuring the encoded provisions in this manner, we loosely categorize building component provisions by design intent since similar building components have similar behavior. One building code class can have several instances that correspond to related provisions in the building code—for example, there may be a class in the building code representation corresponding to the issue of door clearance of which there are several variations or instances. This relationship is analogous to a particular building design having several instances of a door class. The prototype code-checking program currently implements the encodable provisions that can be classified as prescriptive checks. Each building component is analyzed against a set of rules that capture the intent of the building code provisions (in many cases, a rule is some form of geometrical interference tests.) Provisions that address issues such as door width and door clearances are provided as heuristics that test for disabled access. If a door complies with these provisions, then it fulfills the design intent for accessibility.

4.   PERFORMANCE-BASED ANALYSIS USING SIMULATION

While prescriptive code checking is possible for individual building components, global issues of accessibility would require directly capturing the design intent of a set of provisions. Performance-based methods directly test the design intent for usability of a facility as opposed to relying on the prescriptive-based provisions to check for compliance. In the case of disabled access, the design intent is clear: provide the same or equivalent access for disabled persons and non-disabled persons. Focusing on wheelchair access, persons in wheelchairs must be provided the same or equivalent access to a building and its facilities as persons who do not use wheelchairs. "Equivalent" access is somewhat ambiguous, but the intent is that a person in a wheelchair need not go through extreme methods to be able to have access to a building's facilities. For example, if a person not using a wheelchair needs to travel a certain distance to get to a bathroom facility, then a person using a wheelchair should have to travel approximately the same distance to use either the same or a different bathroom facility. The concept of access is a system-wide issue related to the entire floor or building as well as a local issue confined within a defined space. The encoded provisions can be used to analyze local prescriptive issues such as clearances around building components. However, testing for compliance of global issues such as the existence of an accessible path can be more easily done using simulation techniques.

Simulation can be employed to address provisions that are difficult to analyze statically such as the existence of an accessible path in a building design. These provisions examine global issues of a project as opposed to looking at localized phenomena. In examining the issues of disabled access, the design analysis program must consider accessible path. For example, if a door is on an accessible path, the program can check its necessary clearances. However, since these are local and static checks, the program cannot guarantee that in getting from one room to another, even if individual doors meet the code, a disabled person can actually get to these doors.

Simulation of a wheelchair moving through the space is a logical approach. Using motion planning, a research area in robotics, such a simulation is possible [Latombe91]. Here, a wheelchair agent is the robot that searches for a possible path. The robot is constrained to move only forward and with prescribed turning radius. The former constraint is consistent with satisfying a design intent concerning reasonable motion and the latter physical constraint is determined by examining closely the provisions as given in ADAAG. Detailed development of the wheelchair robot is described in [Han00, Han01].

The robot's path is calculated as per [Latombe91] with some modifications. Before the path planner generates a path, we must specify the initial position and the goal position of the wheelchair robot. Based on these two positions, the planner will generate a potential field in the configuration space (the space defined by the open areas, obstacles, and the wheelchair robot) that has a high point at the initial position and a low point at the goal position. The robot starts at the high point and essentially travels downhill to reach the goal position. Fig. 4 shows the tools developed for the simulation of accessible route and wheelchair motion.

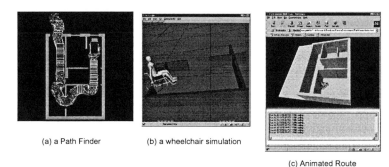

(a) a Path Finder   (b) a wheelchair simulation

(c) Animated Route

Figure 4. Simulation of Accessible Route and Wheelchair Simulation

5.   CASE EXAMPLE

This section presents a case example of disabled access analysis for a floor plan as shown in Fig. 5. Recall that the performance-based approach is able to determine the usability of a facility, and usability does not necessarily equate to code-compliance. Fig. 2 shows the generated analysis report with a view of the modeled floor plan. Specifically, the floor of the entire facility has been set to darker color (red in the generated VRML frame), indicating that there are critical components of the facility that are inaccessible. The comments associated with inaccessible building components have links to the prescriptive provisions of the ADAAG document as an informative guide. The following discuss the results of two facilities, namely the Men's Bathroom and the Women's Bathroom.

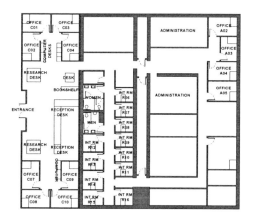

Figure 5. Floor Plan of a Facility

Men's Bathroom

The analysis reports that there is no accessible route to the accessible toilet in the Men's Bathroom as illustrated in Fig. 6. Since there are no other accessible toilets, the bathroom is not considered to be accessible, and in turn, the whole facility is deemed inaccessible.

Fig. 7 confirms the inaccessibility of the toilet. Here, the wheelchair user is not able to pass through the stall's doorway. It is interesting to note that the partition walls were added to the original plan to ensure privacy for the toilet user. Ironically, the addition of these walls has made the toilet inaccessible. With the removal of the partitions, the Men's bathroom would revert back to a single-occupancy from a multiple-occupancy toilet. As shown in Fig. 8, without the partition walls, the motion planner can generate an accessible route to the stall.

Figure 6. Disabled Access Analysis Report for Men's Toilet

Figure 7. Wheelchair User Unable to Access Men's Toilet

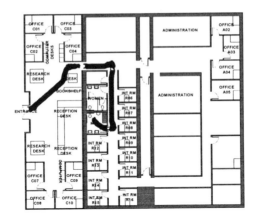

Figure 8. Wheelchair Route to Men's Toilet with Stall Partitions Removed

Women's Bathroom

The analysis also reports that there is no accessible route to the accessible toilet in the Women's Bathroom as illustrated in Fig. 9. The performance-based parameters are developed using the ADAAG toilet stall clearance areas as a guideline for the evaluation of the toilets, and the accessible stall violates these guidelines. Since there are no other accessible toilets, the bathroom is not considered to be accessible, and in turn, the whole facility is deemed inaccessible.

As shown in Figure 10, however, the wheelchair user actually has a comfortable access to this toilet. The user in fact can easily position for side transfer, a position that is more difficult to achieve than a diagonal transfer for this given stall. By slightly adjusting the toilet parameters as prescribed by ADAAG, the analysis shows that the toilet is actually accessible as illustrated in the generated path shown in Fig. 11. This example illustrates that, in this case, the parameter (as given in ADAAG) that was used for evaluating accessibility may be too restrictive, and that the performance-based method is more flexible by describing a range of possible goal areas and orientations.

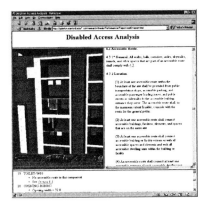

Figure 9. Disabled Access Analysis Report for Women's Toilet

Figure 10. Wheelchair User Access to Women's Toilet

Figure 11. Wheelchair Route to Women's Toilet

6.   SUMMARY AND DISCUSSION

This chapter examines using encoding prescriptive-based provisions and supplementing them with performance-based methods to support compliance and usability analysis for disabled access. Currently, the prototype code-checking program is able to check individual building components as well as a system of building components for compliance and the simulation techniques implemented can analyze access path existence and facility access. The compliance analysis program has been implemented as part of an on-line service framework to take advantage of Internet and web-based technologies.

The automated approach has been applied to analyze a facility for disabled access. As illustrated in the case example, for the Men's bathroom, the analysis can be employed to check for compliance as well as usability of critical building components. For the Women's bathroom, the results and a comparison with an actual wheelchair user's interaction with the facility also reveal some of the shortcomings of using the prescriptive-based parameters to develop the performance-based methods.

In this work, we have compared the analysis results with an individual wheelchair user's ability. It should be noted that the ability to use the facility represents strictly a qualitative test as there are many different levels of disability, but such a comparison still provides important insight into the analysis. The discrepancy between one's mobility and the usage parameters set forth by the ADAAG illustrates the difficulty in providing a performance-based access code that encompasses all wheelchair users and provides guidelines for usage and comfort. However, adjustments to the performance-based analysis tailored to a group of similar users might provide insight to the actual accessibility of a facility.

Ensuring usability of the facility for wheelchair users should be the main priority. All spaces and critical building components should at least be made usable. The performance-based motion-planning accessible route methods developed in this work could be a viable tool to determine the usability of new critical spaces. As the intent of the ADAAG is to give equivalent access to facilities, whether or not these facilities actually meet some set of prescribed measurements should be secondary to providing actual usability. Note that not all possible configurations can be covered by the prescriptive-based code. It is important to make sure that all accessible spaces were at least made usable as measured by some alternative metrics. This work provides a hybrid approach combining prescriptive-based and performance-based methods that may be able to test for usability and compliance of a facility for disabled access.

ACKNOWLEDGEMENTS

This research is supported by the National Science Foundation under Grant No. EIA-9983368 and by the Center for Integrated Facility

Engineering at Stanford University. Any opinions, findings, and conclusions or recommendations expressed in this chapter are those of the authors and do not necessarily reflect the views of the sponsoring agencies. The authors would like to thank Mr. Joe Covanaugh for his participation in this research.

REFERENCES

[ADAAG97] *Americans with Disabilities Act Accessibility Guide.* Access Board, U.S. Architectural and Transportation Barriers Compliance Board, Washington, D.C., 1997.

[Han97] Han, C.S., J. Kunz and K.H. Law, "Making Automated Building Code Checking a Reality," *Facility Management Journal*, pp. 22-28, September/October, 1997.

[Han98a] Han, C.S., J.Kunz and K.H. Law, "Client/Server Framework for On-Line Building Code Checking," *ASCE J. Computing in Civil Engineering*, 12(4):181-194, 1998.

[Han98b] Han, C.S., Kunz, J. and Law, K.H., "A Hybrid Prescriptive/Performance Based Approach to Automated Building Code Checking," *International Computing Congress*, ASCE, pp. 537-548, Boston, MA, October, 1998.

[Han99] Han, C.S., J. Kunz and K.H. Law, "Building Design Services in a Distributed Architecture," *ASCE J. Computing in Civil Engineering*, 13(1):12-22, 1999.

[Han00] Han, C.S., *Computer Models and Methods for a Disabled Access Analysis Design Environment*, Ph.D. Thesis, Department of Civil and Environmental Engineering, Stanford University, 2000.

[Han01] Han, C.S., K.H. Law, J.-C. Latombe and J.C. Kunz, "A Performance Based Approach to Wheelchair Accessible Route Analysis," (under preparation).

[IAI97] International Alliance for Interoperability *Industry Foundation Classes, Specifications* Volumes 1-4, Washington DC., 1997.

[Latombe91] Latombe, Jean-Claude (1991). *Robot Motion Planning*, Kluwer Academic Publishers, Norwell, MA.

Chuck Han currently works for Autodesk, Inc. in the Design Connectivity Solutions division where he is implementing building model and interoperability solutions. Dr. Han holds a Masters in Architecture from U.C. Berkeley and a Ph.D. in Civil and Environmental Engineering from Stanford University. His research interests include automation of building design and construction services including building code checking. He is also a licensed California architect.

John Kunz is a senior research associate with the Center for Integrated Facility Engineering (CIFE) at Stanford University. His principal responsibilities in CIFE are to manage research projects, supervise student research and teach. Current and recent projects include developing models of engineering products and processes, organizational modeling, automated construction planning, developing symbolic P&ID's, and automated code checking. Research interests cross the engineering lifecycle from pre-project planning through design-build, retrofit and decommissioning. An important research and teaching theme is the use of different strategies to validate new formalized theories that have been implemented as computer models.

Kincho H. Law is a Professor in the Department of Civil and Environmental Engineering at Stanford University. His research focuses on the application of advanced computing principles and technology in engineering. Current research projects include management and compliance analysis of regulatory information, distributed and internet-based computing for engineering services.

Chapter 10

COPLINK
Arming Law Enforcement with New Knowledge Management Technologies

Roslin V. Hauck, Michael Chau & Hsinchun Chen
University of Arizona, Tucson, Arizona USA

Abstract: The problem of information and knowledge management in the knowledge intensive and time critical environment of law enforcement has posed an interesting problem for information technology professionals in the field. Coupled with this challenging environment are issues relating to the integration of multiple systems, each having different functionalities resulting in difficulty for the end-user. The COPLINK project ties together the law enforcement domain expertise of Tucson Police Department with the research and technical background of the University of Arizona's Artificial Intelligence Lab. Working closely together as a user-involved project, we have collaborated at all levels of development (design, testing, and implementation) and the result of our efforts are the COPLINK Connect database, Detect criminal intelligence and Collaboration applications. COPLINK offers a cost-efficient way of web enabling stovepipe law enforcement information sharing systems by employing a model for allowing different police departments to more easily share data amongst themselves through an easy-to-use interface that integrates different data sources. This chapter highlights the technologies created as a result of our collaboration.

Key words: knowledge management, information retrieval, law enforcement, information sharing, collaboration, data integration, intelligent analysis

1. INTRODUCTION

The challenges of being a law enforcement officer are many and exist at different levels. There are, of course, the dangers on the street, being the front line as protectors of the community. There is also a large workforce of law enforcement personnel working to solve crimes by searching for critical information. Unlike the popular view propagated by the television and film industries, law enforcement agencies are anything but cutting-edge in their use of information technologies for information sharing and criminal intelligence analyses. In reality, many officers, investigators, and crime analysts are minimally armed with large disparate data stores within their own agencies, which are often times difficult to use and have limited access. This, coupled with little or no information sharing between agencies, makes investigative tasks difficult and time consuming. In a field where time to locate and apprehend a suspect is critical, there is no room for error or for delay.

Under the umbrella of digital governments, the development of cutting edge knowledge management technologies for law enforcement is an important and challenging endeavor. Focusing on a previously neglected domain, issues of dealing with huge amounts of information, different types of legacy systems, security, end user needs and user characteristics all lead to the potential for significant impacts to digital government research and its influence on society. Funded by the National Institute of Justice and the National Science Foundation, the University of Arizona's Artificial Intelligence Lab has teamed with the Tucson Police Department (TPD) under the COPLINK project, focused on the development of different knowledge management technologies, including the Connect Database, Detect Criminal Intelligence Analysis, and Intelligent Agent applications.

The COPLINK project directly targets the problems of information sharing and criminal analyses within and between law enforcement agencies. The approach of this project is not merely one of user-centered design but one of user-involved design. To leverage law enforcement domain expertise and the University's research and technical capabilities, the COPLINK project revolves around the participation of Tucson Police Department law enforcement personnel serving as active members of the development team. This chapter details our story, in terms of law enforcement needs, technology development, collaboration efforts and results from the perspectives of both the University of Arizona's Artificial Intelligence Lab and the Tucson Police Department. It is our hope that by sharing our case study, we can persuade other organizations to create a similar synergistic bond between research efforts and application of technology in digital governments.

The COPLINK Connect Database, COPLINK Detect Criminal Intelligence Analysis and COPLINK Collaboration applications were developed to specifically deal with the problems and issues with information sharing and criminal intelligence analysis facing law enforcement agencies. We utilized a user-involved design methodology that led to the resulting design decisions, including data source identification and functionality. Design principles of platform-independence, stability, scalability, and an intuitive graphical user interface are the underlying foundations of the COPLINK systems.

2. KNOWLEDGE MANAGEMENT PROBLEMS IN LAW ENFORCEMENT

The general area of knowledge management (KM) has attracted an enormous amount of attention in recent years. Although it has been variously defined, it is evident that knowledge management exists at the enterprise level (see (Davenport & Prusak 1998) and is quite distinct from mere information (e.g. see (Nonaka 1994; Davenport & Prusak 1998; Teece 1998)). Also apparent in this area are the challenges that knowledge management poses to an organization. In addition to being difficult to manage, knowledge traditionally has been stored on paper or in the minds of people (Davenport 1995; O'Leary 1998). The KM problems facing many firms stem from barriers to access and utilization resulting from the content and format of information (Jones and Jordan 1998; Rouse, Thomas et al. 1998). These problems make knowledge management acquisition and interpretation a complex and daunting process. Nevertheless, knowledge management information technologies have been developed for a number of different applications, such as virtual enterprising (see e.g., (Chen, Liao et al. 1998)), joint ventures (see e.g., (Inkpen and Dinur 1998)), and aerospace engineering (see e.g., (Jones and Jordan 1998)).

The same problems of knowledge management and information access exist at the specialized organizations of law enforcement. Federal, state, and local criminal justice entities possess vast repositories of information, but the explosive growth in digital information and the need for access within government agencies have made information overload increasingly significant.

A function of the daily routine of many crime analysts and detectives at TPD is to create knowledge from information by analysing and generalizing current criminal records that consist of approximately 1.8 million criminal case reports containing details from criminal events dating back to 1986. Although investigators can access large data stores of criminal data to tie together information needed to solve cases and crimes, they must manually search for connections or relationships in existing in the data. Combining information to create knowledge is often hampered by voluminous information examination of which requires exorbitant time and effort on the part of the investigator. Compounding this problem is the variability of individual investigator's ability to locate relevant information. The problem is not necessarily that the information has not been captured—any officer who fills out up to seven forms per incident can attest to that. The problems are database integration and access to information. Typically, law-enforcement agencies have captured data only on paper or have fed it into a database or crime information system. If the agency involved has more than one of these (that are possibly incompatible), information retrieval can be difficult or time-consuming.

2.1   Database Integration

One important aspect of problem solving is the ability to cluster related information to permit querying across many different data types and sources. This requires the ability to integrate and access the vast number of law enforcement data sources (Sparrow, 1991). In many local law enforcement agencies, criminal information databases exist as isolated stand-alone systems. While many law enforcement agencies depend heavily on crime-related information systems, most of their systems are not networked together; thus deterring collaboration (Pliant, 1996). Inability to share information with other systems prevents an agency's receiving timely information that could be used with that from other data sources to increase the efficiency of crime prevention and investigations (Tucson Police Department, 1997).

2.2   Access to Information

Similarly, law enforcers often have a problem accessing valuable information sources. Because time can be such a crucial factor in the completion of an investigation, access to information in a timely fashion is critical. Obstacles to acquiring information promptly can include restricting access to some systems to certain types of officers and long wait times for query returns. Although a detective may need information within 3-40 hours, he or she may have to wait a few weeks to a month before receiving it. Likewise, secure remote access to textual and multimedia databases is not currently available at many agencies (Tucson Police Department, 1997).

Potent information retrieval tools can provide information sharing abilities as well as alleviate crime analysts' information overload, reduce information search time required for analysis of available criminal records, and advance the investigation of current cases. This chapter introduces three knowledge management systems that can provide the ability to access data from different systems as well as provide the functionality of intelligence analysis and collaboration that currently does not exist in the traditional records management system.

3. TUCSON POLICE DEPARTMENT CASE STUDY

The Tucson Police Department (TPD) recently evaluated its information technology and identified problems of lack of information sharing, integration, and knowledge management. The department agreed to participate in research to investigate the potential of current state-of-the-art, near-term, and cost-effective database, intranet, and multimedia technologies to make computer justice information database integration, management, and access more effective.

Similarly to systems at many other law enforcement agencies, TPD's current records management system (RMS) has many problems pertaining to its interface, access to information and lack of knowledge management. Although users are able to search on name queries, location queries, vehicle queries, etc., they are not able to search multiple fields simultaneously. In addition, users of RMS complain that, depending on the type of query, RMS can take from a few minutes to a few hours to return its results.

The COPLINK project attacks several problems existing in many law enforcement agencies, including TPD, by developing a model integrated system that allows law officers both within and between different agencies to access and share information. An additional goal of COPLINK is to develop consistent, intuitive and easy-to-use interfaces and applications that support specific and often complex law enforcement functions and tasks. While the scope of this project includes a multilevel development plan incorporating different information technologies, the focus of the research reported here is not only on the development of a multimedia database system to promote information sharing, but also the improvement of criminal intelligence analysis.

4. COPLINK CONNECT DATABASE APPLICATION

After analyzing user requirements dealing with the problems of information integration and ease of access, we created the COPLINK Connect application, employing a consistent and intuitive interface which integrates different data sources, such that the multiplicity of data sources remains completely transparent to the user, allowing law enforcement personnel to learn a single, easy-to-use interface. In addition to the interface design, we also developed a model that allows for information sharing both within and between law enforcement organizations.

4.1   Design Criteria

The main design criteria considered for the COPLINK project includes:
- **Platform independence**: Because not all police departments utilize the same hardware or software operating systems, platform independence was critical.
- **Stability and scalability**: The system also had to offer room for system growth and expansion.
- **Intuitive and ease of use**: The front-end user interface should be intuitive and easy to use, yet flexible enough to meet the equally demanding investigative needs of detectives and officers.

Typical law enforcement applications usually are legacy systems having out-dated performance and capability. For example, TPD's RMS took 30 seconds to answer simple requests and up to 30 minutes for more complex queries. Improved response time was critical to restoring departmental efficiency. To ensure application speed, issues of data and network communication, disk access and system I/O needed to be addressed. This also meant carefully distributing logic where it could be most quickly and efficiently executed, i.e., all user-input error checking should be done in the front end, and all database access logic achieved through pre-compiled stored PL/SQL procedures in the database.

Another critical issue, especially in designing a system that could be deployed across multiple law enforcement agencies, was acknowledging that no two agencies would store their incident data in exactly the same way. Therefore, it was important to come up with a data organization design that was flexible enough to be applied to any underlying data set. The database team designed a series of standardized "views" that fitted typical information search and presentation situations. For example, most of the data in the TPD systems were related to "Person," "Location," "Vehicle," or "Incident" information. A set of views was developed for each of these areas of interest, with the underlying data sets mapped to those standard views, making the system more portable to other law enforcement agencies.

4.2   Database Design

Based on the criteria established and after much investigation, the COPLINK team decided upon a three-tier architecture:
- **Front-end interface:** The front-end should be a thin client, consisting of a series of user-friendly query screens matching the four main areas previously discussed (Person, Location, Vehicle, and Incident). The front-end would generate query requests.

- **Middle-ware application server:** The middle-ware would handle secure requests from multiple clients, and execute the stored procedures in the database.
- **Back-end database:** Results from the database would be processed by the middle-ware, and be formatted into return data strings. These return strings would then be sent to the front-end where they would be parsed and displayed to the user.

There are four main query screens, each resulting in a summary listing of information related to an initial query. Figure 1 illustrates relationships among queries. For example, if a user initiates a search on a particular first-name/last-name combination, a summary table is presented as a result of a dynamic SQL query, listing all possible matches, as well as the number of incidents associated with each individual match. From there, the user can select either a secondary listing of incidents related to a particular individual or can access a more detailed summary of the personal information on the individual. For an incident summary, all the pertinent case detail information on a particular incident is presented. For a detailed person summary, the user can select the incident summary for that individual, and from there obtain case details for any incident listed.

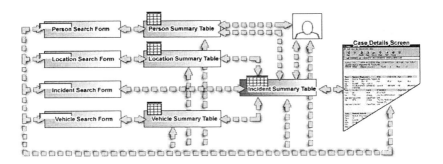

Figure 1. COPLINK Connect Search Schema

4.3 User Evaluations for the COPLINK Database Application

A usability evaluation, involving 52 law enforcement personnel, was conducted to assess the achievement of a number of the goals that guided the design and development of the COPLINK Connect. Items on the questionnaire used to assess and compare the COPLINK and RMS systems were based upon user perceptions of such widely used measures of usability as: *effectiveness* (impact of system on job performance, productivity, effectiveness of information, and information accuracy), *ease of use* (measures of effort required to complete a task, ease of learning how to use the application, ability to navigate easily through the different screens, and satisfaction with the interaction), and *efficiency* (speed of completing tasks, organization of the information on the screens, ability to find information and the interface design itself) (Hauck, 1999).

From both questionnaires and interviews, participants indicated that the quality and quantity of information from COPLINK Connect surpassed those of RMS. In a review of current RMS practices, a number of detectives and officers were actually unable to use RMS but were able to use COPLINK DB to conduct searches. It is evident from this evaluation that COPLINK DB allowed a population of TPD personnel to access information that would have been quite difficult for them to acquire using the RMS system. From both the questionnaire and the interview data collected from this evaluation, it is evident that many participants rated the information found in COPLINK as more useful than the information in RMS.

5.   COPLINK DETECT CRIMINAL INTELLIGENCE APPLICATION

In order to provide investigative support through data mining techniques, a knowledge management tool, COPLINK Detect, was specifically designed to aid law enforcement investigators and detectives in criminal intelligence analysis, helping to improving efficiency and effectiveness. A statistics-based, algorithmic technique, called a concept space or automatic thesaurus, was used to identify relationships between objects (terms or concepts) of interest (Lesk, 1997). The technique has been frequently used to develop domain-specific knowledge structures for digital library applications.

A concept space is a network of terms and weighted associations that represent the concepts and their associations within an underlying information space that can assist in concept-based information retrieval. In addition, co-occurrence analysis uses similarity and clustering functions (Chen & Lynch, 1992) to weight relationships between all possible pairs of concepts. The resulting network-like concept space holds all possible associations between objects, which means that every existing link between every pair of concepts is retained and ranked. The concept space was used as the basis for the COPLINK Detect application.

In COPLINK, detailed case reports are the underlying space and concepts are meaningful terms occurring in each case. Detect provides the ability to easily identify relevant terms and their degree of relationship to the search term. The relevant terms can be ranked in the order of their degree of association so that the most relevant terms are distinguished from inconsequential terms. From a crime investigation standpoint, Detect can help investigators link known objects to other related objects that might contain useful information for further investigation. For instance, like people and vehicles related to a given suspect.

Information related to a suspect can direct an investigation to expand to the right direction, but a case report that reveals relationships among data in one particular case fails to capture those relationships from the entire database. In effect, investigators need to review all case reports related to a suspect, which may be a tedious task. In the COPLINK project, we introduce Detect based upon the concept space algorithm as an alternative investigation tool that captures the relationships between objects in the entire database.

To date, we have successfully adopted our techniques to create COPLINK Detect based on a collection of 1.5 million case reports from the current Tucson Police Department Records Management System. These cases span a time frame from 1986 to 1999 (the entire case record collection for the City of Tucson). Based on careful user requirement analysis, five entity fields from the database were deemed relevant for analysis: Person, Organization, Location, Vehicle, and Incident type. The purpose of this tool is to discover relationships between and among different crime-related entities. It is important not only to know that there is a relationship, but also to know what each relationship is.

5.1   System Design

In general, there are three main steps in building the domain-specific Detect concept space. The first task is to identify collections of documents in a specific subject domain; these are the sources of terms or concepts. For Tucson Police Department, we are using the case reports in the existing database. The next step is to filter and index the terms. The final step is to perform a co-occurrence analysis to capture the relationships among indexed terms. The resulting output is then inserted into a database for easy manipulation (for a more in-depth analysis of the Concept Space algorithm, see Chen & Lynch (1992)). The last two steps have been customized for COPLINK Detect. After optimising the code and tuning the database, we found that the total time required for building COPLINK Detect is approximately five hours, which is acceptable in the given situation.

5.1.1   Term Filtering and Indexing

Due to the nature of the data residing in TPD's database, each piece of information is categorized in case reports and stored in well-organized structures. Theoretically, a concept space can contain any number of term types (e.g., person names, organizations, locations, crime types, etc.). In practice, however, the size of the database, the time required to build the Detect concept space, and the response time of queries are major constraints that limit the number of term types. With the collaboration of personnel from the Tucson Police Department, we identified and created a set of term types for the COPLINK Detect in order to balance performance and comprehensiveness. The index maintains the relationship between a term and the document in which it occurs. Both index and reverse index are required for co-occurrence analysis. The index contains the links from term to document; the reverse index contains the links from document to term.

5.1.2   Co-occurrence Analysis

After identifying terms, we first computed the term frequency and the document frequency for each term in a document, based on the methodology developed by Chen and Lynch (1992). In general, some term types are more descriptive and more important than others and deserve to be assigned higher weights so as to ensure that relationships associated with these types are always ranked reasonably. In COPLINK Detect, crime types are assigned comparatively higher weights. We then performed term co-occurrence analysis based on the asymmetric "Cluster Function".

5.2   User Evaluations for COPLINK Detect

We conducted user evaluations to examine the effects of COPLINK Detect on law enforcement investigation and work practices (Hauck & Chen, 1999). Twelve crime analysts and detectives participated in the four-week longitudinal evaluation, during which they were asked to complete journal entries on searches they had conducted using COPLINK Detect. By utilizing data collection methods of documentation, structured interviews, and direct observation, we were able to evaluate the function and design of the COPLINK Detect system. The journals and interviews revealed that COPLINK Detect provided support for intelligence analysis and knowledge management in the areas of link analysis, summarization, and efficiency.

5.2.1 Link Analysis and Summarization

Participants indicated that COPLINK Detect served as a powerful tool for acquiring information and cited its ability to determine the presence or absence of links between people, places, vehicles and other object types as invaluable in investigating a case (Harper & Harris, 1975). The impact of link analysis on investigative tasks is crucial to the building of cases. An officer assigned to investigate a crime has to have enough information to provide a lead before he/she can begin working. Too many cases have to be closed because of lack of information or inability to utilize information existing elsewhere in the records management system. Detect manages all the data in the records system in such a way that it can be used as knowledge about the suspect.

5.2.2 Efficiency

Perhaps one of the most crucial benefits of the use of COPLINK Detect in law enforcement is its speed. As one of our participants explained, identifying a suspect between 48 to 72 hours after a crime is difficult. Beyond this time frame, a suspect is able to destroy evidence that may tie him/her to the crime or change his/her appearance to avoid identification. Witness/victim memory of the suspect's appearance also fades within this period. Identification of the suspect ideally should occur within 48 hours of the crime, so establishing useful links for identifying and locating the suspect is a crucial step. A number of interviews and journal comments indicated that use of COPLINK Detect increased productivity by reducing time spent per information search.

6. COPLINK COLLABORATION SYSTEM

The rapid advancement of information technologies and the Internet provides great opportunities as well as challenges for law enforcement. These technologies allow better use and sharing of information. With the growing popularity of the Web, information can be shared among agencies or made accessible to the public more easily than ever. On the other hand, however, there are many issues and challenges, which are not yet completely resolved. In this section, we report on our experience in designing a collaborative information-sharing infrastructure in the law enforcement domain. We also review some of the major challenges we encountered. Our project is built on the COPLINK infrastructure at TPD, and given the success of COPLINK Connect and COPLINK Detect, we identify some areas that can be further improved.

6.1   Design Goals and Challenges

6.1.1   Information Access and Monitoring

Besides the data sources incorporated in COPLINK Connect, there are many other external sources that need to be inquired frequently by police officers. These data sources include information or search services that are available on the Web. Examples include search services such as Property Assessor Information, Map Guide, People Search and Reverse Lookup. Without substantial experience and knowledge, it becomes difficult to locate important and accurate information. These resources employ a wide range of different hardware platforms, database systems, network protocols, data schemas, and user interfaces. This poses a great challenge for managing and combining these data sources. Several research groups have proposed the use of distributed ontology or agent technology database to deal with this problem (e.g., Ambite et al, 2001; Bouguettaya et al, 2001). Although these systems can effectively manage multiple data sources, they do not allow users to add a new resource easily or to rate the quality or credibility of an existing data source.

In addition, most of the data sources are passive and lack the ability to push useful information to the users. Police officers often have to track the activities of a particular suspect or the whereabouts of a vehicle. These monitoring functions are usually not available in most search systems. As a result, the data sources have to be checked manually on a regular basis, resulting in heavy mental effort for the user.

6.1.2   Personalization and Collaboration

Personnel with different job duties and geographical locations have very different information needs. Given the large number of data sources, police officers face the problem of finding the right data sources that are relevant to their jobs. One main goal of our design is to provide customizable and personalized information to the users.

Effective collaboration among law enforcement personnel is another important goal in our design. A police officer may obtain some knowledge from the observations during patrol, while a crime analyst may get some particular insights when doing an investigation. Such knowledge however, is tacit and not efficiently shared. When a police officer needs some particular information, he/she does not know whom to contact. We find that there also are situations where two different units are working on two closely related cases (e.g., related to the same person), but none of them know that another unit is working on a related case. As a result the two units are not able to collaborate and share their findings. The issues of sharing knowledge in a collaborative manner and linking together people working on similar cases are to be addressed.

6.2   System Architecture

Taking into consideration the above issues and challenges, we propose the COPLINK Collaboration system, an infrastructure which tries to address those problems to a certain extent.

6.2.1   Linking People Together

We adapt an approach based on collaborative filtering in our system. Collaborative filtering is defined as the collaboration among people to help one another perform filtering by recording their reactions to the information they read (Goldberg et al, 1992). While traditional collaborative filtering relies on documents read (e.g., Konstan et al, 1997) or items purchased by users (e.g., Amazon.com), we make use of the users' search actions and search histories.

The rationale behind this is that when two users search for the same information, it is likely that the users have similar information needs and that they may possibly be working on two related cases. When a user performs a search query through COPLINK Collaboration, the search query will be forwarded to the corresponding data sources. Our system will return the search results to the user and store the search session in the user profile database for further analysis. Collaboration will be performed by applying data mining techniques on these user search profiles. Our previous research has shown that machine learning and data mining techniques such as ID3, genetic algorithms and relevance feedback can be applied in inductive search query analysis (Chen et al, 1998). Using these techniques, the system tries to (1) recommend similar cases to users and (2) identify police officers with similar information needs. If the system finds that two police officers have performed similar searches (e.g., similar search keywords or search criteria), it will alert both users and provide a way for them to contact each other for further collaboration. Since no extra effort is required from the users, we expect them to be more willing to share information. Figure 2 shows a simplified version of the system architecture.

6.2.2   Finding Useful Data Sources

Another measure we use for collaboration is users' ratings of data sources. Users can give ratings to or write reviews for the data sources they use. Our algorithm is based on a hybrid approach, which combines content-based filtering and collaborative filtering (Balabanovic & Shoham, 1997). Data mining techniques are also applied in our filtering algorithm. Useful information sources will be recommended to a user based on one's past search sessions and the recommendations of other users who have similar information needs. This allows users to have a personalized list of data sources they need while irrelevant sources are filtered.

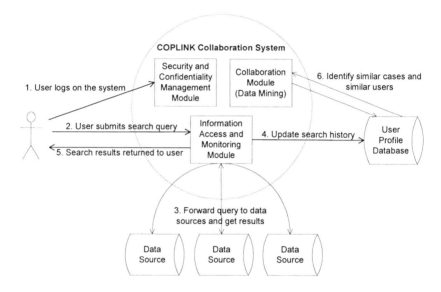

Figure 2. Proposed system architecture to support information sharing and collaboration

6.2.3   Information Monitoring

Users can also set up monitoring tasks through the system. If a user wants to monitor a database for a particular query, the system will store the monitor task in the user profile database and check the corresponding database periodically. When relevant data is updated or inserted into the database, the system will send an alert message to the user through the user interface, email, voice message or cellular phone.

7. CONCLUSION

Criminals do not bound themselves by county borders or jurisdictions. Furthermore, criminals are creatures of habit and being able to understand their habits and close associations is important (Joyce, 1996). The COPLINK applications take advantage of these characteristic by not only promoting information sharing and collaboration between stovepipe information sources and different agencies, but also by capturing connections between people, places, events, and vehicles, based on past crimes. Our evaluation of these knowledge management and intelligence analysis applications support its potential for transforming law-enforcement practices in this age of digital governments.

In this chapter, we have identified the major challenges in designing an information sharing and collaboration infrastructure within the law enforcement domain to promote criminal intelligent analysis and knowledge management. We have proposed and are implementing an architecture that addresses some of the major issues. Currently, the COPLINK Connect database system is fully deployed at the Tucson Police Department, while final user evaluations and modifications on COPLINK Detect are being conducted. A prototype of the COPLINK Collaboration system is being developed. We are excited about the results of the COPLINK project, from both the potential impact in the research community as well as in application as an example of digital government technologies being used to help the general community. We hope our experience can provide useful insight to other digital government research projects.

ACKNOWLEDGEMENTS

This project has been funded by grants from the National Institute of Justice, Office of Science and Technology #97-LB-VX-K023 and the National Science Foundation #9983304 with support from the Digital Equipment Corporation External Technology Grants Program #US-1998004 for its award of an equipment grant. Appreciation also goes to Sergeant Jennifer Schroeder, Dr. Homa Atabakhsh, Dr. Daniel Zeng, other COPLINK team members and the personnel from the Tucson Police Department who were involved in this project.

REFERENCES

Ambite J., Arens Y., Hovy E., Philpot A., Gravano L., Hatzivassiloglou V., Klavans J. Simplifying Data Access: The Energy Data Collection Project. IEEE Computer 2001; 34(2): 47-54

Balabanovic M., Shoham Y. Fab: Content-based, Collaborative Recommendation. Communications of the ACM 1997; 40(3): 66-72

Bouguettaya A., Ouzzani M., Medjahed B., Cameron J. Managing Government Databases. IEEE Computer 2001; 34(2): 56-64

Chen H., Lynch K. J. Automatic Construction of Networks of Concepts Characterizing Document Database. IEEE Transaction on Systems, Man and Cybernetics 1992; 22(5): 885-902

Chen H., Shankaranarayanan G., Iyer A., She L. A Machine Learning Approach to Inductive Query by Examples: An Experiment Using Relevance Feedback, ID3, Genetic Algorithms, and Simulated Annealing. Journal of the American Society for Information Science 1998; 49: 693-705

Chen Y. M. Liao C. C., Prasad B. A Systematic Approach of Virtual Enterprising through Knowledge Management Techniques. Concurrent Engineering-Research and Applications 1998; 6(3): 225-244

Davenport, T. H. Business Process Reengineering: Where it's been, Where it's Going. In *Business Process Change: Reengineering Concepts, Methods and Technologies*, V. Grover and W. Kettinger, eds. Middletown, PA: Idea Publishing: 1995.

Davenport, T. H., Prusak, L. *Working Knowledge: How Organizations Manage What They Know*. Boston, MA, Harvard Business School Press, 1998.

Goldberg D., Nichols D., Oki B., Terry D. Using Collaborative Filtering to Weave an Information Tapestry. Communications of the ACM 1992; 35(12): 61-69

Harper W. R., Harris D. H. The Application of Link Analysis to Police Intelligence. Human Factors 1975; 17(2): 157-164

Hauck R. V. COPLINK: Exploring Usability of a Multimedia Database Application for Law Enforcement. Report 1999, available at http://ai.bpa.arizona.edu/go/datawarehousing/publications/nij.pdf

Hauck R. V., Chen H. COPLINK: A Case of Intelligent Analysis and Knowledge Management. In *Proceedings of the 20th Annual International Conference on Information Systems*, P. De, J. I. DeGross (eds.). 1999 December 13-15 Charlotte, NC: International Conference on Information Systems, 1999.

Inkpen A. C., Dinur, A. Knowledge Management Processes and International Joint Ventures. Organization Science 1998; 9(4): 454-468

Jones P, Jordan, J. Knowledge Orientations and Team Effectiveness. International Journal of Technology Management 1998; 16(1-3): 152-161

Joyce N. ICAM: Chicago's Newest Crime-Fighting Tool. Proceedings of the Conference in Technology, Community Policing sponsored by the National Law Enforcement and Corrections Technology Center, 1996, available at http://www.nlectc.org/txtfiles/confrpt.html

Konstan J., Miller B., Maltz D., Herlocker J., Gordon L., Riedl J. GroupLens: Applying Collaborative Filtering to Usenet News. Communications of the ACM 1997; 40(3) 77-87

Lesk M. *Practical Digital Libraries*. Los Altos, CA: Morgan Kauffmann, 1997.

Nonaka I. A Dynamic Theory of Organizational Knowledge Creation. Organization Science 1994; 5(1): 14-37

O'Leary D. E. Enterprise Knowledge Management. IEEE Computer 1998; 31(3): 54-62

Pliant L. High-technology solutions. The Police Chief 1996; 5(38): 38-51

Rouse W. B., Thomas B. S., Boff, K. R. Knowledge maps for knowledge mining: Application to R&D/Technology Management. IEEE Transaction on Systems, Man and Cybernetics: Part C- Applications and Reviews 1998; 28(3): 309-317

Sparrow M. K. Information systems: A Help or Hindrance in the Evolution of Policing? The Police Chief 1991; 58(4): 26-44

Teece D. J. Research Directions for Knowledge Management. California Management Review 1998; 40(3): 289-292

Tucson Police Department. COPLINK: Database Integration and Access for a Law Enforcement Intranet. Whitepaper 1997, available at http://ai.bpa.arizona.edu/coplink/whtpaper/whitepaper.html

Roslin V. Hauck is currently pursuing her doctorate in Management Information Systems at the University of Arizona and has been affiliated with the department since 1997. She received her Bachelor's degree in Communication Studies from Northwestern University (1995) and her Master's degree in Communication at the University of Arizona (1997). Her research interests include technology adoption and organizational behavior, human-computer interaction, information visualization, usability and software design.

Michael Chau is a doctoral student and Research Associate at the Artificial Intelligence Lab at the University of Arizona. He received his bachelor degree in Computer Science and Information Systems from the University of Hong Kong in 1998. His research interests include information retrieval, natural language processing, digital government, multi-agent technology and Web mining.

Dr. Hsinchun Chen is McClelland Endowed Professor of MIS at The University of Arizona and Andersen Consulting Professor of the Year (1999). He is also the director of the Artificial Intelligence Lab and Founding Director of The University of Arizona Mark and Susan Hoffman eCommerce Lab. He received the Ph.D. degree in Information Systems from New York University in 1989, MBA in Finance from SUNY-Buffalo in 1985, and BS in Management Science from the National Chiao-Tung University in Taiwan. He is author of more than 90 articles covering medical informatics, semantic retrieval, search algorithms, knowledge discovery, and collaborative computing in leading information technology publications. He serves on the editorial board of Journal of the American Society for Information Science. He is an expert in medical informatics, digital library, knowledge management research, and his work has been featured in various scientific and information technologies publications including Science, New York Times, Business Week, NCSA Access Magazine, WEBster, and HPCWire.

Chapter 11

Web-Based Systems that Disseminate Information from Databases but Protect Confidentiality

Alan F. Karr[1], Jaeyong Lee[1], Ashish P. Sanil[1], Joel Hernandez[2],
Sousan Karimi[2], Karen Litwin[2]
[1]*National Institute of Statistical Sciences Research Triangle Park, NC, USA*
[2]*MCNC Research Triangle Park, NC, USA*

Abstract: The Internet provides an efficient mechanism for Federal agencies to distribute their data to the public. However, it is imperative that such data servers have built-in mechanisms to ensure that confidentiality of the data, and the privacy of individuals or establishments represented in the data, are not violated. We describe a prototype dissemination system developed for the National Agricultural Statistics Service that uses aggregation of adjacent geographical units as a confidentiality-preserving technique. We also outline a Bayesian approach to statistical analysis of the aggregated data.

Key words: Data confidentiality, privacy, Web dissemination, digital government, aggregation, statistical analysis

1.   INTRODUCTION

There has been longstanding concern in the United States and elsewhere over the confidentiality of statistical data, especially data gathered by the Federal government in sample surveys and censuses (see Appendix B for examples). Confidentiality may be mandated by law, prescribed by agency practices or promised to respondents. Often, confidentiality must be preserved in order to ensure the quality of the data: respondents may lie if they believe that their privacy is threatened.

At the same time, government agencies have an obligation to report their data, or information derived from the data, and they recognize the need for some balance between strict confidentiality and the benefits derived from the release of statistical information (Duncan, *et al.*, 1993).

The Internet has emerged as a natural and efficient mode for disseminating Federal data (Schorr & Stolfo, 1997). However, the ease of access and potentially large quantities of data that Web-based systems can provide intensify the need for techniques that prevent disclosure of confidential data. Computing power and ubiquity of databases make record linkage (see Appendix A) and other means of breaking confidentiality surprisingly easy (Keller-McNulty & Unger, 1993). On the positive side, the opportunity exists to implement new technologies to protect confidentiality, which can also meet user needs in new ways.

Research on this topic is being carried out at the National Institute of Statistical Sciences (NISS), working with collaborators at Carnegie Mellon University, Los Alamos National Laboratory, the Ohio State University and MCNC under an NSF-sponsored Digital Government project. The project Web site is http://www.niss.org/dg. Several aspects of the problem make this a challenging cross-disciplinary effort: devising strategies, some that reflect the entire history of queries to a system, to evaluate and reduce disclosure risk; and exploring issues of system design, user interfaces, scalable data structures and new Internet technologies.

In this article, we describe a prototype system developed for the National Agricultural Statistics Service (NASS). The system disseminates survey data concerning on-farm usage of chemicals (fertilizers, fungicides, herbicides and pesticides) in far greater geographical detail than previously, but protects the identities of farms in the survey. Confidentiality is preserved by means of geographical aggregation: data from adjacent counties are aggregated to the level of disclosable "supercounties."

2.   THE NASS DATA

The data consist of on-farm use of agricultural chemicals on various crops in 1996-1998, collected by NASS through an annual survey of farms.

The database contains 194,410 records collected from 30,500 farms, with information on the rates of usage of 322 chemicals on 67 crops (field crops, fruits and vegetables). For our purposes, each data record can be thought of as containing Farm ID, state, county, year, farm size in acres, crop, chemical, and the number of pounds of the chemical applied to that crop. (The real database is more complex, involving quantities such as number of applications and adjustment weights.)

User queries to the system are for *application rates* (pounds applied per acre) of certain chemicals on particular crops in geographical regions of interest. Ideally, information would be released at the county level. Currently, however, because of confidentiality concerns, NASS releases application rates only at the state level.

3. AGGREGATION FOR DISCLOSURE RISK REDUCTION

The confidentiality concern of NASS is to protect the identities of farms in the survey. Information cannot be disclosed that would enable a user to estimate accurately the chemical usage on a particular farm (Dalenius, 1977). Such a disclosure would breach the respondent confidentiality promised by NASS. (Adjustment weights are also confidential, for technical statistical reasons.)

For the application rate in a geographical unit to be disclosable, NASS requires that two widely employed rules (FCSM, 1994; Willenborg & de Waal, 1987) be satisfied. The N-rule requires that the unit contain at least $N = 3$ surveyed farms for the specified chemical, crop and year. The p-rule prohibits a dominant farm that comprises more than $p = 60\%$ of the total acreage of all farms surveyed in the unit.

The underlying rationale for these rules, which collectively we term the (N, p)-rule, is that farms in a sample containing too few farms or a farm whose size dominates a sample are susceptible to both identity and attribute disclosure risks (see Appendix A).

At the county level the (N, p)-rule with $N = 3$ and $p = 60\%$ does not work: more than one-half of counties are undisclosable. Simply refusing to answer such queries would lead to unacceptable user frustration. Instead, the NISS system aggregates undisclosable counties with neighboring counties (in the same State) to form disclosable "supercounties," allowing NASS to release data at the highest resolution consistent with the risk criteria.

Aggregations must be computed automatically, since there are too many (State, year, crop, chemical) combinations to permit manual aggregation on a case-by-case basis. We employ two "greedy" algorithms (see Appendix C) based on the following heuristic procedure: Examine the undisclosable (super)counties in a random order and merge them with a neighboring (super)county according to some criterion for desirability of merging. Continue until only disclosable (super)counties remain.

The algorithms differ only in the rule that governs the merging process. The **pure** rule directs the merging of counties in a manner that favors leaving the disclosable counties alone, thereby preserving the "purity" of their data. Instead, it merges the undisclosable counties among themselves insofar as possible. This procedure does preserve purity of as many disclosable counties as possible, but it can create large supercounties comprised of many undisclosable counties.

The **small** rule, by contrast, favors forming small supercounties by merging an undisclosable region with the neighboring region most likely to achieve disclosability. In practice, judging by visual inspection, the **small** rule produces satisfactory aggregations.

Both algorithms randomize the order in which candidate mergers are considered, breaking ties either randomly or on the basis of similarity of application rates. Either can produce aggregations in which some supercounties may be decomposed into smaller but nevertheless disclosable supercounties (see Appendix C). To alleviate this, we employ a two-step process. First, the **small** algorithm is run to produce an initial aggregation, and then the **pure** algorithm is run within each supercounty produced by **small**, in order to determine if it can be decomposed.

This composite procedure works remarkably well. It is also very fast: test runs for aggregation of states containing 100 counties take less than a millisecond per run, even on a 233 MHz Pentium PC running Linux.

Moreover, it produces aggregations that are as good as those produced by complex, formal optimization procedures. The aggregation problem can be formulated as a (NP-hard) combinatorial optimization problem over the edge-set of the adjacency graph of the counties in a state. One advantage of doing this is that the optimization framework allows explicit incorporation of "goodness" of aggregations, allowing preference, for instance, for aggregating counties that lie within the same watershed. The combinatorial optimization problems can be solved using computationally intensive simulated annealing methods, but long running times make this infeasible in practice. In test cases where we have used both methods, there is no significant difference between the characteristics of the aggregations they produce, and we conclude that the heuristic methods are adequate for the application we describe here.

4.   NASS SYSTEM ARCHITECTURE AND OPERATION

The prototype NASS system (Karr, *et al.*, 2001) is accessible at http://niss.cnidr.org. Figure 1 shows schematically the system architecture. The system has been implemented on a Sun SPARCSTATION 10 running Solaris 2.6. The NASS survey database and the Query History Database (QHDB) are maintained by an Oracle 8i relational DBMS. An Apache HTTP server forms the front end, allowing users to interact with the system via a Web browser.

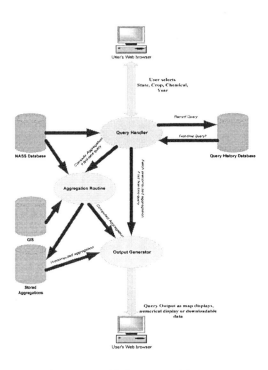

Figure 1. NASS System Architecture

As shown in Figure 2, the user first selects from an HTML form a State containing the counties for which chemical usage information is desired. Once a State is selected, CGI scripts written in Perl query the database and retrieve lists of crops grown in the State and chemicals used there. JavaScript routines then generate drop-down menus that let the user select among only the crops grown and chemicals used in the selected State.

Next, the user either selects a crop, in which case the Perl/JavaScript routines regenerate the menu for the chemicals, showing only those used on the selected crop, or the user selects a chemical, which leads to an updated menu of crops. At this point (or earlier), one or more years may be selected. The user may also override the default map-based output and specify another output format before submitting the query.

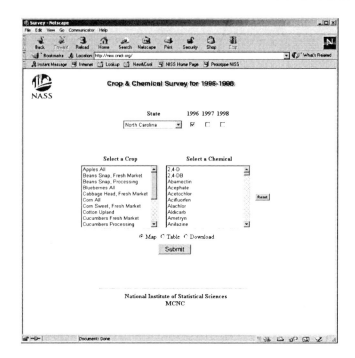

Figure 2. Query Input Screen. (Reprinted by permission of IEEE. Alan F. Karr et al.
"Disseminating Information but Protecting Confidentiality." *IEEE Computer*, February 2001.
© 2001 IEEE.)

A major design decision is to store (in ASCII text files) the result of
every query answered by the system, which can be retrieved if the query is
ever received again. This avoids recomputation of aggregations, but the
primary motivation is to prevent inconsistent and potentially privacy-
threatening responses arising from randomized steps in the aggregation
algorithms.

The result of a query consists of a list of supercounties that arise from the
running of the aggregation algorithm. Each supercounty has associated with
it a set of component counties and the application rate of the selected
chemical on the selected crop in the selected year(s) in the supercounty.

All queries are recorded in the QHDB, which allows usage of the system
to be monitored and facilitates understanding of user behavior. The role of
the QHDB is much more complex in systems for which the risk of answering
a query depends on what data have been released by the system to date.
"Table servers" being developed by NISS have this feature.

For previously answered queries, the stored results are passed to the
output display module. Otherwise, CGI scripts in Perl extract the relevant
raw data from the NASS database, and the adjacency structure for counties is
retrieved from a geographical information system (GIS). The survey and

adjacency data are then input to the aggregation routine, which is a stand-alone program written in C. The output from the aggregation routine is stored in a file, for both future use and access by the output display module. The directory and file naming convention we use makes it easy to identify and retrieve results corresponding to previous queries.

The default mode for reporting query results to the user is a map, as shown in Figure 3. Supercounties are colored according to the application rate of the chosen chemical on the chosen crop, and the color bar also shows the State-wide average rate. Supercounty and county-within-supercounty boundaries are shown, but differently. Multiple years appear on separate maps, but share a common color scale. The aggregations may differ year-to-year for a multiple-year query; this minimizes the degree of aggregation. At the expense of (much) greater aggregation, the system could force the same aggregation for multiple years.

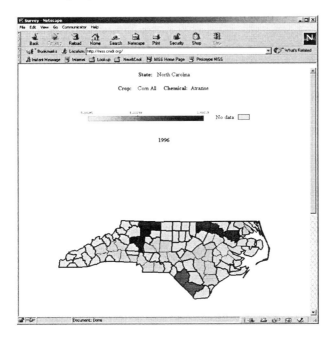

Figure 3. Map Output Screen. Reprinted by permission of IEEE. Alan F. Karr et al. "Disseminating Information but Protecting Confidentiality." *IEEE Computer*, February 2001. © 2001 IEEE.

The user also has the option of viewing in tabular form the numerical values of the application rates underlying the map. Finally, the aggregated data can be downloaded in XML format, using a DTD that reflects the hierarchical nature of data aggregated at the supercounty level.

Navigation aids enable the user easily to modify the current query, or to request different forms of output. Navigation and query updates are facilitated by the storing the current session parameters in a hidden frame on the user's browser. Also, the system maintains internal status flags so that abnormal exits and disruptions can be handled appropriately.

5.   STATISTICAL IMPLICATIONS OF AGGREGATION

While aggregation prevents disclosure, it may also distort the data. Thus, from a statistician's point of view, a question that immediately arises is: How should one go about analyzing the aggregated data in order to make informative inferences about the surveyed population?

In this section, we present a sketch of a Bayesian simulation approach for the analysis of such aggregated data. This methodology is the focus of Lee, *et al.* (2001), to which the reader is referred for details.

We abstract the NASS system as follows. Let $P = \{Y_1, \ldots, Y_N\}$ be the data for the population (of farms) of interest, where N is the size of the population. Initially, we suppose that farms have only one attribute. Suppose that the disseminator samples $S = \{y_1, \ldots, y_n\}$, comprising the surveyed farms, using simple random sampling from P.

The disseminator also draws a partition $\kappa = \{\kappa_1, \ldots, \kappa_k\}$ of the index set $\{1, 2, \ldots, n\}$ from a distribution $p(\kappa \mid S)$, representing the units of aggregation. Often, $p(\kappa \mid S)$ is statistically independent of S. This occurs, for example, if κ_i is defined by geographical units such as counties. On the other hand, in the NASS setting, κ depends on sampled values y_i, which leads to the need for the Bayesian approach described here.

Let n_i be the number of observations in the ith partition set κ_i, for $i = 1, \ldots, k$ The disseminator aggregates the sample over the partition κ and releases $A = \{(\bar{y}_1, n_1), \ldots, (\bar{y}_k, n_k)\}$, where $\bar{y}_i = (1/n_i)\sum_{j \in \kappa_i} y_j$.

To illustrate analysis of aggregated data, consider estimation of the population variance. The usual estimator $s^2 = \sum_{i=1}^{n}(y_i - \bar{y})^2/(n-1)$ of the population variance $S^2 = \sum_{i=1}^{N}(Y_i - \bar{Y})^2/(N-1)$ cannot be recovered from A in general. However, a natural extension of the usual estimator in this case leads to the estimator

$$s_a^2 = \frac{1}{k-1}\sum_{i=1}^{k} n_i(\bar{y}_i - \bar{y})^2.$$

This estimator, though, is not guaranteed to be unbiased unless κ is independent of the sample S.

Thus, the dependence of the partition on the data values of the sample renders the usual estimation procedures deficient. Moreover, to keep this description simple, we have taken the data Y_i to be simple real-valued random variables; whereas in the NASS system they are ratios of pounds applied to acre. The analysis of ratios introduces additional complexities. It is clear that any methodology that addresses the aggregated data problem must not only accommodate the dependency between κ and S but also cope with ratio-valued data.

We briefly outline the general strategy behind the Bayesian simulation method. To keep the outline simple and within the scope of this article, we continue to treat the Y_i as real-valued random variables. A complete version is presented in Lee, *et al.* (2001). The population data $\{Y_1,\ldots,Y_N\}$ are taken as drawn from a parametric density $f(y \mid \theta)$, and $y_1,\ldots,y_k$ are a simple random sample from the population, and are treated as unobserved latent variables. Let θ have a prior distribution $\pi(\theta)$. Denote the sum of the y-values in the ith partition by y_{i+}: $y_{i+} = \sum_{j \in \kappa_i} y_j$. Then, based on aggregated data (n_1, y_{1+}), ..., (n_k, y_{k+}), the likelihood is

$$\prod_{i=1}^{k} f^{*k}(y_{i+} \mid \theta) p(\kappa \mid S),$$

where f^{*k} is the density of k-convolution of f. If f is a Gaussian or Gamma density, f^{*k} is known, but in many cases, of course, f^{*k} is unknown. This does not pose much difficulty in the Bayesian computation we propose.

The joint posterior distribution of $(\theta, P \setminus S, S)$ given the aggregated data A is proportional to

$$\pi(\theta) p(\kappa \mid S) \prod_{i=1}^{k} f(Y_i \mid \theta) \prod_{i=1}^{k} I\left(\sum_{j \in \kappa_i} y_j = y_{i+}\right).$$

Note that the posterior distribution explicitly includes the term $p(\kappa \mid S)$, in order to model the data-dependent partition. Lee, *et al.* (2001) show how $p(\kappa \mid S)$ could be specified.

This posterior distribution will almost always be intractable analytically. However, if we could generate a sample from it, we could: (1) Study the distribution of the population parameter θ; and then (2) Generate several realizations of P and perform a bootstrap analysis (Efron & Tibshirani, 1986) on statistics of interest.

But, the posterior distribution will generally be too complex to allow direct generation of samples. We can, however, employ Markov chain Monte Carlo (MCMC) methods (Gilks, *et al.*, 1996) for the simulation. For MCMC, we simulate a particular Markov chain on the state space (P, θ) such that the stationary distribution of the chain is the posterior distribution. Thus, by running the chain long enough, we can generate samples from the posterior. See Lee, *et al.* (2001) for details of the simulation procedure.

6.   CONCLUSION

Citizen access to data and information is an essential responsibility of the Federal government. The system described here is a step toward using the Web to meet that responsibility efficiently and effectively. Using it, NASS is able to provide information in more detail than previously, yet be assured that confidentiality criteria are fulfilled.

More complex data sets, queries and privacy concerns lead to additional challenges. For example, in many databases, the disclosure risk associated with a query depends on which queries have been answered previously. Integration of multiple databases raises additional issues, especially with risk computation and reduction. At the most basic level, a decision-theoretic formulation of the problem is necessary, in order to allow agencies to balance the value to society of releasing information derived from confidential data against disclosure risk.

ACKNOWLEDGEMENTS

Carol House of NASS stimulated development of this system, and Joseph Prusacki of NASS provided both data and knowledge about them. Hassan Karimi of MCNC set up the GIS routines. We thank NISS summer interns Karen Brady and Christopher Holloman for numerous comments and suggestions. The research was supported by NSF grant EIA-9876619 to NISS. Jaeyong Lee is currently at the Pennsylvania State University.

REFERENCES

Consumer Reports (2000). Who knows your medical secrets? *Consumer Reports*, August 23-26.

Dalenius, T. (1977). Toward a methodology for statistical disclosure control. *Statistik Tidskrit* **5** 429-444.

Duncan, G. T., de Wolf, V. A., Jabine, T. B., and Straf, M. L. (1993). Report of the panel on confidentiality and data access. *Journal of Official Statistics* 9 271-274.

Duncan, G. T., and Keller-McNulty, S. (2001). Mask or impute? *Review of Official Statistics* (to appear).

Duncan, G. T., and Lambert, D. (1986). Disclosure-limited data dissemination (with discussion). *Journal of the American Statistical Association* 81 10-28.

Efron, B. and Tibshirani, R. (1986). Bootstrap methods for standard errors, confidence intervals, and other measures of statistical accuracy (with discussion). *Statistical Science* 1(3) 54-77.

Federal Committee on Statistical Methodology (1994). Report on Statistical Disclosure Limitation Methodology.

Fienberg, S. E., and Willenborg, L. C. R. J., eds. (1998). Special Issue on Disclosure Limitation Methods for Protecting the Confidentiality of Statistical Data. *Journal of Official Statistics* 14(4).

Gilks, W.R, Richardson, S., and Spiegelhalter, D. J., eds. (1996). *Markov Chain Monte Carlo in Practice*. Chapman & Hall/CRC.

Karr, A. F., Lee, J., Sanil, A., Hernandez, J., Karimi, S., and Litwin, K. (2001). Disseminating information but protecting confidentiality. *IEEE Computer* 34(2) 36-37.

Keller-McNulty, S., and Unger, E. A. (1993). Database systems: Inferential security. *Journal of Official Statistics* 9 475-499.

Lee, J., Holloman, C., Karr, A. F., and Sanil, A. P. (2001). Analysis of aggregated data in survey sampling with application to fertilizer/pesticide usage survey. *Review of Official Statistics* (to appear).

Schorr, H., and Stolfo, S. (1997). *Towards the Digital Government of the 21st Century*. Report from the Workshop on Research and Development Opportunities in the Federal Information Services. Available on-line at http://www.isi.edu/nsf/prop.html.

Willenborg, L., and de Waal, T. (1987). *Statistical Disclosure Control in Practice*. Springer-Verlag, New York.

APPENDIX A: A DATA DISCLOSURE PRIMER

In broad terms, two kinds of disclosures are possible from a database of records containing attributes of individuals (e.g., Census records) or establishments (e.g., occupational safety data). An *identity disclosure* occurs when a record in the database can be associated with the individual or establishment that it describes. An *attribute disclosure* occurs if the value of a sensitive attribute, such as income or health status, is disclosed.

The first step in preventing identity disclosures is to remove explicit identifiers such as name and address or social security number, as well as implicit identifiers, such as "Occupation = Mayor of New York."

Often, however, this is not enough, because of the proliferation of databases and software to link records across databases. Record linkage produces identity disclosures by matching a record in the database to a record in another database containing (some of) the same attributes as well as identifiers. In one example, date of birth, zip code of residence and gender alone produced numerous identity disclosures from a medical records database by linkage to public voter registration data (Consumer Reports, 2000).

Identity disclosure can also occur by means of rare or extreme attributes. A data record for an eighty-year old Korean female dentist in North Dakota might easily be re-identified, as might Bill Gates' record in a database containing income of residents of Washington.

Aggregation (geographical or otherwise) is a principal strategy to reduce identity disclosures. The Census Bureau does not release data at aggregations less than 100,000. To prevent disclosing Bill Gates' identity by means of his income, all incomes exceeding $10,000,000 could be lumped into a single category, a procedure called *top-coding*.

Attribute disclosure is often inferential in nature, and may not be entirely certain. For example, AIDS status (a most sensitive attribute) can be inferred with high certainty from prescription records, but with less certainty from physician identity (if some physicians are known to specialize in treating AIDS).

Dominance can lead to attribute disclosure. The University of North Carolina at Chapel Hill is the dominant employer in Orange County, NC, so that the rate of workplace injuries for the county is, in effect, that for UNC. If this value is confidential at the establishment level, it cannot be disclosed at the county level.

There is a wealth of additional techniques (Fienberg & Willenborg, 1998) for "preventing" disclosure, which preserve low-dimensional statistical characteristics of the data, but distort disclosure-inducing high-dimensional characteristics. The (N, p)-rule employed in the NASS system is one example. *Cell suppression* is the outright refusal to release risky entries (typically, small ones) in tabular data. *Swapping* interchanges the values of one or more attributes, such as geography, between different data records. *Jittering* changes the values of sensitive attributes such as income by adding random noise. Even virtual databases can be created, which preserve some characteristics of the original data, but whose records simply do not correspond to real individuals or establishments (Duncan & Keller-McNulty, 2000).

APPENDIX B: FEDSTATS

More than 70 Federal agencies report expenditures of at least $500,000 per year on statistical activities of collecting, analyzing and disseminating data. These include:

- **Bureau of Economic Analysis** (www.bea.doc.gov): Statistics on gross domestic product, personal income and international trade;
- **Bureau of Labor Statistics** (www.bls.gov): Unemployment statistics, consumer price indices, occupational safety and health statistics;
- **Bureau of Justice Statistics** (www.ojp.usdoj.gov/bjs): Crime, victim, criminal offender and sentencing statistics;
- **Bureau of Transportation Statistics** (www.bts.gov): Highway safety, commodity and airline on-time statistics;

- **Census Bureau** (www.census.gov): Population and economic statistics, especially from the decennial Census;
- **Energy Information Administration** (www.eia.doe.gov): Statistics on energy consumption, cost and reserves, as well as projections of future usage;
- **National Agricultural Statistics Service** (www.usda.gov/nass): Statistics on agricultural production and pesticide/herbicide/fungicide usage;
- **National Center for Education Statistics** (nces.ed.gov): Statistics on educational achievement and education finance;
- **National Center for Health Statistics** (www.cdc.gov/nchs): Statistics on births, marriages, divorces and deaths, prevalence of diseases, nursing homes and nutrition.

The Federal Interagency Council on Statistical Policy's "FedStats" Web site (www.fedstats.gov) provides access to the full range of statistics and information produced for public use.

APPENDIX C: ALGORITHMS FOR AGGREGATION

To describe the aggregation algorithms we use the following color code: Red = Undisclosable singleton county; Pink = Undisclosable supercounty (aggregate of singletons); Blue = Undisclosable supercounty containing one or more disclosable singleton counties; Green = Disclosable singleton county; Yellow = Disclosable supercounty.

The basic algorithm is:

1. **Start:** Color all disclosable counties Green and all undisclosable ones Red.
2. **Eliminate Red:** Examine each Red county according to a pre-selected random order. Merge with an appropriate neighboring county or supercounty, creating a Pink, Blue or Yellow supercounty. Continue until no Red counties remain.
3. **Eliminate Pink:** Examine each Pink supercounty according to a pre-selected random order. Merge with appropriate neighbors until no Pinks remain.
4. **Eliminate Blue:** Merge Blues with neighbors in the manner used for the Reds and the Pinks.
5. **End:** All (super)counties are Green or Yellow.

This procedure is guaranteed to terminate with a disclosable aggregation as long as the State-level data are disclosable.

What distinguishes the **small** and **pure** variants of the algorithm is how they define an appropriate neighbor to merge with. Table 1 lists the merging preferences for the two procedures, and should be read as follows. Consider, for example, the "Eliminate Red" section of the **small** algorithm. The preference is first to merge the Reds with other Reds to form disclosable (Yellow) supercounties. Whenever there are multiple candidates, one is selected either at random or on the basis of similarity of application rates. When all such cases have been exhausted, we next merge the Reds with any Blues that would yield a Yellow. We proceed down the list until all Reds have been merged.

It is clear from examining the table that **small** tends to produce small supercounties while **pure** favors leaving the disclosable counties alone and merging the undisclosable counties among themselves.

Table 1. Merging Rules for the **small** (top) and **pure** (bottom) algorithms.

Eliminate Red	Eliminate Pink	Eliminate Blue
R + R γ Y	P + G γ Y	B + B γ Y
R + B γ Y	P + B γ Y	B + G γ Y
R + G γ Y	P + P γ Y	B + Y γ Y
R + P γ Y	P + Y γ Y	B + B γ B
R + Y γ Y	P + P γ P	B + G γ B
R + R γ P	P + B γ P	B + Y γ B
R + P γ P	P + G γ P	
R + B γ P	P + Y γ P	
R + G γ P		
R + R γ P		

Eliminate Red	Eliminate Pink	Eliminate Blue
R + R γ Y	P + B γ Y	B + B γ Y
R + B γ Y	P + P γ Y	B + Y γ Y
R + P γ Y	P + P γ P	B + G γ Y
R + R γ P	P + Y γ Y	B + B γ B
R + P γ P	P + G γ Y	B + Y γ B
R + Y γ Y	P + B γ B	B + G γ B
R + G γ Y	P + Y γ P	
R + B γ B	P + G γ P	
R + Y γ P		
R + G γ P		

The example in Figure 4 illustrates for a hypothetical small "State" made up of seven States in the Western USA. The data are displayed in the box beside each map. For the original data, WA, NV and NM are undisclosable and marked as Red. We first apply the **small** algorithm to produce an aggregation. Select a random order for merging the Reds, say {WA, NV, NM}. From Table 1, after the "Eliminate Red'" step, we get the supercounties displayed in the second map. Note that the undisclosable NM has forced us to create a Blue region, wasting a disclosable county. We get the aggregation in the third map after the "Eliminate Pink" step and the aggregation in the fourth map after the "Eliminate Blue" step.

At this stage, all the regions are Yellow and hence disclosable. However, we see that {AZ, CA, NV, NM} can be decomposed into disclosable regions CA and {AZ, NV, NM}. This large region was created purely as a consequence of the visiting order we selected for the

Red. Running the **pure** algorithm succeeds in breaking up the {AZ, CA, NV, NM} region, leading to the aggregation displayed in the final map.

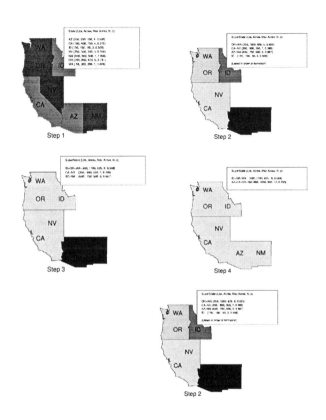

Figure 4. Steps in the Heuristic Aggregation Procedure.

Alan F. Karr is Director of the National Institute of Statistical Sciences, a position he has held since 2000, and prior to which he was Associate Director (1999-2000). He is also Professor of Statistics and Biostatistics at the University of North Carolina at Chapel Hill (since 1993). His research activities are cross-disciplinary collaborations involving statistics and such other fields as transportation, materials science, software engineering, data confidentiality and E-commerce. He is the author of 3 books and more than 70 scientific papers. Karr is a Fellow of the American Statistical Association and the Institute of Mathematical Statistics, and served as a Member of the Army Science Board from 1990 to 1996.

Jaeyong Lee is Assistant Professor of Statistics at the Pennsylvania State University. He holds a Ph.D. in Statistics from Purdue University, and was Postdoctoral Fellow at the National Institute of Statistical Sciences from 1998 to 2000. His research interests span theoretical and computation aspects of nonparametric Bayesian statistical analysis.

Ashish P. Sanil holds B.Sc. and M.Sc. degrees in Mathematics from the Indian Institute of Technology, Kharagpur, India; M.S. in Social and Decision Sciences, M.S. and Ph.D. in Statistics from Carnegie Mellon University. He is a Research Statistician at the National Institute of Statistical Sciences. His research interests involve computationally intensive applications of statistics: confidentiality and data disclosure issues, Internet technologies, and scalable algorithms for the analysis of large data sets.

Sousan Karimi is a program manager at MCNC's Center for Networked Information Discovery and Retrieval (CNIDR), where she leads, designs and develops distributed, interactive Web-based applications. Previously, at the Multimedia Lab at the University of Iowa, she developed multimedia systems for instructional purposes. Ms. Karimi has B.S. in Economics and Computer Science, a M.S. in Computer Science, and has completed her course work towards Ph.D. in Computer Science.

Karen Litwin has a B.S. degree in Computer Science and a B.A. degree in Psychology. She is currently a program manager at MCNC responsible for web-based software development, database application programming and maintenance. She served as the technical lead for the Department of Labor's O*NET, an online occupational system and database.

Joel Hernandez received the B.S. degree in computer science from the University of Central Florida in 1992. He has worked in the areas of system and application software development and networking and telecommunications. Currently he is a Systems Programmer/Analyst at MCNC where he is working on the JumpStart project whose goal is the creation of a signaling protocol and associated architecture for a WDM burst-switching network.

Chapter 12

WebView
A Globally Accessible Geographic Image Database Environment⁎₊

Aidong Zhang and Lei Zhu
Department of Computer Science and Engineering
State University of New York at Buffalo
Buffalo, NY 14260, USA

David Mark
Department of Geography
State University of New York at Buffalo
Buffalo, NY 14260, USA

Abstract: This chapter describes the *WebView* system which supports efficient access to a very large distributed database of geographic images based on content similarity. An integrated metaserver consisting of a metadatabase, metasearch agent, and query manager facilitates such access. *WebView* significantly reduces the amount of time and effort that the user spends in finding the information of interest. We also present approaches to supporting content-based geographic image retrieval. The work is intended to augment image databases held by U.S. government agencies, which now generally must be accessed by location and time of the earth images, rather than similarity of content to a query.

Key words: WWW, Web, content-based retrieval, image databases

1.   INTRODUCTION

   Current airborne and satellite platforms are collecting very large volumes of earth imagery. The U.S. National Aeronautics and Space Administration (NASA) alone are collecting some two terabytes per day! Beginning in 1999 and thereafter, the United States Geological Survey (USGS) has been archiving enormous volumes of data from NASA's Earth Observing System

⁎ This research is supported by National Science Foundation Digital Government Program.
₊ URL of demo: http://picasso.cse.buffalo.edu:8080/META/.

(EOS) and Landsat 7 satellites launched in mid 1999. The archive faces exponential near- and long-term growth in digital data. In the first year after the launch, holdings in the archive were doubled, and this trend will continue with the addition of blocks of declassified intelligence imagery and enormous volumes of digital data from satellite downlinks (see Figure 1).

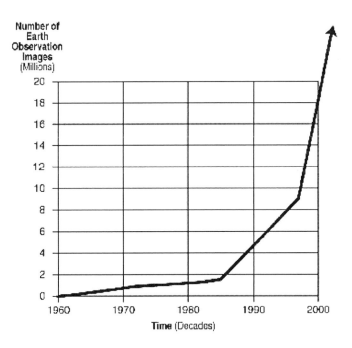

Figure 1. Exponential growth of USGS satellite data archives.

Another example of a large dataset that is managed by the USGS is its digital orthophoto quadrangles (DOQ). These are one-meter resolution ortho-rectified aerial photographs over the United States. By the year 2002 the USGS will have 12 terabytes of DOQ data. This growing dataset is currently stored in 55 megabyte (monochrome) and 150 megabyte (color infrared) files. Providing users with greater access to these data is a challenge. A beginning has been the public browse view available on the TerraServer, developed under a research and development agreement with Microsoft (see http://www.terraserver.com). However, TerraServer provides access only by latitude and longitude, by place name, and by clicking on an index map.

New methods are needed to allow search of very large databases of earth imagery based on image content. To deal with the increasing pool of geographic image data and the inherent complexity in visual data querying, it is crucial to carefully select database sites in order to support efficient queries. Designing a metaserver on top of various geographic image databases can help solve the problem. Given a query, the metaserver first ranks the database sites and then distributes the queries to the selected databases.

In recent research, database selection has focused on directing text queries to databases. For example, web search engines such as Lycos and AltaVista currently create web indices in their search engines by periodically scanning potential web sites and using the text information in their resident HTML pages. Techniques from information retrieval [ODL93,SEKN92] are used for intelligent resource site selection. Examples of such systems include GLOSS (from Stanford) [GGMT94,GGM95] and HARVEST (from University of Colorado) [BDH+94]. These systems employ statistical approaches to record the frequency of occurrence of text keywords from known sites to construct an index of relevant sites for directing a query. More recently, research on image database selection has appeared. MetaSEEk [CSBB97] is a meta-image search engine designed to query large distributed online visual information sources. NetView [ZCSSM98] provides a framework for designing an integrated large-scale distributed image databases.

This chapter describes the *WebView* system which supports efficient access to a very large distributed database of geographic images based on content similarity. An integrated metaserver consisting of a metadatabase, metasearch agent, and query manager facilitates such access. *WebView* significantly reduces the amount of time and effort that the user spends in finding the information of interest. We also present approaches to supporting content-based retrieval for geographic image databases. The work is intended to augment image databases held by U.S. government agencies, which now generally must be accessed by location and time of the earth images, rather than similarity of content to a query.

2. SYSTEM ARCHITECTURE

Figure 2 shows the overall architecture of the system. The three main components of the system include: i) image databases at remote sites, ii) a metaserver consisting of a metadatabase, a search agent and a query manager, and iii) a set of visual display applications at the client machines. In this framework, a visual query submitted by a client is distributed to relevant databases through the metaserver. The metaserver selects the target database site(s) by consulting the metadatabase which houses abstract data about individual image databases. The query is then posed to the selected databases in an acceptable form. The searching mechanism of the local database searches its repository for possible answers to the posed query. The answer is then fed back to the client.

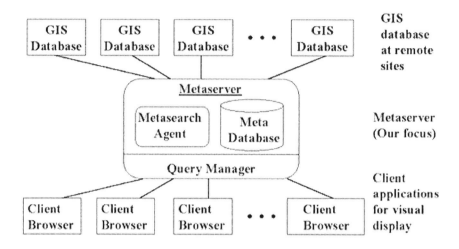

Figure 2. Overall architecture of the system.

The role of the metaserver is to accept user queries, extract the information in the query for suitable matching of the metadata, produce a ranking of the database sites, and distribute the queries to selected databases. The challenging problem is to determine database relevance for visual queries without detailed examination of all images of database for possible matches. Our approach is to extract central metadata to represent the individual databases.

The metadatabase houses both templates and statistical data. A hierarchy of the templates representing image clusters can be built to support efficient retrieval. A template at a higher level represents the coarse features that contain all the features its child templates represent. We observed that such templates can adequately represent the database's content.

The metaserver relates the databases' content to the templates by calculating each database's statistical metadata with respect to the templates. Various statistical data can be computed from the distributions of the similarities between database images and the templates and stored in the metadatabase. The statistical data represent the visual relationships between the databases and templates. The relevant databases for a particular query are determined by a two-level process. This involves determining the similarity of the query with metadatabase templates, then ranking the database sites, based on the visual relationships recorded about the databases and templates. Various database selection approaches can be developed corresponding to the statistical data. We have investigated two approaches, namely, mean-based and histogram-based approaches, for database selection [CSWZ98].

Figure 3 shows a prototype system including seven local geographic databases. At Step 1, a user query is sent to the metaserver, which matches the query to templates with the corresponding metadata of remote databases to select a ranked list of relevant databases for the query. At Step 2, the query is forwarded to the selected databases. The matched images from each selected database are sent to the user.

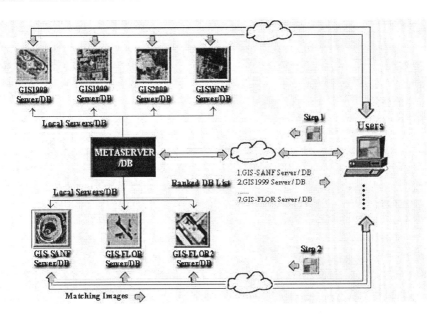

Figure 3. Prototype system including seven local geographic databases.

3. RETRIEVAL FROM REMOTE GEOGRAPHIC DATABASES

Retrieving geographic images differs in many ways from other applications. Computational representation of geographic content is the challenge. The challenge is compounded by the uniqueness of geographic images, such as presence of spatial autocorrelation, scale-dependency of content, and human cognition of content. These are fundamental issues in handling geographic images and need to be thoughtfully addressed in implementation of geographic image retrieval systems.

We have identified a multi-scale data representation method that is most appropriate for geographic images, using wavelet transforms [SZB99]. The wavelet transform process decomposes an image into a low frequency, coarse scale image and several high frequency images that are sensitive to directions. The transform can perform recursively thus representing geographic content at multiple scales. The transformed images require much less storage than that of original images while the original information can be fully recovered.

Wavelet transform has gained much attention in recent years. Different forms of wavelet transform have been developed and some are used in geographic image retrieval to reduce the amount of data needed to be processed. However, little is done to identify the transforms that are most appropriate for geographic images. Geographic content depends on scales. Identifying optimal levels of wavelet transform allows feature extraction to be performed only at the most representative scales. This treatment eliminates redundant processes yet maintains the desired geographic content. Another question related to scale is the size of the sample image in relation to the size of database images. This is a research topic less investigated in a formalized manner. Given the fact that the size of database images is predetermined, the size of the sample image should meet certain criteria to support representation of a particular content and in the mean time to assure search efficiency. Figure 4 shows the features calculated using a wavelet transform at different scales.

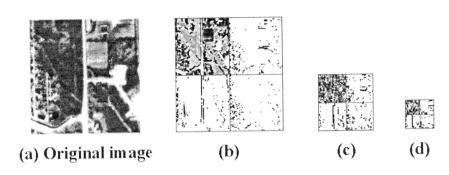

(a) Original image   **(b)**   **(c)**   **(d)**

Figure 4. Multi-resolution wavelet representation of an airphoto image: a) original image; wavelet representation at b) scale 1; c) scale 2; d) scale 3

3.1   Keyblock-based Geographic Image Retrieval

We now present a new approach termed *Keyblock* for content-based geographic image retrieval, which is a generalization of the text-based information retrieval technology in the image domain. In this approach, methods for extracting comprehensive geographic image features are provided, which are based on the frequency and correlation of representative blocks, termed keyblocks, of the geographic image database. Keyblocks, which are analogous to index terms in text document retrieval, can be constructed by exploiting various clustering algorithms.

The keyblock-based image retrieval includes the following main stages:

(1) *Codebook generation*: generates codebooks that contain keyblocks of different resolutions. Although objects are good candidates to be considered as visual keywords in the images, object recognition for natural images is still an unsolved problem and may remain to be an open problem in the long term. With a limited degree of sacrificing the accuracy, one practical approach is to segment the images into smaller regions, and then select a subset of representative regions using clustering algorithms. These representative regions can be used as the keyblocks to represent the image contents.

(2) *Image encoding*: for each image in the database as well as in the query, decomposes it into blocks. Then, for each of the blocks, find the closest entry in the codebook and store the index correspondingly. Each image is then a matrix of indices, which can be treated as 1-dimensional codes of the keyblocks in the codebook. This property is similar to a text document, which is considered as a linear list of keywords in text-based information retrieval. The image can also be re-constructed by using the codebook.

(3) *Image feature representation and retrieval*: extract comprehensive image features, which are based on the frequency of the keyblocks within the image, and provide retrieval techniques to support content-based image retrieval. There are four main components in this stage:

- Database $D = \{I_1, \dots I_j, \dots, I_M\}$: a list of encoded images;
- Codebook $C = \{c_1, \dots c_i, \dots, c_N\}$: a list of keyblocks;
- CBIR model $\varphi = (f,s)$: f is a feature extraction mapping which generates the feature vector for each image, and s is a similarity measure between the feature vectors of two images;
- Q: a set of visual queries, where each query has a feature vector that is similar to the feature vector of an image.

Figure 5 illustrates a flowchart of the keyblock approach. This idea was initially explored in [Lei00b,Lei00a]. This chapter expands the idea and apply it to the geographic image domain.

3.2 GIS Codebook Generation

Keyblock generation is critical to our approach. Two general domains are considered in our approach:

- *Original space*: with a limited degree of sacrificing the accuracy, one practical approach is to partition/segment the images into smaller blocks, and then select a subset of representative blocks, which can be used as the keyblocks to represent the images.

- *Feature space*: another practical approach is to extract low-level feature vectors, such as color, texture, and shape, from image segments/blocks, and then select a subset of representative feature vectors, which can be used as the keyblocks to represent the images.

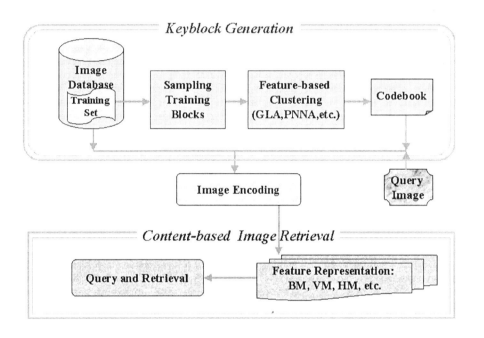

Figure 5. Flowchart of the keyblock-based image retrieval.

We design various clustering approaches to generate keyblocks from either the original image space or the feature space. The keyblocks are selected from the centroids of the clusters of either the original space or feature space. Fundamentally, let $C = \{c_1, \ldots c_i, \ldots, c_N\}$ be the codebook of the keyblocks representing the images, where N is the codebook size and $c_i, 1 \le i \le N$, are the keyblocks. Let F be a mapping:

$$F : R^k \to C = \{c_1, \ldots c_i, \ldots, c_N \mid c_i \in R^k \},$$

where R^k is the Euclidean space of dimension k. Given a sequence $T = \{t_1, \ldots t_j, \ldots, t_l \mid t_j \in R^k \}$, the mapping F gives rise to a partition of T which consists of N cells $P = \{p_1, \ldots p_i, \ldots, p_N\}$, where $p_i = \{t \mid t \in T, F(t) = c_i\}$. For a given distortion function $d(t_j, c_i)$, which is the distance between the input t_j and output code c_i (For example, the Euclidean distance, which is also called the square error), an optimal mapping must satisfy the following conditions:

- *Nearest Neighbor Condition*: For each p_i, if $t \in p_i$, then $d(t,c_i) \leq d(t,c_j)$, for all $j \neq i$.

- *Centroid Condition*: For a given partition P, the optimal code vectors satisfy $c_i = (\sum_{t \in p_i} t) / k_i$, $1 \leq i \leq N$, k_i is the cardinality of p_i.

There are a variety of clustering algorithms available that can be applied to different types of data sets [NH94,WYM97,ZRL96,PFG97, SCZ98,SCZ00]. We use a practical and efficient algorithm. In this algorithm, clustering is applied to the set of data obtained from a training set of the images (either from the original space or the feature space) and then the centroid of each cluster is used as a codebook entry. Two popularly used algorithms are Generalized Lloyd Algorithm (GLA) [GG92] and Pairwise Nearest Neighbor Algorithm (PNNA). We use an integrated approach of the two algorithms to efficiently generate the codebook of keyblocks. Furthermore, we also incorporate the GIS domain knowledge into the keyblock generation process. To generate codebooks that reflect the semantic content of the geographic features, we adopt a 3-stage keyblock generation strategy, which is illustrated in Figure 6.

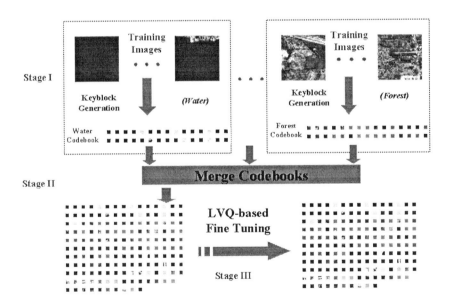

Figure 6. Three stages of the knowledge-based keyblock generation.

At stage I, for each geographic feature (For example, for geographic image database GEO used in our testing, there are five geographic features: water, agriculture areas, forest, grass lands, and residential areas.), a corresponding codebook will first be generated. For each geographic feature, domain experts only need to provide some training images, and then the clustering algorithm mentioned above is used to select the keyblocks. At stage II, codebooks generated in the stage I will be merged to a big codebook. This codebook has keyblocks of different semantic meaning and can be used in image coding and decoding. At stage III, a fine-tuning process, termed learning vector quantization (LVQ)-based approach, will be used.

In our experiments, to generate keyblocks, 405 remote-sensing images are randomly selected as the training set from our GIS test bed. Three block sizes, 2×2, 4×4, and 8×8, are used. Intuitively, blocks with different sizes may capture information with different granularity. Usually smaller blocks exploit local information of the image content, such as edges and regions with high spatial frequency. Larger blocks may provide correlation among neighboring sub-blocks as well as an overview of the global variation.

For each block size, experiments have been performed to generate codebooks of three different sizes 256, 512, and 1024. In the implementation, the distortion, which is the objective function for optimization when generating a codebook, is the square error commonly used for image compression. The square error is the Euclidean distance between the vectors of the intensity values of an original block and that of the corresponding keyblock. In short, the testing is conducted with 9 (3 block sizes × 3 codebook sizes) codebooks. After the codebooks are generated, all images in the database are then encoded correspondingly. As an example, Figure 7 shows an image and its reconstructed images with different codebooks.

To encode an image based on the codebook, the image is partitioned or segmented into blocks and then each block (or its feature vector) is replaced by the index of the nearest entry in the codebook. Now each image is a matrix of indices of the keyblocks. We can re-construct the image using the codebook to measure if the codebook is properly selected. To reconstruct the image, each index is replaced by the code vector in the codebook, which is actually a lookup table. Obviously, the reconstructed image is only an approximation of the original one. Figure 8 illustrates the general procedure for image encoding and decoding.

4. KEYBLOCK-BASED IMAGE FEATURE REPRESENTATION AND RETRIEVAL

Image feature representation models similar to text-based retrieval models can be designed in this context. We have designed various models suitable for geographic images:

- Models based on single keyblocks: the features are calculated based on the appearance of individual keyblocks (termed uni-block models). In particular, we have designed Boolean Model (BM), Vector Model (VM), and Histogram Model (HM).
- Models based on multiple keyblocks: the features are calculated based on the correlations between keyblocks in images. Our purpose is to extract feature vectors that not only include the occurrence information of blocks but also carry context information of the neighboring blocks. We call such models n-block model, where n is the number of blocks considered. Particularly interested models are bi-block and tri-block models.
- Models based on combined features: The above models capture different image content under various contexts. For example, the uni-block model only considers single keyblock's occurrence, while the bi-block and tri-block models consider multiple keyblocks' co-occurrence. It is reasonable to combine them to improve the retrieval performance.

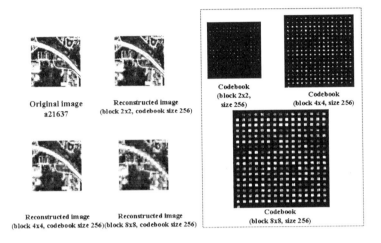

Original image
a21637

Reconstructed image
(block 2x2, codebook size 256)

Reconstructed image
(block 4x4, codebook size 256)

Reconstructed image
(block 8x8, codebook size 256)

Codebook
(block 2x2, size 256)

Codebook
(block 4x4, size 256)

Codebook
(block 8x8, size 256)

Figure 7. A raw image and the encoded images after re-construction with different codebooks. Each codebook is obtained with the same training set.

Codebook (a list of keyblocks)

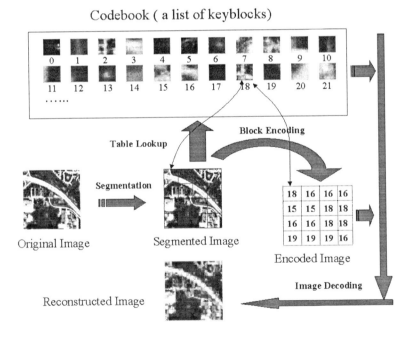

Figure 8. The general procedure of image encoding and decoding.

We have conducted comprehensive experiments to demonstrate the effectiveness of these models. In the GIS domain, users are more interested in ``subimage match'': given a small image pattern which represents kinds of geographic features such as forest and water, find images having similar geographic features and mark out those areas. It is relatively similar to object recognition. We compared these models with the popularly used wavelet-based models.

For wavelet transforms, first, we use the Nona Tree [SRGZ97] to decompose each image to subimages recursively until a certain subimage size (in this experiment, it is 32×32.) is reached. Then, based on these subimages as well as those original images, different types of wavelet transforms such as Gabor, Haar and Daubechies are applied to extract texture features of images at different scales/resolutions from fine to coarse. Similarly, for codebook-based feature extraction and retrieval, we first use the Nona Tree to decompose each encoded image, and then conduct models such as the uni-block model, bi-block model, tri-block model and feature combination model respectively on the subimage level.

There are 33 query images which are subimages of 32×32 chosen from the images in the database by GIS experts from the National Center for Geographic Information and Analysis (NCGIA) at Buffalo. These query images are divided into 5 categories: agriculture, grass, forest, residential area, and water. Their feature vectors are generated correspondingly. For each query, the average precision corresponding to the top 1, 2,..., up to 40 retrieved images is calculated. Finally, the average precision is calculated over all queries.

Figure 9. Example of retrieval results on an agriculture image in GEO.

Figure 9 shows the retrieval results of an agriculture image. The query image is at the upper-left corner. The returned images as well as the marked areas of our approach are apparently better than those of the Gabor wavelet. Figure 10 indicates that the performance of our approach outperforms the wavelet transforms. For example, in the case of Feature Combination Model, the average precision is always 20% to 30% higher than wavelet transforms.

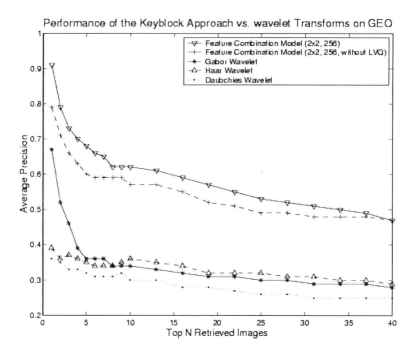

Figure 10. Average precision: comparison of keyblock approach with Wavelet Transforms.

5. CONCLUSION

We have developed the system framework WebView to support global query access to various geographic image databases over the Internet. This framework includes the creation of a metaserver and its major components: the metadatabase, the metasearch agent and the query manager. A new approach for content-based geographic image retrieval is also proposed by exploiting analogous text-based IR techniques. This approach provides methods for extracting image features that are not in favor of any particular low-level feature such as color or texture. Instead, the features extracted for an image is a comprehensive description of the content of the image that is more semantics-related than the existing lower-level features. We have conducted substantial experiments to demonstrate the effectiveness of the proposed approach. Results have demonstrated that our approach is superior not only to color histogram and color coherent vector approaches that are in favor of color features, but also to Haar, Daubechies, and Gabor wavelet texture approaches which have been commonly used for texture-based geographic image retrieval.

REFERENCES

[BDH+94] M. Bowman, P. Danzig, D. Hardy, U. Manber, and M. Scwartz. Harvest: A scalable, customizable discovery and access system. Technical Report CU-CS732-94, Department of Computer Science, University of Colorado-Boulder, 1994.

[CSBB97] S. Chang, J. Smith, M. Beigi, and A. Benitez. Visual Information Retrieval from Large Distributed Online Repositories. Communications of the ACM, 40(12):63-71, December 1997.

[CSWZ98] W. Chang, G. Sheikholeslami, J. Wang, and A. Zhang. Data resource selection in distributed visual information systems. IEEE Transactions on Knowledge and Data Engineering, 10(6):926-946, November/December 1998.

[GG92] A. Gersho and R. M. Gray. Vector Quantization and Signal Compression. Kluwer Academic Publishers, 1992.

[GGM95] L. Gavarno and H. Garcia-Molina. Generalizing Gloss to Vector-Space Databases and Broker Hierarchies. In Proceedings of the 21st International Conference on Very Large Data Bases, pages 78-89, 1995.

[GGMT94] L. Gavarno, H. Garcia-Molina, and A. Tomasic. The Effectiveness of Gloss for the Text Database Discovery Problems. In Proceedings of the ACM SIGMOD'94, pages 126-137, Minneapolis, May 1994.

[Lei00a] Lei Zhu, Aibing Rao and Aidong Zhang. Advanced feature extraction for keyblock-based image retrieval. In Proceedings of International Workshop on Multimedia Information Retrieval (MIR2000), pages 179-183, Los Angeles, California, USA, November 4 2000.

[Lei00b] Lei Zhu, Aidong Zhang, Aibing Rao and Rohini Srihari. Keyblock: An approach for content-based image retrieval. In Proceedings of ACM Multimedia 2000, pages 157-166, Los Angeles, California, USA, Oct 30 - Nov 3 2000.

[NH94] R. T. Ng and J. Han. Efficient and Effective Clustering Methods for Spatial Data Mining. In Proceedings of the 20th VLDB Conference, pages 144-155, Santiago, Chile, 1994.

[ODL93] K. Obraczka, P. Danzig, and S-H Li. Internet Resource Discovery Services. IEEE Computer Magazine, 26(9):8-22, 1993.

[PFG97] E.J. Pauwels, P. Fiddelaers, and L. Van Gool. DOG-based unsupervized clustering for CBIR. In Proceedings of the 2nd International Conference on Visual Information Systems, pages 13-20, San Diego, California, December 1997.

[SCZ98] G. Sheikholeslami, S. Chatterjee, and A. Zhang. WaveCluster: A Multi-Resolution Clustering Approach for Very Large Spatial Databases. In Proceedings of the 24th VLDB conference, pages 428-439, August 1998.

[SCZ00] G. Sheikholeslami, S. Chatterjee, and A. Zhang. WaveCluster: A Wavelet-Based Clustering Approach for Multidimensional Data in Very Large Databases. The VLDB Journal, 8(4):289-304, February 2000.

[SEKN92] M. Schwartz, A. Emtage, B. Kahle, and C. Neuman. A Comparison of Internet Resource Discovery Approaches. Computing Systems, 5(4):461-493, 1992.

[SRGZ97] G. Sheikholeslami, E. Remias, J. Guo, and A. Zhang. Image decomposition and representation in large image database systems. The Journal of Visual Communication and Image Representation, 8(2):167-181, June 1997.

[SZB99] G. Sheikholeslami, A. Zhang, and L. Bian. A Multi-Resolution Content-Based Retrieval System for Geographic Images. GeoInformatica, An International Journal on Advances of Computer Science for Geographic Information Systems, 3(2):109-139, June 1999.

[WYM97] Wei Wang, Jiong Yang, and Richard Muntz. STING: A Statistical Information Grid Approach to Spatial Data Mining. In Proceedings of the 23rd VLDB Conference, pages 186-195, Athens, Greece, 1997.

[ZCSSM98] A. Zhang, W. Chang, G. Sheikholeslami, and T. Syeda-Mahmood. *Netview*: A Framework for Integration of Large-Scale Distributed Visual Databases. IEEE Multimedia, 5(3):47-59, July-September 1998.

[ZRL96] Tian Zhang, Raghu Ramakrishnan, and Miron Livny. BIRCH: An Efficient Data Clustering Method for Very Large Databases. In Proceedings of the 1996 ACM SIGMOD International Conference on Management of Data, pages 103-114, Montreal, Canada, 1996.

Aidong Zhang received her Ph.D degree in computer science from Purdue University, West Lafayette, Indiana, in 1994. She was an assistant professor in the Department of Computer Science and Engineering at State University of New York at Buffalo, Buffalo, New York, 14260, from 1994 to 1999. She has been an associate professor in the Department of Computer Science and Engineering at State University of New York at Buffalo, Buffalo, New York, 14260, since 1999. Her research interests include content-based image retrieval, geographical information systems, distributed database systems, multimedia database systems, digital libraries, and data mining. She serves on the editorial boards of the International Journal of Multimedia Tools and Applications, International Journal of Distributed and Parallel Databases, and ACM SIGMOD DiSC (Digital Symposium Collection). She has also served on various conference program committees. Dr. Zhang is a recipient of the National Science Foundation CAREER award.

David M. Mark is a Professor of Geography at the University at Buffalo, the State University of New York, and is the Director of the Buffalo site of the National Center for Geographic Information and Analysis (NCGIA); he has been a Research Scientist with the NCGIA since its inception. Mark received his Ph.D. from Simon Fraser University (Canada) in 1997 and has been on the faculty at UB since 1981. Mark is Project Director of the University at Buffalos NSF-funded Integrative Graduate Education and Research Traineeship (IGERT) project in Geographic Information Science, and is a member of UB's Center for Cognitive Science. David Mark has written or co-authored over 200 publications, including about 75 refereed articles, 3 edited books, 20 book chapters, 64 conference proceedings articles, and 27 technical reports. He has made about 200 academic presentations, almost three-quarters at professional meetings, and the others as invited talks at universities and government agencies. Mark was involved in the founding of the University Consortium for Geographic Information Science, and later served as President of the UCGIS (1998). Previously, Mark served as Vice-chair (1987-88) and Chair (1988-89) of the Geographic Information Systems Specialty Group of the Association of American Geographers and Chair of the Technology Interest Group, Canadian Cartographic Association (1987-89). He also has served on numerous international editorial boards and program committees, and was program co-chair for Auto Carto 10 (1991), COSIT'99, and GIScience 2000. Mark's research has been funded by the National Science Foundation, the National Institutes of Health, the National Imagery and Mapping Agency, and other agencies, and he has served on several advisory panels at the NSF. Mark's research interests focus on many aspects of geographic information science, notably geospatial ontology, spatial cognition and language, history of geographic information systems, human-computer interaction, digital elevation models, and computer mapping.

Chapter 13

The Federal Government
Meeting The Needs Of Society In The Information Age

Yolanda L. Comedy
IBM, 1301 K Street, NW, Washington, DC 20005 USA

Abstract: The Federal government has two roles in the information age: 1) to lead the society as we define our vision, goals, desired transformation, and strategies in light of the opportunities and newly created problems associated with information technology tools; and 2) to transform the government by becoming savvy users, key innovators and drivers of change with information technology tools.

Key words: information technology, federal government, democracy, information technology research and development, e-government

1.   INTRODUCTION

Information technology is currently a revolutionary force. In many ways, it has transformed our society in the United States and has touched our nation and the world not only economically and politically, but also socially and culturally. The use of information technology tools has become pervasive and with this technology new and wonderful ideas and excitement about future possibilities have emerged as well as a complex set of policy issues. And at the core of many of these possibilities and issues is the federal government. The government is a key player in issues such as access, appropriate use, research, and organizational change. The government, especially the federal government, has found itself at the forefront of many policies, strategies, decisions, and regulations related to information technology. At the same time, the government faces the complex challenge of revolutionizing itself to make pertinent, accessible, and adaptable use of information technology tools for its own benefit and the benefit of the citizens it is designed to serve.

The challenges for the federal government range from it's role in funding and doing the research necessary to help advance information technology, to helping to solve the issues of privacy and security, to figuring out its own technological needs and how to blend those with it's present organizational structure. In essence, the challenge of the federal government is two-fold. First, it is a catalyst for the change that has occurred in the so-called "information age." The government has a responsibility for helping to "manage" the transformation of society spurred by information technology tools. The government is critical to such issues as ensuring that 1) information technology tools are accessible; 2) citizens' rights to privacy and security are not compromised; 3) the educational system can affordably use information technology tools; 4) research remains constant and futuristic; and a plethora of other issues that have and will emerge. The policy decisions associated with these issues are best accomplished with government-industry-academic-non-profit organization partnerships. Second, the government must manage it's own ability to use the tools of the information age, in a timely and economically sound manner. Citizens have grown to expect that the use of technology tools be both demand-driven and user-friendly. It is an exciting, yet complex venture.

2. THE GOVERNMENT'S ROLE IN RESEARCH, INNOVATION AND POLICY IN THE INFORMATION AGE

The tools of the information age were the product of a strong federal government focus on research and development. The federal government funded most of the basic research that led to the creation of information technology tools and it is critical that the government continues to focus both on knowledge creation and funding for basic research. *Technology in the National Interest* notes " [f]or more than 200 years, the Federal government has played a vital role in establishing a scientific and technological infrastructure that has contributed substantially to U.S. economic growth and the competitive success of American industry."[1] Yet, ensuring that the federal government maintains this strong role is a constant concern. Scientists, technologists and industry leaders pay close attention to the funding source and focus of basic research. The Government plays a balancing act with limited resources, realizing both the importance of providing funding for the nation's short-term needs and desires as well as realizing the need to plan and provide for the long-term. It is a difficult issue, but it is certain that a strong, prosperous nation of the future demands a national strategy that is focussed, realistic and well funded.

"A new, more sophisticated, and more complex role for government is emerging, one that makes better use of resources, and that shares more decision making with states and with the private sector. New policies should focus on long-term investments in knowledge-based infrastructure—the capacity of the entire system of private entrepreneurship, human resources, investment and enhancing frontiers of technical knowledge—using tools that encourage and enable rather than direct the deployment of these assets."[2] Government becomes the facilitator of the innovation enterprise.

While most Americans seem to agree that science and technology is important to this nation's prosperity and well being, there is certainly an ideological struggle between those that believe that market forces will keep industry innovative and our economy strong versus those that believe that the government must play a role in the innovation process by funding the basic research that industry requires to develop new products. I am firmly in the camp that believes that the federal government as well as local and state government must play a strong role in funding basic research and providing the "seed corn" for tomorrow's discoveries. "The information technology industry expends the bulk of its resources, both financial and human, on rapidly bringing products to market."[3] While the IT industry does spend money on R&D, it is constrained in making long-term investments based on two realities: the fast turn around time necessary to get products to market and intense global competition. Therefore, the government's role in information technology research and development is key.

2.1   Globalisation

Presently, the world is strongly interconnected which in part is a result of information technology tools and other technologies. This situation creates an interesting and challenging policy arena in that policy-makers must constantly work and rework their strategies. It is impossible and in many cases undesirable for technologies to remain within any geographic border. Therefore, national policies must take this reality in to account and create strategies that are international in scope. Realizing that all innovation will not occur or stay confined within U.S. borders, our policy leaders must foster relationships to cooperate and collaborate, understand the policies of other nations and quickly adapt to new international discoveries and the complex policy-making needs that often accompany them. Further, as Lewis Branscomb and Richard Florida[4] note, policy-makers must strive to make the U.S. the most attractive place for innovators and innovations. In part, this is why federally funded research is so critical to U.S. economic strategy.

2.2   Federal Information Technology Research and Development Management

Management of a science and technology policy for the nation is critical. The White House Office of Science and Technology Policy and President's Science Advisor helps to play this role.[5] To help ensure future generations of information technologies, the National Coordination Office (NCO) for Information Technology Research and Development (ITRD) (formerly the NCO for Computing, Information, and Communications (CIC)) was created to coordinate planning, budget, and assessment activities for the Federal information technology research and development program. The NCO reports to the White House Office of Science and Technology Policy and the National Science and Technology Council and works with 11 participating Federal agencies through the Interagency Working Group (IWG) on IT R&D "to prepare and implement the Nation's $2 B IT R&D budget crosscut, helping to shape the Nation's 21st century information infrastructure and to ensure continued U.S. technological leadership. Since no one Federal agency cites IT R&D as its primary mission, it is vital for agencies to coordinate, collaborate, and cooperate to help increase the overall effectiveness and productivity of Federal IT R&D."[6]

The Federal interagency Information Technology Research and Development Coordinating Groups are focused on the following research areas: High End Computing (HEC), Large Scale Networking (LSN), High Confidence Software and Systems (HCSS), Human Computer Interface and Information Management (HCI&IM), Software Design and Productivity (SDP) and Social, Economic, and Workforce Implications of IT (SEW).

2.3   The President's Information Technology Advisory Committee

The NCO also supports the President's Information Technology Advisory Committee (PITAC). Initially appointed by President Clinton, PITAC provides advice to the Administration regarding the Nation's challenges and constraints in information technology. The committee is comprised of approximately 23 members from industry, academia, and the non-profit sector.[7]

In its report, *Information Technology Research: Investing in Our Future,*[8] the Committee advocates increasing federally funded basic long-term, high-risk information technology research and development. PITAC notes that information technology can help transform our society and recommends both technical and socio-economic research and policy priorities. Finding that the federal information technology research and development investment is inadequate and too heavily focused on near-term problems, PITAC recommends creating a strategic initiative in long-term information technology research and development. Specifically, the Committee recommends increased research in software development, scalable information infrastructure, high-end computing and the socio-economic impact of information technology. PITAC's recommendations have received strong bipartisan support and resulted in increased federal funding for information technology research and development.

2.4   Information Technology Policy Issues

The Government has been a key player in policy issues that have surfaced due to the information age. Citizens have been keenly aware of issues such as the possibility that information tools may cause greater socio-economic divides in this nation; the fear that personal privacy will be decreased or lost; the possibility that unnecessary regulations will hinder the marketplace; and the concern that children can gain access to inappropriate materials, such as pornography. The tools of the information age require an examination of possible unintended consequences and of our society's goals and philosophies in light of the new technologies with which we live.

The information age has forced new questions with which the government must grapple. The Federal government must intervene regarding the increasing cases of identity theft that are occurring, in part, because of information technology tools? The Federal Trade Commission sponsors conferences, handles consumer complaints, and provides consumers with information about identity theft—the Department of Justice, Secret Service Agency, Federal Bureau of Investigation must all deal with this heightened problem.

The federal government has been a force in ensuring that our nation's citizens have access to some of the key tools of the information age, especially personal computers. The Department of Education has funded programs to increase the number of computers and access to the Internet in the classroom and in community centers. Several agencies have been involved in the creation of Community Technology Centers, designed to ensure that all citizens have access to personal computers and the Internet. The Federal Communications Commission (FCC) administers the e-rate program to "insure that all children including those who do not have computers or Internet access at home will have the high-tech tools necessary for the new digital economy."[9] In addition, the government has tried to spur innovative uses of information technology tools through programs such as the Department of Commerce's Technology Opportunity Program (TOP).[10]

The federal government is beginning to sponsor and do research on socio-economic issues associated with information technology. Policy issues abound from the type of education required in the information age and the type of workforce that will be needed, to the social implications of computer use and Internet interactions and the aspects of privacy that the society is or is not willing to forego. Privacy and security are key components to the success of information technology tools. Without a high degree of trust in the systems established, people will have a diminished interest in using information technology tools. With the amount of information now available electronically, people want assurances on issues such as who has access to medical records, how documents can be signed electronically, and maintaining intellectual property rights.

The Federal government is in a unique position to help drive the twenty-first century workforce. Science and technology careers should be promoted, either through the use of information dissemination or economic and other incentives for people who choose to study math and science. Making sure that everyone in our nation has the opportunity to participate (and benefit) from science and technology is critical in order to meet equity goals and international competition. The best employees will know both how to use information technology tools and how to create and apply those tools.

The government's role in research, innovation and policy in the information age is significant. The extent to which the government meets the challenge of sponsoring and doing research, investing in innovation and formulating well-defined strategies and policies is critical to the impact that information technology tools will have on our nation. This important role is further complicated by the government's challenge to be leaders of technology and get it's own house in order.

3.   TRANSFORMING THE GOVERNMENT IN THE INFORMATION AGE

The President's Information Technology Advisory Committee noted the importance of transforming government through the use of information technology tools in order to make services and information more easily accessible to all citizens no matter their location, level of computer literacy or physical capabilities. Citizens will increasingly demand that government provide the same level of technological access to information as the private sector. Services are demanded such as "one-stop shopping, with documents and forms that are easily accessible and able to be completed and returned electronically; requests that are quickly and clearly answered; and critical life-saving needs are able to be communicated and solved using technology tools."[11]

3.1 Transforming Services and Communication

In order to accommodate our twenty-first century lifestyle, the public will expect government services to at least equal business services. Convenience, ease-of-use, and immediate to short-term response will be demanded of many governments throughout the world. Data will need to be readily available to respond to needs as fundamental as filling in tax forms on-line to life-threatening needs such as managing a potentially devastating forest fire. The public cannot and should not endure a twentieth century response to twenty-first century problems. The ability to receive simultaneous responses, to find data easily, and to have human-free interaction are all mainstays of the business world created through information technology. If we can shop on-line, find pertinent information on the Internet, and chat with our friends and family, we will also expect to fill out government forms, find government statistics or hours of operation and communicate with the government agencies without ever leaving our homes or places of employment. The government must have a serious strategy and adequate funding to achieve these goals.

In some ways, federal, state and local governments have been responsive to this problem. We can fill out our tax forms on-line and receive our refund checks through direct bank deposit and we can access some information on-line. Yet the services are not pervasive. There is a monumental difference in what various levels and locales of government can provide. And furthermore there is a tendency toward an arduous process rather than the convenience and ease-of-use that the public craves. One stop shopping is an important goal of the federal government, but many issues make it difficult to impossible to provide.

At present, governments lack the data storage capacity, tools necessary to rapidly access data, and the capability to make the data available to all citizens. There is also a lack of the critical workforce skills necessary to solving these complex constraints.[12] In addition, to make it all happen, information systems will need to be upgraded, new tools will need to be created, and data will need to be located, centralized and be made easy to disburse upon demand. In addition, it is critical that data be secure and that citizens feel safe from data misuse. It is a lot to ask, but nothing less will be acceptable.

3.2   Constraints to Transforming Services and Communication

3.2.1   Skilled Employees

Local, state and federal governments have historically been reputed for lacking top-quality service, although many work diligently to provide citizens with excellent and efficient service. In the information age the government has the added burden of establishing information age service, which requires not only sufficient data and effective management, but also on-line access and one-stop "shopping." To provide service that is information age compliant, governments need multiple tools. First, a technologically savvy workforce is critical. Several types of employees are important. Employees with high-level technical skills are needed to create or adapt tools for government use and to stay abreast of the latest and most effective information technology tools. Employees that understand policy issues associated with the information age will constantly be necessary to ensure that there are procedures and policies, which will help maintain citizens' privacy and security. It is also a requirement to have employees that can manage systems and provide tools to facilitate data input and dissemination in a timely manner as well as to help choose and manage the best long-term information technology solutions. To further complicate the situation, as is historically the case, government must compete with other sectors that also need employees with the same or similar skill-sets.

3.2.2   The data

There is a plethora of data collected by government. The data collected by the federal government is collected and used across agencies for a variety of purposes. The data is disparate with a wide variation in method of collection, analysis of data, use of data, dissemination purposes, etc. Agencies are often stove-piped, communicating better internally than across agencies. In some ways this is an unfortunate occurrence, which makes it difficult to effectively manage data in the information age. On the other hand, the society has traditionally demanded that the government not be given the freedom to collect large amounts of information on organizations or individuals with no apparent cause. As discussed in the section, *Democracy in the Information Age*, this is but one of the many issues related to information technology tools that we must confront as a society.

Information technology tools, along with effective strategies and adequate skilled personnel, can certainly be a catalyst for change in government operations. The government is often slower than industry in taking advantage of information technology tools. Among the constraints are "the scale of the Federal enterprise, the lack of incentives (or the powerful disincentives) to cut costs, the curtailment of capital investments, the cumbersome Federal acquisition process, the risk-averse nature of government management, and conflicting and complex legal requirements for both openness and privacy."[13] In addition, the proclivity toward a short-term focus and an incoherent budget process increases the constraints for government to take full advantage of a much-needed change in process.

3.3 Addressing the Constraints

In order to begin to address the federal government's full submersion into the information age, the federal government has created a variety of vehicles of change, including the Federal Chief Information Officer (CIO) Council and it's portal, FirstGov. The Federal CIO Council was created by executive order in July 1996. The Council "serves as the principal interagency forum for improving practices in the design, modernization, use, sharing, and performance of Federal Government agency information resources. The Council's role includes developing recommendations for information technology management policies, procedures, and standards; identifying opportunities to share information resources; and assessing and addressing the needs of the Federal Government's information technology workforce"[14] The council has dealt with such pertinent issues as: electronic government, accessibility, privacy, security, and management challenges.

FirstGov, launched in September 2000, is a portal created through a public-private partnership and designed to connect the world to all U.S. Government information and services. FirstGov houses 30 million pages of government information, services and online transactions that allows users to access data without a detailed knowledge of the organization and role of individual government agencies. The site is also a catalyst for electronic government by working to transform the way in which citizens interact with government and receive government information and services.[15]

3.4 Electronic Government

Presently, the most important action for the federal government (as well as state and local governments) to take is to create a workable strategy to ensure the full creation of electronic government. Electronic government or e-government is defined as "an organization that connects critical business systems directly to key constituencies (customers, employees, suppliers, constituents) via intranets, extranets and the Web."[16] Data must be collectible, useable and able to be easily disseminated immediately—data must be easily integrated throughout the government in order to provide these services. All information must be secure. And appropriate hardware and software must be utilized. Information technology tools can help create this system of services and communication.

The U.S. Senate Committee on Governmental Affairs is considering Senate bill 803 *E-Government Act of 2001*, sponsored by Senator Lieberman, which is designed to help bring the government further in to the information age by accomplishing three objectives: 1) building an interoperable government infrastructure; 2) creating a catalyst fund for pilot government projects; and 3) establishing a Chief Information Officer position for the federal government.

While the task of providing an excellent electronic government is not easy, the possibilities are endless and exciting. For example, government and citizens can establish a new relationship using the tools of the information age. Governments may begin to view citizens as their key clients and strive to more effectively provide the channels for a two-way communication, which will help foster a better society. Citizens will be able to more easily place requests and complaints and governments will be able to better disseminate pertinent information. In fact, the citizen/government relationship could become the standard for an "information society" which affords us the opportunity to obtain accurate information rapidly in order to help solve short and long-term problems.

The systems that must be designed to meet these challenges require careful, integrated, broad vision planning. Agencies cannot afford to choose inappropriate hardware or proprietary software that will not facilitate cross-agency and intra-agency communication. Even some industry leaders, who by their very nature are competitive, are choosing open standards. Lou Gerstner of IBM notes "[w]e made our commitment to open-standards-based computing long before the Internet was on anybody's radar screen...because you don't get end-to-end enterprise integration and you're not going to be able to build end-to-end e-business infrastructures without open standards."[17] E-government success by its very nature requires the ability to select the best solution for particular situations at key times.

Research projects that encourage e-government should be futuristic, exciting, experimental and daring. Pilot projects can be created to complete research, test theories, and find solutions. Technology centers established by the government could be responsible for providing technical solutions for both governmental and societal problems. At this time, the government is in a position in which it must play "catch-up" with the rest of the economy, but is also very capable of becoming a leading player in the newly forming e-world. Further, the government can tie its internal needs with that of the society and work to ensure that there is equitable access to the tools of the information age, that public education is transformed, and that the democratic process is expanded.

3.5 Democracy in the information age

Information technologies could lead to a greater and stronger democracy by helping to improve communication between citizens and the government as well as between people and businesses, non-profits, education systems, and other entities. However, these possibilities will not be realized without careful attention and strategies to ensure equity of results and technical security.

Conversely, some of the most exciting possibilities of these new technologies create the leading fears of the information age. The ability of both government and business to collect and use personal data is on one hand promising and on the other very scary. Perhaps, we feel comfortable that amazon.com can tell us based on our previous purchases the new artists or new CD's that we may like. Perhaps, we want the government to have all of our information in a central data system so that we may access it more readily. But, the thought of businesses and governments creating extensive profiles on individuals may not be such an exciting possibility. The thought of who may use those files and to what end are daunting.

The ability to severely limit a criminal's ability to steal our identity by using fingerprinted ID cards or eye scans may be acceptable on one hand yet limit our personal freedom on the other. After all, the social security number was never suppose to be a personal identifier, but it is constantly requested before many types of transactions can be completed. Similarly, the idea of voting online from the comfort of our homes may thrill us, but the lack of security presently associated with the web, the amount of inequity that will be caused and the uncertainty about the care, handling and accurate representation of our data is not as appealing.

New technologies bring both positive and negative consequences. For example, "…the negative results of our many individual decisions to purchase automobiles include gridlock, air pollution, urban sprawl, the decline of urban centers, and dependence on insecure sources of imported oil."[18] While it doesn't change our desire to create and use new technology, it is evident that technology changes our lives—it changes the way we interact with people, it changes our expectations about our transactions, it changes our associations, and it changes aspects about the way we think our society should run and the values that we should hold most dear. Information technology tools, human genetics, environmental sciences and the like will all make a substantial impact on us. We must work diligently to ensure that we shape the changes to fit our goals as a society and that we are visionary and questioning and proactive in making technology a catalyst for positive change.

4.   CONCLUSION

Many of us cannot remember how we survived before we could go online to shop, do our research, find articles of interest, and communicate with our co-workers, friends and relatives. We cannot imagine life without ThinkPads, PDA's, or our cell phones. We have come to expect a type of immediacy that makes our life simultaneously easier and more hectic. Many of us are fully immersed in the information age. It's an exciting time and an exciting technology. But, with this new technology come new questions and new responsibilities. It is not a technology that stands alone, but instead one that has and will transform our society. It is up to us to ensure that we achieve the transformations that we most want and that we will envision possibilities in order to tackle constraints and problems that are associated with any new technology. In this, our government holds a key portion of the responsibility to lead our society and to transform itself.

Some of the key issues are laid out in this chapter; many others are not yet imaginable. But, it is certain that the federal, local and state governments are in a position to shape societal change and to reshape it's own organizational structure. Key to success in these areas is well-planned strategies, with clear goals and time frames for achievement and funding adequate to meet the demands. Immediate issues such as privacy and security can turn this exciting technology on its head. Societal goals such as equity of opportunity and a knowledge-based workforce can be facilitated by information technology tools only to the extent that we devise a workable strategy of action, with a strong focus on implementation and results. The federal government and its partners in business, academia, and the non-profit sector must meet the charge. Information technology provides tools, our tenacity and good judgement must provide the ability to solve our multi-faceted problems and make viable, long-lasting changes in our society.

NOTES

1. National Science and Technology Council, Committee on Civilian Industrial Technology, *Technology in the National Interest*. Washington, D.C. 1996. This document along with other National Science and Technology Council documents reflects the Clinton Administration's commitment to science and technology. President Clinton established the Council in 1993.
2. Branscomb, Lewis M. and James H. Keller, 1998. *Investing in Innovation: Creating a Research and Innovation Policy That Works*. The MIT Press. Cambridge Massachusetts: 463.
3. President's Information Technology Advisory Committee, Report to the President, *Information Technology Research: Investing in Our Future*. Washington, D.C. February 1999:8. See: http://www.itrd.gov.
4. Branscomb, Lewis M. and Richard Florida, *Challenges to Technology Policy in a Changing World Economy* in Branscomb, Lewis M. and James H. Keller, 1998. *Investing in Innovation: Creating a Research and Innovation Policy That Works*. The MIT Press. Cambridge, Massachusetts.
5. It is not certain what changes in the present structure will be made under the Bush Administration.
6. See http://www.itrd.gov
7. By Executive Order the committee can have up to 30 members.
8. President's Information Technology Advisory Committee, Report to the President, *Information Technology Research: Investing in Our Future*, Washington, D.C. February 1999.
9. Kennard, William; *E-Rate: A Success Story*, Educational Technology Leadership Conference – 2000, Council of Chief State School Officers, Washington, D.C. January 14, 2000.
10. Formerly the Telecommunications and Information Infrastructure Assistance Program (TIIAP).
11. President's Information Technology Advisory Committee, Report to the President, *Information Technology Research: Investing in Our Future*, Washington, D.C. February 1999: 16.
12. See: President's Information Technology Advisory Committee, Panel of Transforming Government, *Transforming Access to Government Through Information Technology*, Washington, D.C. September 2000.
13. Ibid: 4.

14.From http://www.cio.gov section *About The Council*. See the website for additional information such as CIO membership, meeting minutes and government-wide issues.
15.See http://www.firstgov.gov
16.Kingscott, Kathleen and Ed Gillespie; 2001. A Public Policy Framework for e-Government. IBM document.
17.From Lou Gerstner's delivered opening keynote address at PartnerWorld 2001in Atlanta, Feb. 26, 2001. See: http://www.ibm.com/lvg/
18.Sclove, Richard E., *Democracy and Technology*, 1995.The Guilford Press, New York, NY: 4.

BIBLIOGRAPHY

Branscomb, Lewis M., and James H. Keller. 1998. *Investing in Innovation: Creating A Research and Innovation Policy That Works.* The MIT Press. Cambridge, Massachusetts.
Council on Competitiveness. 1996. *Endless Frontiers, Limited Resources: U.S. R&D Policy for Competitiveness.* Council on Competitiveness Publications Office. Washington, D.C.
International Business Machines Document. 2001. Kingscott, Kathleen and Ed Gillespie. *A Public Policy Framework for e-Government.*
Gerstner, Lou. 2001. Keynote Address. PartnerWorld 2001 in Atlanta, February 26, 2001.
National Research Council. 2000. *Making IT Better: Expanding Information Technology Research to Meet Society's Needs*. National Academy Press. Washington, D.C.
National Research Council. 1998. *Fostering Research on the Economic and Social Impacts of Information Technology*. National Academy Press. Washington, D.C.
National Science and Technology Council, Interagency Working Group on ITR&D. 2000. *Information Technology: The 21st Century Revolution.* Supplement to the President's FY 2001 Budget. Washington, D.C.
National Science and Technology Council, Committee on Civilian Industrial Technology. 1996. *Technology in the National Interest.* Washington, D.C.
President's Information Technology Advisory Committee. 2000. Report to the President. *Transforming Access to Government Through Information Technology.* Washington, D.C.
President's Information Technology Advisory Committee. 2000. Report to the President. *Resolving the Digital Divide: Information, Access and Opportunity.* Washington, D.C.
President's Information Technology Advisory Committee. 1999. Report to the President. *Information Technology Research: Investing in Our Future.* Washington, D.C.
Sclove, Richard E. *Democracy and Technology.* 1995. The Guilford Press. New York.
Teich, Albert H., Stephen D. Nelson, Cecilia McEnaney, and Stephen J. Lita, eds. 2000. *AAAS Science and Technology Policy Yearbook.* American Association for the Advancement of Science. Washington, D.C.
The U.S. Department of Commerce, National Telecommunications and Information Administration. 1999. *Falling Through The Net: A Report on the Telecommunications Gap in America. Defining the Digital Divide.* Washington, D.C.

Dr. Yolanda L. Comedy serves as the Corporate Community Relations Manager in DC/MD/VA for IBM. She joined IBM in February, 2001.

Previously, she worked for the National Coordination Office for Information Technology Research and Development (NCO) as a contractor from Noesis, Inc. At the NCO, Dr. Comedy was responsible for coordinating the activities of the President's Information Technology Advisory Committee (PITAC).

Prior to joining Noesis, Inc., Dr. Comedy was a Senior Policy Analyst/Consultant at the White Office of Science and Technology Policy (OSTP). At OSTP, she worked with the President's Committee of Advisors on Science and Technology (PCAST) on a variety of issues, including science, math, engineering and technology education, and increasing diversity in science and technology.

From 1994-97, Dr. Comedy worked at the United States Agency for International Development's Center for Democracy and Governance and Policy and Program Coordination, Office of Development Partners. At USAID, Dr. Comedy worked on the New Partnership Initiative and issues of civil society and decentralization in various agency missions, including Mozambique, Tanzania, Paraguay and Eritrea.

In 1993, Dr. Comedy served as a consultant to the Ohio Board of Regents, Academic and Graduate Programming where she conducted research and policy studies related to the improvement of graduate education in Ohio's public and private colleges and universities.

Dr. Comedy received her Ph.D. in Political Science from Indiana University in 1993 and her B.A and M.A degrees from the Ohio State University in 1980 and 1983, respectively.

Her awards include, a Ford Foundation Dissertation Fellowship and American Association for the Advancement of Science Fellowship.

Chapter 14

Policy and Portals

A doorway to an electronic government

Patricia Diamond Fletcher
University of Maryland, Baltimore County, USA.

Abstract: The United States government has a rich history of information policy. The U.S. Federal government is the largest creator, disseminator, and maintainer of information, and as such, has paid special attention to the appropriate use and disposal of this information. The recent interest in using the Internet to offer government information, services and transactions has made the information policy environment more complex, and perhaps, more critical. In a society that has become accustomed to twenty-four hour, seven days a week access to high quality information and services, the public has developed the same expectations from the government. Recent advances in Internet technologies have made use of a "portal" model of information and service delivery. A joint venture between the US Federal government and the private sector has enabled the quick launch of a Federal government portal, FirstGov. This article examines the rich policy environment that supports electronic government ventures such as FirstGov. The concept of a portal is explored and an evaluation of FirstGov as a portal model is offered.

Key words: information policy, portals, federal government

1.   INTRODUCTION

In 1986, Harlan Cleveland asserted, "government *is* information.[1]" This comment underscores a history in the United States Federal government of being an information collector, creator, disseminator, and repository – tasks that make up the information life cycle and seek to insure an open and democratic government. There has been a long-standing recognition of the importance of information and information management to the Federal government (Fletcher, et al, 1993; Anderson & Dawes, 1991; Caudle, 1988; Horton, 1979; McDonough, 1988; Sprehe, 1987). The value of information to government has recently skyrocketed, however, as government becomes "digital" and information, ubiquitous.

Government's role in this new information society has not yet been fully explored. Rather it is evolving ad hoc in response to the development of new information technologies, most notably network technology, and the expectation of more "customer-oriented" focus by its citizens. This focus has been nurtured by the private sector in its creation of electronic commerce applications which have created the 24/7 business model, a model that lets customers interface with companies any time, any day of the week. This business model also includes a creation of value for customers that is information-based: infinitely customisable service and products. Through the use of "cookies" and other information collecting practices, companies can learn a range of behaviours and characteristics about visitors to their web sites and turn this information into the ultimate in customer service, individually focused, always available. With this as the business model for electronic commerce, the Federal government has a tough act to follow.

A recent U.S. Department of Commerce report[2] notes that the digital economy is no longer emerging–it is here. The report states that in 1994 three million people used the Internet; in 2000 that number is three hundred million. The report further notes that there are more than one billion web pages on the Internet and that approximately three million new web pages are added daily. The U.S. Federal CIO Council also has reported that more than 1200 electronic initiatives are underway in the Federal government.[3]

This chapter will examine the policy guidelines informing the creation of electronic government, and in specific, will look at the role of the Federal government in creating *the* model to make government accessible and understandable. The remarkably speedy development of FirstGov – the Federal gateway to government information and services - is envisioned to be the government "home" to all who access it, creating a sense of community and connection with all levels of government in the United States.

2.   ELECTRONIC GOVERNMENT AND INFORMATION POLICY

On June 24, 2000, in the first presidential Internet address to the public, President Bill Clinton called for the development of a Federal government Internet portal, or single point of entry, that would provide easy and open access to online government services and information available to the public[4]. The vision for this portal, FirstGov, is to be a high-speed, 24 hours a day, seven days a week, user-friendly entry point to every online resource, be it information, data or service, offered by the Federal government, and ultimately, to all levels of government in the United States. FirstGov is also seen as the vehicle to substantively reduce government bureaucracy, enable a more responsive and customer-focused government, and enable a new and active citizen participation in democratic processes. This citizen-centric focus would eliminate the impact of Federal agency stovepipes and provide service and government information based on service or information category, and not on agency. Thus, FirstGov would facilitate government-to-citizen (G2C), government-to-business (G2B), and government-to-government (G2G) interactions and transactions to occur. The actual launch of the website occurred September 22, 2000[5]

FirstGov contains information from more than 27 million Federal agency web pages, making it one of the largest collections of information on the Internet. Two important questions arise with the development of FirstGov: What policy informs this instantiation of government service and information delivery, and, is the creation and use of such a "gateway" model the best fit for all levels and all branches of government[6]?

3. FEDERAL INFORMATION POLICIES

As mentioned earlier in this chapter, the U.S. Federal government has a significant history of legislatively mandating information management practices, which has been covered well in other publications. [7] Some critical and important pieces of legislation and policy include the Paperwork Reduction Act of 1995 (PRA) (Public Law 104-13), a lengthy and wide-ranging law, first enacted in 1980. It was revised in 1986 with some changes, and then revised again in 1995. The PRA was enacted to reduce the paperwork burden on private citizens and businesses that interact with the government. It emphasizes the effective and efficient use of IT to achieve paperwork reduction. Hand-in-hand with the PRA is OMB Circular A-130 (Office of Management and Budget, 1985), which was created to clarify information management, information systems management, and information technology management for the Federal agencies affected by the PRA. The Circular has been most recently revised in 2000 to include the implementation guidelines for the Government Paperwork Elimination Act of 1998 (P.L. 105-277, Title XVII). The passage of the Government Paperwork Elimination Act (GPEA), while authorized with a minimum of attention and hoopla, could be one of the most influential pieces of legislation pertaining to the management and use of information technology.

A number of experts have suggested that GPEA may be at least as significant as earlier, critical laws enacted to do the same, e.g., the Brooks

Act of 1965, the Paperwork Reduction Act of 1980 and its amendments, and the Information Technology Management and Reform Act of 1996[8]. When fully in place, GPEA promises to facilitate government processes that are more externally focused, that is, to citizens and the business community. Earlier information policy, while important, was more appropriate to the inner workings of government. GPEA creates the play for the stage set by the National Partnership for Reinventing Government – a Clinton Administration program to create citizen-focused, ubiquitous government. With the passing of GPEA, there is a formal recognition that government is and will continue to develop into an electronic presence as it interfaces with citizens and businesses in providing not only information, but further, the capability to transact business directly over the Internet.

GPEA further serves to provide protections to the information from illegal intrusions, altering of the data, or unauthorized use or reuse of the information. Under GPEA, citizens will be able to file information electronically with the Federal government and receive information electronically as well. GPEA requires that by 2003, Federal government agencies must provide an electronic alternative for public access to their records with electronic filing of documents by the public also in place where practicable. Thus, GPEA provides the framework for the acceptance of electronic records as legal, valid and enforceable. It encourages Federal agencies to promote electronic record keeping, filing, maintenance, submission, and archiving. This opens up a wide array of possible types of electronic information interactions including electronic freedom of information requests, submission of bids and proposals for government contracts, application for licenses, loans and benefits, receipt of benefits such as social security, online procurement processes, and citizen commentary on legislative issues.

This last interaction – citizen involvement with the governance of the United States – was furthered by the development of the innovative web site "E government – An Experiment in Interactive Legislation[9]." Senators Fred D. Thompson (R-TN) and Joseph L. Leiberman (D-CT) sponsored the development of this web site and on May 20, 2000 it was open for business. The business here was to create a venue for public discourse on how the government should provide information, services and benefits in an online environment. The timing of this venture led to the concept of electronic government becoming a policy issue in the 2000 Presidential election[10].

Another law that helped set the stage for electronic government is the Information Technology Management Reform Act of 1996 (later renamed the Clinger-Cohen Act). As introduced by Senator Cohen, the intent of the Act was to be:

A bill to facilitate, encourage, and provide for efficient and effective acquisition and use of modern information technology by executive agencies; to establish the position of Chief Information Officer of the United States in the Office of Management and Budget; to increase the responsibility and public accountability of the heads of the departments and agencies of the Federal Government for achieving substantial improvements in the delivery of services to the public and in other program activities through the use of modern information technology in support of agency missions; and for other purposes. (S.946)

Coincident with the passage of the Clinger-Cohen Act was Executive Order 13011, "Federal Information Technology" of July 16, 1996. This integrates provisions of the Clinger-Cohen Act of 1996, the Paperwork Reduction Act of 1995, and the Government Performance and Results Act of 1993. More importantly, it put the Presidential "seal of approval" on the value and importance of information and its attendant technologies to government. This Executive Order is but one of many information-focused policies created during the Clinton Administration. The implementation of the National Performance Review on March 3, 1993 (later renamed the National Partnership for Reinventing Government) represented the Administration's intent to use information technology to create a more responsive and fast-acting government.[11]

3.1 Electronic Government Policy under President Bush

It is still too early to tell how the Bush Administration will define the importance of information technology and electronic government as part of its national agenda. Early reports, however, are not encouraging. One indicator of the trend is the Bush Administrations' revitalizing the use of the word "citizen" as opposed to the Clinton Administrations' focus on "customers." A recent mention in FCW.COM noted that electronic government is low on the totem pole of the President's agenda[12]. In the President's budget draft for 2002, a fund of $100 million has been allocated towards electronic government initiatives. The paucity of this is clearly seen when considering that the Federal government annually spends approximately $40 billion on information technology. The E-Government Act of 2001[13], as proposed by Senator Joseph L. Lieberman (D-CT), advocates for a $200 million annual e-government fund to go to cross-agency projects. Lieberman's bill would create a Federal CIO in the Office of Management and Budget. This CIO would be responsible for a newly created Office of Information Policy and would provide the leadership, oversight, vision, communication and coordination necessary to create the citizen-centric electronic government. Explicit in this is the use of Internet technologies to create easy access by citizens to government information and services. With the recent shift in the control of the Senate going to the Democrats, is becomes more likely that the Lieberman bill will receive the necessary support to pass. With this, we come back now to the implementation of FirstGov, the centralized online gateway to government information and services.

4.   GOVERNMENT AND ELECTRONIC GATEWAYS

The gateway or portal concept of electronic commerce has become a dominant theme in today's Internet environment. At its most basic, a portal is a main doorway for users to access the Web. It becomes like a homepage, becoming not only a favourite entryway to the Web, but also, a place Internet users come back to which meets a range of their information needs. The ability to create this "come backness" is often referred to as stickiness, the ability of a portal site to keep users faithful to repeated use of their services. In a business sense, portals are viable in their ability to aggregate thousands of Internet users to one "home" location. This move to a portal concept makes sense when one considers that home access to the Internet for April, 2001 was estimated at 167.5 million in the United States[14]. Recent IBM data indicates that there are more than two billion web pages currently populating the Internet universe and that number is expected to double by the year 2002[15]. Given this unruly and poorly indexed wealth of web pages, the notion of aggregating and providing a common entry guide to the Web makes good sense. Such extensive market penetration and the enhanced 24/7 access to information and services in the business sector makes government's move to an electronic presence an evolutionary move. The idea of using a gateway to simplify access builds on the experience of the private sector.

Government is moving towards a quasi-portal model of business in an effort to offer a more integrated or horizontal view of government – one that minimizes the "agency" aspect of services and information and capitalizes on the "content" aspect, or the subject of the information need. This will streamline a user's access to relevant government services and information, cutting back on the need to know what agency at what level of government offers the information or services needed by citizens. The development and use of a single portal point of access to the Web is seen as a necessary condition for horizontal government (Steyaert, 2000; Deloitte Research, 2001; Jupp, 2001; Council for Excellence in Government, 2001). It is envisioned that an electronic government portal will transform the citizens' relationship with their government. Governance will also be facilitated, with portals creating communities of interest that will function around political issues and elected officials, enabling an unprecedented flow of conversation between citizen and government.

Researchers have noted, though, that government is not just like business in its processes. A report from a 1998 Workshop on digital government, sponsored by the National Science Foundation (Dawes et al, March 1999) calls for the government, in its rapid move to the Internet, to not lose site of the fact that governance is also a necessary condition for democratic rule; that electronic government incorporate both government information and service delivery, and the provision of mechanisms to enable and facilitate governance.

As mentioned earlier, the creation of FirstGov represents the Federal governments most significant entry into the portal realm. At a hearing before the House Subcommittee on Government Management, Information, and Technology (October 2, 2000)[16] Senator Horn (R-CA) called for government to be up-to-date in its information management, be well organized for information retrieval and be accessible to the public. In her testimony to the House Subcommittee Sally Katzen, Deputy Director for Management, Office of Management and Budget, praised the early efforts already seen in the opening of the FirstGov doorway. She made reference to the quarter of a million users that visited the site in its first four days of business. She further reinforced the idea that FirstGov should be intuitive to citizens, access to it being organized by need and not by agency.

Is the public ready for such a venture? It would appear that both the technology and demand are in place. The response of U.S. households to making Internet portals their "home" suggests that the diffusion of the Internet is well underway and recent reports attest to the public's interest in government information. A recent Hart-Teeter study conducted under the auspices of the Council for Excellence in Government indicates that citizens already use the Internet for getting government-based information and overwhelmingly support the development of an electronic government. [17] Sixty-six percent of the survey respondents indicated they had already used government web sites, and 71 percent of these rated the electronic interaction as good or excellent. Interestingly, 51 percent of the survey respondents expressed the belief that the move to an electronic government would lead to a "better" government; 68 percent said it would improve access to information; and 64 percent felt that an electronic government would make transactions with the government more convenient. A study by the Momentum Research Group (July 26, 2000) had similar findings. Sixty-five percent of those surveyed had at least one electronic interaction with government, 20 percent of these in the previous thirty days. Forty-seven percent of the respondents noted that they wanted to use the Internet, or electronic government, to renew their driver's licence, 38 percent expressed the desire to have access to government in a one-stop shopping mode, and 36 percent wanted to be able to use the Internet to vote in major elections. This study also reported that citizens wanted to access government through a portal-type interface, but at the local level, not federal. Clearly the public interest in electronic government is evident, and the access mechanisms and range of services and information wanted would suggest the utility of a portal.

5.   WHERE DO WE GO FROM HERE?

The Presidential Memo on Electronic Government called for the creation of one web site that would "promote access to government information organized not by agency, but by the type of service or information that people may be seeking.[18]   FirstGov's early efforts point to this as an outcome. It uses the powerful Inktomi search engine, donated for three years, free of charge by Fed-Search, a foundation developed by Dr. Eric Brewer. Both individual citizens and businesses can purchase government goods at this web site. Transactions such as procurement, licensing, and registration can be accomplished online at FirstGov. At this time, FirstGov has indexed more than 20 million existing federal government web pages. And FirstGov has an ambitious set of goals to accomplish. As stated on their homepage:

- We are working across government to accelerate the growth of a secure seamless, electronic government.
- We are encouraging cross-agency portals to serve specific customer groups such as those already created for kids, workers, seniors, and more.
- We are reaching out to businesses, non-profits, associations, and other groups. We have more than 90 FirstGov partners and the number is growing.
- We are transforming the way government at all levels deliver services to you and the way you interact with your government. (http://www.firstgov.gov/top_nav/about.html?ssid=992271455394_172)

While the current instantiation of FirstGov is a web presence, it is important to note that this model is not constrained by the ability to access the Internet or computers in one's home. Many governments are successfully deploying information kiosks in local government offices and public spaces such as shopping malls or schools (Norris, Fletcher & Holden, 2001).

Internet connections in public libraries are also a well-used venue (McClure). Citizen to government transactions have also been available for many years using ATM technology and public-private partnerships. The telephone is also a conduit for citizen to government conduct. For example, the IRS is making use of this device interactive for tax filing. There is a seemingly endless array of options, and more appearing daily on the horizon.

A final thought here has to do with the perpetual inefficiencies in data redundancy and duplication. The Internet, by virtue of its ease of use and access, is compounding information overload. And government, in its rush to get online, is guilty of contributing to this overload. The creation of the FirstGov portal does not mean that all government information will reside in one format, in one location. FirstGov uses existing Federal agency databases for its content, and it has been well established that these agency web developments are often less than optimal (McClure and Sprehe, 2000). What we have seen is government agencies putting their paper products online, without first thinking about reengineering for an online environment, and without attention to thinking about what data needs to be provided and in what format. That is, we are receiving the electronic version of our paper government rather than seeing government reengineered for an electronic environment. There is the further complication in that all U.S. state governments have web sites, many of these being all-inclusive gateways to state government. One need only go to North Star, the official home of Minnesota government (http://www.state.mn.us/) or AccessWashington (http://access.wa.gov/) to see innovative and diverse approaches to online information and service delivery. Is there a need for one mega-gateway to subsume all these local efforts? And would such an application take away from the great sense of "localness" offered on state, city and county homepages? We have long been a nation where government touches us most where we live, in towns and villages, in major metropolitan areas, counties, school districts, forest preserves, and the like. Can a federal government gateway create and maintain a local feel? Should it? While the ideal of one-stop-24 hours seven days a week-service is enticing and noteworthy in private commerce, the convenience of one web portal providing all government related information and services to all people might not be feasible, or even desired. There are many important questions to be thought through as we move forward in our electronic world.

NOTES

1. Harlan Cleveland, "Government is Information (But Not Vice Versa)," Public Administration Review, 46 (1986): 605-607.

2. Daley, W.M. Digital Economy 2000, Office of Policy Development; U.S. Department of Commerce Economics and Statistics Administration: Washington, DC, 2000: 1-71.

3. Webcast of November 15, 2000 CIO Council Meeting. http://www.cio.gov/text/whatsnew.htm (accessed November 20, 2000).

4. Remarks by the President in the First Internet Webcast; June 24, 2000. http://www.whitehouse.gov/WH/new/html/internet2000-02-24-text.html (accessed October 10, 2000).

5. President Clinton Launches FirstGov: A Single Easy-to-Use Website for Government Services and Information; September 22, 2000. http://whitehouse.gov/WH/html/Fri_Sep_22_124445_2000.html (accessed October 10, 2000).

6. As noted in the vision statement of FirstGov, an ultimate goal for this gateway is to be the one central source for all U.S. government information, accessible anytime, anywhere, by anyone. Retrieved from the World Wide Web http://www.firstgov.gov/top_nav/about.html?ssid=992024031962_172 June 2, 2001.

7. The Federal information policy landscape has been well detailed in Hernon, P.; McClure, C.R.; and Relyea, H.C., Eds. Federal Information Policies in the 1990s: Views and Perspectives; Ablex Publishing Corporation: Norwood, New Jersey, 1996; 340 pp. Another, more recent examination of these policies can be found in McClure, C.R.; Sprehe, J.T.; and Eschenfelder, K. Performance Measures for Federal Agency Websites: Final Report; this report can be accessed at http://fedbbs.access.gpo.gov/libs/measures.htm. Another good conceptual and legislative overview of information management policy is contained in "Electronic Commerce: A Conceptual Overview." May, 2001. Harold C. Relyea. Washington, DC: Congressional Research Service.

8. GPEA is a giant Step Toward Hassle-Free Government. Government Computer News, December 12, 1998. Retrieved from the World Wide Web http://www.gcn.com/archives/gcn/1998/december14/23.htm May 28, 2001.

9. "E government – An Experiment in Interactive Legislation." Available at http://gov_affairs.senate.gov/egov

10. Dorobek, C.J. "Gore and Bush make E-gov a campaign issue." Government Computer News, June 19, 2000: 6.

11. "A Brief History of Vice President Al Gore's National Partnership for Reinventing Government. http://govinfo.library.unt.edu/npr/whoweare/historyofnpr.html (accessed May 24, 2001).

12. Sarkar, D. "E-gov a low priority for Bush." FCW.COM. May 10, 2001. (accessed May 10, 2001 at http://www.civic.com/articles/2001/0507/web-bush-05-10-01.asp)

13. The E-Government Act of 2001. 107th Congress, First Session. May 1, 2001. http://www.senate.gov/~gov_affairs/050101_press-bill%20text.pdf

14. Nielson//Net Ratings. (accessed May 24, 2001 at http://www.nielsen-netratings.com/)

15. "Fast Growing Cyveillence Analyzes Millions of web pages daily." IBM. (Accessed May 20, 2001 at

http://www2.software.ibm.com/casestudies/swcsdm.nsf/customername/0F5B6E9E210F3F
CC87256A0F002C071D)

16. For the complete witness testimony go to
http://www.house.gov/reform/gmit/hearings/2000hearings/001002.FirstGov/001002h.htm

17. Hart-Teeter

18. The White House, Memorandum for the Heads of Executive Departments and Agencies on Electronic Government. December 19, 1999.

Patricia Diamond Fletcher is associate professor in the Department of Information Systems, UMBC. She has published extensively in the area of government information policy and electronic government. She is currently studying new models of multi-partner collaboration for electronic government projects, a project funded by the National Science Foundation under the direction of the Center for Technology in Government. She will be on sabbatical leave at the US General Accounting Office for the 2001 academic year, where she will be conducting projects in information policy, privacy law, and strategic planning for information technology. Fletcher received her MLS and PhD from the School of Information Studies at Syracuse University.

Chapter 15

Citizens' Perspectives on E-government

Sharon Strover
University of Texas, Austin, Texas USA.

Abstract: This article presents the results of a survey conducted in the state of Texas to the assess issues and concerns citizens have in having government provide services over the Internet. The survey presents one vision of what people believe about network-mediated government services and how they interact with them, and it contributes ideas about the sorts of policies and considerations our government agencies might adopt as they move toward a fully realized e-government

Key words: public opinion survey, e-government services, privacy

1. INTRODUCTION

Using the Internet for public and private information transactions has developed significantly over the last five years. As the citizens gain more experience with emerging online tools and information resources from private sector services, a similar level of service is being expected from government entities. In the many states in the US, legislatures and state leadership are promoting an electronic government agenda. State efforts typically focus on multiple aspects of an Internet-based model of service delivery such as providing information or allowing people to register or apply for certain permits or licenses, often with the intention of simply automating existing services. Other models either proposed or being implementing go beyond simple automation and attempt to re-think the broader nature of government services. Most e-government initiatives include some variation of promises for more or better citizen participation or e-democracy, sometimes noting the new ease with which people can "reach" elected officials or staff. Yet few state government efforts actually have been able to realize a model that substantially changes the relationship between citizens and government.

At minimum, state governments should ensure that citizens, the potential users of e-government services, are at least prepared to accept and use electronic services, particularly since their implementation can come at substantial cost. This chapter reports on the efforts of one state, Texas, as it attempted to assess citizens' perceptions about and attitudes toward e-government. The results of the effort were not precisely what the state expected or wanted to hear, but by the same token these unexpected findings are what make them so important.

2.   ELECTRONIC GOVERNMENT MISSIONS

In early 2001, the US National Commission on Libraries and Information Science reviewed trends in providing public documents to American citizens, and commented that a crisis was brewing around the country (U.S. National Commission on Libraries and Information Science, 2001). The specific event catalyzing their study was the imminent closure of the federal office, the National Technical Information Service, which had been charged with making public documents available to the public, cataloging them, and maintaining a repository for public information. As various federal agencies were publishing those same documents on the Web, this agency found itself with less to do and a reduced budget, even though no single agency had assumed the repository or cataloging functions. The Commission wrote, "Public ownership of information created by the federal government is an essential right. It not only allows individuals to fulfill their civic responsibilities, but also contributes to an overall improvement in their quality of life. Current information technology not only brings with it expanded opportunities for using government information but also a number of difficulties, including adequacy of finding tools, technological incompatibilities, and sometimes just the overwhelming amount of information" (p. 4). The core problem was not simply one of new agencies performing the same duties as the NTIS; rather, the problem was that not all information was being shared on the Web, that not everyone could necessarily access information that was there, and that there was no repository – no history – for the documents.

The Commission went on to offer 36 recommendations, and several are relevant to ongoing state efforts to launch e-government efforts, particularly their admonishment that the public's most critical unmet requirements for public information resources be identified.

This speaks to the need to understand how people seek information from the government, and how they would like to interact with government for various information and service transactions. This "demand" perspective is uncommon in the efforts of most state e-government efforts to date. For example, one survey of state initiatives identified few states that have literacy or language barrier policies, that only one state had a program designed to ensure that residents could access e-government resources, and that few state portals had explicit policies addressing privacy concerns (Texas Department of Information Resources, 1999).

Texas established an Electronic Government Task Force to assess citizen and business interaction with government, and it reviewed other states' practices to identify key issues, including the fact that some underlying benefits of e-government can include convenience, greater access to information, and the potential to reduce costs of individual transactions. However, they found that few states had surveyed actual public interest in these potential benefits. Consequently they sought to assess public opinion on these sensitive public issues before proceeding with a design of an e-government model.

3.   PUBLIC OPINION SURVEY

A public opinion research project was conceived as a way to assess a variety of issues related to public access necessary to use e-government services as well as public opinion about the proper form and emphasis of those services among the residents of Texas (Strover and Straubhaar, 2000). Such feedback could positively influence the development and use of e-government services in the state.

How we use computers and the Internet intersects several policy issues now that more social and civic practices, economic transactions, and government programs rely on technological mediation. In all state e-government plans, services will be dependent on a Web-based or computer network-based delivery system. Consequently, how people use computers and the Internet, their attitudes toward both, and how they feel about various privacy and security issues associated with sharing personal information on the Internet are important considerations.

This research project had several specific questions, a few of which this chapter will address:

(1) Would people use government services if they were available on the Internet? How much would they pay?

State government provides numerous services to residents, ranging from constructing highways to undertaking epidemiological studies to supporting a higher education infrastructure. Some services are likelier than others to be early candidates for being provided via the Internet. Which services are people most amenable to using over the Internet? What factors might discourage them from using those services?

(2) What are the privacy and security concerns of Texans with respect to e-government applications?

Numerous studies have found that people in the United States are increasingly wary about maintaining the privacy of personal information. Various well-publicized "cracks" in Internet security have underscored that this technology is not failsafe. Moreover, it is amply clear that the Internet itself generates information about people as they use the Internet, which in turn raises more concerns from people regarding the use of information based on their Internet transactions. In addition, the sale of data about people that the state has collected is a growing source of revenue for Texas government; the Internet and digitization generally enable that data collection (and sale) to be lucrative. What are peoples' attitudes toward the state's handling of what many believe is personal information? How might these influence attitudes toward using e-government services?

(3) What are citizen opinions with respect to financially supporting e-government services?

Internet-based government information and services will incur certain costs. Texas, like several other states, faces several choices with respect to supporting this change. Using revenues from general funds or charging people who use electronic services are among the alternative payment schemes being considered. How do Texas residents feel about such payment plans?

3.1   Sample and Procedures

The database for this study is based on a survey conducted in March-April, 2000. This survey used a Computer Assisted Telephone Interviewing (CATI) system at the University of Texas to conduct telephone interviews with 1,002 respondents. Of those, 800 comprise a random sample survey of households in the state, while an additional 202 households represent a sample of people exclusively from rural counties. Consequently, 328 respondents represent people from rural areas while 674 respondents are from non-rural regions. We interviewed individuals (in Spanish as required) in households over 18 years of age, using last birthday in order to randomly sample within the household. The telephone interview took approximately 14 minutes to administer.

3.2   Utilization of Electronic Services

In order to investigate how people might feel about using government services on the Internet, the survey asked a series of questions about peoples' current use of various services. If they already made use of a service, the survey followed this up by asking if they would use it if available on the Internet; if they indicated they would use that service on the Internet, they were asked how much they might pay for the convenience of using it that way.

Perhaps not too surprising, the most *frequently used* services included renewing a driver's license, filing and paying taxes, registering to vote, and voting.[1] As the tables below (Tables 1 and 2) indicate, many of the actual users of the services are very interested in having an Internet-based delivery system:

- 55% indicated they would use the Internet to register to vote,
- 53% of the entire sample said they would use the Internet to renew a driver's license,
- Nearly 47% said they would use it to actually vote,
- 39% said they would use the Internet to file and pay taxes.

With respect to how much people might pay for the convenience of such services, responses varied depending on the nature of the service. People were willing to pay more to renew a driver's license over the Internet, for example, than they were for a fishing license. These results do indicate that people are willing to pay a fee to use Internet-based services, and that prices perhaps could vary depending on public demand.

Table 1. E-government services: Use, Internet Interest, and Payment

	Voted in state or local elections	Filed and paid taxes	Registered to vote	Renewed a driver's license	Paid Traffic or vehicle tickets or fees	Enrolled in educational programs	Requested Personal Information
Use service	87.5%	82.1%	80.4%	79.0%	54.7%	53.8%	53.4%
Would use service if on Internet	46.8%	39.1%	55.3%	53.1%	32.3%	40.4%	34.2%
How much would you pay?							
Under $3	**N/A**	4.6%	**N/A**	11.7%	7.3%	5.6%	8.4%
Up to $10		9.0%		16.9%	8.3%	10.1%	9.3%
Over $10		7.5%		10.1%	5.1%	7.3%	1.6%
Nothing at all		10.6%		8.1%	7.9%	11.0%	8.6%

Table 2. E-government services: Use, Internet Interest, and Payment

	Obtained fishing or hunting licenses	Participated in Community or State mtgs.	Received professional licenses from state agencies	Obtained info. on public safety/ environment	Obtained paperwork for building or other sorts of permits	Applied for health, social, or welfare services
Use service	38.1%	27.8%	24.8%	23%	22.3%	15.6%
Would use service if on Internet	26.6%	17.6%	14.9%	21.2%	14.2%	9.6%
How much would you pay?						
Under $3	7.9%	3.7%	2.5%	3.9%	2.8%	2.5%
Up to $10	5.7%	3.9%	3.7%	3.1%	4.2%	2.4%
Over $10	4.4%	1.1%	3.7%	2.0%	2.2%	1.2%
Nothing at all	4.9%	6.8%	3.4%	9.6%	2.6%	2.4%

* Each number represents a percentage of the entire weighted sample.

3.3   Which services are ideally suited for the Internet?

Tables 1 and 2 above illustrate several services that are likely candidates for e-government services since much of the public is ready to accept their electronic provision, and may even be willing to pay for them. In assessing other attitudes toward e-government services, the survey asked people some more general questions about their ideas of computer-based delivery of government services.

The results indicate that there are contradictions in the sample when it comes to evaluating the Internet's usefulness for government services (Table 3). While on the one hand most of the sample evaluates the Internet as potentially very useful and that having government services on it would be useful, people also agree that they would prefer to see someone in person when using a service, and that they are concerned that the Internet is not sufficiently <u>available</u> to make public services available through that means. They also show some concern for the quality of services they would receive on the Internet.

Table 3. Percentage Agreement on Internet & E-government

	Prefer to see someone in person	Internet makes govt. more available	Internet not sufficiently available	Concerned about the quality of services
Strongly disagree	9.5%	4.1%	8.1%	7.6%
Disagree	17.5%	8.1%	20.5%	23%
Neither agree nor disagree	11.9%	7%	10.9%	10.2%
Agree	31.6%	49.7%	44.5%	42.5%
Strongly agree	29.4%	31.1%	16%	16.8%

As is evident from these data, it is especially encouraging that the great majority of the sample – 81 percent - believes that the Internet can make government more available. On the other hand, 61 percent agreed or strongly agree that they prefer to see someone in person, and 59.3 percent have concerns regarding the quality of services they would receive over the Internet. About the same percentage acknowledge that the Internet is not sufficiently available to everyone in order for the government to rely on it for providing services. Older people were particularly likely to be concerned about the quality of services and to prefer to see someone in person.

Internet Not Sufficiently Available

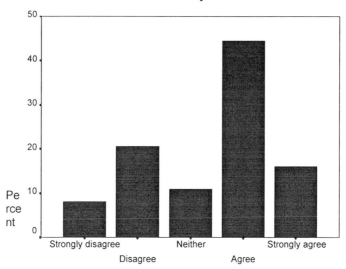

Figure 1. Agree/Disagree "The Internet is not sufficiently available to everyone to use it for providing government information and services."

Makes Govn. More Available

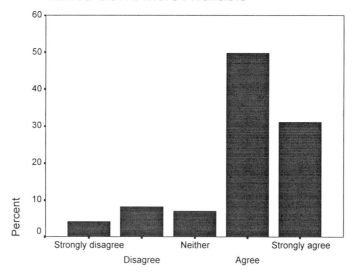

Figure 2. Agree/Disagree "Having government information on the Internet would make government more available to the people."

When examining responses on the questions by demographic factors such as income and education, we find overwhelming agreement across all income and educational levels that having government information on the Internet would make government more available, although more highly educated and higher income groups tend to agree most strongly.

3.4 Privacy and Security Issues and Attitudes

In line with other current survey results in the U.S., nearly 70 percent of Texans agreed that they were worried about privacy on the Internet.[2] Beyond privacy, this study also asked if people found certain government information handling practices acceptable. Because Texas already sells some data produced through its normal functions (licensing drivers, recording births, etc.), and because e-government will produce much more data about people, the state is interested in public perceptions regarding the acceptability of selling that data as well as public concerns about security and privacy associated with state government's handling of personal data.

As a rule, people who used the Internet less frequently expressed more concerns than did those who used it more often. The survey asked people how they felt about the release of personal information (using driving history as an example), and what permission method regarding releasing personal data they would prefer. Nearly 53 percent of the sample felt that the release of this sort of information was "unacceptable," while 14 percent were uncertain and another 29 percent thought it was acceptable. People with higher incomes and more education particularly felt this practice was unacceptable.

3.5 Data Release Policies

The generally acknowledged methods that policymakers discuss when it comes to releasing personal information are the opt-in and the opt-out strategies. Opt-in refers to people actively deciding what personal data can be released; without explicit permission, no data would be released. Opt-out, the strategy generally preferred by organizations collecting data, allows people to request that their data be withheld; without such an affirmative request, personal data are released. Consequently, there is a greater burden on the individual in the latter strategy.

When asked if people would prefer to opt-in (give permission ahead of time) or opt-out (notify the state when they would like to be removed from an existing database), the <u>overwhelming</u> majority, 72.4 percent, preferred the opt-in strategy of giving permission ahead of time.

3.6 Confidence and Concern Regarding Use of Information

Previous studies have shown that people are sometimes less concerned about the handling of non-financial personal information than about financial personal information.[3] This sample was, on average, extremely concerned about giving financial information about themselves on the Internet to government agencies. Roughly 70 percent were either "very concerned" or "concerned."

There was also substantial concern regarding providing non-financial information over the Internet to government agencies as well, although these same two categories total roughly 60 percent of the sample, slightly lower than the percentage expressing concern over financial information handling.

Finally, whether people feel confident that the state will use their personal information appropriately is another area pertinent to e-government services. Whether people trust the state or Federal government to responsibly divulge or shelter such data may have a strong bearing on how well people accept e-government services in the future. The survey illustrates a weak level of confidence in either type of government handling personal, confidential information. Only very small percentages of the population express strong confidence in how government will handle their personal information.

3.7 Attitudes Toward Possible Support Schemes for E-government

The survey assessed attitudes toward four alternative methods of financially supporting e-government services, and opinions were most favorable toward two plans: (1) using advertising to underwrite the costs of the service or (2) having users of such services pay a fee. Figures 3 and 4 illustrate the percentages of people who found these options acceptable. People at lower income levels found the idea of a fee-for-use more palatable, while older people did not favor this option. Interestingly, Internet users were more likely to find the idea of using advertising on state pages acceptable.

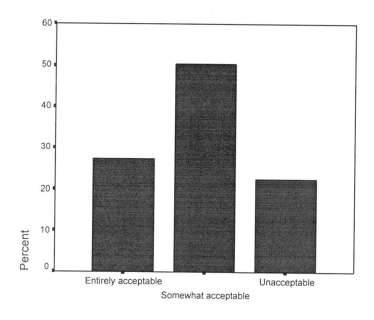

Figure 3. Acceptability of Users Paying for E-government

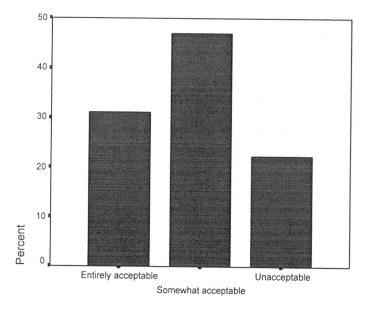

Figure 4. Acceptability of Advertising on E-government Web Pages to Support Service

The other two options we mentioned in the survey were having the state use general revenue to support e-government services or the state using the revenue from selling data generated by using e-government services as a means of support. Both were resoundingly deemed "unacceptable" by this sample.

Over 60% of the sample finds the option of the state selling data to obtain financing for e-government objectionable. An only slightly smaller percentage feels the same way about using the general fund for support. These results suggest at least two conclusions: that people are unaware that the state already sells data it gathers on residents, and that in any case people believe that such data should not be part of an economic equation for e-government; second, that there should be some quid pro quo when it comes to finding money for such services, making a fee-for-service or paid advertising basis of support more acceptable.

4.   SUMMARY

This survey sought to assess issues and concerns citizens have in having government provide services over the Internet. Key findings of the survey include the following.

–   While people see the Internet as potentially very useful and think that having government services on it would be useful, people also agree that they would prefer to see someone in person when using a government service. They also show some concern for the quality of services they would receive on the Internet.
–   People are also concerned that the Internet is not sufficiently <u>available</u> to offer public services through that means.
–   The e-government services that people are most likely to use include registering to vote, paying traffic tickets or vehicle fees, voting, enrolling in educational programs, filing and paying taxes, and requesting personal information. People were also somewhat interested in using e-government services to obtain hunting or fishing licenses and obtaining information on public safety or the environment. Of interest to smaller groups were participating in public meetings, receiving or renewing professional licenses, filing paperwork for building or other permits, and applying for health, welfare or social services.
–   The e-government services that the most people are willing to pay for include renewing driver's licenses, paying traffic tickets, enrolling in courses, filing taxes and requesting personal information.

– People are very concerned about how the government will handle their personal information. They do not want data about them or their transactions sold in order to support e-government, and they want to have a choice regarding how the state will sell or release their personal information.

These results highlight some possible directions for e-government efforts:

– Continue to monitor Internet use among the population in order to assess who does and does not use the Internet, and why;
– Consider ways to target the groups using the Internet the least and conduct pilot experiments with different settings, technologies, or interfaces that can address such individuals' hesitations about the Internet and e-government services;
– Develop and publicize privacy and security standards that address people's concerns;
– Implement a method of facilitating opt-in data sharing/disclosure strategies.

Plans to base government services on a Web interface have the potential to extend more government services to more people, to achieve substantial cost savings and efficiency, and to open the door to new ways that government can be accountable. However, designing new government systems runs the risk of losing sight of precisely what people want and how they currently think about and use government services and the Internet. This survey presents one vision of what people believe about network-mediated government services and how they interact with services, and it contributes ideas about the sorts of policies and considerations our government agencies might adopt as they move toward a fully realized e-government.

NOTES

1. Although the Texas state government does not assess property taxes, this question was used in part because it is increasingly common to use electronic means to pay a variety of bills.
2. A 2000 "WWW User Survey" survey (the 8th) from the Graphics, Visualization and Usability (GVU) Center at Georgia Tech revealed that 72% of Internet users believe there should be new laws to protect privacy on the Internet. The survey also found that 82% of users object to the sale

of personal information. The survey suggests a sharp increase in privacy
concerns since the Center's prior GVU poll. In their prior poll, users
favored anonymity and new laws to protect privacy and opposed direct
marketing and the sale of personal information, according to the GVU's
Seventh WWW User Survey. See
http://www.gvu.gatech.edu/user_surveys/survey-1997-10/.
3. See the Federal Trade Commission 1997 privacy hearings, for example,
for reports on this issue.

REFERENCES

Federal Trade Commission (1998). Privacy Online: A Report to Congress. Available at
    www.ftc.gov/reports/privacy3/index.htm. See also FTC (1999). Self Regulation and
    privacy online: A Report to Congress. Available at:
    www.ftc.gov/os/1999/9908/privacy99.pdf.
Georgia Institute of Technology, Graphics, Visualization and Usability (GVU) Center (2000).
    WWW User Survey. Available: http://www.gvu.gatech.edu/user_surveys/survey-1997-
    10/.
Strover, S. and J. Straubhaar (2000). E-government services and computer and Internet use in
    Texas. Available: www.utexas.edu/research/tipi.
Texas Department of Information Resources (1999). A survey of state portal initiatives.
    Available: www.dir.state.tx.us/egov/Surveys/State_survey/indenx.html.
U.S. National Commission on Libraries and Information Science (2001). A Comprehensive
    assessment of public information dissemination. Available:
    www.nclis.gov/govt/assess/assess.execsum.pdf

Dr. Sharon Strover is the Director of the University's Telecommunications
and Information Policy Institute, which undertakes research on
contemporary communication policy issues. Recent subjects include
children's Internet use and privacy, telecommunications infrastructure
planning, and international "information society" efforts. She also directs the
College of Communications Office of Survey Research, which conducts
studies on various social concerns. Dr. Strover has contributed chapters to
several books and monographs, is co-editor of books on urban and rural
telecommunications and is working on a volume examining the cable
television industry and another book examining rural America, economic
development and communications. Current interests include cable and
television policy and regulation, urban telecommunications policy, trends in
audience research, the social effects of media, and European communication
policy. She has conducted research for the National Association of
Broadcasters, Children's Television Workshop, the National League of
Cities, The European Union, the Ford Foundation and various media
companies. Electronic Byways: State Policies for Rural Development

through Telecommunications (Westview, 1992), and Democracy and Communication in the New Europe (Hampton, 1995) contain some of her recent work. Other current research projects include an investigation of linguistic markets for audio-visual products in Latin America and North America.

Chapter 16

Building Collaborative Digital Government Systems
Systemic constraints and effective practices

Sharon S. Dawes and Theresa A. Pardo
Center for Technology in Government, University at Albany/SUNY

Abstract: Successful digital government policies and applications often depend on the ability of multiple organizations to collaborate toward shared objectives. Despite compelling benefits, these efforts are fraught with problems, and often fail. The developmental experiences of 18 collaborative digital government initiatives in New York State reveal five systemic constraints that account for the common difficulties: divergent roles, multiple missions, operational diversity, changing technology, and limited ability to adapt to change. The project experiences also offered ten guiding principles that can help make collaborative systems more successful. These focus on purpose, stakeholders, partnership, leadership, managing complexity, skills, resources, communication, work processes, and explicit design methods.

Key words: interorganizational collaboration, intergovernmental collaborations, integrated services, integrated systems, partnerships

1.   THE NEED FOR COLLABORATIVE SYSTEMS

In the last decade, important changes in public expectations and service delivery technologies have made more understandable, accessible, and cost-effective government services possible. To make the possibility a reality, program managers and system designers are learning that they need to know a great deal about both technology and collaborative ways of working.

When the US National Performance Review (NPR) recommended that government agencies "re-engineer government activities, making full use of computer systems and telecommunications to revolutionize how we deliver services" (NPR, 1993, p. v), it opened the door to more aggressive and innovative use of technology to support enhanced public services. The Access America Plan issued in 1997 strengthened this commitment to IT, calling for "new IT-based information systems and improvements in the process by which they are managed . . . in programs ranging from health care to law enforcement" (Heeks, ed., 1999, p.232).

Governments have since turned more often to the private sector for the IT expertise needed to implement these new service delivery systems. At the same time, relationships between government and non-profit organizations have been changing. The emergence of new technologies has encouraged a tighter coupling of work processes and information flows across these sectors. Age-old intergovernmental and interagency relationships have been affected as well. For example, the welfare reform initiative offers more flexibility at the service delivery level, but in exchange for intergovernmental information sharing mandates that far exceed the reporting requirements of the programs it replaced. Integration of justice information systems connects defense attorneys, probation departments, police agencies, courts, and others. Electronic interchanges links medical providers, insurance companies, health maintenance organizations, and Medicaid and Medicare payers into a business partnership facilitated by IT.

In 1998, the National Science Foundation launched a Digital Government research initiative to encourage investigations into this combination of technology and service delivery issues. In one of the early agenda-setting workshops, government managers identified their needs for research. Three of these needs focused in some way on collaborative systems: interoperable systems that are trusted and secure, models for electronic public service transactions and delivery systems, and models of public-private partnership and other networked organizational forms. The workshop report (Dawes, et al, 1999) points out how the remarkable increase in information sharing capability makes the complexity of these arrangements both organizationally and technologically daunting. These arrangements raise issues related to the use of advanced networking and other information technologies; to the negotiation of roles, rules, and resource sharing; and to the effect of such collaborations on the quantity, quality, and accessibility of services. They also highlight the importance of institutional and social constraints on the change that advanced IT introduces into organizations (Dutton, 1999). These issues are of great interest in the US and many other parts of the world.

The research literature on cooperative and collaborative systems tells us that these efforts are fraught with problems, and often fail. Despite compelling reasons for private and public organizations to embrace participative systems, significant, deeply embedded barriers to success include dispositions against cooperating with prior adversaries, the costs of collaboration in complex social and political systems, the difficulties of engaging deep conflicts, and leadership incentives favoring control (McCaffrey, et al. 1995). The desire to undertake interorganizational information sharing may come from a variety of different problem situations (Dawes, 1995), but the same problem situation maybe viewed as a catalyst for action in some cases and not others (Weiss, 1987). Moreover, there may be substantial disagreement among participants about the level or exact nature of the problem to be addressed (Dawes et al., 1997a).

Management and organizational factors also come into play. Leadership, sponsorship and management philosophy affect the success or failure of collaborative systems (Pardo, 1998; Burt, 1997; Larson, 1992). A study of local governments found officials to be greatly concerned with structural change, intergovernmental arrangements, substantive policy issues, and effects on internal operations (Cigler, 1994). Policy, legal, and data gaps and conflicts also stand in the way of such initiatives (Landsbergen and Wolken, 2001). Private sector collaborations face similar economic, social, and political conflicts. (Kumar, et al. 1996).

2.   RESEARCH PROGRAM

Since the mid 1990s, the Center for Technology in Government (CTG) at the University at Albany/SUNY has been studying technology-enabled interorganizational collaborations. During that time, we have been involved in eighteen projects in New York State in which public organizations have engaged in system development projects that demand complex relationships with other public agencies, non-profit organizations, or private businesses. These organizational relationships are not new to government, although the possibilities for service integration, administrative reform, customer service, and new efficiencies have been heightened considerably by the emergence of network- and user-oriented technologies. Our research has covered all three common types of interorganizational collaborations:

– **Public-Public Collaborations:** This category includes both horizontal agreements between agencies or departments at the same level of government and vertical agreements or intergovernmental alliances between federal, state, and local levels. These vertical forms are by far the most prevalent, representing a wide array of programs and services ranging from food stamps, to road building, to public safety. These intergovernmental arrangements are often authorized by federal law, elaborated by state rules and decisions, and operated by local agencies. Despite their denigration as myopic "stovepipes," these arrangements benefit from both concentrated expertise and strong programmatic focus.

– **Public-Non-profit Collaborations:** In certain service sectors, most notably health and human services, non-profit service organizations are a major (sometimes sole) channel of service delivery at the community level. This form of interorganizational relationship is also very common. In the past, these relationships have been characterized by fee-for-service or annual contracts specifying the conditions under which a government agency will pay the non-profit to deliver those services. Today, we are beginning to see joint development of service programs in which the public and non-profit participants share responsibility for program design, performance, and evaluation.

– **Public-Private Collaborations:** Contracting and outsourcing are the most familiar collaboration methods that link the public and private sectors. In these cases, the government remains accountable for a service that is totally or partially operated by the private sector. Public private partnerships imply a sharing of resources, responsibility, risks and benefits. In these arrangements, government relinquishes some management responsibilities while retaining enough control (through law, regulation, or contract) to protect the public interest. Although these are the least common forms of collaboration, they generate a great deal of attention -- and the most debate.

Coordinated, collaborative information systems offer the hope of integrated services to citizens and streamlined operations within government, but the prospects for success are low. Many government and professional organizations are searching for ways to make these essential systems more successful. Three recent studies at CTG are among the first attempts in the US to analyze the issues that attend these systems and to document practices that lead to success.

The first project was a development effort to prototype a statewide geographic information system cooperative (Kelly, et al., 1995). The objective of the second project was to identify and document the practices associated with successful state-local information systems by studying the experiences of eleven initiatives in New York State (Dawes, et al., 1996a, Dawes, et al., 1997b). The third project investigated various ways government agencies use information internally to design, operate, or evaluate programs (CTG, 2000). Together these studies involved 18 different collaborative information system initiatives, which are briefly characterized in Table 1.

Table 1. Collaborative Digital Government Projects Studied – 1995-2000

System Project	Main Purpose	Participants
Geographic Information System Cooperative	Data access & sharing	State-local-non-profit-private-federal
Aging Network Service Management System	Case management	State –local-private
Electronic Local Financial Reports	Fiscal administration	State-local
Electronic Death Certificates	Vital records	State-local-private-non-profit
Electronic Transfer of Dog License Data	Licensing	State-local-private
Hunting and Fishing Licenses	Licensing	State-local-non-profit
Immunization Information Systems	Health care	State-local-private-non-profit
Probation Automation Project	Case management	State-local
Real Property Assessment System	Tax Administration	State-local-private
Real Property Sales Network	Records management	State-local-private
Local Social Services Imaging Project	Records management	State-local
Electronic Voter Registration	Records management	State-local-federal-non-profit
Homeless Information Management System	Program planning & evaluation	State-local-private-non-profit
Kids Well-being Indicator Clearinghouse	Program planning & evaluation	State-local-federal-federal
New York City IT Knowledge Repository	Knowledge sharing	Multiple local agencies
Municipal Affairs Contact Management	Technical assistance	Multiple regions of a state agency
Statewide Accounting System	Financial administration	State-local-private
Annual Real Property Assessments	Tax administration	State-local

Programmatically the projects range from human services to law enforcement to general government functions. Seven projects can be thought of as "G-to-G" applications in which government agencies and jurisdictions transact some kind of business with one another. The Electronic Local Financial Reports project is one of this type. It replaced a cumbersome and ineffective manual reporting process with one in which local governments used simple technology-supported templates to record and transmit their annual financial statements to the state. Two others were designed specifically for public access to government information. The Kids Well-being Indicator Clearinghouse, for example, integrated data formerly collected and published in a book of statistics into a searchable web-based repository with built-in data analysis features. Six other projects, such as the Aging Services Network, supported direct client or citizen services. Three others supported the operational or planning needs of the participating agencies. For example, the Homeless Information system aims to collect client data from non-profit and government shelters in order to produce an integrated database that all participating agencies can use to evaluate the effectiveness of shelter programs. This broad sampling of collaborative government systems offered a rare opportunity for systematic investigation.

CTG's role in the 18 projects took several forms. In the group of 11 state-local projects, we conducted surveys and interviews with the participants, and conducted document analysis to both describe and explain the structure and dynamics of the projects. In the others, we worked directly with the participating organizations as they established their goals, sought good practices to emulate, evaluated their business processes, and data resources, prototyped and tested systems, and constructed business cases for full system development.

3.   CONSTRAINTS ON COLLABORATIVE SYSTEMS – AND THEIR CONSEQUENCES

The eighteen projects revealed a working environment of extraordinary complexity. The research unveiled a consistent set of five environmental factors that interact, and almost inevitably lead to some undesirable consequences. Every project operated in the context of these systemic constraints which reflect the policy, legal, and economic environment; technology infrastructure and capabilities; program rules; business processes; management techniques; and human and organizational limitations. Figure 1 below shows how these factors combine to produce these undesirable consequences.

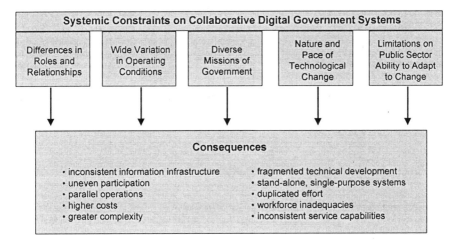

Figure 1. Systemic Constraints on Effective Collaborative Systems

3.1 Roles and relationships

We found that the roles of different organizational actors are complicated, changing, and often poorly understood. In state-local relationships, for example, the two levels of government operate on both shared and separate bodies of law. They interact differently with citizens, one usually at some distance, the other in a much more personal way. They attract and rely on different kinds of professionals; state officials tend to be specialists in various professions, local officials are more often generalists. State and local levels are organized according to a mixture of constitutional, programmatic, financial, traditional, and geographic dimensions. In addition, they engage in a variety of relationships with one another: collaborative, contractual, regulatory, and adversarial. Public and private sector roles and relationships reflect other differences: the profit motive so crucial to successful business is absent in government; methods of staff recruitment and rewards for performance are widely different.

3.2 Variety

Organizations that participate in collaborative service delivery systems also exhibit great variation even within the same type. Local governments are an especially good example. In New York, local government is organized into 57 counties, 62 cities and 932 towns. There are also thousands of special districts that manage schools, fire protection, water systems, transportation, and other specialized activities. Local jurisdictions exhibit an infinite variety of conditions based on population, economic conditions, and physical geography. Federal and state agencies vary widely as well in size and distribution of staff and funding. Often each agency's work culture is dominated by a single profession – medicine in health departments, engineering in transportation agencies, and so on, Similarly, non-profit and commercial organizations can be of almost any size, focus on any of a myriad of goals, and be organized and managed in widely different ways.

3.3   Missions

Every level of government tries to carry out a large number of unrelated missions: build roads, educate children, protect the environment, fight crime, and create jobs. Even within the same agency, specialized programs usually divide the organization into clear sub-units of responsibility. Systems that support service programs reflect this "stove pipe" way of organizing work, partly because they are designed to respond to these specific missions, partly because the entire authorizing environment from Congressional committees to budgeting and accounting practices are set up to reinforce programmatic integrity. Moreover, all of government's many missions are important and therefore they all compete for resources from the same pool of tax dollars, a situation that sets up adversarial conditions even when agencies are trying to collaborate on common goals.

3.4   Technology

In the past decade, and particularly since the emergence of the Internet, powerful new computing and communications technologies have been introduced into to government operations. However, the electronic revolution has not reached into every corner of our society nor every government office that serves local communities. Large agencies and businesses are well equipped, while others are not. Wide discrepancies in technical capacity from one place to another severely limit the degree to which these new tools can be applied consistently to program management and information sharing goals. Network infrastructure is often built by individual units of government paying some portion of the cost to build or at least connect to high-speed networks. In small, poor, and rural places, and in many non-profit service organizations, this often means no connection at all. Similarly, computing capabilities often reflect the ability of each agency and jurisdiction to pay for its own needs, resulting in a patchwork of technology that does not support a consistent level or quality of service.

3.5 Adaptability

The very structure of our government allows significant change only when there is strong agreement among a wide variety of individuals and institutions. The laws and regulations that codify government activities ensure stability in operations, but they also make change difficult to achieve. The budgetary process, civil service requirements, and procurement and ethics laws all act as brakes on the ability of any one actor to make and implement decisions. Moreover, federal, state, and local electoral, budgetary, and legislative cycles may not coincide, making intergovernmental initiatives even more difficult to define and implement. When juxtaposed against the more rapid and flexible change capabilities of successful businesses, it is no surprise that government moves more slowly and continually looks for ways to engage business in its operations.

The environmental factors described above have specific consequences for using information systems effectively:

- Technological capacity (hardware, software, networking), and the ability to pay for it, varies widely from place to place and organization to organization.
- Inadequate intergovernmental, interagency, and inter-program communications lead to fragmented and duplicate development efforts.
- A limited repertoire of relationships with private businesses and stringent "arms-length" relationships often result in inadequate communication and limited working-level interaction between the government and the private sector.
- Program-specific funding and legal requirements encourage stand-alone, single-purpose systems.
- Uneven local capacity to participate fully in new systems, often requires state agencies to support two or more variations.
- Technical workforce inadequacies reduce the ability of all governments and most non-profit agencies to take advantage of new technologies.

4. GUIDING PRINCIPLES FOR COLLABORATIVE DIGITAL GOVERNMENT APPLICATIONS

The research went beyond the identification and explanation of these problems to explore instances where projects were successfully meeting at least some goals or expectations. These goals included satisfaction across all participants with goal setting, decision making, system design and implementation, and user support. By focusing our analytical lens below the level of the entire system, we uncovered a number of good, effective strategies and practices. These findings generated useful lessons even from projects that were not otherwise highly successful. This body of knowledge and experience suggests some powerful principles that can help collaborative digital government systems develop more successfully.

4.1   Have a clear purpose and realistic, measurable expectations

Common understanding of a shared and clearly articulated purpose is crucial in collaborative initiatives. Realistic, measurable expectations about ability to achieve that purpose are equally important. Together, these represent decisions about what specific goals the project should address and what realistically can be achieved given the resources available. We saw in some projects how clear statements of purpose and scope fostered the ability to set measureable performance goals, which increasingly critical to continued funding and political support for systems initiatives.

4.2   Identify and understand all stakeholders

In order for different organizations to work toward the same or complementary goals, they need to understand and appreciate one another's abilities, strengths, and limitations. Stakeholder considerations must encompass all those who are directly involved in the process of designing, delivering, and paying for the system. Customers, of course, represent another critical stakeholder group. Stakeholders also include those who are indirectly affected by the outcome of a new system or program. Stakeholder analysis must include not only positive impacts. It is equally important to know who can be hurt and how.

4.3   Commit to serious partnerships

The concept of "partnership" has become so overused that it has begun to lose its meaning. In the projects where effective partnerships were in place we saw active, trustful relationships focused on common goals; real sharing of risks, resources and benefits; and healthy interdependence as well as clear and logical division of responsibilities.

4.4   Choose a well-skilled and respected project leader

The project leader is a critical success factor in collaborative system projects. The leader must be able to span the psychological and political distance between different agencies, levels of government, or sectors of the economy. The best leaders had a good understanding of the real world operations of each participant, they enjoyed the confidence and support of top-level executives, were excellent communicators, resourceful managers, and were flexible and willing to seize opportunities.

4.5   Adopt tools and techniques to manage complexity

These projects require tools to manage people, time, relationships, partnerships, ideas, conflicts, resources, information, and processes. Project managers need a range of techniques to manage multiple streams of formal and informal communication and activity. Successful techniques usually combined some rigor in design, but also common sense adaptations to particular problems or situations. Techniques that harness group (rather than individual) analysis and decision making were especially useful.

4.6   Recruit a balanced project team.

The most effective work teams included strength in three areas: management, technology, and policy. They could handle traditional project management functions (time lines, work plans, budgets, recruiting). They understood both the capabilities and limitations of various technical choices and implemented them well. They also included well-informed program and policy staff, including those engaged in direct service functions, who kept a constant eye on substantive service goals.

4.7   Expect to assemble a mixture of resources

Most collaborative systems operate on a variety of funding and in-kind resources contributed by different organizations, with different rules of accountability. These resources may include regular appropriations, grants, and in-kind contributions of material or expertise. Successful financing strategies in these projects often entailed not only the usual budget management skills, but also the ability to convince others to contribute resources, to compete successfully for grants, to "leverage" existing resources, and to balance the constraints and rules imposed by multiple funding sources.

4.8   Communicate as if survival depends on it

Good communication practices ensured that all stakeholders (both those actively involved and those who would eventually be affected) were continuously and adequately informed about project goals and progress. The best communications plans used a variety of communication techniques suitable for different audiences. Contacts were tailored in content, detail, frequency, and medium to the specific information needs of each audience

4.9   Pay attention to work processes and practices

Project teams often found that a significant amount of the improvement they expected from a new system actually came from understanding and improving their business processes before they applied any technology. It was very worthwhile to analyze and improve processes as part of the design stage. Moreover, in many instances even very standard business processes were conducted in very non-standard environments. Tools such as data dictionaries, and process and workflow analysis helped identify ways that different organizations could participate in a new system or service. Organizations unable to implement a sophisticated automated system in the short term began by focusing simply on the new or improved business process. An organization that needed to retain its reliance on paper processing could still adopt the standard data definitions that were built into the computerized system. In this way, each organization could begin to integrate the useful elements of the new system into its own environment, given its own operational and resource constraints.

4.10   Demonstrate and refine ideas before implementing

We saw how prototypes and demonstrations made ideas tangible to users and open to improvement throughout the design process. The philosophy behind prototyping is that system development is more effective when customers are partners in the design process. Prototyping allows for the building of the system to begin much earlier in the development process, and allows customers to see and influence the system as it is being built. The projects that included prototypes made tangible all the ideas that both designers and customers usually try to communicate to one another in words. These projects were better able to engage users, to see and understand the functionality and limitations of the design, and to alter it as needed.

5. CONCLUSION

Across the 18 initiatives, we observed many effective applications of these principles. While some of the projects were especially effective, none of them could be characterized as a complete success. Nevertheless, each one offered some insight into various aspects of collaborative system design, development, or implementation. These insights serve as lessons in effective practice that revolve around three main considerations: accounting for the needs and capabilities of all stakeholders, understanding the details of all the work environments in which the system will operate, and managing not only the work, but the complexity of the relationships that underlie collaborative systems.

REFERENCES

Burt, R. S. (1997). The contingent value of social capital. *Administrative Science Quarterly*, 42: 339-365.

Cigler, B.A. (1994). "The County-State Connection: A National Study of Associations of Counties." *Public Administration Review* 54(1): 3-11.

Center for Technology in Government. (2000). The Insider's Guide to Using Information in Government at http://www.ctg.albany.edu/guides/usinginfo. Albany, NY: Center for Technology in Government, University at Albany/SUNY.

Dawes, S. (1995). Interagency Information Sharing: Expected Benefits, Manageable Risks. Journal of Policy Analysis and Management, 15(3): 377-394.

Dawes, S., et al. (1997.) *Tying a Sensible Knot: A Practical Guide to State-Local Information Systems.* Albany, NY: Center for Technology in Government, University at Albany/SUNY.

Dawes, S., Pardo T., Connelly, D., Green, D., & McInerney, C. (1997). *Partners in State-Local Information Systems: Lessons from the Field,* Albany, NY: Center for Technology in Government University at Albany/SUNY.

Dawes, S., Bloniarz, P., Kelly, K., & Fletcher, P. (1999). *Some Assembly Required: Building a Digital Government for the 21st Century*, Albany, NY: Center for Technology in Government, University at Albany/SUNY.

Dutton, W. H. (1999). *Society on the Line: Information Politics in the Digital Age.* Oxford University Press.

Heeks, R. (1999). Reinventing Government in the Information Age in Heeks, R., ed. *Reinventing Government in the Information Age: International Practice in IT-Enabled Public Sector Reform.* New York: Routledge.

Kelly, K. et al. (1995.) *Sharing the Costs, Sharing the Benefits: The NYS GIS Cooperative Project.* Albany, NY: Center for Technology in Government, University at Albany/SUNY.

Kumar, K. & van Dissel, H.G. (1996 September). "Sustainable Collaboration: Managing Conflict and Cooperation in Interorganizational Systems." *MIS Quarterly:* 279-287.

Landsbergen, David and George Wolken. (2001). "Realizing the Promise: Government Information Systems and the Fourth Generation of Information Technology." *Public Administration Review* 61:2:206-220.

Larson, A. (1992). Network Dyads on Entrepreneurial Settings: A Study of the Governance of Relationships, *Administrative Science Quarterly* 36: 76-104.
McCaffrey, D.P., Faerman, S.R., & Hart, D.W. (1995). The Appeal and Difficulties of Participative Systems, *Organization Science* 6(6): 603-627.
National Performance Review (1993). *Report on the National Performance Review.* .Washington D.C: Government Printing Office.
Pardo, T. A. (1998.) Reducing the risks in innovative uses of information technology in the public sector: A multidisciplinary model. Unpublished Doctoral Dissertation, University at Albany-SUNY, Albany, NY.
Weiss, J.A. (1987). Pathways to Cooperation among Public Agencies, *Journal of Policy Analysis and Management* 7(Fall): 94-117.

Sharon Dawes is the Director of the Center for Technology in Government at the University at Albany, State University of New York, an applied research center devoted to effective use of information technology in the public sector. As Director, Dr. Dawes is responsible for programs, projects, and partnerships that increase productivity, reduce costs, increase coordination, and enhance the quality of government operations and public services. In 1995, the Center was named an Innovations in American Government Award winner.

From 1987 to 1993, Dr. Dawes was Executive Director of the NYS Forum for Information Resource Management, a network of state government organizations and public officials interested in information management, policy, and technology. Forum programs of research, outreach, and education involve a wide variety of public officials, as well as private corporations and academic institutions interested in information policies and technologies.

Dr. Dawes also has a dozen years experience in the Executive Branch of New York State government. From 1977 to 1984, she was Associate Commissioner for Income Maintenance with the NYS Department of Social Services, a position with responsibilities for the state's multi-billion dollar intergovernmental public assistance programs. There she was instrumental in the development of the Department's statewide Welfare Management System (WMS).

Dr. Dawes has written research reports, articles, and case studies that take a variety of perspectives on information as a public resource. She is co-author of Government Information Management: A Primer and Casebook, published in 1991 by Prentice-Hall, and has lectured on information policy and management in the public sector before numerous professional, academic, and government audiences.

Dr. Dawes holds a Ph.D. in Public Administration from the Rockefeller College of Public Affairs & Policy at the State University of New York at Albany.

Theresa Pardo is the Project Director at the Center for Technology in Government, a public-private-academic partnership designed to reduce the risks of applying information to public problems. The Center is a 1995 *Innovations in American Government Award* winner. Dr. Pardo is currently a Co-Principal Investigator in two research projects sponsored by the National Science Foundation: *Knowledge Networking in the Public Sector* and *Digital Government: Developing an Information Technology and Organizational Design Research Agenda for Evaluation and Management of Research Proposals*. She has also directed two projects addressing electronic records issues funded by the National Archives. Dr. Pardo teaches in the information science and public administration programs at the University at Albany, State University of New York and has written articles, research reports, and case studies focusing on information use and information technology innovation in the public sector. She holds a Ph.D. in Information Science from the Rockefeller College of Public Affairs and Policy at the University at Albany, State University of New York.

Chapter 17

E-Government in Canada
Meeting The Digital Imperative

Jeffrey Roy
Centre on Governance, The University of Ottawa, Ottawa, Ontario Canada.

Abstract: This article examines the evolution of digital government in the Canadian context. Key policy documents that have established the foundation for Canada's digital government plans are discussed. In addition, the views of a cross section of senior Canadian government officials on the development of digital government are presented. The views discussed by these officials address issues of system and organizational capacities, cultures of innovation and technological adoption, competencies, drivers and inhibitors of the evolution of digital government, and design principles.

Key words: policymaking, design, decision-making, technology adoption, organization

1.   INTRODUCTION

E-government is expanding. As online activity grows across private, public and civil spheres of organizational life, and as governance transformations impact organizations across these sectors, governments are not immune. The most relevant question is whether public sector leaders can orchestrate change by fostering adaptive capacities and coherent strategies for renewal - or whether the emerging digital era will impose change in a fashion more reactionary.

This chapter begins from the premise that e-government presents a real transformation in democratic governance, including design, decision-making and service delivery capabilities. Importantly, e-government takes place within a changing governance context where technology itself may only be one driver – as people debate the extent to which it is a tool for improving current systems or an enabling platform for redefining them for more fundamental ways.

Whatever the balance here, the lesson here is that understanding the digital architecture is only one element of the e-government challenge, and it may not be the primary one at that. E-government, in deploying new technologies and reorganizing governance and managerial processes in order to adapt to an inter-connected world, presents today's leaders with a daunting task in looking toward tomorrow.

In Canada, the foundation for the e-government movement has been established by three key policy documents put forward by the Management Board of the Government (Treasury Board of Canada Secretariat, www.tsc-sct.gc.ca):

1. A Blueprint for Renewing Government Services using Information Technology (1994)
2. Strategic Directions for Information Management and Information Technology: Enabling 21st Century Services to Canadians (April 2000)
3. A Framework for Government On-line (February 2000)

This movement was inspired and prioritized by the October 12th, Speech from the Throne in which the federal government vowed that by 2004, it would be known around the world as the government most connected to its citizens. This e-government initiative has been labelled "Government Online" (GOL) in Canada - although online service delivery is just one of the many components of GOL. A high level committee of senior public sector executives was subsequently created to act as the senior advisory and oversight committee ("champion") for GOL.

In terms of implementation, the leadership or oversight role was given to the Chief Information Officer Branch (CIOB) in the Treasury Board Secretariat. Within this Branch, an Office for Government Online was established to coordinate GOL efforts across the federal government. The office determined three key areas of implementation: technology, people, and business processes. The backbone of the technology component is the Strategic IM/IT Infrastructure Initiative (SII) aimed at developing a federated architecture for the federal government.

This chapter examines the efforts of the Government of Canada to harness information and communication technology (ICT) as an enabling force. Various forms of e-government are now clearly on policy and managerial reform agendas of the public sector. The extent to which the challenges are well understood, however, is the source of much debate. Some managers and politicians remain sceptical in the face of spectacular claims of external commentators that the Internet is a revolution in both citizen expectations and service delivery; yet, others are more optimistic and e-champions are gathering strength as public service renewal is increasingly intertwined with technological change.

2. THE VIEW FROM WITHIN

In speaking with a cross-section of senior public servants across both operational departments and central agencies, we probed them on their views about the likely opportunities and challenges ahead with respect to e-government[1].

Specifically, this dialogue was guided by three broad directions: i) capacities – the overall vision and approach requires; ii) culture – the adaptive challenges, the new decision-making approaches, and the changing leadership requirements; and iii) competencies – the necessary skill sets and human resource considerations for managing people.

2.1 Capacities

The short-term vision for the federal government is to ensure that all government services are on-line by the year 2004. According to government leaders, this vision must be viewed as the realization of an environment where citizens have a choice of delivery channels. And if they are using the electronic channel, services must be organized in such a way that on-line engagements are meaningful and accessible through a single-window.

For many senior managers, the rapid acceleration of technological innovation is challenging government's capacity to adapt in an unparalleled manner. For instance, the government put in place major telephone call centres roughly 25 years ago, and even today issues arise as to their effective utilization. In a digital world, planning for the next three years will be a challenge, to say nothing of achieving a coherent forecast of the world in ten years time.

Another emerging challenge for e-government lies in the balance between corporate direction and departmental flexibility. Federal executives accept that flexibility is crucial in order to facilitate innovation at the department level. At the same time, they believe that new capacities are required on a government-wide basis, as departments need to have a shared approach to common objectives, much like integrative Y2K efforts.

One result is that on-line government means taking a government-wide approach to agenda setting. Infrastructure is key to enabling such inter-connectivity and responsiveness at a government-wide level. The notion of a federated architecture model is meant to be sensitive to the difficult balancing act at play by achieving government-wide coordination in a fashion that equally respects departmental flexibility and front-line innovation.

Industry is also a critical reference point for the emergence of e-government, and business may have multiple roles to play. The extent to which the private sector is a competitor, a model, or a partner of government is an issue of strategic importance. Executives believe that the constant pressure to respond to a changing marketplace also forces government to become more innovative itself. The main reason lies in public expectations, shaped by a variety of service delivery experiences that create points of comparison between private and public models. Thus, innovation being spurred by electronic commerce translates into higher public expectations toward government.

In terms of contrasts, however, others suggest that adopting a business case approach with the sort of return on investment tests prevalent in the marketplace may not be the most appropriate route for government. In the short run, much of the effort in fostering a digital architecture may not carry such returns, and what is required is a business case accounting for this form of strategic investment. In this sense, government's mission is partly distinct from business in serving broader questions of the public good, such as infrastructure, in a digital era.

The shared view across executives is that *complementarity* is more important than commonality. There was broad agreement that there is much to be gained from bringing private sector people into government—adding that creativity, rather than conformity, should be encouraged. The uncertainty so prevalent in a digital environment also challenges relations between business and government.

If the public sector possessed a clear blueprint of what it wanted to achieve, with few unknowns, then it would be relatively easy for industry to be able to promise to help reach specified targets. The absence of any such certainty makes collaboration a challenge. In terms of realizing new forms of private-public partnerships, some respondents point out that the public sector carries unique attributes that may augment the complexity in forging such arrangements. The greater role of public scrutiny, for example, may make it difficult to foster a culture conducive to risk. As a result, there is a need for collective education—including all stakeholders and the public in order to learn to better acknowledge when a certain amount of failure must be tolerated.

2.2 Culture

Many respondents stressed that in a world of greater electronic connectivity, aligning leadership is a critical challenge. The key is to provide leadership that ensures an integrative strategy of technology, people and performance. Providing a culture that unleashes creativity and focuses on outcomes must be a key priority of public sector leadership today.

In terms of the new type of leadership required for e-government, not everything is new however. Clear direction and sound judgement remain critical success factors, although the systems within which they are being applied are rapidly changing. A unique challenge in government is the lack of clear equivalent to the CEO and Board of Directors of a private sector company, which means that the politicians and the public are key stakeholders.

Government's complex agenda, along with the uncertainty of how to couple bottom line considerations with what is in the public interest may well increase the risk associated with IT investments. A holistic assessment of government requirements is necessary, both to provide adequate funding for the digital foundation of e-government and to better guide decision-making as layers are built upon this base.

A major leadership challenge will be to find ways to create momentum for such innovation and creativity, and to guide this momentum in a coherent direction. An additional role for an e-government leader is to ensure that all components of the organization (corporately or at the department level) understand the ramifications of new technology for every aspect of decision-making, policy formulation, and service delivery. Building this understanding requires a culture of learning. This need for multiple forms of direction and accountability creates a particular challenge for senior public sector managers at the Deputy and Ministerial level. Leadership means blending specific targets and mandates with horizontal agendas, and IT is a critical driver in this regard.

New forms of trust are said to be required across government, and this type of connectivity, often much more horizontal than in the past, cannot be easily rooted in hierarchy. One government executive estimates that on a scale of organizational complexity, Y2K may be viewed as perhaps a 4 out of 10. Subsequent phases of on-line government and digital governance, in contrast, should be viewed as more akin to an 8 of 10. Y2K was largely remedial; these next steps are about process realignment and designing something entirely new.

In terms of information flows and transparency, many of the executives agree that the explosion of information is altering government decision-making in far reaching ways. As one example, much of the legislative framework adopted for an industrial era, designed to protect and control information flows, may no longer be appropriate in an era of information sharing and knowledge management.

However, many see this shift, at least, in a potentially positive way. As information becomes more readily available, there is greater transparency across government, and the public will not only demand more, they will also know more. The result will be that people will feel a higher sense of value for their investments in government, and if the value is not there, a more informed public means greater accountability.

Practically, the growth of information also carries enormous consequences for workflows within government. Responding to electronic mail, maintaining adequate records, and learning to separate data that is largely noise from strategic information, are all organizational challenges of an unprecedented magnitude in a digital era.

For the time being, these challenges may raise more questions than answers. Government managers must ask themselves—how much do you negotiate and how much do you dictate, when do you devolve, and when is centralization necessary?

This central – flexible balance is a crucial theme. Some individuals point to a careful, but strategic role for central agencies to assist in this transition, although it must be one of facilitation rather than dictation. Central agencies may be best positioned to provide a neutral forum for cross-departmental learning and sharing strategic advice.

Yet, central agencies must prepare for this role by becoming a focal point of relational knowledge as to how government interacts with other stakeholders—citizens, businesses and social groups, and other levels of government. Here again, a new federated approach to governance requires a balance of autonomy and coordination.

How are these changes sustained? According to several executives, there must be an organizational culture that empowers ownership to those taking decisions. In turn, accountabilities are multiplied, and the central management challenge is to link individual and collective performance. The latter must also be a part of people's accountabilities, and it must be measured.

Some respondents foresee a more networked model of government where technology both empowers public servants with more information and connects them to their clients in a much more direct fashion. This shift entails a much greater need for partnering within government, as well as between government departments and their external agents in the network[2].

2.3 Competencies

Executives link the renewal of leadership with a focus on people: they also point to the need to start with the most senior managers across government. One individual underlined that since the background of a significant proportion of Deputy Ministers is in policy, their sensitivity to the impact of a digital transformation may be limited.

Government must invest more in training, and think about systemic ways to reward those who promote innovation and risk in a manner that recognizes government's uniqueness, rather than being captured by it. A new balance between performance and process is required, and e-champions must be nurtured to lead the way. Once again, others are equally insistent on the responsibility of senior management, suggesting that there should be a basic IT proficiency test for potential EX candidates.

The risks and rewards associated with IT and e-governance are also important factors in managing staff. One leader comments that IT failures are often more visible than those in policy or program areas, and there must be attention accorded to this point. Similarly, traditional governmental processes may not support the same types of rewards for success in a highly charged IT environment than those found in industry.

The result is that government must pay closer attention to its human resources efforts, and in particular, to its capacities to train and retain highly skilled workers. The public sector, according to many, has much to offer in terms of interesting work and flexible work styles.

Fostering a dynamic and supportive work environment is as much a part of the foundation for digital government as technology itself. The digital transformation is all encompassing; it is therefore necessary that the process of reform be as open as possible. While communications tools are one component, the process must also involve consultation, listening and dialogue.

The challenge extends to all layers of the public sector. For example, program managers in government have not traditionally thought about electronic service delivery and its various dimensions, such as the need for horizontal governance. These types of issues are indicative of the ongoing challenge facing public servants.

3. LOOKING AHEAD – DRIVERS AND INHIBITORS

Overall, four main drivers emerge from discussions with executives, and while their order may be arguable each is important. The first and most recent policy driver is the 1999 Speech from The Throne and its pledge to ensure that all government services will be on-line by 2004. This type of political support creates somewhat of a *burning platform* to make things happen.

The second key driver is the government wide-priority of improving service delivery to citizens and businesses, electronically or otherwise. The strategic challenge here involves embracing a citizen centric model based on a single window, enhanced accessibility and efficiency, reliability and security. This logic sees clients shaping governments, and the expectation is a growing client base moving on-line.

The third driver is part of the overall strategy to modernize government—a process in which technology is now recognized as a key factor. Fourthly, the federal executives suggest that a successful evolution toward e-government will yield synergies with the private sector, increasing their competitiveness internationally. There is broad agreement that the 21st century context of globalization and digitization accelerates the importance of each of these points.

In terms of inhibitors, a key consideration is cost. In fact, there are huge amounts of resources required to create a digital infrastructure. Yet, cost may also be perceived incorrectly if bottom line considerations are not weighted properly against a complete picture of government's agenda. Since strategic investments into digital government play an important public interest role, carrying many spin-off benefits for industry and communities alike, there can be no simplistic return on investment calculations.

Another challenge of moving to e-government is the issues of acceptance and accessibility. Several executives pointed out that, on average, connected Canadians are probably better off citizens, and the danger of a growing digital bias is an issue not only for government, but rather for all stakeholders in our society.

Thus, certain segments of our population will require special efforts in order to develop the skills necessary to benefit from the promises of a digital world. At the same time, a service provider government must be prepared to offer the necessary advice and support for aspiring users of on-line channels.

Although all executives concur with the dangers of a digital divide, some also perceive a strategic opportunity for government. Electronic channels, and innovative approaches to deploy them may allow governments to become more creative in reaching out to these same Canadians, demonstrating a commitment to both connectivity and cohesion.

4.   EMERGING DESIGN PRINCIPLES

There is the basis of a shared belief that an effective strategy to realize e-government must re-balance traditional administrative and political-cultural frameworks and the adaptive and collaborative requirements of e-governance. This process requires a *renewed culture in government*, one more open to the enormous potential of technology in its main forms.

From the preceding discussion, four main guiding principles are proposed that – taken collectively – provide a template for shared thinking and action.

First, *efficiency* remains a key principle for government - tied, in part, to an inter-connected global arena carefully monitoring the fiscal performance of all countries. A key component of the potential of ICT is the capacity for reduced costs as new media channels create a compelling business case for delivering services on-line.

Yet, the uniqueness of the "business case" in government has been underscored: it is not driven by maximizing profits as in the marketplace, but rather by maximizing the collective potential of all Canadians, individually and organizationally, to lead productive and prosperous lives in a more electronic and knowledge-driven age. Thus, efficiency gains must be weighed along with the investment being made to encouraging people to develop on-line skills. Cost savings is one variable in a more complex equation.

Secondly, *adaptability* is increasingly important as a principle. A critical part of the e-government challenge is the sobering recognition that the environment is not static: whether the federal government succeeds in getting all services on-line by 2004 is perhaps less important than the reality that the social, economic and political contexts of 2004 could well by very different from today.

This principle implies a public sector comfortable with technology in different forms. Adaptive e-government means deploying technology as an "enable" force for better learning and knowledge management. Information, communication and social networks will transcend traditional structures and boundaries: they must be unified less by control and more by a common mission and collective leadership.

Such learning requires dialogue in order to allow government to become both digital and *deliberative* – the latter being the third principle. The challenge of deliberative government extends beyond the need to improve existing capacities today. Deliberative government must engage its partners and the citizenry and define the future as well: *Deliberative democracy underpins social learning, and it justifies the growing pursuit of public and multi-stakeholder consultation techniques today.*

Government must not only accept input: it must seek it and demonstrate how participation helps to define policy and improve service delivery. Perhaps the most contentious, and certainly the least discussed aspect of e-government is the role of deliberation in reforming democratic governance.

A useful, and indeed necessary component of e-government readiness will be strengthening the deliberative capacities of the public service, and anticipating the potential consequences for the democratic processes so closely interwoven. What is required is an alignment of new skill sets within the public sector, of new relational ties to specialists outside of, but engaged with the public sector, and of the broader public in their dual capacities of both customer of government services and citizen of the democratic polity.

Such alignment will invariably remain elusive - and as such, the best one can strive for is to foster ongoing capacities for improvement and adaptation. Such capacities are underpinned by learning - and as a result, e-government must be about working in a more strategic and collaborative fashion in order to strengthen overall capacities across traditional boundaries.

This governance challenge means undertaking both a structural and cultural shift from, moving from *independence* to one where *interdependence* becomes the fourth guiding principle. Building e-government on this premise provides the fourth design principle for bettering governance. In sum, four crucial design principles of e-government are:

- *Efficient*   - *Adaptive*
- *Interdependent*   - *Deliberative*

5.   CONCLUSION

What are the lessons to be drawn? First, realizing the promise of e-government is perhaps best viewed as an evolving process of learning and adaptation. As digital connectivity grows, a mix of technical and social forces will transform the shape of our public institutions over time.

Yet, precisely how this transformation will occur depends greatly on the citizen, and the manner by which public expectations are shaped by collective education and experiential learning. This evolution will likely be neither predictable nor common across all segments of the population. Consequently, digital governance must meet many needs via multiple challenges simultaneously.

For this reason, the federal executives understand the need to move beyond the somewhat simplistic comparisons of the *old* and the *new* model of governing. The holistic challenge is to seek innovation while recognizing that redesigning governance requires buy-in and ongoing support, as much from public servants working in government as from clients of the services they provide.

A related and quite important message emerging from both the literature and our respondents is that governments will operate with heightened interdependence. Partnerships are now central to public management, and it must be a priority for all governments to foster and strengthen capacities for collaborative action.

In a digital world, relationship management will become a core competency of the new public servant. The digital infrastructure must be complemented by human ingenuity, and trust among all partners becomes an essential ingredient in order to navigate an environment of heightened change and uncertainty.

In sum, there is a need for expanding, deepening and sustaining dialogue—across all stakeholders and the citizenry. E-government must be an engaged and constructive partner in shaping the new governance patterns that will otherwise render it rudderless.

These governance patterns must bridge traditional administrative and political-cultural frameworks to the adaptive and collaborative requirements of a connected and interdependent world – a world that requires a *new culture in government*, one open and enabled to take advantage of the enormous potential of the digital and information age.

NOTES

1. The primary set of interviews, undertaken by Deloitte Consulting took place over the winter of 2000, during the adoption phase of the Government Online agenda. Follow-up interviews, led by The Centre on Governance also took place in the fall of 2000. The initial set of interviews was published jointly by Deloitte Consulting and The Centre on Governance in the monogram series, governance (#4), E-Government in Canada: A Dialogue with Federal Executives on Meeting the Digital Transformation (Barb Kieley, Greg Lane and Jeffrey Roy). For more information, please consult The Centre on Governance (www.governance.uottawa.ca).
2. The Government of Canada has recently launched a renewed portal which features three "clusters" or streams of services, integrated across functions for separate clients groups (citizens, businesses, and non-Canadians). For many observers, such a step marks the tentative beginning of reorganizing government internally to better orient information, services and functionality externally.

3. The research assistance of Paul Faya is both duly acknowledged and greatly appreciated.

REFERENCES

Browning, J. [1998] "Power to the People - Government isn't disappearing. It's being Disintermediated" in WIRED Magazine (January 1998).

Canadian Defence Industry Association [1999] "CDIA Procurement Committee, Industry Proposals for DND Procurement Reform"(www.cdia.ca/committee/procure.htm).

Carr, G. [1998] "Public-Private Partnerships: The Canadian Experience"(speech to Oxford School of Project Finance, available at http://home.inforamp.net/~partners/oxford.html).

Center for Technology in Government, "Making Smart IT Choices" [1998] (Albany: www.ctg.albany.edu/resources)

Chief Information Officer's Branch (CIOB), Treasury Board of Canada Secretariat [1998] "Supporting Electronic Government: The Government of Canada Public Key Infrastructure" (Ottawa: http://www.cio-dpi.gc.ca).

Corden, S. [1997] "The Australian Government's Industry Commission Examines Competitive Tendering and Contracting by Public Sector Agencies" reported in Public Administration Review (March/April 1997, Vol.57, No.2).

Duff, Angus. [1997] "Outsourcing Information Technology - Human Resource Implications" IRC Press, Industrial Relations Centre, Queen's University, Kingston.

Essex, L. and Kusy, M. [1999] Fast Forward Leadership - How to exchange outmoded leadership practises for forward-looking leadership today (Financial Times / Prentice Hall).

Ferris, N. [1999] "CIOs on the Go"in GovExec.com, March 1999 (www.govexec.com/features).

Gagnon, Y. and Dragon, J. [1998] "The Impact of Technology on Organizational Performance" in Galliers, R.D. and Baets, W.R.J. [1998] Information Technology and Organizational Transformation (Wiley Series in Information Systems: Toronto).

Globerman, S. and Vining, A.R. [1996] "A Framework for Evaluating the Government Contracting-Out Decision with an Application to Information Technology" in Public Administration Review (Nov/Dec 1996, Vol.56, No.6)

Guillaume, G.[1999] L'empire de réseaux (Paris: Descartes & Cie.).

International Council for Information Technology in Government Administration [1998] "Procurement Study Group Report" in An International Journal on Information Technology in Government {ICT: www.ica.ogit.gov.au).

Jayes, D. [1998] "Contracting out information technology services at the UK Inland Revenue" in OECD, Contracting Out Government Services (Paris: OECD=s Public Management Occasional Paper No.20).

Jelich, H., Poupart, R., Austin, R. and Roy, J. [2000] "Partnership-Based Governance: Lessons from IT Management" in Optimum Vol. 30, No. 1. pp. 49-54).

Kobrin, S. J. [1998] "You Can't Declare Cyberspace National Territory: Economic Policy-Making in The digital Age" in Tapscott, D. with Lowy, A. and Ticoll, D. Blueprint to the digital Economy: Creating Wealth in the Era of E-Business (McGraw-Hill).

Moritz, R. and Roy, J. [2000] "Demographic Insight on Canada's Federal Information Technology Workforce: Community Renewal and Tomorrow's Leadership Imperative" in Canadian Government Executive (July).

Mornan, B. [1998] "Results-Based Procurement: A Model of Public-Private Sector collaboration" in Optimum Vol.28, No.1.

Nelson, M.R. [1998] "Government and Governance in the Networked World" in Tapscott, D. with Lowy, A. and Ticoll, D. [1998] Blueprint to the digital Economy: Creating Wealth in the Era of E-Business (McGraw-Hill).

New Zealand Public Service [1997] Information Technology Stocktake (Wellington: State Services Commission).

Newcombe, T. [1998] "Multistate On-line Procurement Project Under Way" in Government Technology, Oct 1998 (www.govtech.net/publications/).[3]

OECD [1997] "Information Technology as an Instrument of Public Management Reform: A Study of Five OECD Countries" [OECD: www.oecd.org/puma/gvrnance/it).

Papows, J. [1998] Enterprise.com - market leadership in the information age (Perseus Books: Reading).

Paquet, G.[1997] "States, Communities & Markets: The Distributed Governance Scenario" in The Nation-State in a Global Information Era: Policy Challenges [Queens University Bell Canada Conference].

Public Works and Government Services Canada [1998] "Benefits Driven Procurement" A Paper Presented to the Ninth International Public Procurement Association (Copenhagen: www.pwgsc.gc.ca/sos).

Rifkin, Jeremy [2000] The Age of Access - The New Culture of Hypercapitalism (New York: Jeremy P. Tarcher/Putnam).

Rosenau, P.V. [2000] Public-Private Policy Partnerships (Cambridge, Mass.: The MIT Press).

Tapscott, D. and Agnew, D. [1999] "Governance in the Digital Economy" Finance and Development December 1999, pp. 84-87.

Tapscott, D. with Lowy, A. and Ticoll, D. [1998] Blueprint to the Digital Economy: Creating Wealth in the Era of E-Business (McGraw-Hill).

Thorton, K. [1998] "Living in the Information Society - Rethinking Government" (http://www.ibm.com/ibm/public).

Weill, P. and Broadbent, M. [1998] Leveraging The New Infrastructure - How Market Leaders Capitalize on IT [Harvard Business School Press].

Wyatt, S., Henwood, F., Miler, N. and Senker, P. eds. [2000] Technology and In/Equality – questioning the information society (Routledge: London and New York).

Yankelovich, Daniel. [1999] The Magic of Dialogue: Transforming Conflict into Cooperation (New York: Simon and Schuster).

Dr. Jeffrey Roy is Director of The Centre on Governance and an Assistant Professor of The Faculty of Administration, The University of Ottawa. He holds a B.A. in Economics from The University of Waterloo, an M.B.A. from The University of Ottawa, and a Ph.D. in Public Policy from Carleton University. He teaches courses in Governance, Public Administration and Public Management, Negotiation and Consultation, and New Models of Collaborative Governance in Economic Development and Information Technologies. Current research activities focus on new governance dynamics tied to knowledge, innovation, and new information technologies. Present research projects include an international study on regional learning and collaborative governance and an examination of digital government challenges in North America - emphasizing new forms of private-public partnerships and new models of citizen engagement and multi-stakeholder consultation. Professor Roy may be reached at – roy@admin.uottawa.ca {*visit our Centre @ www.governance.uottawa.ca*}.

Chapter 18

Laying out the Foundation for a Digital Government Model Case Study
Tunisia

Noureddine Boudriga and Salah Benabdallah
National Digital Certification Agency (ANCE), Tunisia
University of Carthage, Tunisia

Abstract: The objective of this chapter is to describe the foundation for a digital
government. It will define the steps for governments to follow to develop
services based on information and telecommunications technologies and the
Internet. Governments need to define objectives and develop a thorough plan
to implement on-line services. Planning will be based on a set of
interdependent tasks constituting three major aspects. They are the
telecommunications infrastructure, the legal framework, and the digital divide.
A model to implement such a plan will be presented and discussed in this
chapter. The model can be implemented by any country, especially emerging
ones. The Tunisian government effort to move toward a digital government
will be presented as an example.

Key words: e-government, info-communication society

1.   INTRODUCTION

Information and communication technologies and the Internet are
changing the world economy and transforming societies in countries around
the world. The use of information by public agencies, businesses, and
citizens has grown rapidly within the last decade in different countries.
Governments that fully use the potential of networked information
technologies will not only increase the quality of their services, but will also
cut the costs of those services. In addition, the use of these technologies will
help to promote the use of information technologies among businesses and
citizens, leading to rapid economic growth and employment, and creating
their information and telecommunications society.

Government entities and agencies play a major role in promoting the digital economy by providing a number of online services, such as access to a wide range of data sets (e.g., public databases, regulation texts, and transportation analyses and forecasts), online tax filling, and bill payment; as well as making available an environment that helps companies embrace the digital economy. But for these objectives to be achieved, they must be intimately associated with reengineering these entities themselves. Economic success will increasingly be determined by:

– how effectively the government can promote technological innovation, encourage entrepreneurship, and improve education and workers skills; and
– how actively the transition is carried out in all organizations, public and private, from traditional hierarchies to networked structures.

In this chapter, a model to implement a digital government is presented and discussed. The model would be a guideline for governments to follow to promote information and communication technology in a society and move toward a digital society. The model is based on thorough planning that includes laying out telecommunications infrastructure, developing information and communication technology pilot projects, preparing the required legislation, securing payments, creating a public key infrastructure for digital certification, and implementing on-line government services.

The proposed model can be implemented by any government, especially governments of emerging countries. In this chapter, Tunisia's experience in implementing such a model will be presented.

The policy issues that Tunisia has undertaken for the implementation of an info-communication society address several measures that can be categorized into four main sets as follows:

1. Expanding the use of information technologies in the public sector by improving use of the Internet to guarantee public access to administrative information and procedures, and promoting the use of information and communications technologies in all departments.
2. Putting down the groundwork for the promotion of electronic commerce by promoting electronic payment and electronic money systems, encouraging the development of electronic authentication procedures, protecting privacy, consumers and intellectual property rights, and developing security measures.
3. Building a legal framework and reforming the institutions for advancing information and telecommunications technology by changing relevant existing regulations that would make the implementation of current technical standards difficult or extremely inefficient.

4. Installing a communication infrastructure capable of supporting the creation, distribution, and sharing of information and knowledge, as well as giving support to basic and advanced research and development in information and telecommunications technologies.

The remaining part of this chapter is organized as follows. Section 2 presents the e-government model and describes the different tasks that a government should follow to implement the online services. Section 3 describes the Tunisian government experience in implementing the model. It will present the Tunisian achievements in implementing a modern communication infrastructure. It will describe the legal framework developed to promote an Info-Communication society. Lastly, this section will present the main measures that the Tunisian government has implemented to reduce the digital divide. Section 4 is the conclusion for chapter.

2. DIGITAL GOVERNMENT MODEL

2.1 Principles of an Info-communication Society

An information and telecommunications society (or info-communication society) is a new socio-economic system where people can accomplish cost-effective innovation that will be available on a network, access data worldwide, and share intellectual products. People in an info-communication society will have easier access to culture and have the ability to make better contributions to economic development. This new type of system is intended to replace the current system, which is based on mass production and mass consumption. It will widen economic frontiers, lead to new waves of reforms, reengineer several administration processes, reduce the need for high-cost structures, develop regional activities, and promote tele-activities.

The move toward an info-communication society in a country will change the structure of the country's economy, implying deep changes that will affect its productivity and modify its organizational structures. It will also improve the rationalization of products, advertisement and distribution. The development of digital economic activity will promote global economic competition. It will also result in higher speed information exchange and improved efficiency in electronic transactions. In addition, it will lower social costs, increase real income, and improve quality of life.

However, the applications of electronic commerce in many areas of economic activities are expected to increase in complexity and size.

Telecommunications technologies and services will continue to develop to meet increasing demand and to improve service quality. Related industries will continue their rapid growth, consolidating their roles as leading industries in the new economy. New industries will be developed in various areas related to information and telecommunications technologies, creating new jobs. New types of companies will be created. They will produce and get managed virtually, no matter where the employees are located.

In today's digital revolution, governments will not have a choice only to promote information technologies (IT) in their perspective societies. Otherwise, they will be left behind economically. The developed (or industrial) countries are well advanced compared to the rest of the world in promoting IT, since their telecommunications infrastructures already exist.

In building the info-communication society, governments need to follow a model. In this chapter, a model that governments can follow to implement e-government is proposed. An e-government is more than a web site. It is connecting a government with its citizens in a scale that until now has been unimaginable. It will change the government work where citizen services and government operations are reformed with a robust technical enterprise platform.

2.2   Digital Government Model

The move toward an info-communication society will result in great use of online services. To achieve such a comfort, prior tasks need to be undertaken, such as laying out the appropriate infrastructure, legislation, and training. The process of implementing e-government will be longer for some countries than others depending on the country's technological advances. Nevertheless, the proposed model is applicable (*Figure 1*) to any government since it is modular. Governments may choose not to apply all the modules depending on their technological advances.

Before presenting the model, a definition for e-government is proposed. An e-government is the installation of online government services where citizens can access government services at any time and from any location, and where government departments and agencies can share and exchange information securely. The government will be modelled as a multi-location large company where the citizens are customers and government agencies are departments of the company, spread all over the country. The model described below details the different steps that any government, especially those that belong to emerging countries, would follow to implement e-government.

In implementing the model (*Figure 1*), governments need to establish a thorough plan. The plan will be based on sequential and parallel phases.

They are three major phases in the planning, the infrastructure, the legal frameworks and the digital divide. These phases are described below. To refer to *Figure 1*, the set of phases are the set of tasks $\{S_i : 1 \le i \le 10)$. It is organized as a workflow as it is shown.

Task S_1: Political Decision to build E-Government: The development of e-government requires a political decision. Governments need to set up objectives in realizing their e-government. They must analyse needs and requirements, evaluate risks, and, finally design a strategic plan.

Task S_2: Infrastructure Evaluation: Governments must determine if their telecommunications network can handle the new traffic resulting from the use of these new services and whether it can provide a high level of service quality. The cost to modernize the network should also be estimated.

Task S_3: Legal Framework: The existing legal frameworks of many governments need to be amended to accommodate new concepts of the digital economy. From a policy perspective, such a legal framework would have to address all the different factors and challenges that are associated with using an information and communication technology platform. Governments need to formulate a legal framework for e-commerce, electronic document exchanges, and telecommunications regulations. Organizational framework should be established to define the legal relations between different ICT actors.

Task S_4: Pilot IT Projects: To implement e-government, governments must start a number of pilot IT projects depending on their country needs. These projects will be a measure to introduce the IT in the society. But before starting these projects, objectives should be defined.

Task S_5: Construction of an Advanced Technology Network: Governments should build a nationwide back-bone network using fiber-optics, advanced switching techniques, and a mobile communications system with global reach. The network will allow access to multiple services including the next-generation Internet, as a foundation to support the conversion to digital broadcast systems to create a global digital network.

Task S_6: Reduce ICT Illiteracy: To make full use of e-government services, governments should reduce IT illiteracy. Political decisions have to be made to connect research centers, universities, and schools to the Internet, to create community centers to promote the use of ICT by the population, and to formulate incentives for companies to train their employees in ICT.

Task S$_7$: Reduce Digital Divide: Governments should give all of its citizens the chance to access computers and the Internet. Incentives should be formulated such as promoting low price, good quality computers, lowering Internet connection fees, and encouraging companies to train their employees in ICT.

Task S$_8$: Develop Digital Payment: The challenges that governments face in electronic payment relate particularly to emerging payment mechanisms that can either be network based or be stored-value cards. The payment mechanisms should be adapted to the local practice. For example, if credit cards are not widely used by a local population, the government should come up with payment mechanisms that will promote on-line transactions.

Task S$_9$: Establish a Certification Authority: In developing on-line government services, governments should formulate a legal framework and technical solutions for handling secure transactions. The technical solutions should be based on building a local public key infrastructure (PKI), developing local expertise in digital certification and signatures, and promoting, in particular, network security procedures.

Task S$_{10}$: Develop On-line Government Services: on-line government services should provide a one-stop government information service. The goal will be to create a friendly easy-to-use mechanism for the public to locate information and services available on the net. In addition, government administrations and agencies should access, share and exchange information securely.

Each of these tasks should be carefully planned and progressively implemented. The temporal dependency between tasks and/or subtasks should be observed. The whole implementation process can take several years depending on the availability of qualified human resources, a country's financial capabilities, and the level of commitment of decision makers.

The following section will present the implementation of the e-government model in Tunisia and describe the results achieved thus far.

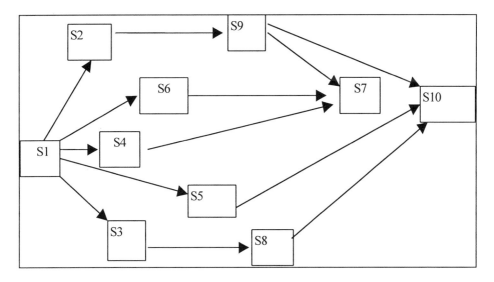

Figure 1. E-government Model

3. CASE STUDY: TUNISIA E-GOVERNMENT

The Tunisian experience in building the e-government and achieving the realization of an info-communication society is based on a strategic plan that first lays out some basic principles that drive the Tunisian information technology planning efforts. These principles have guided the set of strategic goals based on the urgency that drives their implementation. These principles can be describes as follow:

– The Tunisian government would provide access to non-classified information and processes for all citizens and businesses to verify and to modify the information collected about them.

– Tunisian's infrastructure would support universal access to government information and services through reduction of social and economic barriers. It would also provide secure electronic transactions.

– The Tunisian government would consider information technology as a strategic asset and give it a key role in re-engineering government processes to increase efficiency, effectiveness and availability.

– The Tunisian government would establish incentive actions to help its private sector embrace information technology, promote electronic commerce, and develop their workers' skills.

– Information must be adequately secured and protected to insure confidentiality, integrity and availability, and to prevent, detect and minimize loss from intentional or accidental hazards.
– The Tunisian government should build a countrywide economy and infrastructure that supports a broad spectrum of opportunities for all citizens while improving their quality of life.
– Tunisian government should improve the education system by providing an environment that supports continuing life learning and training in information technology.

Based on these principals, three goals were identified by the Tunisian government in September 1997 as strategic phases that would define the current focus and efforts in building the Tunisian Info-Communication Society and foster the realization of digital government. They are the infrastructure, legal frameworks and the digital divide.

3.1   Building an infrastructure for Info-communication Society

To implement an e-government, the Tunisian government has decided to set up a high performance network capable of providing good service quality for high speed traffic and offering complete connectivity to a worldwide network. The national network has been built on three components:
– The Tunisian Gigabit Network (TGN) infrastructure uses 6500 km of fiber optics cables (see Figure 2). It will offer varied speed from 10 Gbps at the end of year 2001 and 40 Gbps by the end of year 2004. The TGN includes 55 loops using Synchronous Digital Hierarchy (SDH) technology. It permits advanced switching techniques, IP transmission, and a mobile communication system with global reach.
– The Tunisian Multi service Network (TMN) is built on the TGN and allows access to multiple services. TMN uses ATM technology and will include the next generation Internet as a foundation to support conversion to digital broadcast systems. It guarantees the creation of a global digital network, and provides ADSL access with up to 1 Mbps.
– The access network would allow countrywide access to Internet services. It offers by the end of year 2001 high-speed access to business and homes. All companies would be connected via dedicated lines. Internet access reached 319, 100 at the end of March 2001 and is expected to reach 7% of the homes by 2004.

The building of this modern telecommunications infrastructure is based on what has been achieved from 1988 to 1997. During this decade, Tunisia has installed 1300 km of fiber optics cables connecting major cities with a speed of 2.5 Gbps. X.25 networks have been available, offering 64 Kbps connections. The number of companies connected to X.25 networks was only 1,400, using 29% of the network capacity. Several technologies have been experimented with through this period. They include ATM technology, GSM communications, and ISDN services.

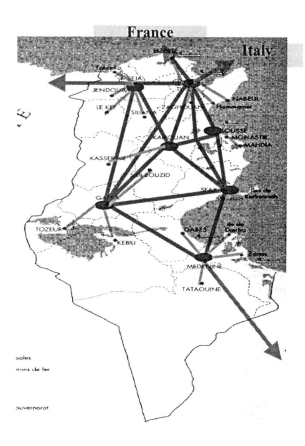

Figure 2. The Tunisian Gigabit network

3.2 Building a legal frame for Info-Communication Society

The 2000 Tunisian legislature passed the electronic transactions and commerce bill[1] (August 9th, 2000), which created the National Digital Certification Agency (NDCA) and defined its role and missions. It guaranteed legal enforcement of digital signatures and established the requirements for the provision of certification service activities. It also defined public key infrastructure rules and provided protection policies and measures for the consumers. The main missions of the NDCA are:

– to license the activities of certification service providers (certification authorities) across the country,
– to ensure that certification service providers (CSP) carry out its duties in full respect of the Electronic Transactions and Commerce Act and its provisions,
– to define specifications for signature establishment and verification packages,
– to establish a public key infrastructure for the certification of public agents and governmental entities, and
– to contribute to the activities of research, training, and studies related to digital exchanges and commerce.

In addition, the NDCA will be responsible for cross-certification with international certification bodies, and will provide certification guidelines that will guide the definition of certification practice statements, the management of digital certificates, and the obligations to customers for public keys based on the international levels of assurances.

The National Telecommunications Authority[2] (NTA) was officially launched at the beginning of January 2001 after the adoption of the new Broadcast, Radio and Telecommunications Act by the Tunisian Parliament. As an independent body, the NTA will pave the way for bringing new players into the telecommunications industry, plan for efficient use of national resources (radio spectrum, phone numbering, IP addressing and naming), and issue all new licenses in the sector in future. Furthermore, the authority's mandate is to ensure that reliable and efficient telecommunication services are made available to citizens and to ensure that every operator employ the technical, managerial and financial resources required to provide these services.

The NTA mission is to effectively co-ordinate standardization and related activities to meet the needs of the Tunisian community in accordance with internationally recognized standards and practices that enhance economic efficiency and competitiveness, to fulfil the community's demand for consumer protection, quality of service, and safe and a sustainable environment. The NTA must also encourage the exercise of effective and fair competition to the advantage of customers, and to monitor the provisioning and financing of the universal telecommunications services.

The legal framework has been amended by several complementary legal provisions that aim to complete the environment in which a competition will take place in July 2001 with arrival of a new GSM operator and the opening of telecommunication services. Examples of these provisions address inter-networking, servers, cryptography, and digital signature issuing systems.

3.3   Reducing the Digital Divide

To reduce the digital divide, the Tunisian government has implemented three programs: the Publinet program, the Cyberpark project, and the Technopole park project for information technologies. However, these programs were preceded by several main measures for reducing illiteracy and decreasing communication and access costs.

The Publinet program aims to promote information technology and digital culture through the creation by young entrepreneurs of computer centers offering the following services to their communities:
–   access to the Internet with a speed of nx64bps,
–   a resource center including computers, software and documentation,
–   technical support and training provided by qualified technicians trained through several sessions organized by the government.

The program has attracted important interest by the private sector after the success of the first fifty Publinets, which the government financed by 50%. Thirty months after the program was launched (in October 1998), the number of Publinets is now about 300.

The Cyberparks program offers a space equipped with ICT facilities. It serves as a virtual incubator for young engineers and technicians who would create their own companies to produce services and products related to ICT. The Cyberparks support tele-working activities. The technical support for the Cyberpark managers and incubators is assured and provided through a virtual network by highly qualified engineers and researchers of the Technopole park and the School of Communications, respectively. Five cyberparks are under construction and are expected to start offering their services by the end of 2001.

The Technopole park for ICT was inaugurated in November 1999. It was built to bring together the ICT industry, ICT R&D organizations, and ICT schools. By the end of March 2001, the Technopole park counted 320 engineers, 100 faculty members, and 1,000 students. It includes 7 private companies, the School of Communications, The Institute for Communications Technology, the Continuous Education Center, The Center for Research and Studies in Telecommunications, and the Research Institute for Computer Science and Telecommunications.

The second phase in the construction of the Technopole park will be completed in 2002. The number of companies will be 21 and the number of engineers will exceed 1,000. It will also include tele-centers and it will establish certification programs for engineers.

These efforts to reduce the digital divide in Tunisia are additions to ongoing programs and continuing efforts to connect all the universities, high and junior high schools by 2001, and primary schools by 2004, to reduce Internet subscription and access fees, and to provide low price and high quality PCs for average income families.

3.4   Building the Tunisian E-Government

To develop on-line government services (task S_{10} in *Figure 1* above), governments should complete tasks S_3, S_4, S_5, S_8, and S_9. The Tunisian government's achievements with tasks S_3, S_4, and S_5 have already been described previously. Tasks S_8, S_9 and S_{10} will be presented in this subsection.

In September 1997, the Tunisian government outlined several key goals for adapting electronic commerce technologies and implementing a digital government. It created an electronic commerce task force and planned to make available to citizens and companies a large range of information categories, including official reports, regulatory requirements, census data, financial data, etc. However, several issues have to be addressed before year 2004. They include the identification of data sources, data collection and update practices, the forms under which data are to be made available, data security measures, and the price of access to these data.

The government would identify the departments and agencies that produce data for the public. At the same, it would define common procedures for data collection, updating, formatting, and security. For the pricing issue, two policies have come into conflict. Open approach encourages making on-line access easy and cheap, and even free, while financial pressures on departments encourage cost recovery and maximization of returns. To start, the Tunisian government has implemented various electronic services free of charge. These services include procurement of requests for proposals, permits for telecommunications related services, a Tunisian merchant gallery, on-line registration at schools and institutes (e.g. School of communication, the institute of communication technologies, and the institute of multimedia) for students, digital libraries, reservation systems, and on-line payment.

In implementing these projects, it has been found that there is a need to develop a payment platform. Payment may be made using bankcards; however, the number of credit card holders is low, thus, slowing the development of the e-government process. It was decided, therefore, to come up with a payment platform adapted to the local society. The result was the development of an efficient payment system and the creation of a type of virtual money called "e-Dinar". This system is based on the need to uniquely identify individuals seeking to use electronic links to government services. It will be done via electronic card technology (see *Figure 3* for picture of an e-Dinar card), which carries individual electronic information and may allow storage of dynamic information to perform processing functions required for authentication.

Figure 3. The e-Dinar card

The e-Dinar payment system as described by *Figure 4* uses the SSL protocol with:
- two secured connections (c_1 and c_2) between a certified merchant gallery, a secured payment gateway managed by the Tunisian Internet Agency (ATI), and the e-Dinar platform (managed by the Tunisian Post);
- the establishment of two successive https sessions s_1 and s_2 for each transaction; and the use of two independent sets of confidential parameters. The first set is static and related to the e-Dinar card. The second is related to the user and can be modified any time. The two sets are sent separately on s_1 and s_2.

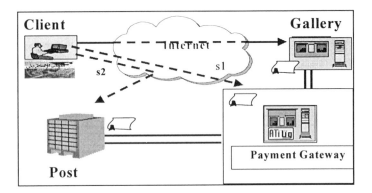

Figure 4. The e-Dinar card system.

4.   CONCLUSION

The e-government model proposed in this chapter is a guideline for governments to implement on-line services. To implement such a model, governments need to set up objectives and strategies. The example of Tunisia has been presented as a case study.

The Tunisian government has set up a strategy that aims to introduce the country in the Info-Communication Society, and to make all of its administrative services for citizens and businesses available on the Internet. The strategy has addressed three main components: the telecommunication infrastructure, the legal framework, and the promotion of a digital services and content industry.

A number of important realizations have been achieved. They include the implementation of electronic money and the creation of the National Telecommunication Authority and the National Digital Certification Agency, as well as a set of pilot projects and commercial web sites. By 2004, the government plans to maximize the contribution of ICT to growth and employment and expects an ICT ratio of 8% of GDP and an ICT ratio of about 25% of new job offers. Tunisia has shown a strong potential in ICT services. The realization of the e-government will stimulate ICT activities through the development of new services, the implementation of a secure governmental intranet, and the expansion of wireless and Internet infrastructure.

NOTES

1. See the URL http://www.bmck.com/ecommerce/tunisia.htm for an English version of the law.
2. See the URL http://www.maktaba.mincom.tn for a copy of the act.

Noureddine Boudriga is a Professor of Telecommunication at the University of Carthage Tunisia, and Head of the distributed systems and networks research laboratory. His research and consultancy interests have focused on network engineering, system modelling, and network security. He has taught undergraduate and graduate courses as well as developing courses and tutorials for industry in high-speed networks, network security, quality of service in telecommunications, software engineering and e-commerce. Particular research activities include network synthesis and design, resource allocation in ATM networks, QoS in networks, security protocols, and protocol engineering. The dissemination of the results of Dr. Boudriga's interdisciplinary research has involved logic programming, software engineering, distributed database, network traffic engineering. Prof. Noureddine A. Boudriga is currently the CEO of the National Digital certification Agency (ANCE) in Tunisia

Dr. Salah Benabdallah worked at IRSIT, an R&D center in Computer Science and Telecommunications, in Tunis, TUNSIA. In 1997, he became the Executive Director General of IRSIT. In 1998, IRSIT was transformed into an IT company, IRSIT Inc. Dr. Benabdallah became the Founder and the CEO of the company. In 2001, Dr. Benabdallah joined the National Digital Certification Agency (ANCE) in Tunisia. His research interests are decision support systems, computer simulation, mathematical modelling, e-government, and e-services. During his carrier, Dr. Benabdallah has been a principal investigator in a number of national and international projects. He also served in many IT related committees at the national and international levels.

Chapter 19

Aveiro - Digital Town
A Social Services Experiment

Nelson Pacheco da Rocha
Universidade de Aveiro, Portugal

Abstract: The chapter presents the framework of the Aveiro Digital Town Programme. It focuses on the social services area of the Programme, both the long-term objectives and the first stage results.

Key words: Digital Cities, Disabled and Elderly People, Social Support Institutions

1.   INTRODUCTION

The "Information Society" creates a unique opportunity to lead economic and social development in Portugal, but it may also represent a way to increase the gap that still separates our country from others more developed ones. Thus, it is urgent to find the best practical ways that will make it possible to achieve the Information Society in Portugal. The Aveiro Digital Town Programme attempts to respond to this important challenge through the search for better approaches to the development and introduction of information and communication technologies in a town scale, as well as by showing evidence of the advantages they can provide.

The town of Aveiro is a medium sized town (70 000 inhabitants) located in a very dynamic region, in which is located: the R&D branch of Portugal Telecom; a highly distinguished and proactive University, with a strong tradition in information and communications technologies; and a Local Government committed to the promotion of Internet and other new technologies. The development of the Aveiro Digital Town must be accomplished more on the basis of a radical transformation of the habits and behaviour of the citizens and institutions, rather than just providing the town with the necessary infrastructures and systems. Therefore, it has been considered of great importance that the Programme should promote the involvement of all on a volunteer basis while keeping a flexible and motivational attitude toward relevant, spontaneous initiatives among the most interested agents in the town. Society must be motivated and mobilized and participants must be flexible in the search for dynamic actions and new initiatives. The final aim of this effort, it must be kept in mind, is the improvement of the quality of life in the town, in all its dimensions. Toward that end, several strategic areas have been considered: i) Building the digital community; ii) Local government and local public services; iii) Schools and education community; iv) University and academic community; v) Health services; vi) Social services; vii) Economic sector; viii) Culture and leisure.

The Aveiro Digital Town Programme, in general, and the implementation of the defined goals in the various areas, in particular, are scheduled to be developed over eight years, subdivided into two stages. The first stage has already been implemented on an experimental basis, and is to be followed by a six-year second stage, which was designed to become a sustainable process. In the first stage, there was a budget of 5.99 MEuro for 38 projects. These projects allowed the development of 33 sites, 9 CD ROMs, 20 new services and the involvement of more than 4300 users.

2.   LONG TERM AIMS OF THE SOCIAL SERVICES AREA

Concerning the integration of citizens with special needs, social services are an area of great importance for the creation of a Digital Town. Information and communication technologies should contribute to a more fair society, providing an equality of opportunities for all and, thus, avoid the introduction of new barriers and social differences. Support should be provided for less privileged groups of people as well as making use of new approaches to solving access problems experienced by disabled people. These new perspectives have raised a fundamental issue: the social involvement of disabled people, the study of their abilities and the development of technologies to accommodate a wide variety of disabilities are resulting in a normalization of access. Thus, the state of one's physical disability is becoming less of a determinant of ability to make use of digital resources. Lack of technological means available in a community, rather, is now the main access barrier. Any person at any time can find himself or herself in an underprivileged situation, which means the discrepancy between a person's abilities or capabilities and the existing resources in a community.

The social services element of the Aveiro Digital Town Programme is based on this paradigmatic pattern, having as its central goal to raise the level of autonomy of a disabled person within an environment as high as possible. The application of this paradigm must be evident in the new programmes of specific intervention, leading to larger equality of opportunities regarding both the normalization process of daily life and the social integration. Furthermore, wider flexibility of systems and services is needed in order to satisfy the needs of people in general, and the less privileged in particular. This process demands a particular awareness of the new technological developments, which are usually associated with new barriers. This must be largely taken into account, not only in the sphere of social services but also in all areas covered by the Aveiro Digital Town Programme. These general aims underlie the set of goals that follow.

2.1   Contributing to a Wider Accessibility to Systems and Services

The community will only be accessible (or inclusive) if all its members can manage to use it, that is, being able to move within it and make good use of its services and social equipment while showing a high level of autonomy.

In Portugal, the national process of providing assistance to assistive technology is anachronistic and needs serious rethinking. However, there are things that can be done on a regional level: i) provide training programmes for educational and institutional agents [1]; ii) establish integrated competence centres focusing on disability (i.e. not deficiency: the substitution, "compensation", or prevention of functions necessary for the execution of a particular activity); iii) perform post-design and implementation review and consulting; iv) evaluate and review components that may regularly provide researchers in this area with systematic important insights; v) create a system of knowledge which catalogs problems and solutions that may be useful to other regions of the country.

Removing existing barriers is as important as preventing the creation of new ones when new services are introduced. Since the main motivation of the Digital Town is to promote the use of new technologically supported services, there is an urge to guarantee that no new limitations are added by the new services to certain groups of the population. To avoid this, one must: i) make the society aware of accessibility problems; ii) promote accessibility to the Internet; iii) increase emphasis on universal design related themes in the syllabuses of the schools of technology; iv) invest in the development of accessibility solutions for new digital services through an intensive and systematic process of reviewing users' demands and promoting expert authorities to evaluate less accessible systems and services.

2.2   Information Systems for the Institutions

Digital towns are also based on the modernization of social services -- to make them easier for users to access -- by reorganizing their management and administrative procedures, as well as providing new services. All of this will be possible with a new attitude towards financing, equipment, training and strategic partnerships with those who have the competence and know-how.

The first priority is the introduction of the information and communication technologies into institutions. Since the expense for human resources is the most significant part of an institution's budget, it is then necessary to carry out an important reform in an organization's procedures in such a way that its human resources can be made more available to provide good quality services. One must welcome every strategy used to reduce repetitive administrative tasks so that more time is left for the "moments of attention" to users.

There is an enormous need to provide institutions with integrated information systems to be applied not only to accountancy but also to information management. Apart from that, one must take into account that a social worker is mainly an information manager. Consequently, the new technologies should be used to introduce more objectivity to different social tasks. However, changes in procedures cannot be achieved only by the introduction of new equipment. It will be necessary to: i) invest largely in training; ii) create best practices for the introduction of new information and communication technologies; iii) develop line partnerships between the institutions and between these and the scientific entities; iv) introduce the workflow and remote cooperation methodologies in the making of individual educational plans (PEIs), thus demystifying the necessity of a large number of meetings which are not always productive; v) make the bureaucratic processes dependent on the information and communication technologies in order to increase their general use.

Creating a digital town may as well have a strong impact on the relations between the institutions and the local, regional and national structures of the public administration, including: i) providing remote access to frequently required services, such as asking for documents and filing forms by citizens; ii) creating new relations between institutions with responsibilities over local social issues, namely in the exchange of information and flow of documents; iii) introducing workflow and remote cooperation methodologies in the work between the institutions and the local welfare structure, with the purpose of reducing the burden associated with an indefinite number of meetings and to optimise the productivity level of human resources; iv) generalizing the sharing of data among the different entities of the social fabric, particularly concerning responses in problematic areas which demand close cooperation among the social and governmental entities involved.

2.3   Promoting the Production of Multimedia Contents Adapted to Citizens with Special Needs

Multimedia content may play an important role in helping citizens with special needs to not only optimise rehabilitation programmes but also to help people acquire new capabilities, or even to provide new strategies for overcoming daily difficulties [2].

There has been evidence of the growing interest in the use of the new technologies for these purposes and some content have already been produced. Nevertheless, the limited amount of content written in Portuguese, especially for children, is not easily applied to certain groups of the population. Since many programmes do not fit the particular needs of certain groups of people, the production of new material meant to satisfy their particular needs has become a priority. Therefore, it is necessary to develop content for orientation and mobility programmes (space orientation, adoption of conventions, association of concepts and connection of the cultural knowledge with the cognitive information), daily routine learning programmes (moving in the house and in the street, getting dressed, eating, communicating, etc.) as well as programmes meant to assist in the individual's integration in the labour market.

2.4   Remote Support Services

New information and communication technologies can be used to provide remote support to elderly or disabled people living alone or professionals and families living in geographically and socially isolated areas with relatives having some kind or impairment. This is particularly important because Portugal is a country where there is a lack of qualified professionals; a marked asymmetry between regions in general, and, in particular, between some rural and urban areas concerning access and distribution of health, education and social support services and resources [3].

The application of new concepts of social support could strengthen the role of the existing auxiliary networks composed of trained staff currently working in institutions that do not currently easily contact by citizens who are seeking support services. In the particular case of the elderly, we mustn't forget that the present tendency of Portuguese policies is one of allowing poor quality elderly homes to be replaced by host families. New information and communication technologies may help establish contacts between professionals within these auxiliary networks as well as with all the basic units operating for the social support system.

There is a whole range of remote services that must be taken into account, which can be used to help end-users such as the elderly, the disabled or families with disabled young children, as well as to provide support to geographically isolated people (e.g. security, surveillance, advice and companionship, response to emergency situations, medical monitoring). Remote services should also be used to increase inter-institutional relations. This includes both cooperation between similar institutions (cooperation among partners or technical support by the resource or competence centres), and cooperation among the complementary institutions such as a telemedicine service meant to support an elderly home. Finally, to carry out such services there should be previous research on the professionals' expectations as well as on the kind of best practices needed for the introduction of the remote support services.

2.5   Integration of Disabled People in Working Environments

Information and communication technologies are usually foreseen as a way to promote the integration in the working environment of disabled people. However, a sustainable social movement must follow technological opportunities. Disabled people, apart from their productive capacity, have many special needs that must be satisfied in order to be able to work efficiently (for example, satisfaction of daily life needs).

As far as the Aveiro Digital Town Programme is concerned the creation of multi-service telecentres has been considered essential [4]. They should be given the support of mediator entities ("social operators") whose tasks are, among others, the following: i) supporting the training for and the upkeep of the work developed by eventual telecentres; ii) working as the "visible face" of the telecentres and as the initial guarantee of the quality of the services provided, to alleviate a certain mistrust of companies due to recent history; iii) creating a sustainable set of clients and activities, as well as strengthening the commercial loyalty of those clients; iv) providing adequate training; v) providing the teleworker with support in the negotiation of contracts that fit the needs and expectations of both employers and employees; vi) providing the teleworker psychological support whenever needed; and vii) keeping strong ties in the relationships with the employers.

2.6   Training

The success of such projects as the Aveiro Digital Town Programme is basically dependent on the following conditions: i) the minimum required training level in information and communication technologies, ii) an acceptable capacity of work within multidisciplinary teams, iii) awareness of social problems and spirit of citizenship.

Therefore, apart from establishing an intensive training plan for institutional staff, it is more important to include real problem solving plans rather than teaching word processing or worksheet skills. All related paramedical and social schools, for example, should put emphasis on the potentialities of the new information and communication technologies in their study plans and they should also be aware that an high training level should mean the capacity of working efficiently in a multidiscipline team.

3.   FIRST STAGE RESULTS

The first stage of the Aveiro Digital Town Programme has already been implemented on an experimental basis, and must be followed by a six-year second stage. During the first stage, the University of Aveiro is coordinating the intervention plan of the social services area due to a set of unique conditions: i) a long lasting experience in the development of services, applications and equipment especially thought of and designed to help and support people with special needs; ii) large experience dealing with specific groups of people, namely people suffering from impaired eyesight and hearing, mental disability, people with cerebral palsy and elderly people; iii) wide experience with multidisciplinary teams involving engineers, psychologists, sociologists, therapists and social workers; iv) a strong connection with several social service institutions working both locally and nationally; v) established links with national and international institutions with recognized research in this area, through participation in several R&D European projects; and vi) international cooperation with some local administration entities that have achieved success in the implementation of support services for the disabled and elderly people.

The well recognized experience and capacity shown by the University of Aveiro has proven the usefulness of its work in the four projects that managed to contribute to the achievement of the goals in the social services area established by the Aveiro Digital Town Programme: RESEA (Network services of APPACDM), NET ALIMENTAR, IST (Social Integration Through Telework) and MEU (Mobility in the Urban Area).

The RESEA sought to systematize the introduction of information and communication technologies into social service institutions. The project has integrated training with the new technologies and has introduced a new dynamic approach in the APPACDM (Portuguese Association of Mental Disabled Children's Parents and Friends). APPACDM has promoted both the reorganization of the institution's services and the creation of new ones, making it easier to communicate between people and remote advice services (e.g. communication between residential homes and a technician). Last but not least, the project has promoted the use of multimedia adapted to children with special needs, including those concerning space orientation, mobility, colours, volume, learning basic daily life tasks, civic behaviour and road safety.

As far as the social service institutions are concerned, the project NET ALIMENTAR has promoted the creation of new methods of interaction between institutions and civil society by means of information and communication technologies, initiated through a permanent campaign intended to collect food and recruit volunteers.

As a result of this work, a group of physically handicapped people managed to be actively involved in the production of some multimedia content for the Aveiro Digital Town Programme. Furthermore, the project has developed a telework model, which can be used in other situations, including other Portuguese towns. Such a model has been intended to identify the kind of tasks that, in a digital town, can possibly be successfully accomplished by citizens in general, and the disabled people in particular. This telework model also considers the possibilities for integrating disabled people into the workforce of the companies in Aveiro through telework; and, it attempts to identify the most suitable types of telework and the telework activities most likely to be developed by these companies.

The community ought to provide accessibility to all its members. The disabled and elderly people have the right to access all of the technologies offered to the population in general[1]. This is, the underlying philosophy of the MEU project. In fact, the community will only be accessible (or inclusive) if all its members can be able to use it, that is, having the possibility to move within its area as well as use its social services and equipments as much autonomy as possible. The underlying perspective of the MEU project was, on the one hand, to create a line of a public means of transport meant to make clear both the useful methods of accessing information by all citizens and the interfaces with other means of transport subsystems. On the other hand, the MEU project has promoted the use of citizenship through the Internet, thus creating a service that allows any citizen to give their opinions, to praise and to criticize the accessibility conditions in public places (public institutions, schools, banks, hospitals, etc.). Once available, the information is effective not only for notifying every one of the locations or services that are easily accessible, but it is also useful for encouraging the correction of accessibility problems.

The dynamic processes developed among the different elements and projects within the social services area have promoted a future partnership to work together to build a critical mass to promote an inclusive information society. These partnerships have already helped to create a portal, which aims to be the integrating centre of all information about rehabilitation. Although still in its first stages, it already includes a digital library and a centre meant to display information about assistive technology.

The digital library, which has already been created, will contribute Portuguese multimedia content. This library already features a set of outstanding material for social services, such as, case studies, outstanding experiences, dissemination of good practices, an on-line updated law collection, and relevant information about all the institutions of the region. To achieve all of this, the institutions must adopt a cooperative attitude, especially concerning the updated information.

In terms of assistive technology, the portal aims to address the increasing necessity of obtaining useful and systematized information about assistive technology, because everyone needs to know the best way to supply one's needs or the best place to get the right information. Furthermore, social service institutions lack access to information about vendors who manufacturer systems which meet ISO 9999 standards for technical systems and aids for the handicapped.

Apart form making people aware of the potentialities of the information and communication technologies, the implementation of a support network for the assistive technology makes possible the understanding of the role of the information society. The development of integrated solutions suitable for each specific case is probably more important than any specific technical aid. As the role of a technical aid is not necessarily different in the case of employment, education or ever within an institution, a limited sector perspective should be abolished. Being connected to the University allows us to transfer new solutions and create systematised knowledge of problems and solutions that may be useful in other regions of the country.

4.   CONCLUSION

The technological means to integrate and disseminate information are now available to all. On the other hand, there is a great variety of knowledge and long experience as a result of projects that have already been completed. There was a considerable effort to systematize procedures and disseminate methodologies, knowledge and results of the various projects of the social services area of the Aveiro Digital Town Programme.

One of the main goals of the experimental phase of the programme has been achieved: the town has become aware that the use of information and communications technologies can mean a whole methodological revolution in the care of disabled and elderly people. Clearly, in the second stage of the Programme, social services will be driven by the institutions and end-users not associated with the University of Aveiro.

The Aveiro Digital Town Programme at mid-term has already been validated as an appropriate guide for other e-government projects. While the programme has been useful in expanding services, the main result has been the creation of a "confidence network" for paving the way to the future.

NOTES

1. Art. 38 of "The act for the 80s" for the International Rehabilitation.

REFERENCES

[1] Rocha, N., *et al.*, "A Distance Training and Telework Experiment for People with Cerebral Palsy", Assistive Technology on the Threshold of the New Millennium (Christian Buhler and Harry Knops, ed.), IOS Press, 1999.

[2] Montgomery, A., *et al.*, "Identifying Computer Assisted Instruction for People with Severe Intellectual Disabilities: A literature review", European Journal on Mental Disability, vol. 3, N.9, pages 32 to 46, 1996.

[3] Pereira, L.M., *et al.*, "Distance Support and Elderly People: Overview on Three Projects", Assistive Technology on the Threshold of the New Millennium (Christian Buhler and Harry Knops, ed.), IOS Press, 1999.

[4] Santana, S., *et al.*, "Teletrabalho e Incapacidade: Análise de um Inquérito a Empresas Portuguesas", to be published in Revista Portuguesa de Gestão.

Nelson Pacheco da Rocha received his Electronics and Telecommunications Engineering degree in 1983 and his Ph.D in 1992, both from the Electronics and Telecommunications Department at the University of Aveiro, Portugal. He has been teaching Computer Science and Electronics Engineering at the University of Aveiro since 1983. During the past ten years, his research interests are related with information and communications technologies for elderly and disabled people and he has been involved in several European projects. Since April 1999 he is Vice-Director of the Health School of the University of Aveiro.

Index

access, 191, 211
    ability and convenience, 147
    administrative, 23
    asymmetry between rural and urban,
        309
    autonomy principle, 124
    barriers, 29, 30, 165
    citizen, 190
    control (security), 127
    control (security), xvii, 121, 122, 126,
        133
    control matrix model, 129
    control models, 122, 127, 131
    cost, 300
    data, xviii
    database, 47, 167, 197, 199
    dial-up, 4
    disk, 168
    domain, 124
    ease of, 9, 167, 182, 236, 239, 308
    efficient, 38
    equitable, 224
    facilitating, 17
    fees, 300
    geographic, 29
    global layer, 128
    inability to access information, 244
    information, xix
    integrated, 166
    interactive, 92
    interfaces, 99
    Internet, xix, 29, 30
        FirstGov, 238
    lack of, 313
    low latency data, 111
    multi-lingual, 101
    network, 296
    on-line, 93, 222, 300
    paths, 59
    points, 30, 146
    policies, 220
    policy, 215
    public, 245, 290
    query, 87
    rapid, 221
    remote, 308
    restricting, 16
    rights, 24, 312
    rules, 123
    security, 124, 125, 132
    security principle, 124
    speed of, 299
    to agency data, 40
    to data, 41, 59, 62, 99, 164, 165, 166,
        198, 223, 225, 263, 290, 291
    to democratic processes, 146
    to e-government, 245
    to FirstGov, 237
    to geographic image databases, 210
    to government databases, 38

to government information, 41, 232, 238, 263
to government services, 40
to inappropriate information, 219
to information, 4, 10, 15, 128, 130, 165, 166, 167, 169, 170, 220, 221, 231, 237, 245, 294
to networks, 3, 8
to non-classified information, 295
to records, 234
to services, 1, 50, 232, 236, 292, 293, 296
to statistical data, xvii, 9, 193
to technologies, 29, 219, 294
to technology, 145
unequal technical capabilities, 141
universal, 131, 295
user, 81
Web, 86, 236
Access America, 259
accessibility
compliance, 160
accessibility, 6, 17, 19, 20, 21, 23, 26, 31, 40, 139, 141, 149, 150, 154, 158, 223, 260, 282, 307, 312
code, 160
compliance, xv, 150, 151, 156, 159
design analysis, 155, 156, 159, 160
design intent, 154
laws and policies, 25
performance-based analysis, 150
performance-based approaches, 150, 156
physical, 158
problems, 306
regulations, 149, 150
solutions, 307
standards, xv
techniques, 20
testing for, 154
to buildings, 149
to facilities, 160
Africa, xvi
agriculture, 6, 9, 182
statistics, 193
AIPA, ix, xi, xvii, 5, 10, 53, 54, 65
America, 5, 33, 51, 228
American Sign Language (ASL), 20

Americans with Disabilities Act, xviii, 8, 25, 26, 34, 149, 151, 161
Amsterdam, 5, 34
annotation service, 22
AOL, 3
application integration, 13
ARPANET, 2, 3
Australia, 24
Austria, 24
authentication, 15, 16, 26, 28, 115, 122, 131, 290, 301
bandwidth, 17
BBC, 2
Bildschirmtext, 3
Bistro, xvii, 10, 111, 113, 114, 115, 116, 117, 118
Braille, 20, 21
Britain, 2
budget management, 269
bulletin boards, 3
business process reengineering, 58, 178
business rules, 70
cable television, 2, 30
caching, 11
CAD, 151, 153
cadastral data, 54, 59, 60, 62
Canada, xix, 12, 24, 103, 104, 135, 212, 275, 276, 285, 286, 287
case management, 263
CEEFAX, 2
Center for Technology in Government, 4, 32, 259, 261, 271, 272, 286
CERN, 4
certification authorities, 16
CGI, 4, 143, 185, 186
chat rooms, 3, 110
childcare, 9
citizen-government interaction, 1, 19
citizens, xvi, xviii, 1, 3, 4, 8, 9, 17, 22, 23, 24, 25, 26, 27, 29, 215, 216, 219, 220, 222, 224, 243, 285, 292, 296, 302, 312
acceptance of on-line services, 244
access, 295
access to documents, 244
access to government information, 30
access to information, 221, 236, 300, 312
accessibility, 39

attitudes, xvi, xix
behavior, 305
benefits, 45
Canadian, 276
choice, 277
comments, 23
communication, 30, 225
conceptions, 5
concerns, 254
connected, 282
democratic participation, 138
digital divide, 29
disadvantaged, 40, 41
document retrieval by, 11
economically disadvantaged, 18
efficient access, 38
expectations of, 70, 232
experience with on-line technologies,
    243
filing information, 234
filing of comments, 6
filing of documents, 11
filing of forms, xvii
focus on, 234
freedom of information, 25
government interaction with, 280
government relationships with, 265
indigent, 38
information use, 289
interactions with government, xvi, 7,
    19, 223
Internet use, 237
needs of, 13, 39, 41, 236, 306
needy, 50
paperwork burden on, 233
petitions, 139
political issues, 15
portal requirements, 237
privacy, 40
privacy concerns, 130
processing requests by, 72
remote access, 308
rights, 24
seeking services, 309
service delivery, 282
services, 9, 69, 262
socially marginalized, 22
special needs, 40, 309
unequal technical capabilities, 141

use of ARPANET, 2
use of FirstGov, 238
use of networks, 3
city council, 60
classification, 12, 13, 56, 122, 127
    government standards, 12
    of documents, 12
    schemes, 12
classification schemes, 13
client push, 112
Clinton, 26
collaboration, xviii, 31, 85, 163, 164, 166,
    172, 174, 175, 176, 177, 259, 260,
    262, 278, 287
    systems, 268
collaborative design, xvi, xix
collaborative digital government projects,
    xix
Columbia University, 4, 32, 85, 86, 101,
    102
commercial off-the-shelf software
    (COTS), 70
commercial service, 2, 6
commit, 115
communication, 2, 4, 22, 29, 168, 224,
    225, 259, 276, 289, 290, 291, 296, 311
    agent, 128
    costs, 299
    inadequate, 267
    infrastructure, 59, 291
    intra-agency, 224
    managing, 269
    many-to-one, 110
    of private data, 16
    one-way, 8
    practices, 270
    privacy of, 131
    processes, 6, 30
    protocol, 153
    society, 291, 292, 295
    technologies, 310, 311
    two-way, 8, 224
    videotext, 3
compatibility, 18
competencies, xx, 275, 277
compliance, xviii, 8, 26, 149, 151, 154
CompuServe, 3
computer centers, 299
concept space, 170

confidentiality, xviii, 9, 111, 115, 118,
    122, 146, 181, 182, 183, 190, 191, 296
    of statistical data, 181
Congressional Record, 14
content-based retrieval, xviii, 197, 199
cooperative information system, xvii, 53,
    54, 63
Cooperative Information Systems, 9, 10,
    65, 66
cooperative system, 59
cooperative tasks, xvi, 38
COPLINK, xviii, 10, 163, 164, 167, 168,
    169, 170, 171, 172, 173, 174, 175,
    177, 178, 179
CORBA, 37, 47, 50, 60, 61, 80, 82, 127
criminal intelligence analysis, xviii, 164
criminal justice, xv, 165
cryptography, 16, 117
CSNET, 3
culture, 18, 277, 283, 285, 306
    access to, 291
    creativity, 279
    digital, 299
    heterogeneity, 73
    learning, 279
    of work, 266
    organizational, 280
    risk, 278
data collection, xvii, 8, 107, 108, 109,
    111, 112, 113, 116, 117, 172, 300
    by government, 246
    infrastructure, 108
    performance, 113
    procedures, 300
    scalable, 117
data dissemination, 182
data integration, 6, 85, 89, 93, 94, 163
data management, 7, 11, 15, 37
data quality, 6
data transfer, 41, 110, 111, 112, 114, 115,
    116
    many-to-one, 118
    scalability, 118
    secure, 118
data warehouse, 92
database, 47, 87, 163, 167, 168, 185, 199,
    200, 201, 202, 203, 206, 209, 212
    access, 197
    administrative, 58

adminstrators, 43
autonomous, 38
autonomy, 128
back-end, 169
co-database, 44
coherence, 60
criminal analysis, 172
criminal information, 166
design, 168
disclosure risk, 190
discovery, 42, 46
distributed, xviii
federal agencies, 239
federated, 128, 134
geographic image, 9, 210
global access policy, 128
government, 38, 41, 50, 130
heterogeneity, 39
heterogeneous, 39, 85
image, 197
integrated, 264
integration, xv, 166
interactions between, xvii
interface, 102
live data, 92
locating, 44
mapping to, 40
metadata, 44, 86
monitoring, 176
multi-database, 85
multimedia, 166, 167
ontologies, 13, 39, 43
ontology, 95
personal information, 131
privacy, 131
proliferation of, 192
public, 290
queries, 47, 87
record matching in, 192
recovery, 81
relational, 89
relationships, 171
reliance on, 38
schema integration, 128
server, 143
statistical, 16, 87, 182, 184
stored procedures, 169
structure, 99
systems, 174

terms, 96
types of disclosures, 191
updates, 59, 93
user profile, 175
virtual, 192
warehouse, 59
workflow, 78
workflow management, 70
database integration, 39, 86, 88, 99
database management, 7
  technology, 39
database management system
  security mechanisms, 16
  views, 14
database systems
  access methods, 13
database warehousing, 91
databases, 4, 31, 37, 41, 43, 44, 46, 47,
    48, 122, 123, 182, 197, 198, 199, 200,
    201
democracy, xviii, 5, 6, 8, 35, 108, 110,
    123, 135, 137, 138, 141, 142, 146,
    147, 215, 222, 225, 228, 231, 233,
    243, 275, 283, 284
  conditions for, 237
Department of Finance, 62
deployment, 37, 40, 53, 217
design, xvi, xviii, 17, 18, 26, 53, 100,
    151, 163, 204, 223, 275
  building, 150, 151, 154, 155
  data organization, 168
  intent, 150, 154, 155
  methods, 259
  of e-democracy systems, 141
  principles, xx, 275, 284
  process, 151
  processes, 270
  review, 307
  simulation, 150
  system, 182
  techniques, 269
  usability, 150
  user-centered, 18, 164
developing nations, xvi, xix, xx, 25
development, xix, xx, 1, 2, 3, 4, 81, 99,
    121, 127, 216, 217, 218, 232, 234, 311
  of digital government, xvi
  of information technologies, 232
  problems, 267

process, 301
processes, xvi, 31
technological, 306
digital certificate, 16
digital city, xix, xx, 5, 26, 305, 306, 307,
    310, 311, 312, 314
  development of, 305
digital divide, xx, 29, 30, 137, 282, 289,
    291, 293, 294, 296, 299, 300
  policymaking, 30
digital government, xvii, xix, xx, 1, 2, 3,
    4, 5, 6, 7, 8, 9, 10, 11, 14, 15, 17, 19,
    22, 23, 25, 26, 27, 28, 29, 39, 107,
    108, 109, 117, 121, 129, 137, 177,
    181, 259, 275, 282, 289, 290, 296, 300
  attitudes about, xix
  collaborative systems, 268
  concept of, 24
  data collection, 107, 113
  definition of, 31
  design of, 293
  development, 245
  development of, 4, 31, 237, 275, 293
  digital divide, 30
  digital signatures, 28
  evolution of, 275
  financing of, 254
  history of, xvi
  IEEE *Computer* special issue, xiii
  information, 10
  infrastructure, 129, 130, 131, 132, 133
  internal systems, 7, 9
  issues, xvi
  models of, 245
  multidimensional data, 91
  needs, 117
  policy, xix
  privacy laws, 27
  research, xvi, 164
  services, 70, 78
  survey of, 6
  system architectures, 7
  systems, xv, xvi, xix
  systems architectures, 8
  technologies, 23
  Web sites, 30
  work environment, 281
  workshop, 237

Digital Government Research Center,
  xvii, 10, 32, 85, 86, 87, 103
digital government systems, 2, 5, 7, 9, 11,
  15, 16, 17, 18, 21, 22, 23, 24, 25
  design of, xv
  integration of, 31
digital signatures, 16, 34
disabilities, xvi, 17, 19, 20, 21, 26, 40, 48,
  149, 306
disabled, xv, xvi, xx, 17, 23, 25, 31, 43,
  46, 48, 49, 149, 150, 154, 155, 156,
  159, 160, 306, 307, 309, 310, 311,
  312, 314
distributed architectures, xv, 80
DNS, 110
document processing, 9
documents, 12, 15, 220, 227, 275, 308
  access to, 244
  cataloguing, 12
  classification of, 12, 13
  collections, 171
  costs, 25
  data type, 14
  downloading, 11, 29
  dynamic relations, 14
  electronic filing, 234
  filtering, 175
  flat (ASCII), 97
  geographic relationships in, 15
  government, 30, 69
  interpretations of, 23
  locating, 11
  management, 150
  management of, 11
  managing relations between, 10
  MARC, 13
  paper, 58
  parsing, 14
  policy, xix, 14
  public, 24
  retrieval, 11
  uploading, 10, 11
  XML, 21
downloading, 11
Dublin Core, 13
DWFMS, 10, 74
dynamic associations, 14
eCitizen, 8, 32
economic development, 291

educational attainment, 29
efficiency, 2, 11, 202, 282, 283, 298
  increasing, xvii
  of crime prevention, 166
  of transactions, 291
  organizational, 10, 53, 54
eGovernment, 79
elderly, xvi, xx, 309, 310, 311, 312, 314
e-mail, 2, 3, 9, 20, 54, 110
encryption, 28, 122, 131, 133
energy, 86
  data, 97
  information, xv
  statistics, 193
Englebart, 2
enterprise integration, 224
e-petitioner, xviii, 8, 137, 138, 140, 141,
  142, 143, 144, 145, 146, 147
e-speak, 37, 47, 50, 51
Europe, xvi, 2, 5
European Union, 26, 28
evolution of digital government, xx
externalizing systems, 7
fault tolerance, 115, 116, 117
federal government, xix, 215, 216, 217,
  219, 220, 221, 222, 223, 224, 226,
  231, 239, 276, 277, 283
  Canadian, 276
  public ownership of information, 244
  Web page indexing, 238
Federal Register, 11
finance, 59
  digital government, 308
  of universal services, 299
  strategies, 269
financial management, 9
Finland, 24
firewall, 130
FirstGov, xix, 223, 231, 232, 233, 236,
  237, 238, 239, 241
  goals of, 240
  launching of, 240
  partners, 238
Ford Foundation, 5
France, 3, 4, 23, 24, 33, 103
freedom of information, 23
  laws, 24
FREENET, 3, 5
FTP, 2, 4

gatekeeper, 22
gender, 29
geographic, 6, 144, 197, 198, 199, 201,
    202, 203, 205, 206, 207, 209, 210,
    213, 217
    organization, 265
geographic images, 9
geographic information, 13, 14, 15, 35,
    197, 201, 202, 209, 212, 213
    relationships, 15
geographic information systems (GIS), 7,
    78, 81, 186, 190, 203, 205, 206, 209,
    263, 271
    development of, 262
geographical, 144, 181, 182, 183, 188,
    212
    locations, 174
geographical data
    aggregation of, 192
geography, 19, 29, 89, 90, 192, 266
Global Information Locator Service
    (GILS), 12
government
    efficiency, 295
government agencies, xvi, xvii, xviii, 6, 7,
    8, 9, 10, 11, 15, 24, 27, 38, 69, 72, 75,
    85, 97, 108, 113, 117, 121, 122, 123,
    165, 181, 197, 199, 213, 221, 223,
    234, 239, 243, 252, 255, 259, 262,
    263, 292
government officials, xvi, xix, 7, 9, 10,
    14, 22, 23, 30, 275
hardware, 7, 18, 168, 174, 224, 267
    failure, 17
    limitations of, 17
health, 3, 41, 47, 191, 248
    departments, 266
    services, xv, 254, 262, 309
    statistics, 192
health care, 260
health insurance, 13
health maintenance organizations
    (HMOs), 260
higher education
    infrastructure, 246
history, xvi, 1, 3, 32, 182, 213, 231
    driving, 251
    for documents, 244
    legislative, 233

housing, 41, 47
HTML, 4, 21, 47, 60, 88, 151, 185, 199
HTTP, 2, 4, 60
    server, 184
human factors, xv, xvi, 1, 6, 17, 31
human services, xv, 262, 263
human-computer interaction, 20, 31
illiteracy, 293
impairments, 19, 20, 21, 31
income, 29
index, 315
indexing, 13, 35, 172
information and communication
    technologies, 1, 5, 6, 19, 20, 22, 31,
    276, 283, 286, 293, 294, 299, 302,
    308, 313
information infrastructure, 5
information integration, 167
information management, 231, 233, 237,
    308
information monitoring, 176
information needs, 22, 24, 174, 175, 176,
    236, 270
information retrieval, 163, 166, 170, 199,
    202, 203, 237
information sharing, xviii, 10, 108, 163,
    164, 166, 167, 176, 177, 260, 261,
    266, 280
    infrastructure, 173
information technology
    development of, xix
information use environments, 22
infrastructure, 5, 19, 23, 38, 39, 55, 113,
    121, 122, 123, 125, 133, 175, 177,
    216, 217, 218, 219, 224, 278, 282,
    285, 291, 292, 293, 295, 296
    public, 117
innovations, xix, 217
integrated solutions, 313
integrated systems, 259
integration, 6, 123
    multi-agency, xv
    service, 121
    systems, 163
interactive computing, 2
inter-agency integration, 9
interface design, 70, 167
Internal Revenue Service (IRS), 41, 107
internal systems, 7

Internet, xix, 2, 4, 6, 10, 32, 33, 34, 35,
    107, 108, 109, 111, 112, 114, 118,
    122, 134, 147, 181, 211, 219, 220,
    221, 224, 236, 243, 248, 249, 252,
    255, 256, 289, 301, 302
    access, 29, 30, 238, 250, 294
    access fees, 300
    access to services, 296
    accessibility, 307
    accessing databases over, 210
    advancement of, 173
    advertising on, 252
    appliances, 18, 30
    attacks over, 131
    attitudes toward, 247, 249
    availability of, 254
    availability of services on, 246
    citizenship, 312
    connectivity, 113
    data collection using, xvii
    data dissemination over, 182
    delivery system, 247
    digital divide, 29
    driver's license registration, 247
    ease of use, 236
    Federal agency Web pages, 233
    federal government portal, 232
    filing taxes, 247
    first presidential address, 232
    frequency of use, 251
    government information on, 250, 251
    government's move to, 237
    hacking, 132
    hotspots, 109
    impact of, 289
    improving use of, 290
    information overload, 239
    infrastructure, 107, 302
    interest in, 231
    monitoring of, 255
    next-generation, 293, 296
    number of users, 232
    petitions, 140
    political decisions about, 293
    portals, 237
    President's Webcast, 240
    privacy, 129, 251, 252
    promotion of, 305
    resources, 116

    revolution, 276
    security, 130, 144
    security risks, 246
    speed of access, 299
    technologies, 182
    transactions over, 234
    universal access, 131
    uploading, 114
    use of, 38, 243, 245, 248, 255
    usefulness of, 249, 254
    voter registration, 247
    voting, 40
interoperability, 6, 18, 70, 79, 123, 124,
    126, 151, 153
    of security mechanisms, 128
intranet, 167, 302
intranets, 8, 223
Ireland, 24
IT², 38
Italy, xvii, 5, 9, 10, 53, 54, 58, 60, 61, 62,
    63, 65, 66
Japan, 2, 5, 24, 65
Java, 46, 50, 60, 66, 130, 153
job placement, 49
Justice Department, 41
keyblock, xviii, 203, 204, 205, 206, 207,
    210, 211
knowledge management, 10, 163, 164,
    165, 166, 167, 170, 172, 177, 280, 283
knowledgement management, xviii
labor market, 309
Landauer, 17, 18, 33
Landsat, 198
language translation, 7
law, 12, 14, 24, 25, 26, 27, 41, 57, 59,
    181, 233, 234, 255, 261, 262, 265,
    267, 303, 313
    privacy, 27
law enforcement, xviii, 9, 10, 163, 164,
    165, 166, 167, 168, 169, 170, 172,
    173, 174, 177, 260, 263
legacy systems, 168
legal framework, 289, 290, 291, 293, 294,
    299, 302
legal system, xx
legislation, 1, 11, 14, 15, 26, 233, 234,
    240, 267, 290, 292
    amendments to, 140
    citizen commentary on, 234

framework, 279
tracking, 15
legislative processes, 1
library catalog, 12
Library of Congress, 12, 33
Licklider, 2, 33
management, 1, 9, 14, 61, 62, 123, 135, 143, 147, 222, 223
  challenges, 280
  government, 262
  issues, 63
  of services, 308
  philosophy, 261
  public, 285
  responsibilities, 281
  security, 125
  techniques, 264
  work teams, 269
MARC, 12, 13
mediator, 87, 88, 92, 94, 310
mental health, 46
metadata, 13, 30, 37, 44, 47, 88, 89, 94, 95, 200, 201
middleware, 47
military, 132
Minitel, 3, 4, 33, 34
MIT, 2, 33, 227, 228, 287
multi-database, xvii
multimedia, 309
Napster, 113
NASA, 197
NASS, 184, 186
National Information Infrastructure, 4, 23
National Science Foundation, xiii, 5, 50, 81, 108, 160, 164, 177, 197, 212, 213, 260
  workshop, 237
NATO, 2
network, 5, 53, 124, 294, 297
  access, 296
  adapting to, 113
  backbone, 293
  capacity, 297
  data, 4
  delivery system, 245
  for assistive technology, 313
  gigabit, 296
  global, 296
  high performance, 296

infrastructure, 113, 266
interconnection services, 54
links, 115
of databases, 38
of institutions, 39
protocols, 174
public, 8
security, 130, 294
society, 291
speed, 168
technologies, 261
technology, 232
telecommunications, 293
virtual, 299
wide-area, 38
network layer
  protocol, 116
networks, 147
  auxiliary, 309
  citizens' use of, 3
  communication, 4, 283
  community, 3
  cooperative architecture, 55
  costs, 266
  development of, 2
  information, 44, 283
  of databases, 43
  private, 117
  security, 130
  social, 283
  X.25, 297
New York, x, xi, xiii, xix, 4, 16, 32, 33, 34, 134, 191, 197, 212, 228, 259, 263, 271, 287
  information systems, 262
  local government, 265
  systems development in, 261
non-repudiation, 16, 28, 115
Nora and Minc, 3, 33
North America, xvi, 3, 12
North American Free Trade Agreement (NAFTA), 12
North American Industry Classification System (NAICS), 12
NSFNET, 3
objects
  distributed infrastructure, 47
OLAP, 91, 94, 103, 104
ONIX, 13

ontological integration, 9
ontologies, 9, 10, 13, 43, 44, 46, 48, 85, 98
   design of, 38, 43
   distributed, 38, 42
   integration, 13, 39, 98
   mapping of, xvii
   remote, 44
ontology, xvi, 13, 39, 42, 43, 47, 48, 85, 86, 92, 95, 96, 97, 98, 100, 101, 102, 213
   distributed, 174
   integration, xv
   relationships between, 44
operation, 1, 221
ORACLE, 2
P3P, 27
packet switching, 2
Paperwork Reduction Act, 233
parliament, 147
Parliament, ix, xvii, xviii, 6, 8, 53, 137, 138, 139, 140, 141, 142, 143, 144, 145, 147, 298
performance, 109, 118, 149, 207, 209, 223, 279
   fiscal, 283
   goals, 268
   individual and collective, 280
   staff, 265
   system, 102
performance study, 118
personal computer, 3
petition, 137, 139, 140, 141, 142, 143, 144, 145, 146
   progress of, 145
petitions, xviii, 6, 8, 137, 138, 139, 140, 141, 142, 144, 145, 146, 147
   security of, 144
planning, xx, 5, 41, 149, 218, 263, 277, 290, 293, 295
   in federal agencies, 40
   motion, 155, 160
   needs, 264
   systems design, 224
policy, xv, xix, 1, 6, 7, 23, 26, 28, 31, 34, 35, 123, 124, 125, 126, 127, 128, 129, 134, 216, 217, 218, 219, 220, 222, 227, 228, 231, 232, 233, 235, 271, 272, 282, 284, 286, 287, 293

   accessibility issues, 17
   as barriers to initiatives, 261
   competencies, 281
   data release, 251
   development, 240
   digital divide, 29
   documents, 23, 275, 276
   environment, 264
   failures, 281
   federal information, 240
   for distributed agents, 128
   formulation, 279
   framework, 26
   freedom of information, 25
   industrial, 3
   information, 231, 234
   information management, 240
   informing creation of digital government, 232
   innovation, 30
   issues, xvi, 23, 215, 234, 245, 261, 290
   perspectives, xvi
   privacy, 28
   public, 131
   reform, 276
   research and innovation, 227
   security, 125, 129, 133
   statistical, 193
   work teams, 269
policymaking, xvi, xix, 1, 23, 275
politics, 137
Portugal, x, xx, 5, 305, 306, 307, 309, 310, 311, 312, 314
precision, 12, 209, 210
President's Information Technology Advisory Committee, xix, 23, 34, 218, 220, 227, 228
President's Information Technology Advisory Committee (PITAC), 23, 34, 38, 218, 219
Prestel, 2
privacy, xv, xvii, xix, 6, 18, 23, 24, 26, 27, 31, 40, 115, 117, 121, 122, 123, 133, 134, 181, 216, 219, 220, 223, 226, 246, 255, 256
   attitudes, 245, 251
   attitudes toward, 26
   citizen, 243

citizens concerns, 130
concerns, 190, 245, 246
constraints, 131
data, 27, 91, 114, 118
definition of, 129
models, 27, 134
of communications, 15
of statistical data, 186
physical, 157
policies, 222
protecting, 290
risks, 130
standards, 255
process management, 15
procurement, 267
government, 4
of software, 18
on-line, 234, 238
services, 300
program design, 262
program management, 266
public administration, xvii, 5, 9, 10, 53, 54, 55, 63, 239, 271, 286
QUBE, 2
query, 12, 13, 44, 46, 168
access, 87
aggregate, 16
aggregation, 90
answering, 186
approximate, 94
cooperative system, 58
datacube, 93
disclosure risk, 190
efficiency, 166
estimates, 94
evaluation, 94
evaluator, 94
global, 210
high-speed processing, 85
inductive search, 175
integrated, 86
interface, xvii, 85, 99, 100, 168
keyword, 99
language, 99
languages, 87
lengthy, 167
main memory, 101
management, 101
matches, 169
mechanisms, xvii, 13
mediator, 94
multi-database, 166
multiple databases, 41
multi-year, 187
natural language, 14
navigational aids, 188
of services, 46
output format, 185
overhead, 43
parameters, 100
partial match, 93
performance, 93
plan, 88
planner, 92
precision, 12
processor, 46
range sum, 94
recall, 12
reformulating, 90
result, 49
results, 89, 94, 128, 186, 187
screens, 169
search, 175
services, 59
query mechanisms, 14, 15, 49, 85, 185, 197, 198, 199, 200, 201, 203, 209, 210
query processing, 39
query processor, 47
race, 29
RAND, 2
recall, 12
record management, 167, 173, 263
regulation, 262
regulations, 79
relationship management, 285
research and development, xix, 5, 179, 198, 215, 217, 218, 219, 228, 291, 299, 305, 311
research in digital government, 4
scalability, xv, xvii, 11, 41, 43, 107, 108, 109, 116, 117, 118, 164, 168
of workflow management, 73
Scotland, xviii, 5, 6, 8, 31, 65, 137, 138, 139, 144, 146, 147
Scottish, ix, xviii, 8, 137, 138, 139, 140, 143, 144, 147
searching, 14, 163, 200
content-based image, 14

costs, 25
for jobs, 47
full-text, 12
keyword, 99
key-word, 14
security
  public-key infrastructure, 127
security, xv, xvii, 6, 7, 23, 26, 31, 40,
    111, 112, 115, 117, 118, 121, 122,
    123, 124, 125, 126, 127, 129, 132,
    133, 141, 146, 164, 191, 216, 220,
    223, 226, 282, 310
  assurance, 131
  attitudes, 245
  concerns, 246, 251
  data, 300
  data collection, 300
  denial of service attack, 131
  development, 133
  development of models, 126
  digital certificate management, 298
  distributed computing, 127
  hacktivism, 131, 132
  information, 125
  insider breaches, 133
  issues, 70
  management of, 126
  measures, 290
  multi-domain, 128
  national, 24
  of agent systems, 134
  of petitions, 144
  officer, 126
  policies, 222
  policy, 126
  policy enforcement, 126
  policy management, 133
  policy selection, 128
  processes, 16
  public-key infrastructure, 294, 298
  risks, 130, 246
  role-based access, xvii
  role-based access model, 126, 127,
    129, 133
  standards, 255
  statistical databases, 16
  survey, 132
  systems integration, 133
  technical, 225

technologies, 133
threats, 132
workflow, 81
workflow management, 79
SENSUS, 85, 86, 88, 95, 98, 99, 100, 102
server pull, 112
service integration, 261
services, 110, 116, 122, 133, 143, 220,
    221, 223, 224, 232, 234, 243, 248,
    249, 255, 256, 286, 290, 296, 307, 309
  acceptance of, 248
  access to, 293
  administrative, 302
  attitudes toward, 246, 247
  autonomous agents, 75
  barriers to, 307
  citizen, 264, 292
  citizen-centric, 70
  clients, 285
  commercial, 2
  content, 236
  control of, 54
  convenience of, 239, 247
  cooperative workflows, 58
  cost-effective, 259
  costs of, 246
  data management, 11, 14
  delivery of, 235, 238, 259, 262, 283
  desired, 254
  development of, 262, 289, 292, 294,
    299, 302, 311
  digital government, 29, 73, 126, 244,
    248, 293, 300
  document delivery, 15
  efficiency of, 255
  efficient, 298
  e-government, 243, 245
  enterprise, 54
  e-services, 46
  exchanging, 54
  expansion of, 314
  externalizing, 8, 9, 10, 16
  externalizing, 8, 9, 10
  financial support for, 246, 252
  financing of, 254
  flexibility of, 307
  for the disabled, xvi
  form filing, xvii
  frequently used, 247

government, 6, 10, 19, 22, 29, 31, 37, 38, 40, 41, 50, 129, 236, 249, 250, 284, 301, 308
government information, 232
improving, 58
information, 3, 23, 39, 231
installation of, 292
integrated, 259, 262
Internet, 4, 296
ISDN, 297
legal, 30
network, 311
network-mediated, 243, 255
obtaining, 75
offering of, 254
on-line, xx, 3, 42, 45, 46, 47, 277, 282, 283, 290, 291, 292, 294, 295, 302
on-lines, 300
organization of, 48
paying for, 254
pervasive, 221
portal, 236
primitive, 114, 115
privacy, 252
private sector, 243
provisioning, 1
public, 2, 26, 306
publish model, 58, 59
quality of, xix, 249, 260, 289, 308, 310
range of, 69, 238, 261, 310
regulations, 75
remote access to, 308
reorganization of, 312
reuse of, 64
search, 174
searching for, 49
security, 15
social support, 309
state government, 246
streams, 285
telecommunication, 299
telecommunications, 29
use of, 246, 293
usefulness of, 254
Web-based, 7, 245, 255
simulation, 149, 155, 160, 189, 190
Bayesian, 188

Singapore, 5, 8, 32
social development, 305
social integration, 307
social security, 129, 192, 225, 234
social services, xvi, 9, 13, 37, 38, 40, 50, 254, 305, 306, 307, 311, 312, 313, 314
modernization, 308
software, xvi, 4, 7, 18, 19, 21, 27, 29, 70, 73, 78, 110, 114, 115, 146, 153, 168, 192, 219, 224, 267, 299
criminal analysis, 10
distribution, 110
errors, 17
incompatible, 18
limitations of, 17
security issues, 133
structure, 115
universal design, 20
South Africa, 24
speech-to-text conversion, 19
SQL, 47, 88, 89, 92, 103, 143, 168, 169
statistical analysis, xviii, 181
statistical data, xvii, xviii, 16, 92, 94, 99, 101, 200
confidentiality of, 181
survey, xix, 31, 35, 183, 191, 243, 256
agricultural, 182
attitudes toward digital government, 248
citizens, 254
data, 186
data dissemination, 182
geological, 9
of citizens, 237
of state initiatives, 245
of Texans, 247
of use of services, 247
of Web managers, 6
privacy attitudes, 251
public opinion, 243
security, 132, 133
system architectures, 7
system design, 267, 271
system development, 264, 270
systems development, 17
systems integration, 54
Taubman Center for Public Policy, 6, 35
taxes, 71, 78, 107, 116, 221
codes, 11

deadlines, 11, 109, 110
file electronically, 107
filing of, xvii, 239
forms, 107
on-line filing, 290
payment of, 80
processing, 112
returns, 10
revenue allocation, 266
security, 130
submission service, 111
submitting forms, 109, 110
uploading forms, 111
withholding, 80
Taylor, 2, 33
TCP/IP, 2, 4, 62, 109
technological adoption, xx, 275
technology
   deployment, 129
   development, 129
   infrastructure, 264
technology adoption, 275
technology deployment, 29
telecommunication
   infrastructure, 302
telecommunications, 3, 26, 29, 259, 289,
   290, 291, 293
   industry, 298
   infrastructure, xx, 29, 289, 290, 292,
      296
   integration, 19
   services, 300
   technologies, 291, 292
télématique, 3
telephone, 239
   bandwidth limitations of, 17
   call centers, 277
   interaction via, 70
   videotext, 2
   Web browsers, 21
Télétel, 3, 4
teletext, 2
temporal relations, 15
testing
   simulation, 155
Texas, xi, xix, 243, 245, 256
   attitudes toward digital government,
      244

Department of Information Resources,
   245
on-line services, 246
public opinion, 245
sale of data, 246, 251
text-to-speech conversion, 19, 20
timestamp, 112, 114, 115
timestamping, 115
town, xix, xx
transactions, 16, 26, 116, 127, 225, 301
   citizen to government, 239
   complex, 8, 16
   costs of, 245
   digital government, 126
   economic, 245
   electronic, 291
   government, 19, 231, 245
   government-to-
      government,government-to-citizen,
      233
   identifying the originator of, 16
   information, 243
   Internet, 246
   legislation, 298
   monitoring of, 130
   on-line, 223, 237, 294
   privacy, 255
   processing, 16
   public service, 260
   repudiation of, 16
   secure, 294, 295
   security of, 129
transformation, xix, 23, 215, 216, 275,
   281, 284, 305
   impact of, 281
Tunisia, xx, 289, 291, 295, 296, 297, 298,
   299, 300, 301, 302
U.S. Congress, 24, 107
United Nations (U.N.), 24, 26
United States, 2, 4, 5, 6, 11, 12, 14, 23,
   24, 25, 26, 27, 28, 29, 30, 33, 34, 35,
   38, 89, 94, 161, 181, 197, 198, 199,
   215, 216, 217, 218, 223, 228, 231,
   232, 233, 234, 235, 237, 240, 244,
   251, 256
   citizens' privacy concerns, 246
   Senate, 224
   state government Web sites, 239

Universal Declaration of Human Rights, 24
universal design, 17, 20, 21, 307
universal service, 299
University of Southern California, 5, 85, 86
uploading, xvii, 10, 11, 107, 108, 109, 110, 111, 112, 113, 114, 115, 116, 117, 118
   performance, 109, 116
   types of, 111
urban planning, 29
usability, xviii, 17, 18, 20, 21, 141, 146, 149, 150, 159, 160
   evaluation, 169
   extending, 150
   of facilities, 156, 160
   testing, 102, 154
videotext, 2, 3
view mechanism, 14
Viewdata, 2
voting, xviii, 8, 40, 108, 110, 116, 126, 129, 144, 254
   on-line, 225
   registration, 247
VRML, 151, 156
wavelet, 94, 201, 202, 209, 210
Web, xvii, xix, 4, 6, 15, 17, 18, 22, 26, 31, 33, 34, 35, 37, 38, 41, 62, 65, 82, 97, 103, 118, 134, 135, 152, 181, 182, 190, 193, 197, 223
   access, 236
   accessibility, 21
   advertising on, 253
   applications, 20
   architectures, 8
   browser, 46, 184
   content, 21
   databases, 38
   documents on, 244
   infrastructure, 38, 80
   popularity of, 173
   portals, 236
   security risks, 130
   servers, 11
   services, 174

   specialized browsers, 21
   technologies, 60
   XML, 45
Web sites, 11, 23, 27
   triggers, 15
Web-based, xvii, xviii, 4, 6, 9, 31, 37, 50, 65, 82, 103, 182
   application, 42
   government, 39
   infrastructure, 40
   publication, 25
   services, 245
   system, xvi, 9
Web-based system, xviii
WebDG, xvi, 9, 37, 38, 39, 40, 43, 45, 46, 47, 48, 50
WebView, xviii, 9, 197, 199, 210
work environment, 310
workflow, xvii, xx, 8, 10, 56, 58, 59, 61, 63, 69, 70, 71, 73, 74, 76, 77, 78, 79, 80, 81, 126, 127, 270, 280, 293, 308
   concurrent, 73
   conventional model, 75
   customized, 75, 80
   decentralized, 71, 76, 78
   dependencies, 72
   design, 74
   distributed scheduling, 79
   exception management, 81
   infrastructure, 71
   inter-agency, 71, 72, 80
   interface, 78
   internal, 58
   inter-organizational, 73
   management, xvii
   performance bottleneck, 73
   self-describing, 77, 78
   semantics of, 77
   server, 78
   specification, 75
World Health Organization, 25
World Wide Web, 4, 21, 35, 103, 118
World Wide Web Consortium (W3C), 27
XML, 13, 21, 28, 35, 45, 59, 60, 61, 62, 187